# The V
# 100 BOAT DESIGNS REVIEWED

## DESIGN COMMENTARIES BY THE EXPERTS

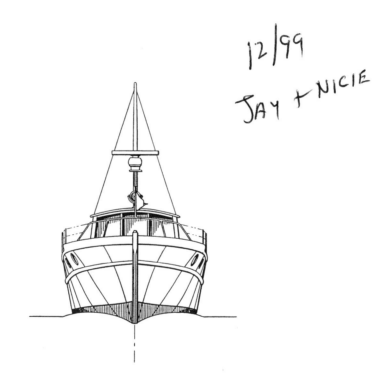

12/99
JAY + NICIE

*Series Editor, Peter H. Spectre*

Text design by Richard Gorski and Lindy Gifford
Cover design by Richard Gorski
Proofreading by Patricia J. Lown
Printed in the United States of America
Cover photograph by Benjamin Mendlowitz

Published by WoodenBoat Publications
P.O. Box 78, Naskeag Road
Brooklin, Maine 04616-0078

# Introduction

*"The joy and satisfaction of planning a lovely thing like a cruising yacht, and of watching her grow until she is there beneath you, with her guiding helm in your own hand, trembling with the life that you, her creator, have given her — why it is the most satisfying thing in the world."*

— Maurice Griffiths

*I*t is no secret that the anticipation of something can be equal to the achievement of it. In many cases it can be even better. That is why the search for the ideal boat is generally more satisfying than the finding of it, and why more books and magazines on boats are sold than there are boats afloat. All that reading matter represents anticipation: of the next boat, of the best boat, of the boat of your dreams.

This book is the anticipator's dream sheet. It contains reviews of some of the most interesting boat designs of our time, and a few from times past. Some even contain intimations of designs of the future.

These reviews are objective and subjective at once. Objective, because they are written by reviewers with training and/or years of experience in design. Subjective, because these same reviewers are no different from the rest of us — they, too, are boat lovers, and they, too, have in their mind's eye the ideal boat, and for years they have been searching for it. Our reviewers, like us, are anticipators.

All of these reviews have their origins in *WoodenBoat* magazine, which for nearly 25 years now has attempted to maintain a noble tradition of boating and yachting magazines of the past. That is, to be a forum for designers and their audience. Nearly every issue of the magazine contains a detailed look at a boat or yacht design; nearly every review includes more than one view of the design in question; almost always at least one of the views is the lines plan, the very essence of the design. (Without the lines plan, or a lines perspective, any expression of what the boat is really like is merely conjecture.)

A design forum such as *WoodenBoat*'s is more than an entertainment, more than an outlet for the output of professional designers, more than floss for dreamers. It is a tool for anyone seeking an understanding of what makes a good boat and, by inference, what makes a bad boat. By reading the reviews and by comparing the commentary to the plans depicted, eventually anyone with an interest in boats will come to understand enough about design to separate the good from the not-so-good. In short, reviews allow one to become at least an educated dreamer, at most an educated chooser of boats.

This book is a collection of many of the best reviews that have appeared in *WoodenBoat* magazine. They have been selected for many reasons, not the least of which is that they are timeless: They are excellent boats now, and they will be excellent boats in the future. Why? Because the sea is timeless; anything that can now take to the sea will always be able to take to the sea. Other criteria are the quality of the writing, the source of the perspective, the clarity of the analysis, and, of course, the ability of the boat to meet the needs of those who called for the design in the first place.

I should mention that the vast majority of these reviews are from the last 10 years or so of *WoodenBoat* magazine. That is because since the mid- to late-1980s Mike O'Brien has been the design review editor at *WoodenBoat*. Mike, a designer and boatbuilder in his own right, has an eye for a good boat and the understanding to choose the proper analyst for that boat. He is the one of late who has encouraged designers and naval architects to submit their plans for review, and he is the one who commissioned a good many of these reviews (he has written a great number of them, too). In editing this book, how could I go wrong? I was able to pick the best of Mike's best.

I should also include a few cautions for readers of this book. All boat designs are an amalgam of compromises and should be judged in that light. All reviewers are subjective, and what they have to say should be compared to your own knowledge and experience. All beautiful boats are not necessarily good, and all good boats are not necessarily beautiful. And this book does not even attempt to include all the good, beautiful boat designs available today.

If you can enjoy this book half as much as I enjoyed putting it together, you have many happy hours of reading — and anticipation — ahead of you.

—Peter H. Spectre
Spruce Head, Maine

## About the Authors

**MAYNARD BRAY,** contributing editor of *WoodenBoat* magazine, is the former superviser of the shipyard at Mystic Seaport Museum, a boatbuilder, a sailor, and a writer. He lives in Brooklin, Maine.

**SAM DEVLIN** is a West Coast designer and boatbuilder best known for his stitch-and-glue craft. He lives and works in Olympia, Washington.

**WILLIAM GARDEN** is a naval architect with hundreds of designs to his credit. He lives, works, sails, and writes in Victoria, British Columbia.

**MIKE O'BRIEN,** senior editor of *WoodenBoat* magazine, is a boatbuilder, boat designer, enthusiastic sailor and paddler, and editor/publisher of *Boat Design Quarterly*. He lives in Brooklin, Maine.

**JOEL WHITE,** owner for many years of Brooklin Boat Yard, Brooklin, Maine, where he lives, is a naval architect, boatbuilder, sailor, and writer.

# *Table of Contents*

*continues*

*continues*

# Reading the Drawings

by Mike O'Brien

*I*n an attempt to represent three-dimensional boats on two-dimensional pieces of paper, designers resort to four basic drawings: the sail plan (or profile), accommodations (or arrangement), hull lines, and construction. Inexperienced eyes seem to view hull lines as being the least accessible of these presentations. In truth, reading the drawings isn't difficult. Once you learn the tricks, the lines will float from these pages as fully formed hulls.

Boat design used to, and sometimes still does, begin with a wooden model of a hull. Imagine, if you will, taking such a model and slicing it as a loaf of bread (see Figure 1). Working to a common centerline and baseline, trace the outline of these slices or sections on a piece of paper. The resulting drawing (inset, Figure 4) gives a picture of the hull's shape as seen from the bow or stern. Usually, the designer shows only half of each section — relying on the builder's inherent sense of symmetry to produce a reliable mirror image. All of the half-sections are presented in a single drawing, the body plan. Most often, the right side shows the hull as if it were coming at you. The left side represents the view looking forward from the boat's wake.

In your mind's eye, reassemble the wooden model. Slice it again, but this time cut the hull horizontally into layers (Figure 2). Trace the shapes of these slices (waterlines) on paper about a common centerline. This drawing shows the hull as seen from below (Figure 5). You should look at it much as you would study a contour map.

Once again, put the model together with imaginary glue. Run your make-believe saw vertically and longitudinally through the hull (Figure 3). The shapes revealed by these cuts are buttock lines, and they can be traced as were the other lines (Figure 4).

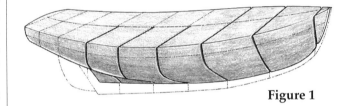

Figure 1

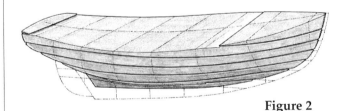

Figure 2

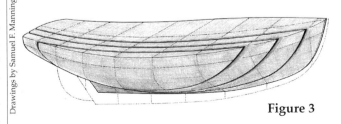

Figure 3

Drawings by Samuel F. Manning

All of the lines described above appear in their own drawings as curves. They also show up in the other drawings, but they are seen there as straight lines. That is to say, the sections display their shape in the body plan, and appear as straight lines in the elevation (profile) and waterlines (half-breadth) drawings. The shapes of the other lines in various views should yield to study of Figures 4 and 5.

Although the three sets of lines we've discussed define the shape of a hull, designers almost always include a fourth set. Diagonals emanate from the centerline in the body plan as straight lines that intersect the curved section lines at more or less right angles. And therein lies the key to the diagonals' value. Nearly perpendicular crossings provide the greatest accuracy for fairing a set of lines, whether on the drawing table or, at full scale, on the loft floor.

*Plans for Blue Moon are available from The WoodenBoat Store, P.O. Box 78, Brooklin, ME 04616; 800–273–7447.*

## Blue Moon
### Designed by Thomas C. Gillmer

*In these specially labeled drawings of Blue Moon's hull lines, the sections are marked with Arabic numerals in all views. Note how they take on shape in the sections drawing or body plan. In the other views, the sections appear as straight lines. Similar reasoning can be applied to the waterlines (upper-case letters) and the buttock lines (Roman numerals). Lower-case letters mark the diagonals in the body plan.*

### Blue Moon
### Particulars

| | |
|---|---|
| LOD | 22'10" |
| LWL | 19'8" |
| Beam | 8'7" |
| Draft | 4'1" |
| Displ | 7,750 lbs |
| Sail area | 380 sq ft |

## Figure 4
## Elevation and body plan (inset)

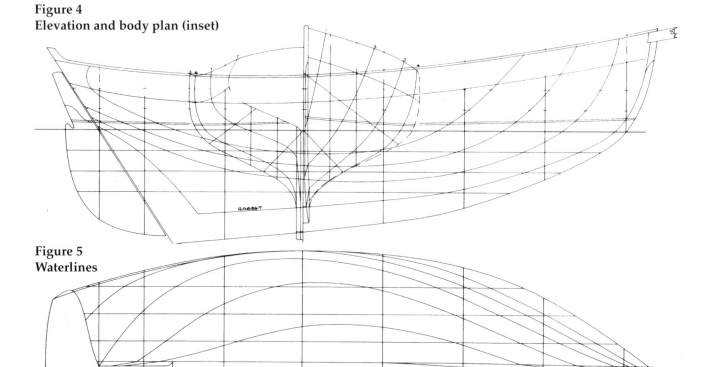

## Figure 5
## Waterlines

# Nesting Dinghies

Designs by Kaufman Design, Inc., Danny Greene, and Charles M. Strayer
Commentary by Mike O'Brien

Consider a tender's design criteria: The boat must be small, yet it will be called upon to carry huge loads; it should row easily, but it will be wide relative to its meager length in order to gain capacity; in the interest of easy handling, it ought not weigh too much, yet we know it will suffer terrible abuse. No doubt about it, drawing a proper dinghy can be an exercise in contradiction.

The three dinghies shown here address the problems of stowage, performance, and capacity by splitting apart amidships. The resulting pieces will nest neatly on the deck of a cruising boat or in a shoreside storage shed. The smallest of the trio, Danny Greene's 10-foot 4-inch Chameleon, folds into a 5-foot 3-inch package that lives on the forward deck of his 34-foot ketch. After bisection, Mike Kaufman's and Charles Strayer's longer (about 16-foot) boats can be nested — or they can sail off as separate, more or less equal, 8-foot halves.

Kaufman describes the advantages of the type while explaining the reasoning behind his J.P. Downs Memorial Bifurcating Dinghy (hereafter, the JPDMBD): "No one," he says, "gets stranded at a mooring while the dinghy is ashore, heavy loads can be carried, and argumentative siblings can be sent off — in different directions."

Strayer's design allows "break-apart" racing: The boats could sail the outward leg as separate 8-foot dinghies, join together at the windward mark, and run home as 16-foot schooners. Or the process might be reversed — that is, the boats could head out in their long configuration and sail for the finish as 8-footers. Given the latter format, I suspect that volunteers for the race committee might be difficult to find.

All of the designs shown here specify plywood construction for stiffness, light weight, and ease of build- ing and upkeep. They all have pram bows in order to make the best use of space and to provide adequate buoyancy forward. But, whatever similarities in concept these three (five?) boats might share, they are quite different from one another in shape and detail. Chameleon's V-bottom, with considerable twist and deadrise in its forward sections, shows the influence of the British Mirror Dinghy (an early stitch-and-glue design). The flat-bottomed JPDMBD has dory-like sections, and Strayer's Longsplice displays a multi-chine hull.

Danny Greene might lay claim to being the dean of nesting-dinghy designers. By his count, more than a thousand boats have been built to the 10 break-apart designs that have come from his drawing board. He describes Chameleon as "my best all around...by far." Construction is dirt simple: Cut out plywood panels for sides and bottom, and join them with temporary butt blocks (where they will be separated later). Lace the hull together with monofilament fishing line. Insert the "mating bulkheads." After the "inside joints" have been filleted with epoxy and fiberglass, and the rails and quarter knees have been installed, the boat can be separated into its forward and after halves. You should understand that, although the hull goes together quickly, considerable detail work is required for a two-piece dinghy. The designer, who built the prototype for his own use, estimates construction time at 100 hours for the rowing version, with an additional 40 hours required to complete the sailing rig and appendages.

Two ½-inch stainless-steel bolts located at the upper outboard corners of the mating bulkheads and an interlocking latch at the daggerboard trunk hold Chameleon together when she's in the water. The boat can be assembled while afloat.

Because Greene enjoys recreational rowing, he has fitted Chameleon with a nicely devised, removable sliding seat and outriggers. Of course, a hull of these proportions and dimensions can't use all the power generated with this setup, and there is little gain in speed compared to the fixed-seat arrangement. But, as the designer points out, "The sliding seat offers a good workout, and the little boat certainly is faster than a stationary rowing machine — the view and the air are better, too."

Kaufman describes a modified stitch-and-glue construction for the JPDMBD, but he writes that conventional methods (involving chine logs, glue, screws, and such) will work as well. Most of the plywood involved measures ⅜-inch thick. The prescribed sails are leg-o'-mutton with sprit booms. The self-vanging nature of this arrangement, and the easy sheeting and gentle disposition of the rig will be most appreciated in so small a boat. Relatively tall masts (well, they're only 12 feet 9 inches) are spliced up out of two 7-foot sections joined with aluminum-tube sleeves to permit stowing them in the nested dinghy.

The drawings for the JPDMBD indicate that the forward and after halves should be joined with purpose-made hinges and latches. Allowing that this method works well but might be expensive, the designer notes that four common ½-inch bolts, one at each corner of the mating bulkheads, will be sufficient and less costly.

For Longsplice's multichine hull, Strayer specifies a clean, frameless blend of fiberglass and ¼-inch plywood assembled in the stitch-and-glue fashion. The virtual symmetry of this boat's forward and after ends should assure a particularly easy job of construction. A rig evenly divided between two spritsails will provide plenty of economical power. I should say that sailors not brought up with this equipment sometimes have problems getting everything set just right. The usual errors seem to be insufficient luff and snotter tension. In any case, once it's understood, the rig will work well enough.

For all their advantages, nesting dinghies tend to be heavier and more complex than their non-folding counterparts. If you don't need, or want, to have your boat break apart, any of these designs would make a fine non-bifurcating daysailer.

*Plans for Longsplice are available from Strayer Yacht Design, 1744 Oak Grove Cir., Green Cove Springs, FL 32043.*

*Chameleon's plans can be had from Danny Greene, Offshore Design Ltd., P.O. Box GE#213, St. George's, Bermuda GEBX.*

*Kaufman Design, Inc., P.O. Box 4219, Annapolis, MD 21403, sells plans for the JPDMBD.*

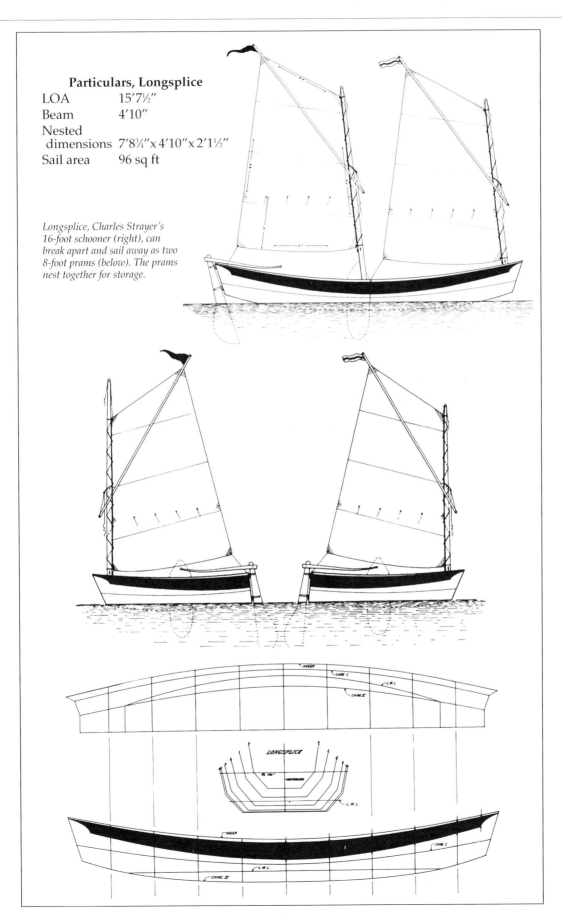

**Particulars, Longsplice**

| | |
|---|---|
| LOA | 15'7½" |
| Beam | 4'10" |
| Nested dimensions | 7'8¾" x 4'10" x 2'1½" |
| Sail area | 96 sq ft |

*Longsplice, Charles Strayer's 16-foot schooner (right), can break apart and sail away as two 8-foot prams (below). The prams nest together for storage.*

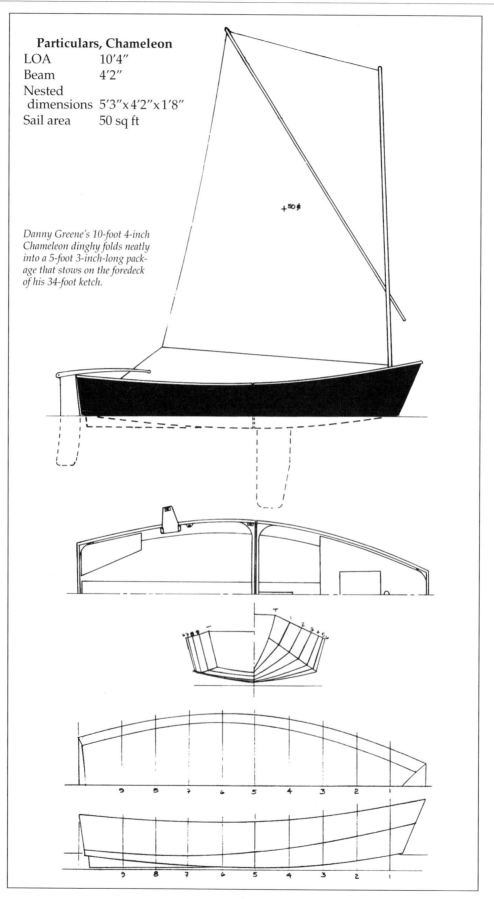

**Particulars, Chameleon**

| | |
|---|---|
| LOA | 10'4" |
| Beam | 4'2" |
| Nested dimensions | 5'3" x 4'2" x 1'8" |
| Sail area | 50 sq ft |

*Danny Greene's 10-foot 4-inch Chameleon dinghy folds neatly into a 5-foot 3-inch-long package that stows on the foredeck of his 34-foot ketch.*

**Particulars, J.P. Downes
Memorial Bifurcating Dinghy**

LOA            15'7"
Beam           5'3"
Nested
 dimensions  8'0" x 5'3" x 2'11"

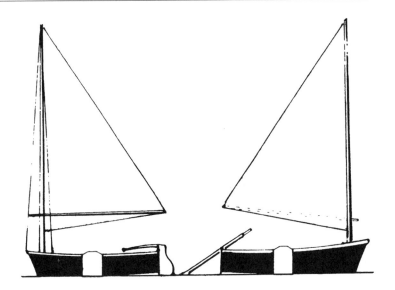

*Kaufman Designs' "bifurcating"
dinghy, shown assembled and nested
here, can sail away from itself (above).*

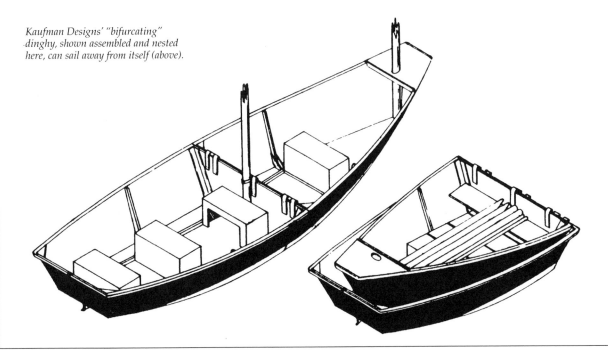

# Simple and Able Touring Kayaks

Designs by Michael B. Alford and Erik Wahlman
Commentary by Mike O'Brien

Kayaks can provide considerable fun, but North Carolina designer Michael B. Alford writes that he developed Tursiops for purely practical purposes: "My goal was to get across four or five miles of open water from the mainland to a string of uninhabited barrier islands. I needed to carry a fair amount of camera gear and a day's rations. Any number of boats might seem satisfactory for this purpose, but the catch was that I didn't want to stake a boat out or worry about vandalism or motor theft. A sea kayak offered all the mobility and rough-water survivability called for — and had the added advantage that it could be stowed under a bush."

Alford wanted a workboat with plenty of reserve stability, and he gave Tursiops a substantial width of 28 inches (many "Northwest" touring kayaks carry about 25 inches beam, and some "Greenland" derivatives are narrower than 20 inches). Due in part to strong flare that produces a relatively narrow waterline beam, Tursiops's great overall width takes little from its top speed and virtually nothing from its cruising pace.

Perhaps we should note here that, although Eskimo-rolling a wide boat is no piece of cake, Tursiops can be rolled by a competent paddler. The point is that this kayak won't capsize easily — and if it does go over, wet rescues will be easier than for narrow boats.

Tursiops's graceful lines belie its simple plywood and web-frame construction. Ample deadrise ("V") to its bottom, the good flare to its sides, and chines that sweep up toward both ends help ensure docile manners in rough water. And this boat avoids the slab-

sided appearance that plagues some sheet-built kayaks.

Out in Shingletown, California, Erik Wahlman has developed a kayak that is similar to, and yet different from, Tursiops. Erik built his Greenland-style prototype by eye, and drew formal lines only after a photograph of the boat in *WoodenBoat* magazine elicited requests for plans from readers in Japan, Australia, and New Zealand, as well as the United States.

The Wahlman kayak shows a V-bottomed plywood hull not unlike the 15-foot Tursiops, but the West Coast boat's greater length (18 feet) and narrower beam (25 inches) probably will make it somewhat faster and slightly less stable. Because maximum speed for this type of boat varies more or less according to the square root of its waterline length, and because stability is gained by increasing length, differences between these kayaks in both categories might be less than one would suspect. Certainly, the boats could cruise in company and arrive at the campsite on the same evening. Be that as it may, if you're racing for cash money, choose the Wahlman design.

On Tursiops, Mike Alford has made a nice job of working the tricky transition from the peaked forward deck (for shedding water and providing foot room) to the flat (for securing gear) after deck. The sloped deck sweeps back past both sides of the cockpit and later blends with the flat center panel of the after deck.

Designer Wahlman tackled, or perhaps avoided, the deck transition problem by specifying a choice of strip planking, cold molding, or a combination of both techniques. These options are more labor intensive, if not more difficult, than Alford's clever plywood solution;

## Particulars
## Tursiops
LOA    15'0"
Beam    28"
Weight   45 lbs

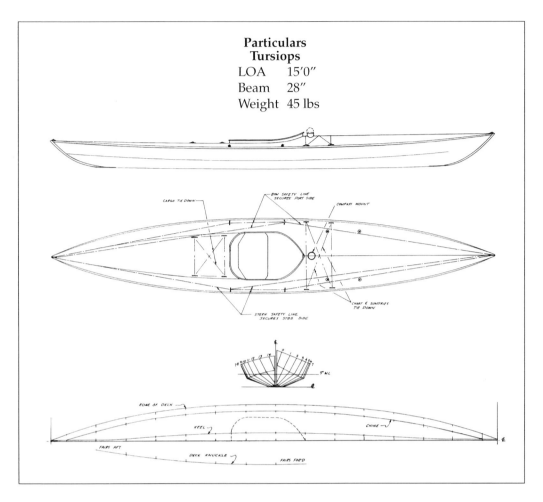

## Particulars
## Greenland-style Kayak
LOA    18'0"
Beam    25"
Weight   70 lbs

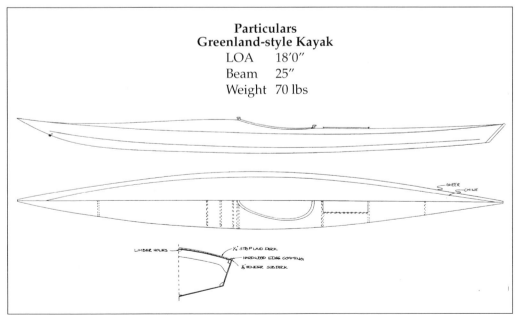

but the builders' efforts will be rewarded by the resulting voluptuous organic curves.

Neither of these boats contains watertight bulkheads. So much the better. No boat, no matter the material of its construction, can be guaranteed to remain tight forever. If your kayak develops a leak, you'll want the bilgewater to collect in the cockpit from where it can be dumped overboard.

Alford specifies foam for positive flotation. Builders of the Wahlman boat can, and should, install airbags. Paddlers of either kayak might consider sitting in a sea sock — a large nylon sack that is secured over the cockpit coaming and prevents excessive amounts of water from entering the boat if the occupant is forced to leave.

Both Wahlman and Alford drew boats that do not require rudders for control. By so doing they lowered building costs, increased reliability (what's not there can't break), and essentially assured that the owners of these kayaks will improve their paddling skills.

In the final analysis, it is the paddler's ability that completes the equation for safe kayaks. Without competent handling, these boats are little more than remarkably unstable devices with high centers of gravity. Paddlers who are unwilling, or unable, to learn the Eskimo roll and proper braces, might be better served by choosing a double-paddle canoe.

Paddlers who are inclined to perfect technique and evaluate risks will find kayaks to be most personal and versatile watercraft. They can traverse wild water that would overwhelm open canoes or small pulling boats and then penetrate streams inaccessible to powerboats. Properly handled, kayaks leave tranquility untouched.

*Building plans for Tursiops are available from The WoodenBoat Store, P.O. Box 78, Brooklin, ME 04616; 800–273–7447.*

*Plans for the 18-foot Greenland-style Kayak can be ordered from Erik Wahlman, Brightcraft Boats, 9395 Mountain Meadow Rd., Shingletown, CA 96088.*

# A Strip-Planked Touring Kayak

———— Design by Steve Killing ————
Commentary by Mike O'Brien

Most of the time, designer Steve Killing draws sailboats — often large, nearly always fast sailboats. His work with paddling boats, though less well known, seems of the same high order. He drew this particularly striking 17-foot touring kayak for canoe builder Ted Moores.

The finely crafted lines drawings show an easily driven, slightly Swede-form hull. That is to say, the maximum beam is carried abaft amidships. This approach tends to produce kayaks that can be paddled fast; and, if the asymmetry isn't exaggerated, the boats handle predictably.

If we're designing a small boat to put out in tall waves, specifying some deadrise (transverse V-shape to the bottom) and rocker (longitudinal, upswept curve to the keel) won't hurt. Skilling calls for about 6 degrees deadrise amidships. He indicates 2 inches of rocker aft and 3 inches forward. The hull is fine-ended, but not particularly so for a kayak. A sharply raked stem and well-shaped forward sections will provide increasing buoyancy as the Endeavour 17 punches into large waves. The fine run, and nearly vertical sternpost, will help ensure positive control when we're running off in a big sea (one of the scariest elements of sea kayaking). In all, this hull has a friendly and competent look to it.

The Endeavour 17 does not need a rudder. That's fine. Store-bought rudder systems cost about $150. They clutter the after regions of the hull. They usually result in spongy foot braces. And they seem to pick awkward times at which to fail. (Traditional Inuit kayaks apparently showed no trace of rudders until after the type had been degraded by modern, foreign influence. Should we ignore several thousand years of design evolution?)

We'll build Endeavour's hull and deck with ¼-inch-thick cedar strips, sheathed inside and out with fiberglass cloth set in epoxy. The strips' bead-and-cove edges will facilitate our fairing the hull and almost preclude the appearance of gaps between the planks. (We are going to finish this boat bright. Right?)

Rather than the common (for kayaks) fiberglass-tape hull-deck joint, Ted Moores suggests that we employ a ¾-inch by ⅞-inch filleted sheer clamp. He explains that this arrangement allows easier hull-deck assembly and ensures a quality joint all the way to the ends of the boat.

Endeavour's plans call for a forward and an after bulkhead — along with the hatches needed to access the resulting compartments. I suggest eliminating the whole works. This strong, monocoque hull seems less likely to sustain damage if it is allowed to flex upon impact. Of course, we'll install inflatable float/storage bags in both ends of the hull, and we'll sit in a sea sock (a fabric sack whose rim attaches to the cockpit coaming under the spray skirt — drastically reducing the amount of water that will enter the boat should we need to wet-exit).

With the above in mind, let's increase the overhang of the coaming's lip from the specified ½ inch to about 1 inch. We don't want the spray skirt and sea sock popping off every time we inhale.

All right, if we get rid of the bulkheads and hatch covers (and sheathe our Endeavour with 4-ounce fiberglass cloth — rather than the specified 6-ounce cloth), I'll wager we can bring this boat out of the shop at less than 38 pounds. Not bad for a kayak that will take us just about anywhere along the coast. And won't it look sharp!

*Plans for the Endeavour 17 are available in the U.S. from The WoodenBoat Store, P.O. Box 78, Brooklin, ME 04616; 800–273–7447.*

*Canadian readers can obtain plans from Ted Moores at Bear Mountain Boat Shop, 275 John St., Peterborough, ON, K9J 5E8, Canada.*

*Designer Steve Killing can be reached at P.O. Box 755, Midland, ON, L4R 4P4, Canada.*

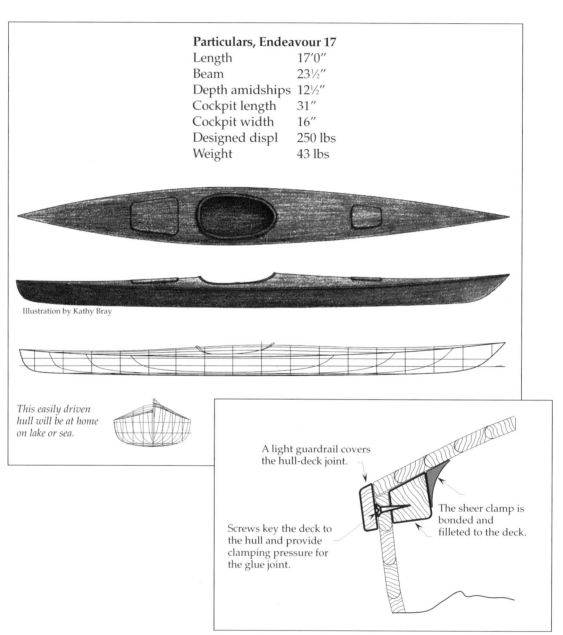

**Particulars, Endeavour 17**

| | |
|---|---|
| Length | 17'0" |
| Beam | 23½" |
| Depth amidships | 12½" |
| Cockpit length | 31" |
| Cockpit width | 16" |
| Designed displ | 250 lbs |
| Weight | 43 lbs |

Illustration by Kathy Bray

*This easily driven hull will be at home on lake or sea.*

A light guardrail covers the hull-deck joint.

The sheer clamp is bonded and filleted to the deck.

Screws key the deck to the hull and provide clamping pressure for the glue joint.

*The sheer clamp is secured to the deck first (rather than to the hull, as is the usual sequence). This procedure allows for accurate positioning of the hull and deck for their final assembly.*

# V

# *Two Sea Kayaks*

Designs by Rob Bryan and Glen-L Marine Designs
Commentary by Mike O'Brien

Rob Bryan's 17-foot 10-inch Seguin and Glen-L Marine's 17-foot Sea Kayak might come from the same family, but they are second cousins — not identical twins. The boats share the hard chines and upswept ends of their Greenland ancestors, and they share clean stitch-and-glue plywood construction. But the comparatively low (7-inch-high sides at the cockpit) and narrow (21½-inch) Seguin is a high-performance touring boat that will challenge and reward experienced paddlers. Glen-L's Sea Kayak (9-inch-high sides at the cockpit and 24 inches wide) is a pickup truck that will build beginner confidence and carry a lot of gear.

These kayaks show a similarity of form that belies their variance in proportion. Beyond any reasonable doubt, Seguin, with its finer lines and less beam, will be the faster, more easily driven of the pair, and the Glen-L will be initially more stable.

Both boats have little flare in their topsides. This configuration combines a relatively wide bottom for stability with a narrow deck for light weight and ease of double-bladed paddling, and it might soften the shoulder of the stability curve.

We should be able to lay Seguin right over on its side and hold it there with a good high paddle brace. Eskimo rolling will prove smooth and easy. Bryan's drawings illustrate the thigh braces and other foam padding needed to fit the cockpit to our own dimensions if we're to pursue such sport.

The Glen-L boat, similarly outfitted, can be braced and rolled, too — though the final 180 degrees might prove difficult for some paddlers.

Bryan has designed a retractable skeg for Seguin to combat potential control problems.

Spectators watching sea kayaks working into a heavy chop sometimes comment on the daring of the pad-dlers. In fact, blasting to windward is the easiest part of rough-water kayaking in terms of the skill required. Sea kayaks, with their low profiles and pointed noses, love that game. The real test of operator ability occurs when paddling across, or off, the wind. Some kayaks tend to dig in and root when traveling with wind and wave.

With the wind on the beam, many kayaks insist upon rounding up to windward as predictably as a well-oiled weather vane — whether or not we want to go in that direction. In simple terms, here's the reason: As we propel the kayak ahead through flat water, pressure builds evenly on both sides of the bow. But, if a breeze springs up, say, over our right shoulder, it will nudge the boat to the left, causing the pressure under the lee (port) bow to increase and turning us to windward. The harder we paddle, and the stronger the wind, the more the boat wants to weathercock.

We can mitigate the problem by pushing hard against the weather foot brace (the right one in this case). This simple, if somewhat unnatural, act leans the boat into the wind, which creates effectively asymmetrical waterlines (more convex on the weather side and somewhat straighter on the lee side) that tend to turn the boat away from the wind. Also, pushing hard with our weather foot automatically increases the power in our weather arm.

Of course, altering various elements of hull shape — such as building in more freeboard forward and more draft aft, or reducing the prismatic coefficient — can help us. If we wish, a fixed skeg can be fastened to the bottom, well aft. But this solution often isn't totally effective, and it forever limits the kayak's maneuverability and increases its draft. Another remedy involves fitting an instantly adjustable sliding seat. Moving this seat aft while underway trims the boat down by the stern, reducing weathercocking. It's efficient, but some paddlers don't like the loose fit of the large cockpits required by sliding seats.

All of the above notwithstanding, foot-controlled rudders supply the most commonly applied cure for sea kayak control problems. Modern store-bought rudder systems can be impressive pieces of engineering, and they work well. But they are expensive, they're not immune to breaking, and their foot-pedal controls tend to be less firm than we would like. Despite clever on-deck storage systems, the rudder blades are never completely out of the way. They can ruin themselves, or the paddler, in surf or rescue situations. When cocked at an angle to the hull's centerline in order to prevent weathervaning, they can cause more drag than a simple skeg. And, contrary to popular opinion, rudders usually make kayaks less — not more — maneuverable. As may be, some designers are loath to spoil the symmetry of their creations by mounting oddly shaped aluminum plates on the kayaks' sterns.

When paddling Seguin, we'll lower its retractable skeg (a small quadrant-shaped centerboard, really) to balance the kayak on a beam reach and to improve directional control when running off. We'll raise it to let the boat head into the wind and to carve tighter turns. Note that the skeg fills its trunk below the waterline at all angles of adjustment, thus reducing turbulence.

Both boats are built using virtually the same construction sequence: cut the hull panels (4mm plywood for Seguin, and 4mm or ¼ inch for the Glen-L) to shape, bend them around two permanent bulkheads and one temporary mold, and stitch them together with copper wire. Then, work thickened epoxy fillets into the seams on the interior of the hull, and remove the wire ties. Apply fiberglass tape to those inside seams. Add decks, coaming, and hatches. Fair external seams, and apply fiberglass tape.

The working plans for these kayaks are extraordinarily complete. Bryan supplies a five-page set of well-crafted drawings and a 40-page instruction book. Glen-L furnishes several booklets, 28 sequential construction photos, and full-sized paper patterns for virtually every component in its kayak. Perhaps because I designed and built boats on the humid shores of Chesapeake Bay, paper patterns make me nervous (their dimensions vary wildly with fluctuations in humidity, and the changes in size are not necessarily equal in all directions). As may be, Glen-L's builders have employed paper patterns for decades, and my friend Joel White supplies full-sized paper station patterns for several of his designs. We've heard no complaints, and I'm beginning to suspect that my concern amounts to tilting at windmills.

No matter how we might arrive at the end products, these stitch-and-glue composite boats tend to be stiffer and lighter than either fiberglass or roto-molded plastic kayaks.

I'll offer just one suggestion to potential builders: Drill a small (say, ¾-inch) hole near the bottom of each bulkhead, and plug the holes with softwood stoppers attached to a ⅛-inch leech line, or some such, running to the cockpit. If leaks develop in either end of the boat while we're offshore alone, we need to have the water drain to the cockpit so that we can pump it overboard, so in the event pull on the lines to pull the plugs. (For this reason, among others, my own sea kayak has neither bulkheads nor hatches.)

*Plans for Seguin are available from The WoodenBoat Store, P.O. Box 78, Brooklin, ME 04616; 800–273–7447.*

*Glen-L Marine Designs sells its Sea Kayak plans at 9152 Rosecrans Ave., Bellflower, CA 90706. Glen-L also offers construction kits for this kayak.*

## Particulars, Seguin

| | |
|---|---|
| LOA | 17'10" |
| Beam | 21½" |
| Weight | 42 lbs |
| Cockpit size | 21"x16" or 28"x16" |

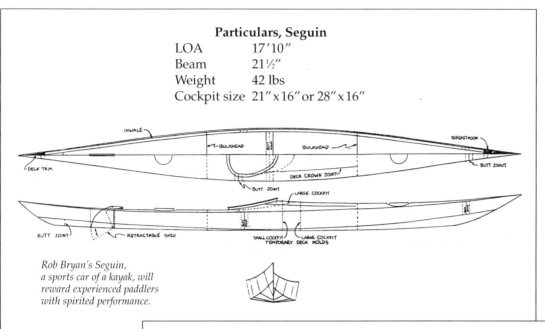

*Rob Bryan's Seguin,
a sports car of a kayak, will
reward experienced paddlers
with spirited performance.*

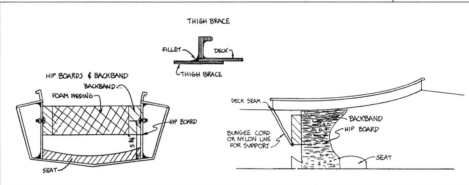

*Seguin's cockpit details show the custom-
fitted padding helpful for bracing and rolling.*

**Particulars, Glen-L Sea Kayak**

| | |
|---|---|
| LOA | 17'0" |
| Beam | 24" |
| Weight | 40 to 60 lbs |
| Cockpit size | 29½" x16" |

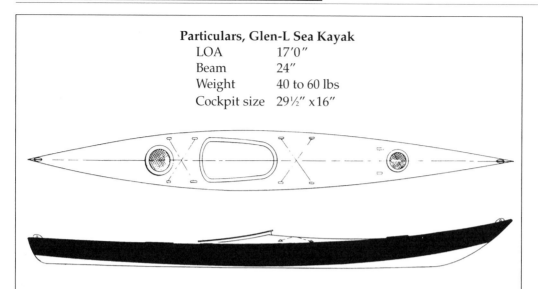

*The commodious Glen-L Sea Kayak offers healthy stability and room for lots of gear.*

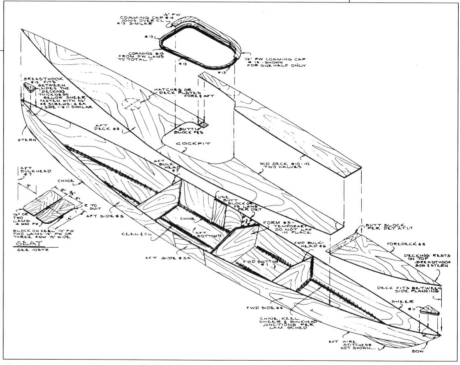

*The Glen-L Sea Kayak's stitch-and-glue, plywood construction, illustrated here, combines quick building time with stiffness and light weight. Sequin goes together in similar fashion.*

# Two Double-Paddle Canoes

———— Designs by Iain Oughtred ————
Commentary by Mike O'Brien

Nothing, absolutely nothing, communicates the feeling of being afloat quite so purely as a light, human-powered boat. This pleasant fact has not escaped contemporary builders. During the past two decades, pulling boats and "Indian" canoes (the British would say Canadian canoes) have enjoyed a renaissance in form and numbers. Now, with help from the striking Iain Oughtred designs shown here, and similar boats drawn by Pete Culler and others, double-paddle canoes seem poised for the same fate.

To many late-nineteenth-century paddlers, "canoe" implied a lightly built, half-decked, lapstrake boat propelled by a double-bladed paddle. John MacGregor usually receives credit for the introduction and early development of the type. Described by small-craft historian Atwood Manley as an "odd mixture of religious zealot, intellectual, and sportsman," this Scottish philanthropist and adventurer journeyed to North America in 1859 — eventually traveling as far as the Bering Sea. Upon his return home, he designed the first of his Rob Roy canoes, which were based loosely on kayaks he had studied.

MacGregor later paddled his Rob Roys through Europe, packing, among other supplies, copies of the New Testament and his own religious writings. He detailed his adventures in a series of engaging books and lectures, the proceeds from which went to charity. How MacGregor fared as a missionary for his faith remains unrecorded, but it is certain that he converted thousands to canoeing.

MacGregor's writings carried Rob Roy's stories across the Atlantic, where they influenced the growing sport of canoeing. For the next few decades, the sale of double-paddle canoes provided a major source of income for many boatbuilders. The most successful — or at least the best remembered — operation was run by J.

Henry Rushton. This master builder from Canton, New York, benefited from having articulate customers such as outdoor writer Nessmuk (George Washington Sears) praise his work in print. Sears, a frail man, cruised extensively in his 9-foot by 26-inch 10½-pound Rushton canoe *Sairy Gamp*.

These days we have a changed environment for double-paddle canoes. Rushton was assured that, used where intended, his elegant small craft would never encounter large, breaking waves. He could afford to give many of his boats low sides and hungry bows. Today, a proliferation of high-speed powerboats complicates the design equation — metal-flaked monsters might lurk around any bend. Iain Oughtred's canoes are prepared for this. Each, having a cutaway forefoot and buoyant lines, resemble baby whaleboats. They should cope comfortably with confused manmade seas as well as with the natural variety.

Many contemporary canoes are destined to spend considerable time bouncing along on cartop racks, where they're dried by speed-limit winds and baked until well-done by the sun. The wood/epoxy lapstrake construction specified for the boats shown here will, no doubt, survive this torture with less trauma than traditional types — though it should be said that conventional lapstrake canoes also handle drying fairly well, and their solid planking absorbs abrasion better than can plywood's thin veneer hide. Perhaps the modern construction's most important advantages for amateur builders lie in off-the-shelf availability of materials, clean frameless design, and the superb gap-filling properties of epoxy.

Iain Oughtred tends to the details in his drawings. Builders' questions are few, and I've never seen a bad boat come from his plans. Much of a lapstrake boat's beauty depends upon properly lined-off planking. If you spot a droopy garboard or squeezed plank after you've finished your canoe, she'll lose her appeal. Oughtred shows where the planks should land on each mold — he has a good eye for it, and little is left to chance.

The relatively narrow (28 inches beam) Wee Rob can be built as a 12-footer, but her length can be increased to 13 feet 7 inches or 15 feet 2 inches for greater speed and capacity. The 31-inch-wide MacGregor is shown at 13 feet 7 inches LOA, and Oughtred has included 15-foot 8-inch and 17-foot 3-inch options. Drawings for both boats detail open and decked versions.

The balanced lug rigs combine short spars and low-centered power with easy reefing, and they're more or less self-vanging. This last is most important, as it reduces sail twist that can lead to rhythmic rolling when running in a breeze — an annoying phenomenon in any sailing boat and downright dangerous for narrow, slack-bilged canoes. I should say that these boats are suited primarily for paddling, and individual builders will have to justify the expense and complication of adding the sailing rigs. No doubt both canoes — particularly the wider MacGregor — will sail creditably.

At the risk of offending proponents of the oar, I'd like to make a case for the double-bladed paddle. First, I'll concede the power of oars for moving heavy loads. Also, fitted to specialized craft with sliding seats or riggers, oars can produce higher speeds (though their advantage is not so great as one might expect). But, for moving people at pleasantly acceptable rates with a minimum of strain, the double-bladed paddle seems better in several ways. It allows the canoeist to sit lower than the oarsman — increasing stability and decreasing windage. As nothing is lost to recovery, the paddle's power stroke is virtually continuous — particularly helpful when working to windward in a breeze. Facing forward clearly is safer than staring over the stern, and a backrest reduces fatigue. Lifejackets can be worn comfortably for paddling, but they're awkward at best if you're rowing.

Nearly everyone acknowledges the advantages of paddles for work in tight quarters. I'm inclined to think that they are superior for open water, too. Although there are variations in rowing strokes, oars literally are locked to their fulcrums; they can provide propulsion and act as crude outriggers. Paddles, on the other hand, can attack the water from many angles with an almost limitless variety of strokes and braces — increasing maneuverability, sport, and possibly your chances for survival.

Double-paddle canoes might well be the ultimate "impulse" boats. Light and simple, they'll sit happily atop your car waiting to explore small streams that flow barely noticed under highway bridges. Yet they're able to handle serious coastal cruising. And you'll be welcome in any harbor because of your complete control, absence of wake, and silence.

*Plans and instructions for building Wee Rob and MacGregor are available from The WoodenBoat Store, P.O. Box 78, Brooklin, ME 04616; 800–273–7447.*

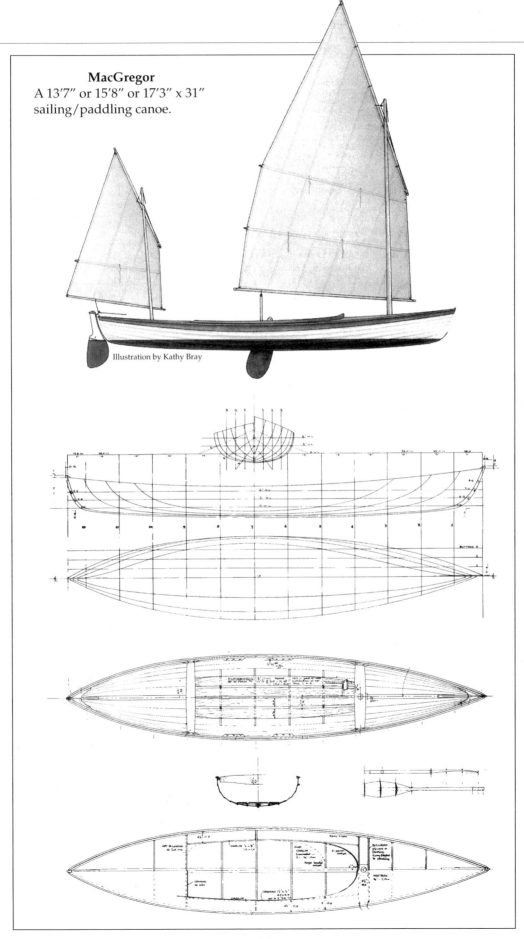

**MacGregor**
A 13'7" or 15'8" or 17'3" x 31"
sailing/paddling canoe.

Illustration by Kathy Bray

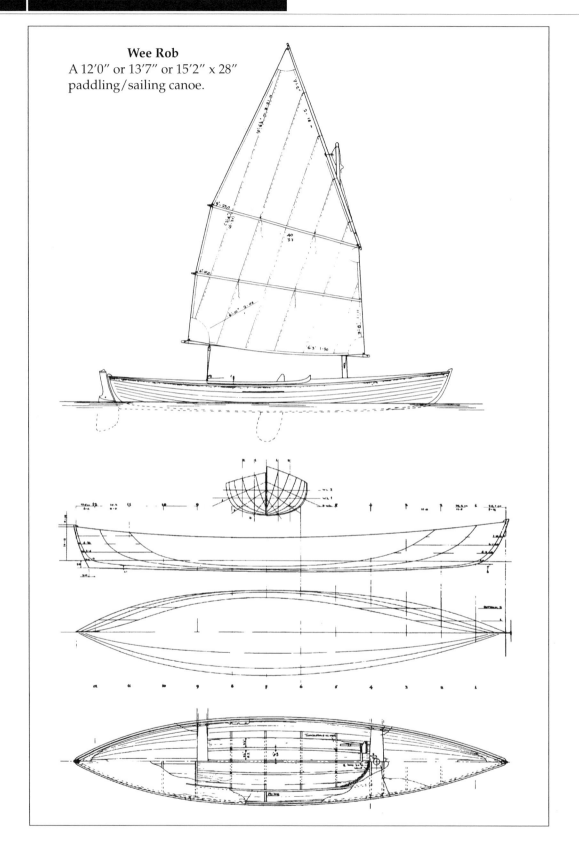

**Wee Rob**
A 12'0" or 13'7" or 15'2" x 28"
paddling/sailing canoe.

# VII

# A Sailing Canoe

—— Drawn by Ned Costello ——

The accompanying lines were taken from a 14-foot 6-inch sailing canoe discovered in the yard of a curiosity shop in Belfast, Maine, by members of the small craft department of Mystic Seaport. Two brass plates bore the legend "William F. Wiser, Builder, Bridesburg, Pennsylvania."

The hull of the Wiser canoe represents a modification of the sailing canoes of the early 1880s. This was the height of their development, before all advances pointed toward speed. The rockered keel and rising floor give an easy motion and a dry bow. The decks and watertight bulkheads make her virtually unsinkable. She has rather moderate sail area, which permitted Wiser to design a much larger cockpit opening than usual, nearly 6 feet in length. Thus, two people could share an afternoon sail, or one could venture on a cruise.

Dixon Kemp's *A Manual of Yacht and Boat Sailing*, first published in 1878, provided drawings from which I adapted her rig. About one-seventh of the sail projects forward of the mast, shortening the boom over the cockpit without reducing sail area. The full-length battens allow quick reefing with a simple pulley system. The vertical seams help to support the weight of the boom, allowing lighter sail cloth. Using this rig, centerboard, and hull shape, she would sail like a dream, though no closer than 45 degrees off the wind. The use of a double paddle with a reefed mizzen would be an excellent way to go straight upwind.

In a time when machines have soured the natural beauty of our land, and when people are turning again to sports that demand intellectual and physical agility, sailing canoes like this one may well enjoy a renaissance. The relative sizes of the canoeist and the canoe set up a close, interdependent relationship seldom achieved. The canoe becomes an extension of the body.

Imagine sitting with legs wedged against the hull, feet controlling the rudder, leeward hand on the main sheet, and windward arm pulling your weight to windward, while flying along at 8 or 10 knots!

*For further information, contact: Mystic Seaport Museum, Ships Plans Division, P.O. Box 6000, Mystic, CT 06355.*

**14' 6" Wiser Sailing Canoe**

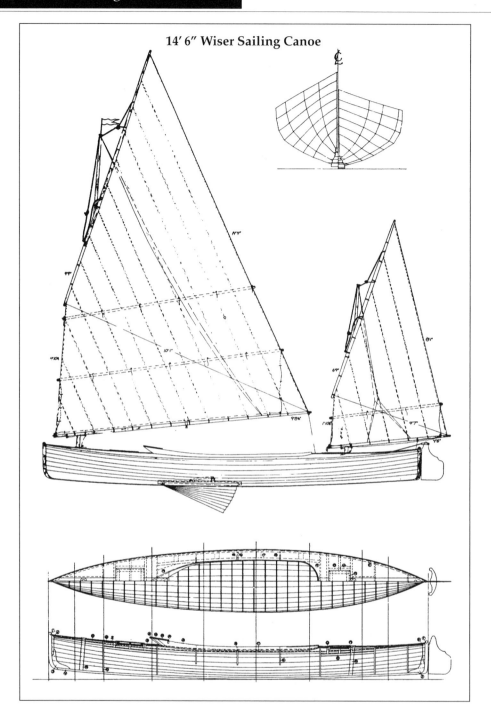

# Two Daysailers, Chesapeake Fashion

——— Designs by Karl A. Stambaugh and Howard I. Chapelle ———
Commentary by Mike O'Brien

*E*asily built and distinctive in appearance, Chesapeake Bay sailing skiffs come from rugged stock. Predecessors, simply rigged and steady on their feet, served as seafood harvesters and common transportation. Often regarded as little more than waterfront equipment, the boats survived in spite of sometimes desultory care. A measure of their strong character can be seen in the two skiff "yachts" shown here. Neither is a direct copy of a traditional design, but both bespeak their Bay origins.

In his search for a trailerable daysailer, designer Karl A. Stambaugh discovered plans for a 21-foot 7-inch crab skiff built by Bill Reeves at Wingate, Maryland, in 1909. But the Reeves boat is large and heavy by most daysailing standards, and the traditional cross-planked Bay construction does not take well to travel by trailer. The old boats lived in the water and got where they were going on their own bottoms — frequent drying and the stress imposed by roller flanges were not considerations back then.

In drawing the Windward 15, Stambaugh combined the crab skiff's flavor with contemporary materials. Plywood, his choice for planking the hull, forces some decisions. And the decisions start right up forward. In no way can sheet plywood be talked into bending around a traditional deadrise forefoot. Most Chesapeake builders would stave the forefoot (use short, thick planks worked to shape); but this technique can be tricky for the inexperienced, and the staves don't mate well with the plywood you might want to apply to the remainder of the bottom. The forefoot could be carved from a single block of timber, as seen in some early deadrise skiffs, but that construction is heavy and prone to rot. In this age of epoxy, cold molding provides an elegant solution — if you can tolerate the increased building time and expense.

The Windward's designer chose a simple path. He drew shallow forward sections that should present no impossible obstacles to sheet plywood. In a light boat intended for sailing, any compromise in performance will prove minimal. To make this hull even more compatible with sheet construction, he raked the stem — thus reducing twist in the sides up forward.

The powerful rudder, styled nicely in keeping with the old Bay skiffs, will give sharp control and carry a fair portion of the lateral plane load. But, for its protection, you might consider tucking the blade up behind the ample skeg. A Neoprene strap bridging the gap between the bottoms of the rudder and the skeg would preclude your snagging pot warp.

Despite the best efforts of Howard Chapelle, Phil Bolger, and others, the joys of sailing a sprit-boomed leg-o'-mutton rig seem to remain little known. This rig's simplicity speaks for itself — no blocks, no standing rigging, simple sheet leads, solid mast and boom. Its sophistication might not be so evident. Because the boom can't lift appreciably (the foot of the sail tightens, reducing lift), the affair is self-vanging. Sail twist is reduced, often resulting in higher speeds and more docile steering. The sheet is needed only for trimming in the boom.

As it need not provide much downward force, this arrangement can be simpler and lighter than if it had to control a conventional boom. Draft can be changed, to an extent, by varying the tension in the snotter — tight to flatten the sail for heavier air and/or windward work, eased off for lighter breezes and/or reaching and running. Sail twist can be adjusted by moving the sprit boom up or down the mast — lower for more twist, higher for less. Of course, draft can also be affected by changing the down-haul tension. Without a single piece of store-bought hardware, this rig will do everything but sit up and say please.

Howard I. Chapelle needs no introduction here. All of us devoted to simple, traditional boats are indebted to him. Best known for his descriptions — some would say interpretations — of historical types, the master draftsman also left behind a body of his own work. Often unpublished, Chapelle's originals contain an enlightening blend of workboat features recombined to create robust pleasure craft.

Though she's clearly no crab boat, Chapelle's 14-foot Sharpie Sailing Dinghy (read skiff) has her Chesapeake origins deeply etched in her style and detail. As she'd not be called upon to carry a heavy catch, Chapelle gave her less rocker than you'll see in any square-sterned Bay skiff — save for those driven by outboard motors. This boat won't get up on top as quickly as an International 14, but no doubt she'll plane, given the right conditions.

Her skipper likely won't be hauling pots or tending trot lines, so her strong flare won't be cause for a sore back. The sharply angled sides provide reserve buoyancy, a wide base for the shrouds, and room for substantial washboards (side decks) — all combined with a relatively narrow bottom. Most observers will appreciate the resulting appearance.

Sharpie sailors learn early not to sheet in too hard or too soon after coming about. A shallow forefoot sometimes won't "hold on" to the new course. Chapelle gave this skiff an impressive gripe (a forward skeg, if you will), and it should help see her through those awkward post-tacking moments. Also, it offers a measure of protection to both the bottom and the slot when beaching. (Some opinion holds that the gripe reduces pounding in a chop.)

The standard dinghy rudder shown on the plans is simple and powerful, but it can be a pintle-breaker in serious shallow-water sailing. A kick-up blade would seem a reasonable modification.

The advantages inherent in sprit-boomed leg-o'-mutton rigs were detailed earlier; Chapelle's drawings indicate an additional worthwhile wrinkle. Aesthetics aside, I've never known a sharpie to take much notice of a sprit boom lying hard against the lee side of its sail (skippers often seem more bothered by asymmetry than do their boats). In any case, if you're disturbed by the resulting crease, this skiff's half-wishbone fitted with offset jaws provides a solution. The sail will fill nicely on either tack, and this arrangement is simpler than a full wishbone boom.

A spread of 130 sqaure feet of canvas (Dacron?) represents considerable sail area for this 14-foot skiff. Perhaps in deference to the Chesapeake's light summer winds, Chapelle drew the larger jib in solid lines, which suggests that he intended it to serve as working sail. The small 28-square-foot headsail is dashed in for stronger breezes and/or lighter crews.

The apparently squat rig is, in fact, of moderate aspect ratio for native Bay boats. Although our eyes have become accustomed to taller and leaner configurations, the mainsail shown will provide more usable power and will set on less expensive spars. It's well to remember that extremely high-aspect rigs sometimes have developed in response to artificial sail-area limits and the search for ultimate windward performance. The limits for this sharpie are imposed by cost and the ability of boat and crew to handle sail — no sense sticking a C-class wing in her.

Construction for this little daysailer is straightforward skiff fashion. Any questions you might have about the details should yield to a careful reading of Chapelle's book, *Boatbuilding*. We haven't been able to find a table of offsets defining these lines, and the plans available from the Smithsonian provide little more information than appears here. Still, I recommend ordering a set if you're intent on building the boat. The larger scale (¾ inch equals 1 foot) and lack of photographic distortion will help ensure that everything goes down right and proper.

If your skiff will live on a trailer, ½-inch plywood makes a good alternate bottom construction. By all means, plank the sides as drawn — including the lapped "rising strake" that will cast a shadow emphasizing the strong flare and nicely drawn sheer. Properly detailed, this boat can sail in any company. She's simple and inexpensive, but there's nothing cheap about her.

*Plans for the Windward 15 are available from Karl A. Stambaugh, 794 Creek View Rd., Severna Park, MD 21146.*

*Plans for the 14-foot Sharpie Sailing Dinghy can be obtained from the Smithsonian Institution, Division of Transportation, NMAH 5010/MRC 628, Washington, DC 20560. Ask for plan HIC-103.*

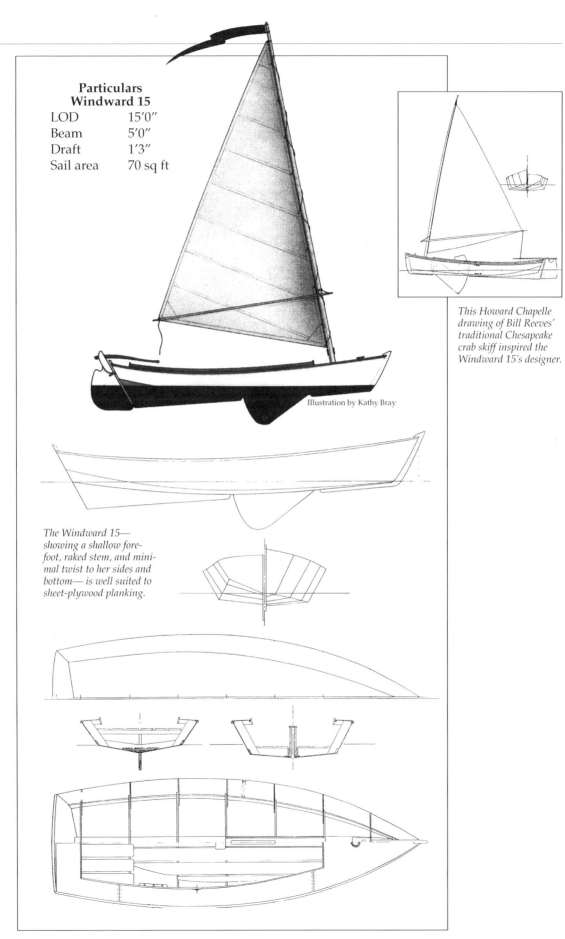

**Particulars**
**Windward 15**

| | |
|---|---|
| LOD | 15'0" |
| Beam | 5'0" |
| Draft | 1'3" |
| Sail area | 70 sq ft |

Illustration by Kathy Bray

*This Howard Chapelle drawing of Bill Reeves' traditional Chesapeake crab skiff inspired the Windward 15's designer.*

*The Windward 15— showing a shallow fore-foot, raked stem, and mini-mal twist to her sides and bottom— is well suited to sheet-plywood planking.*

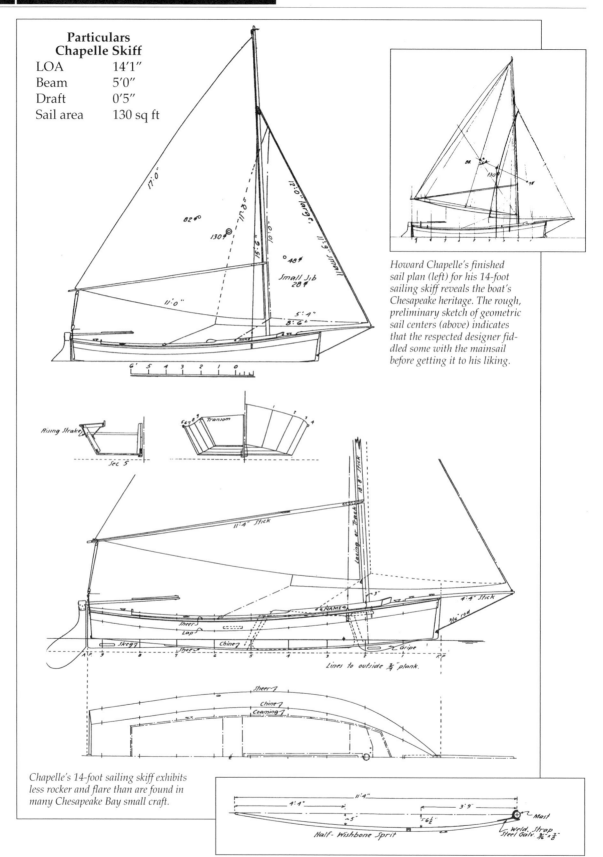

**Particulars
Chapelle Skiff**

| | |
|---|---|
| LOA | 14'1" |
| Beam | 5'0" |
| Draft | 0'5" |
| Sail area | 130 sq ft |

Howard Chapelle's finished sail plan (left) for his 14-foot sailing skiff reveals the boat's Chesapeake heritage. The rough, preliminary sketch of geometric sail centers (above) indicates that the respected designer fiddled some with the mainsail before getting it to his liking.

Chapelle's 14-foot sailing skiff exhibits less rocker and flare than are found in many Chesapeake Bay small craft.

The half-wishbone sprit boom allows for good sail shape on either tack, and it is simpler than the more common full wishbone.

# Schooner and Flashboat

————— Designs by Paul Gartside —————
Commentary by Mike O'Brien

*I*s there one among us who has never lusted after a schooner? For sailors confined — by necessity or choice — to small craft, the pursuit can be particularly frustrating. Paul Gartside has drawn a solution for the problem: a 15-foot cold-molded daysailer/beach cruiser that will let you have your schooner and trailer it, too. Though it lacks the majesty of the schooner-yacht *America* or the great fishing schooners, his design displays grace in full measure.

Admired for its beauty but maligned for what are perceived as technical deficiencies, the schooner rig is not often selected for contemporary designs. As may be, Gartside's boat will withstand fairly rigorous assault by logic. The divided rig breaks the sail area into small, easily handled patches, and, as stability won't be this hull's strong suit, the low center of effort will be appreciated. The foresail might prove just close enough to the main to improve the airflow around the larger sail. In any case, backwinding won't be so great a problem as with the more popular cat-ketch. A sloop directs the flow with its headsail — and saves one mast in the process. The cost comes in the form of standing rigging you'll probably want to add to keep the jib's luff tight.

Strongly raked masts lend much to this boat's appearance and help keep the sails out of the water in rough going. Also, the masts bury in the hull at most convenient locations — clear of the cockpits but handy for use as tent poles. Technical considerations aside, Gartside presents an unanswerable defense for his dropping a cat-schooner rig into this hull: "I like the way it looks."

Well-executed construction drawings reveal a distinctive stern treatment intended, in the designer's words, "to hide the outboard motor." That job it will perform quite nicely while keeping the unpleasant mechanical crew member isolated from the rest of the party. The motor can be tilted clear of the water — a matter of no small importance, as dragging a lower unit all over the bay would prove unacceptable under sail and heartbreaking when rowing. Although the drawings show a bent aluminum pipe tiller (designed to clear the motor's powerhead), I suspect many builders will glue up wooden sticks to the same pattern for a more elegant look.

The centerboard trunk and mainmast are located off center for the usual reasons of strength and simplicity, and to keep the slot clear of the ground. We might notice this modest asymmetry, but the boat most certainly will not.

This little schooner offers plenty of sprawling space for the crew and ample stowage for camping gear — or, rather, it would if it were slightly larger. In fact, the designer believes the boat would work better as a cruiser if it were increased properly in size to about 18 feet by 6 feet. Concern for her rowing characteristics dictated the present 15-foot 3-inch length, and she ought to row quite acceptably with her rig lowered and her appendages raised. This is a true combination boat, and it'll be a rare day when her skipper can't get home, using either the sails, the motor, or the oars.

*A* small downwind sailing rig lends visual interest to the Flashboat's drawings, but this is a thoroughbred pulling boat, pure and simple. Based on a class of raceboats in Gartside's native Cornwall, she's intended for high speed in relatively open water.

Discussing the extremely slack-bilged sections the designer explains, "If you want to make a normal rowing boat faster — without resorting to sliding seats and outriggers — this shape evolves naturally." The resulting narrow load waterline speaks of speed, and it suggests a possible lack of sufficient stability.

I've not yet had the pleasure of rowing a Flashboat, but I have pulled various West Coast designs that display remarkably similar sections. If you'll allow me the luxury of extrapolation....

Stability should be no problem — if you're accustomed to canoes, kayaks, or high-performance pulling boats. This boat will feel tender at first, much in the manner of a light dory, but she'll seem to stiffen once you're settled down on the rowing thwart. Additional loading (say, a compatible passenger and a picnic lunch) will make her even more solid.

At low and moderate rowing effort, the Flashboat will pull much in the manner of a Whitehall — easily and with good carry — though you'll notice her light weight. The revelation will come when you pour on the power. Pulled with sufficient vigor, a typical rowing boat eventually will dig itself a hole in the water and fall into it. No matter how hard you row, you'll go no faster — a textbook demonstration of "hull speed."

The Flashboat, on the other hand, will reward additional effort with increased speed to a degree that feels almost unnatural. A glance at her lower hull lines removes some of the mystery; the water doesn't have to move far or fast to get out of her way.

The construction drawings show each side planked up with four highly "tortured" (twisted to produce compound curvature) strakes of 4mm Bruynzeel. This is expedient design for accomplished builders, but the less experienced will want to be wary, as tortured plywood can bend in strange and subtle ways.

Flashboat is little heavier than some tandem canoes, but she's roomier and better suited to open water. She ought to be almost as fast as some recreational rowing shells, but she's simpler and less expensive. Weighing only 90 pounds, she'll travel happily on cartop — and that's packing a lot of performance on your roof.

*Plans for the 15-foot Schooner and Flashboat are available from Paul Gartside, 10305 W. Saanich Rd., RR #1, Sidney, BC, V8L 3R9, Canada.*

# Particulars
## Schooner

LOA     15'3"
Beam   5'0"
Sail area  108 sq ft

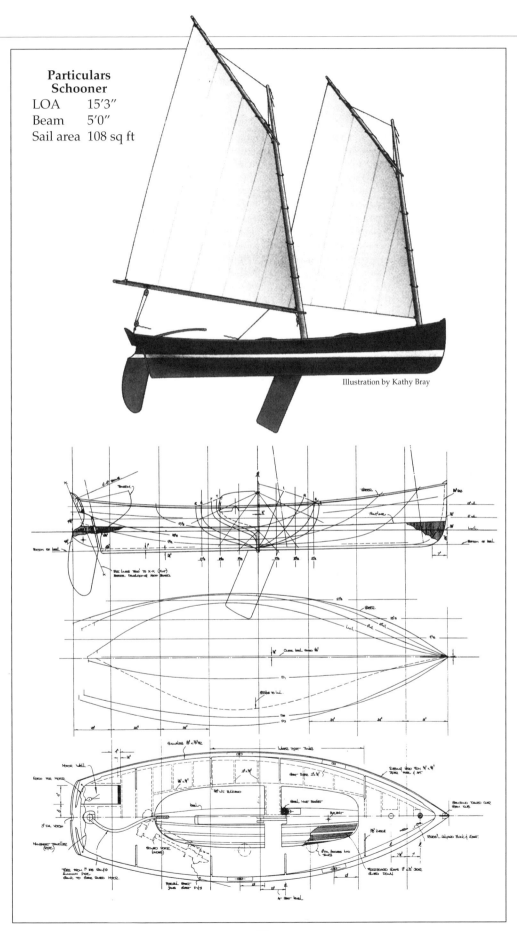

Illustration by Kathy Bray

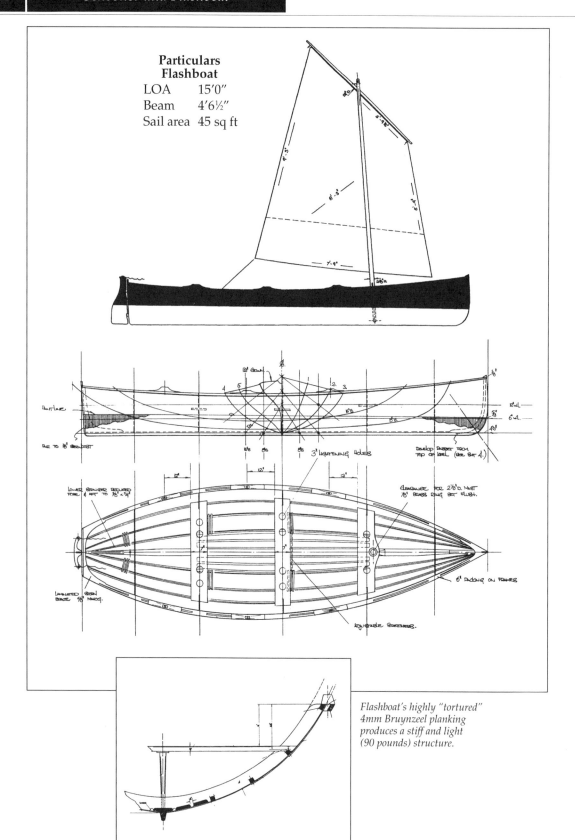

**Particulars**
**Flashboat**
LOA      15'0"
Beam     4'6½"
Sail area  45 sq ft

*Flashboat's highly "tortured"
4mm Bruynzeel planking
produces a stiff and light
(90 pounds) structure.*

# X

# Two Chesapeake Skiffs

——— Drawn by Howard I. Chapelle and Reuel Parker ———
Commentary by Mike O'Brien

Chesapeake Bay sailing crab skiffs can, with little alteration, make fast and able daysailers. These skiffs first appeared on the big estuary during the last years of the nineteenth century. The type — perhaps we should say "types" — varied wildly from creek to creek. Depending upon local conditions and prejudices, an observer at the time would have found single- and two-stick rigs, with or without headsails. Deadrise amidships (amount of V to the bottom) ranged from 0 degrees to about 12 degrees. Hulls were double-ended or transom-sterned. In fact, the diversity in skiff design allowed watermen to identify a boat as the product of a particular county, if not a particular builder.

In addition to serving as their name suggests, the skiffs earned their keep in general waterfront transportation and by handling odd jobs. Although these boats went extinct half a century ago (at least as working watercraft), many of their characteristics survive in contemporary Chesapeake outboard-powered skiffs. Cross-planked bottoms, strong sheerlines, and sharp forward sections still can be seen in the working powerboats at public landings along the Bay's convoluted 5,000-mile shoreline.

The 16-foot 8-inch sailing skiff shown here must be one of the most handsome of the old boats. According to Howard Chapelle, who wrote about her in the June 1943 issue of *Yachting* magazine, this striking deadrise hull was hammered together by a builder named Simmons in 1910 at Cambridge, Maryland. Mr. Chapelle took the lines off the old boat on September 11, 1942 in the same town. We're told only that the hull construction was "of the usual Bay deadrise type." This suggests a V-bottom cross-planked in herringbone fashion with little internal framing. Although he might have shaped a "chunk" forefoot from a single

timber, Mr. Simmons more likely accomplished the considerable deadrise up forward by staving the forefoot. (That is, he filled the space between the backbone and chines with short, thick planks fashioned to the required twist.)

With its 3¾-inch by 3¾-inch keelson and 1-inch bottom planking, this is not a light hull. Good, old-fashioned inertia will make the boat steadier to work in the notorious Chesapeake chop and will give it the power to punch through now-ubiquitous powerboat wakes. No matter what miracle goops and goos we might employ in building this skiff today, I'd suggest not taking too much weight out of its structure.

We're told that most of the Cambridge boats shared the springy sheer, considerable deadrise, flared sides, and raking ends seen here. Chapelle suggests that the rough water often found at the mouth of the Choptank River provided ample incentive to build able skiffs. Unlike some flat-bottomed skiffs, these deadrise hulls tend to maintain headway when coming about; they don't pay off excessively before settling in on a new tack. (The habit of falling off before heading up to a new course constitutes a potentially dangerous character flaw in half-decked boats. Unless the sheets are carefully tended, a nearly stationary skiff can be knocked down as the wind fills its tightly strapped sails. Builders sometimes fitted flat-bottomed Bay skiffs with substantial foregripes to lessen the risk.)

This Cambridge skiff's rig is fairly representative of those seen elsewhere on the Bay. Its sprit-boomed leg-o'-mutton sails provide their usual advantages: They are self-vanging (the angled foot of the sail tightens and prevents the boom from lifting). They can live with light booms and simple sheeting arrangements. Draft in the sails can be controlled, to a degree, by adjusting the tension in the snotter (the line that secures the boom to the mast). Sail twist can be varied by changing snotter tension and/or by sliding the snotter up or down the mast.

Although the curve drawn into the foot of each sail looks fine, our sailmaker will know to cut the bottoms of the sails dead straight to better handle the tension. While we're at it, let's ask him to cut the mainsail somewhat fuller — and with the point of maximum draft farther forward — than he would for, say, a tautly strung sloop. Because the mizzen often will be sheeted closer than the mainsail, among other reasons, it ought to be sewn relatively flat.

At the size we're discussing, these rigs need no ready-made hardware. Absolutely none. Dumb sheaves (well faired and lined holes worked through the sticks near their heads) will substitute for halyard blocks. The single-part sheets need only a bowline at one end and a figure-of-eight knot at the other. Rope snotters do the work of stainless-steel or bronze gooseneck fittings — and then some.

*I*n *The Sharpie Book* (International Marine, Camden, Maine, 1994), Reuel Parker gives us drawings for classic designs that have been adapted for sheet-plywood construction. Here is a fine single-sail skiff, Parker's variation on Figure 115 from Howard Chapelle's *American Small Sailing Craft* (W.W. Norton & Co., New York, 1951). The old boat is believed to have been built on Hoopers Island about 1906. Chapelle took the lines off her at Crisfield, Maryland, in 1943.

This hull's shallow, almost flat-bottomed, forefoot allowed Parker to sheathe its virtually unaltered lines with sheet plywood. (The deeper, sharper forefoot of the Cambridge skiff would, most likely, have demanded some fancy on-the-spot laminating in order to mate with a sheet bottom.)

We might note that this skiff and the Cambridge boat have their centerboards located far forward by yacht standards, and the boards are slightly smaller than expected. This arrangement has obvious advantages in working skiffs, and the added cockpit room will be appreciated in the daysailing derivatives. The happy configuration is made feasible by the forward bias of the sail plans' geometrical centers and by the far-aft lateral plane offered by large skegs and rudders.

Before dropping the rig from the old skiff into the new skiff, Parker lopped about 20 inches off the mast. As indicated by the vertical dashed line drawn on the sail, he added a traditional vertical slab-reefing system that was sometimes used for larger sharpies. Details of this arrangement can be found on page 66 of Chapelle's book, *Boatbuilding* (W.W. Norton & Co., New York, 1941).

Casual inspection of the contemporary waterfront suggests that too many raceboats masquerade as daysailers — their shallow cockpits fouled by nests of lines, and nary a seat in sight. Old skiffs from the Chesapeake offer secure and comfortable alternatives.

*Plans for the Simmons Cambridge skiff, as drawn by Howard I. Chapelle, can be obtained from Ship Plans, NMAH 5010/MRC 628, Smithsonian Institution, Washington, DC 20560. Ask for CBCS plan No. 4.*

*Plans for Reuel Parker's version of the Hoopers Island skiff are available from Parker Marine Enterprises, P.O. Box 4102, Key West, FL 33041. Ask for the 18-foot modified sharpie skiff.*

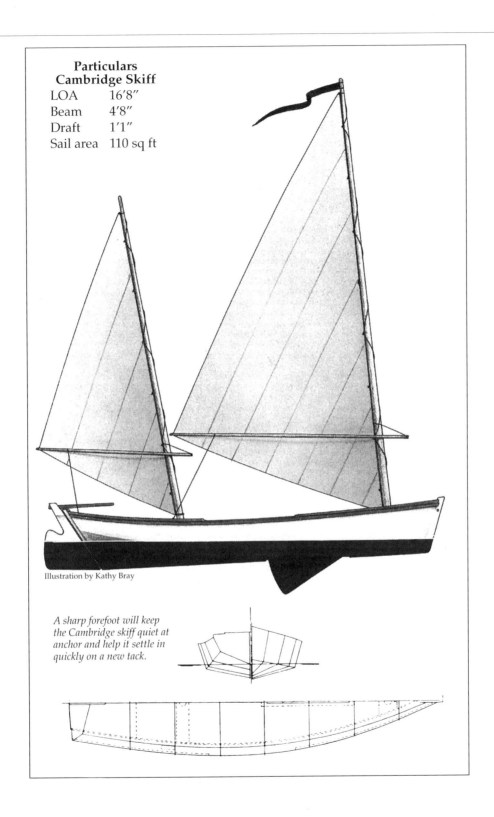

**Particulars**
**Cambridge Skiff**

| | |
|---|---|
| LOA | 16'8" |
| Beam | 4'8" |
| Draft | 1'1" |
| Sail area | 110 sq ft |

Illustration by Kathy Bray

*A sharp forefoot will keep the Cambridge skiff quiet at anchor and help it settle in quickly on a new tack.*

**Particulars**
**Hoopers Island Skiff**
  LOA      17'10"
  Beam     5'6"
  Draft    1'3"
  Sail area  106 sq ft

*Reuel Parker derived his
18-foot sheet-plywood skiff
from a cross-planked hull
drawn by Howard Chapelle
in 1943. The original boat
was built on Hoopers
Island about 1906.*

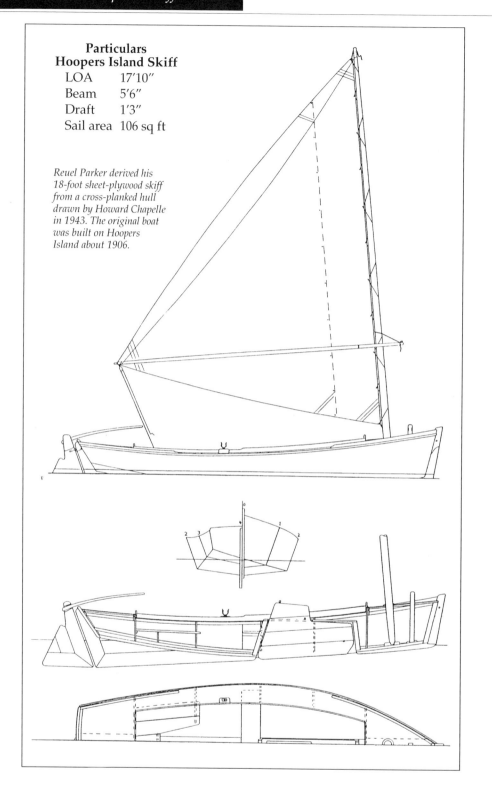

# A Rowing and Sailing Skiff

——— Design by R.D. "Pete" Culler ———
Commentary by the editors of *WoodenBoat*

This skiff was designed by Pete Culler in 1976 for our neighbor, Anne Bray. The boat is intended to serve as a tender for the Brays' summer camp on a rocky island, here in Maine.

Because the island has no beach or dock, the boat must be loaded and boarded over the stern, from a sloping granite ledge. This gave rise to the boat's most unusual feature: The bottom aft has no skeg and is rounded up sharply to roughly match the curve of the ledge where she will be landing. The stern is quite flared and buoyant, and is quite broad for what is a relatively narrow boat, making it very difficult to submerge, and yet providing a smooth run. There is considerable rake to the transom "bringing it closer to you" when boarding. She could be built with a more conventional afterbody if it was wanted. (The conventional version is shown in the design section of the book *Boats, Oars, and Rowing*, [International Marine, Camden, Maine, 1978] by Pete Culler.)

This skiff is intended to be easy to row, with her relatively narrow bottom, clean lines, and low freeboard. As a sailboat she can be anything from a good workhorse to a real flyer, with her three possible sail plans (main and mizzen, main alone, or mizzen alone, stepped forward). Her low freeboard serves as a kind of safety valve, when sailing. While her flared sides will keep her dry and add considerable reserve stability, she will start taking water over the rail long before she reaches the point of no return and capsizes. She will sail best on her bottom, at any rate. The spritsail and Chesapeake mizzen are strong, simple, and light to handle, and easy to construct. There is no boom to conk you on the head when you're rowing out of a tight spot.

The rudder and centerboard have been kept shoal, to preserve the boat's ability to tiptoe in around the rocks and ledges without touching bottom. The rudder looks too shallow, but it is expected to "swim lower" when underway. It is hung in the manner of the English beach boats, with a very long lower pintle, which looks wrong end to, making it easy to ship or trice up, when landing. It is hoped that it will rise up if it hits an obstruction. The pintles and gudgeons are intended to be very stong, since of necessity they must be mounted unusually close together.

Compared to round-bottomed boats, skiffs tend to weigh a lot, and as drawn this one would be no exception. Culler preferred his skiffs on the heavy side, but, in view of this boat's intended use, he thought it would be perfectly okay if the following steps were taken to cut down on her weight:

- The planking reduced from ½ inch to ⅜ inch and using four laps instead of three.
- The frames of cedar instead of oak but spaced 2 inches or 3 inches closer together.
- The bottom planks made thinner, ⅝ inch instead of ¾ inch and their seams splined.
- Except for the chines, all else that was normally made of oak could be made of cedar.

It would be difficult to imagine a handier, more versatile boat for working the shore and beachcombing. She should be a joy to row or sail, and will be an eye-catcher wherever she goes.

*Plans for the 17-foot Culler skiff are available from George B. Kelley, 20 Lookout Ln., Hyannis, MA 02601; 508-775-2679.*

**Particulars**
**17-foot Culler Skiff**
  LOA    17'10"
  Beam   5'0"
  Draft   5¾"

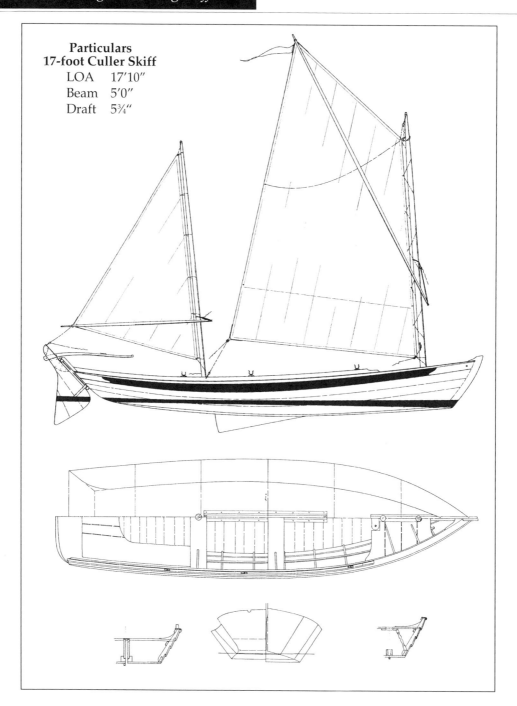

# XII

# A Lapstrake Open Boat

Design by Rob Pittaway
Commentary by the editors of *WoodenBoat*

*Robin* is 18 feet LOA, with 5 feet 1 inch of beam and a depth of 22 inches amidships. She is an open boat, arranged with three rowing positions and a ketch rig for sailing. The mainsail is rigged with a diagonal sprit, and the mizzen with a horizontal sprit. There are no headsails.

*Robin* was designed in 1975 by Rob Pittaway for Nat French of Westport, Massachusetts, and she was built in 1976–78 by his stepson Steve Goodale. The concept was for a boat that two people could use for coastal cruising under sail or oars, yet be small enough to be trailered. Two of the prime requirements were that she be able to carry quite a lot of weight and be reasonably stable when beached. That led to this full but easy shape and the plank keel.

The sail type was chosen for its simplicity, and the two-masted rig to achieve various combinations of sail. The masts are the same size so they can be stepped in either location. Three rowing positions were provided, although the use of two is most frequently anticipated.

All told, nine different woods were used to build this boat: red oak, white oak, hackmatack, Honduras mahogany, native white cedar, Maine cherry, white ash, yellow pine, and white pine. Each wood was chosen not only for function, but also for looks, as the inside of the boat was to be finished bright. Hardware for the boat was custom designed and made by Steve Goodale. This included mast collars, oarlock sockets, centerboard lever, rudder hardware, and stem band

*Robin* has proved to be a fast, able boat under sail and oars, with or without a large load of people. She spends her time between Penobscot Bay, Alamoosook Lake in Bucksport, Maine, and Westport Point, Massachusetts, serving well in each location.

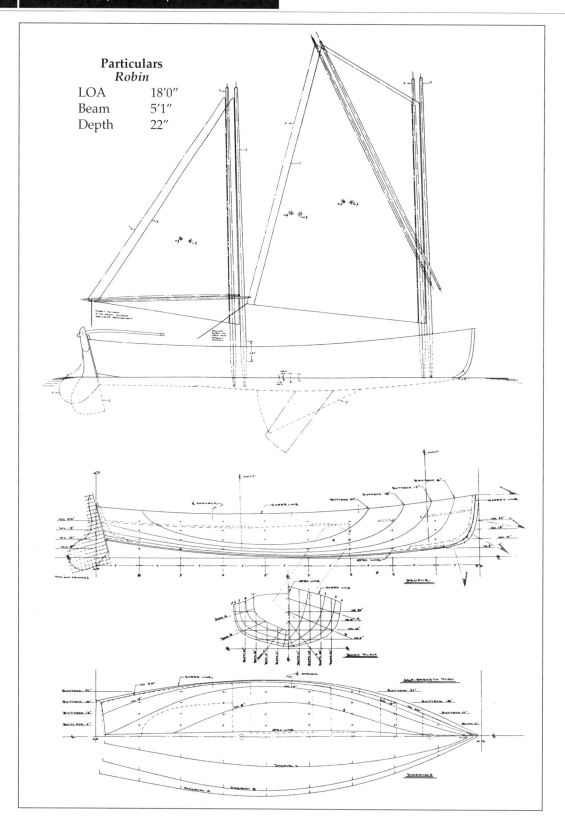

**Particulars**
*Robin*

| | |
|---|---|
| LOA | 18'0" |
| Beam | 5'1" |
| Depth | 22" |

# XIII

# *A Sloop Boat*

———— Design by R.D. "Pete" Culler ————
Commentary by Mike O'Brien

*I*should admit up front to having lusted after the Buzzards Bay Sloop for years. How could I not want this boat? With every subtle curve and detail, her hull demonstrates Pete Culler's gift for proportion and his sense of appropriate decoration.

We can trace the lineage of the traditionally styled 18-foot 8-inch Buzzards Bay Sloop directly to the designer's 17-foot 8-inch Concordia Sloop Boat, and that daysailer has its roots in small working craft. In *Pete Culler's Boats*, by John Burke (International Marine, Camden, Maine, 1984), the Concordia Company's Waldo Howland recalled considerations that led to the Sloop Boat's design and construction:

"Such a boat," Howland said, "would have to be attractive to look at and shipshape in appearance. She would have to be well built with special attention to detail. For a number of reasons, wood seemed to be the best and only medium for construction. Wood has natural virtues so far as appearance, sound, feel, smell, and flotation are concerned. Variations and modifications by [the boat's] owner are easy. And [wood] can be painted, polished, and puttered with. In short, it can be loved."

During their search for an appropriate model, Howland and his fellow conspirators talked about Scituate lobsterboats, Connecticut River shad boats, and Bahama dinghies. All having been said, Culler kept a Kingston lobsterboat firmly in mind while drawing the hull lines for Concordia's daysailer.

Although Burke's book bristles with accounts of the Sloop Boat's ability in a breeze of wind, this is a light and narrow craft that carries a healthy spread of canvas. It can jump up and bite a sailor who dismisses the mainsail's deep reefs as mere affectations. For all its virtues, stability and power are not the Sloop Boat's strong suits.

In 1977, Wyatt Garfield asked Culler to draw him a more able version of this design for sailing off the exposed shores of Cuttyhunk Island. Captain Pete stretched the hull to 18 feet 8 inches, made it 1 foot wider, added 6 inches to the draft, cranked some deadrise out of the bottom, and included 700 pounds of outside ballast for good measure. He increased the sail area sparingly. He swept up the sheer back aft. (So far as I know, nobody ever accused the old Sloop Boat of dragging its tail; but, with a lazy helmsman loafing against the transom, the little boat appeared to be perpetually climbing uphill.) Lapstrake planking replaced the smooth set work specified for the original design. Shadows cast at the laps would accentuate the new hull's sweet lines.

The gains in stability and power provided by these changes might surprise a casual observer until he remembers that "size" increases essentially as the cube of a hull's length. Of course, the unseen lead ballast adds considerable inertia to the equation and stability to the boat.

Grant Robinson finished the first Buzzards Bay Sloop at his shop in Marblehead, Massachusetts. Since then, the good people at The Landing School near Kennebunkport, Maine, have built about twenty boats to this design — well, almost to this design. They added an afterdeck to create a usable lazarette and to provide a solid base for mounting a bronze outboard-motor bracket. (Some of us believe that hanging an internal-combustion engine on a boat of such elegance represents at least a minor crime against nature. As may be, the bracket is removable.)

The Landing's instructors and students faired the hull lines first on the drawing table and then on the loft floor. They drew about 1 inch of additional freeboard at the stem to obviate any chance of the three-dimensional sheer appearing to powderhorn (take on a reverse or S curve forward) in the finished hull — no matter from what angle it might be viewed. Most boatbuilders consider the above modifications to constitute "builder's prerogative." Some designers will disagree. That's the way it is.

When the folks at The Landing School asked if I'd like to sail one of their Buzzards Bay Sloops, they didn't have to wait long for a reply. I drove up to Kennebunkport on an October Indian-summer afternoon. The sun was warm, the air crisp, and the visibility stretched far beyond the limits of middle-aged eyesight — a day to pull from my mind's closet in the dead of this winter.

I found the sloop resting in a borrowed slip at the local yacht club. The low autumn sun reflected from white topsides and mirrored the lapped planks on the water. Oiled teak decks and rails glowed like honey in a glass jar. Oh, my.

Once aboard, I was surrounded by comfortably shaped details. From the steam-bent coaming and slatted benches to the carefully tapered spars, this boat bespoke first-class professional quality. Never mind that she was built as a learning experience. Looking forward from the helm, my eyes followed the ever-tightening arches formed by closely spaced bent frames. They define the hull's shape. Of course, most of the frames are redundant in this glued lapstrake hull. Landing's president John Burgess explains that they were included for their "educational value." Yes, and I'll wager that the students had grand fun bending them in, too.

The sloop's cockpit is, indeed, good space. But I had come to sail, and we fired up the iron breeze for the run to open water. The flooding tide roared at us through the narrow mouth of the Kennebunk River. Any moral objections to internal-combustion machinery conveniently disappeared just long enough for us to power through the cut. (King Kong himself would have had to think twice before rowing against that current.)

As we worked clear of the gentrified Kennebunkport waterfront, Jamie Houtz (Landing's director of boatbuilding) hoisted sail. He had plenty of strings to pull:

throat and peak halyards for the mainsail, a jib halyard, too-tight reef lines, etc. While the sloop is underway, the halyards' falls hang neatly from belaying pins at the turn of the coaming up forward. They look right, and they come easily to hand — a fortunate arrangement on this day as the new three-strand running rigging stretched as if made from rubber.

We reached off under a moderate breeze to the good sound of a lapstrake hull cutting through waves. (Lapstrake boats don't make noise. They make sound, lots of sound, pleasant sound.) The sloop's fine forefoot blends smoothly into flaring topsides to produce a smart bow. This boat understands that she should brush aside small waves but climb over the tall ones. Her motion is easy and comforting.

The helm is light but firm. Culler's sloop wants to keep to its heading, although not to the point of being stubborn. Nudge the tiller, and the boat will change course smoothly — almost imperceptibly. She is certain, but stately, in stays. I'd not want to drive her into a tacking duel with, say, a Herreshoff 12½-footer. If you're accustomed to sailing light centerboarders with big rudders, you'll be able to send out for lunch while putting the sloop about.

The low gaff-headed rig suits this boat aesthetically and functionally. While looking at Culler's drawings, we might wish he had peaked up the gaff just a wee bit to preclude its sloughing off to leeward. But, out on the water, it works fine just as drawn. The gaff's relatively short length, an efficient angle of pull for the peak halyard (allowed by a mast that extends well above the height of the gaff jaws), and a good angle to the mainsail's leech combine to keep the gaff where it ought to be.

The total joy of sailing any boat comes from the sum of a thousand discrete parts — aesthetic and technical. Aboard the Buzzards Bay Sloop, everything adds up perfectly; and she's almost as much fun to watch go as to sail. This was Captain Pete's last design. It might well have been his best.

*Plans for the Buzzards Bay Sloop and other Pete Culler designs are available from George B. Kelley, 20 Lookout Ln., Hyannis, MA 02601.*

## Particulars
## Buzzards Bay Sloop

| | |
|---|---|
| LOA | 18'8" |
| Beam | 6'0" |
| Draft | 2'0" |
| Sail area | 177 sq ft |

Illustration by Stephen Davis

*Firm bilges and outside ballast help keep the Buzzards Bay Sloop on her feet. Culler's original drawings, shown here, specify traditional lapstrake construction. The boat we sailed had a glued plywood lapstrake hull.*

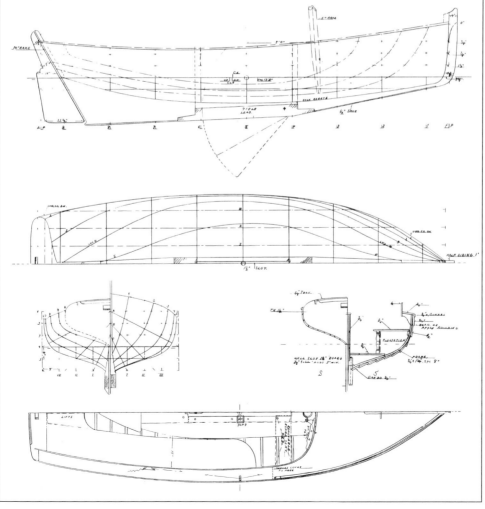

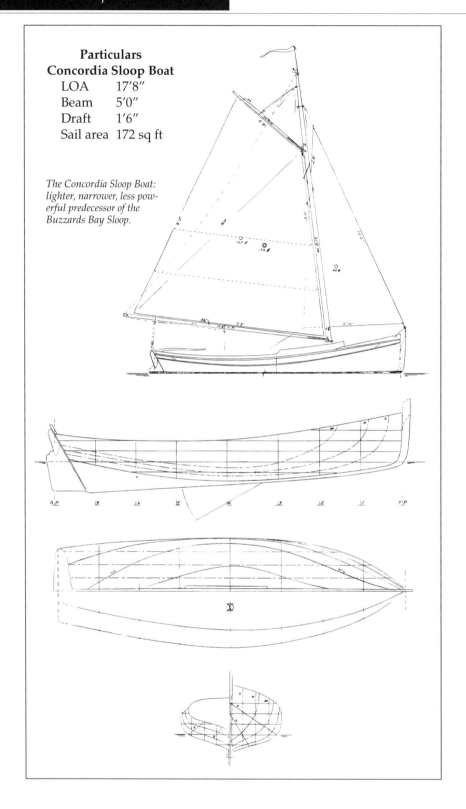

**Particulars**
**Concordia Sloop Boat**

| | |
|---|---|
| LOA | 17'8" |
| Beam | 5'0" |
| Draft | 1'6" |
| Sail area | 172 sq ft |

*The Concordia Sloop Boat: lighter, narrower, less powerful predecessor of the Buzzards Bay Sloop.*

# A Beach-Cruising Yawl

Design by Iain Oughtred
Commentary by Mike O'Brien

*A* long time ago, I cruised the Chesapeake in a 15-foot peapod. A typical summer's day would unfold in no particular hurry: Up at first light (more or less) after having slept on the beach; take a short and slow walk along the waterfront, drag the stranded boat down to the water, stow the meager camping gear, and row off into the morning calm. Breakfast about a mile offshore, safe from at least some of the biting insects; row on until the climbing sun makes the effort uncomfortable (usually about 10 a.m.); go ashore and find a proper shade tree under which to doze until lunch (the insects have disappeared in the heat of a dry day). At the first sign of the afternoon sea breeze (some time between 12:30 and 1:30) set up the unstayed lug rig and sail to wherever. In the evening, when the thermal fades, strike the rig, and pull the last mile or so to a secluded cove. Such are the simple delights of beach cruising.

Because several types of boats are suitable for this pleasant mode of travel, perhaps a functional definition of the breed will serve best. A competent beach cruiser should be simply rigged; capable of carrying large loads; light enough to be dragged over bar and beach by its crew; safe in moderate surf; able to sail, not just float, in shallow water; able to work its way up small creeks under sail, oar, or paddle; comfortable to sleep aboard; sufficiently rugged to withstand frequent and terrible abuse. A beach cruiser need not be flat bottomed, or carry only a single mast, or have only one hull.

The design shown here, Iain Oughtred's 19-foot 6-inch Caledonia Yawl, will make an excellent beach cruiser. It will be faster under sail and will carry more gear than my peapod (though we can be certain that the old pod will be easier to row and less of a challenge to horse around the beach).

Oughtred, known for applying an artist's touch to his light lapstrake creations, admits to being under the influence of Shetland ness yoles and sixerns while drawing this handsome double-ender. And those highly regarded workboats can trace their pedigree to older Norwegian small craft — a strong heritage. The Caledonia has relatively high ends and shows considerable reserve buoyancy above the waterline throughout her length. Her hull lines resemble those of many surfboats that have evolved to meet the rigors of working off exposed beaches on different continents. (Similarities between the world's beach boats often are more striking than regional idiosyncrasies.) This yawl has well-balanced ends. Oughtred gave her a run that is finer and shows more deadrise than might be ideal for extremely high speed under sail. The resulting gains in helm balance and civilized behavior in waves make the compromise profitable.

Caledonia's builders can rig their boats with either balanced lug or high-peaked gaff-headed mainsails. The balanced lug has the advantage of being self-vanging, and it sets on an unstayed mast. Less time will be required to raise and strike the lug rig — good news, as beach cruising often involves repeating the exercise four or five times every day.

The control and balance provided by the tiny (33-square foot) leg-o'-mutton mizzen probably pay for its cost — and for the complication it introduces into the steering equation. The mizzen will almost always be the first sail set. It will keep the yawl squarely into the wind while you fuss about stowing the lunch and setting the mainsail. To assure positive tacking, simply back the mizzen to the inside of the turn as you come about (this boat shouldn't need help often). When you're ready to eat lunch, strap the mizzen in hard, and drop the main (lugsails come down as fast as lead balloons). In this configuration, Caledonia will sit quietly during most summer weather. At the end of the day, if you're of a mind to show off, the mizzen can be used to back the boat down under sail into a slip. Just be sure to remember the boomkin, and keep the mainsheet free to run; if it fouls, you'll be courting disaster of front-page proportions.

The steering difficulty caused by the far-aft location of the mizzen is obvious — the tiller wants to cut clean through the mast. Oughtred could have solved the problem by specifying a fancy curved tiller, or by drawing an inboard rudder with its post forward of the mast, or by using a yoke and lines. He chose the simplest solution: a push/pull tiller. A short tiller arm (half a yoke, if you will) attaches to the rudderhead perpendicular to the centerline. A long, light tiller is hinged to the shorter stick and run forward. As drawn here, pulling the tiller forward will turn the boat to starboard. Some practice in open water will suffice to get the technique under control. On your first day with the boat, you might want to row out of the harbor.

For serious shallow-water sailing, Oughtred chose a pivoting centerboard in preference to a daggerboard. This arrangement requires a longer trunk, but the boat has room to spare. A rowing thwart supports the trunk solidly.

The kick-up rudder (shown as an option) would add to Caledonia's shoal-water ability, but you might want to alter the design to provide for more bearing surface between the blade and cheeks when the blade is in its raised position. Sooner or later, someone will use the kicked-up rudder to scull the boat off a mud bank, and....

Caledonia's lapstrake construction makes good use of plywood and epoxy. The hull is built in an inverted position, and the backbone and building jig are fairly conventional. Four wide strakes for each side are spiled, hung over temporary molds, and beveled. Drywall screws can act as clamps until the epoxy sets. Solid timber shouldn't be used for planking this boat, even if you're fortunate enough to find boards of appropriate width. Lack of cross-grain strength makes it prone to splitting — especially along the laps. Solid planking works fine for similar designs, but here there are subtle differences in shape and considerable differences in framing. Find the best mahogany marine plywood you can, and go to it. Oughtred's yawl is well worth the expense.

The plans specify ⅜-inch planking for Caledonia's sides and bottom. Her frameless hull will be strong and stiff, but it's well to remember that plywood's outer surface — no matter how thick the sheet — consists of one extremely thin layer of veneer. You might consider adding hardwood beaching strips, one on each side, at the first lap just below the turn of the bilge. They needn't be too long. Three or four feet of length should do — just enough to catch the fullness of her hull as she lies on the beach.

As for accommodations, Oughtred shows a version with considerable built-in closed space (similar to a Drascombe Lugger's interior) and a more open model. The open boat will be simpler and lighter — and for beach cruisers, light is good. Builders can choose various combinations of the two layouts. In all cases, the decks are kept below the rails. This arrangement gives better access to the yawl's ends, and it permits secure on-deck stowage of light gear. Also, the sunken decks allow our eyes to follow the full, unbroken sweep of the sheer from stem to stern. I can't look at this boat without wanting to push her into the surf and take off.

*Plans for the Caledonia Yawl can be obtained from The WoodenBoat Store, P.O. Box 78, Brooklin, ME 04616; 800–273–7447.*

*Iain Oughtred can be reached at Altyre Stables, Forres, Moray IV36 0SH, Scotland.*

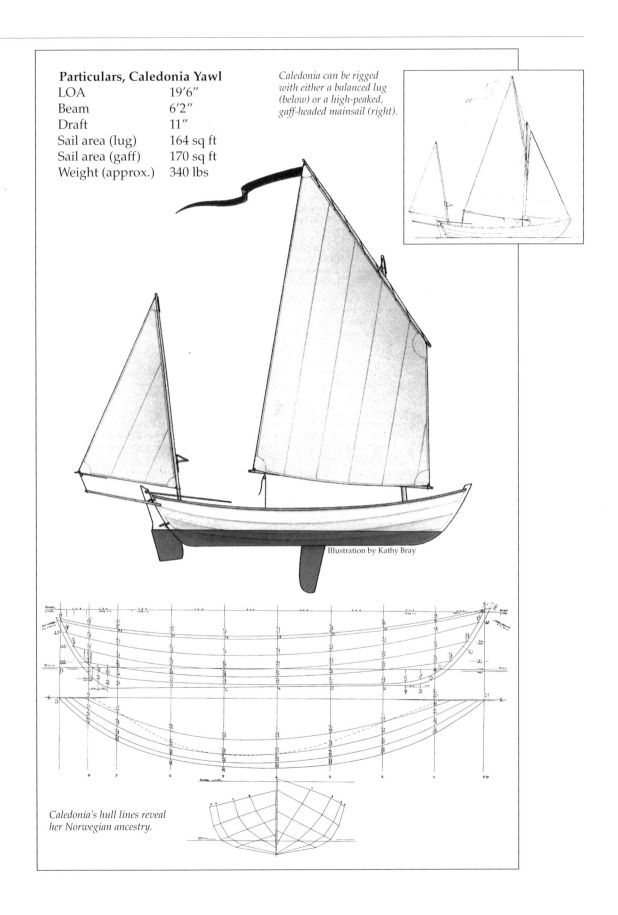

**Particulars, Caledonia Yawl**

| | |
|---|---|
| LOA | 19'6" |
| Beam | 6'2" |
| Draft | 11" |
| Sail area (lug) | 164 sq ft |
| Sail area (gaff) | 170 sq ft |
| Weight (approx.) | 340 lbs |

*Caledonia can be rigged with either a balanced lug (below) or a high-peaked, gaff-headed mainsail (right).*

Illustration by Kathy Bray

*Caledonia's hull lines reveal her Norwegian ancestry.*

## Caledonia Yawl

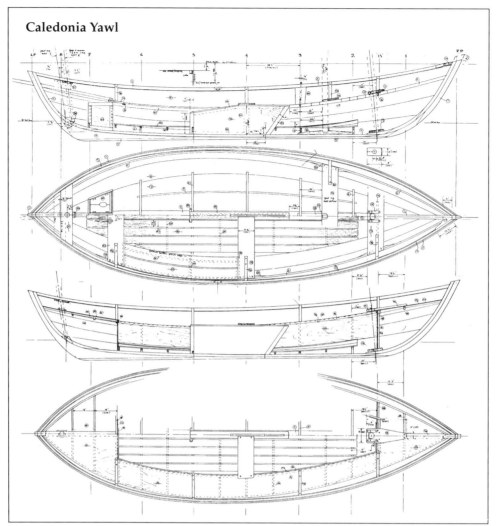

*Builders can choose a simple, open interior (top), a
model with built-in furniture (bottom), or a combination of both arrangements.*

# An Interclub Racing Dory

—— Design by John G. Alden ——
Commentary by the editors of *WoodenBoat*

As the refinement of the Swampscott dory type reached its zenith, the need arose to depart more distinctly from the workboat origins — where rowing was as important as sailing — and to develop a dory type specifically for sailing in interclub races. And, as John Alden never failed to appreciate the trends of his time, he set Sam Crocker, then in his employ, to work on a sailing dory one-design class in early 1921. The result was a beautifully modeled 21-footer with a marconi rig that carried 350 pounds of inside ballast.

The advantages of the new design over the traditional Swampscott were greater beam and firmer bilges, brought aft to the transom, which afforded the opportunity to carry more sail and thus perform better (on a triangular course). With its generous side decks and inside ballast, the design provided a margin of safety without diminishing the excitement factor. It was, in fact, a boat well suited to clubs with limited budgets and many young sailors.

William Chamberlain built the first boats (and many of the rest), which were first sailed in 1921 at Marblehead's Eastern Yacht Club. So successful were the boats that other clubs ordered more built, and the Indian class was well on its way.

In an age of high-performance planing craft, the Indian class has little to offer today's racing sailor, but before it vanishes into obscurity, we ought to take another look. It is, after all, a fine performer itself, and one that will sail well in all sorts of conditions. Given its relative simplicity of construction, the Indian should be relatively inexpensive to build.

The Indian is built dory-style, with the bottom, stem, transom, and six sawn frames being set up first. After the planking is completed, four pairs of steam-bent frames are set in place between each pair of sawn frames, the combination providing a light, stiff hull. Because of that construction, full lofting is unnecessary and dimensions can be picked up from the plan. An interesting option offered in the design is the so-called V-stern, wherein the garboard and broadstrake lap together at the transom without a knuckle, affording, presumably, somewhat less drag at this point.

The round-sided dory types require a wider-than-usual garboard, the stock for which can be very difficult to find these days. There are, of course, a number of ways of creating one wide plank from two narrow ones, but the cheapest and simplest solution might be to join them with typical riveted dory laps, perhaps made flush so as not to show. For the best guidance on dory history and construction, John Gardner's *The Dory Book* (Mystic Seaport Museum, Mystic Connecticut, 1987) is unmatched.

*Plans of the 21-foot Indian Class are available from The WoodenBoat Store, P.O. Box 78, Brooklin, ME 04616; 800–273–7447.*

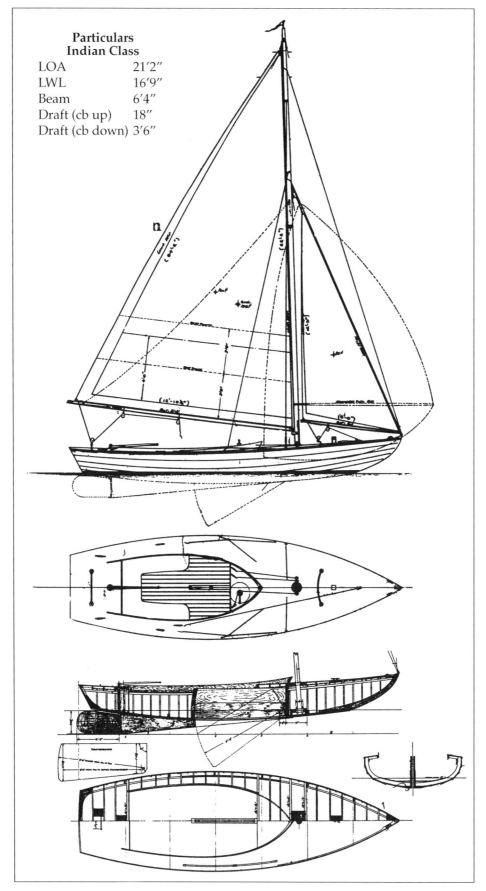

**Particulars**
**Indian Class**
LOA              21'2"
LWL              16'9"
Beam             6'4"
Draft (cb up)    18"
Draft (cb down)  3'6"

# An Experimental Daysailer

Design by Henry Scheel
Commentary by Joel White

Henry (Harry) Scheel is no longer with us, but what remains is a 50-year legacy of designs (and boats) that came from the drawing board of this most creative man.

Scheel was an early hero of mine — his designs always stood out from the pages of the boating magazines over which I misspent so many youthful hours. His boats had a flair, a bold profile, a youthful zest, so much like the man I later came to know. His early career was based in New York City and Connecticut, but later years were spent here in Maine. Before he died, his design work had begun to reach international circles, and three large designs were built at the Royal Huisman Shipyard in Holland, necessitating many trips abroad to oversee construction. To my eye, these are among the loveliest of his creations. They represent the culmination of a lifetime of design.

The Scheel keel, with its cross sections shaped like the profile of an axe head, is another reminder of Harry's inquisitive mind. Designed to concentrate ballast weight low and to reduce tip eddies to a minimum, the Scheel keel is offered by many stock builders around the world — especially where draft reduction is important.

Always an innovator, at the time of his death he was working on a series of designs for a new hull shape that he believed would make a better, faster boat — one in which wave-making would be suppressed by the addition of a chine in the after sections of the boat. He pursued this idea with a series of sailing models, most of them radio-controlled, and it was a common sight around Rockport, Maine, to see Harry fooling with his models. He even made one that had the usual round-bottomed hull shape on the starboard side while the port side had the added chine. Sailing this model on first one tack, then the other, demonstrated to Scheel the value of the chine, and he was able to photograph the different wave patterns coming from each side.

Several years ago, a 25-foot daysailer was built to this idea — the boat illustrated here. Scheel had named the new series Bestyet, and the boat in question was the Bestyet 25.

A look at the Bestyet's plans will show that innovation did not stop with the added chine. The boat has a most interesting drop keel combined with a triangular fixed fin amidships. The sail plan shown is conventional, with a self-tending jib trimming to a track just forward of the mast, but Scheel was experimenting with more radical mainsail shapes — fully battened, and shaped much like windsurfer sails.

The lines plan, especially the body plan, shows what Scheel was doing. A light-displacement shape with long, straight buttock lines and a nearly flat bottom has been modified by starting a chine near the midship section. The chine runs to the stern, where it dies out between the last station and the stern itself. The effect of this in the body plan is to widen the LWL in the after sections, to straighten the buttocks even more, and to produce a shape that will handle higher speeds without too much quarter-wave production. I suppose the idea of drawing the chine at the stern is to eliminate drag when the corner of the transom is immersed, and perhaps for looks.

The displacement is 2,200 pounds, and the displacement/length ratio 125 — very much on the light side. The sail area/displacement ratio, a sort of horsepower rating, works out to 25, which is very high. Anything over 20 gives sports car performance to most boats. The plans we have do not show how much the drop keel weighs, but judging by the light construction of the hull, I would guess that it is perhaps 40 percent of the displacement, or nearly 900 pounds.

The only thing I find surprising about the lines is the large amount of forward overhang. I would have thought that in a boat of this type, Scheel would have gone for more waterline length and less overhang. But this overhang does make for nicely V'd forward sections and a drier boat.

The boat is quite beamy for her length, but the sections have considerable flare in the topsides, and the waterline beam is moderate. The boat is light enough and small enough to gain some of her stability from the weight of her crew sitting to windward. With the lead drop keel down, and a couple of crew on the rail, her stability should be good enough to handle the large sail plan shown.

The boat is built of cold-molded wood — a nice job by Steve Van Dam. This 25-footer has a light, multi-layer veneer skin over a framework of bulkheads and longitudinal stringers, and a thin plywood deck covered by teak strips. This type of construction produces a stiff, strong boat with minimum weight, but it creates an interior that is very much cluttered up with structural pieces.

Scheel elected not to have a cockpit in the strict sense of the word, drawing instead two footwells separated by a bridge deck for the main traveler, and letting the crew sit on the wide side decks. When I sailed the boat, I did not find this a very comfortable arrangement and, with four of us aboard, felt that we were unduly crowded in a 25-foot boat. But we must remember that the boat has very little depth of hull — she reminds me most of an overgrown Lightning — and to expect a deep, comfortable cockpit with seat backs is probably unreasonable. After all, what we are pursuing here is a new and faster way of sailing, not creature comforts.

There is a hatch in the forward deck for access to the forepeak and for storing sails. On each side of the cockpit, a section of the side deck hinges up to allow stowage of smaller gear items. The drop keel trunk comes through the deck just forward of the cockpit, and there is a winch and two-part tackle arrangement for handling this heavy unit. The mast is stepped just forward of the trunk.

When I sailed the boat the day gave us only light airs. The mainsail on board seemed to me to be about half size, reaching as it did only two-thirds of the way up the mast and halfway out the boom. These two facts combined to make for a less than satisfactory chance to try the boat's potential abilities.

I am used to daysailers with lots of lateral plane and a good grip on the water. By comparison, the Bestyet's minimal keel area and small expanse of sail made her very sluggish, and caused her to make a lot of leeway when beating out of the harbor. Outside the lighthouse we lay off on a longer reach, looking for more air, but never found it. The best sailing of the day came just as we returned to her mooring, when the wind picked up a bit and we zigzagged amongst the closely packed boats and she began to pick up her heels just a bit. I had the feeling that I had saddled up a racehorse that never quite got out of a trot, but might someday answer the trumpet with a charge that would take your breath away.

What about the new and improved underwater shape, and the claims of better performance from it? Had there been 15 or 20 knots of wind that day, I might have an answer for that question.

Having been an interested observer of boat design for more than half a century, I know how little comes along that is truly new and revolutionary. Design evolution is inevitably a series of very small steps forward, interspersed with backslides and side excursions. But Henry Scheel was always a man eager to take any track that offered promise, and he was undiscouraged when left floundering in the puckerbrush. I suspect that with this boat he was on the threshold of one of those very small steps. Whether it will develop into a large gain remains to be seen. But, bless the man for stepping forward. Good sailing, Harry!

*The original drawings for the Bestyet 25 are now at Mystic Seaport Museum, Ships Plans Division, P.O. Box 6000, Mystic, CT 06355.*

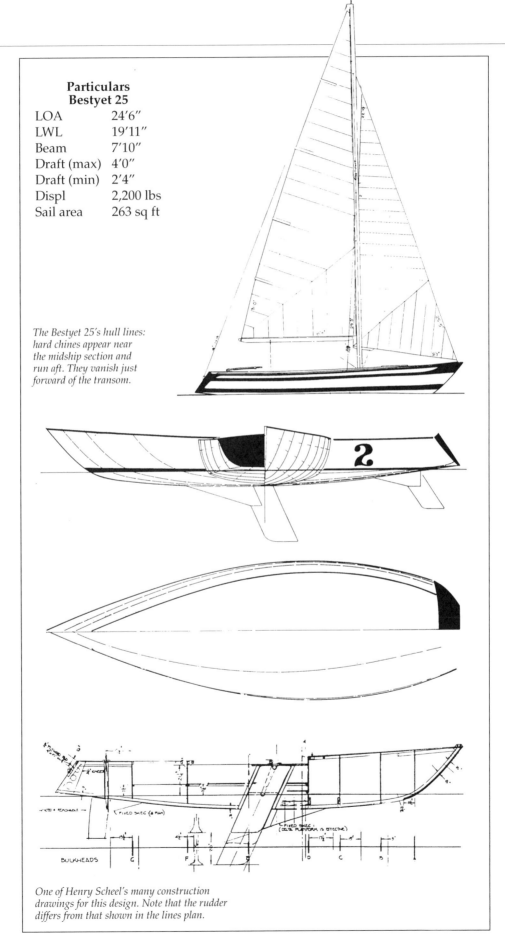

**Particulars
Bestyet 25**

LOA        24'6"
LWL        19'11"
Beam      7'10"
Draft (max)  4'0"
Draft (min)  2'4"
Displ      2,200 lbs
Sail area   263 sq ft

*The Bestyet 25's hull lines:
hard chines appear near
the midship section and
run aft. They vanish just
forward of the transom.*

*One of Henry Scheel's many construction
drawings for this design. Note that the rudder
differs from that shown in the lines plan.*

# Three Knockabouts

—————— Designs by B.B. Crowninshield ——————
Commentary by Maynard Bray

From the time the first 21-foot WL knockabouts *Nancy* and *Jane* appeared in 1892, the nearly fin-keeled jib and mainsail cabin sloops — day boats, really, of up to about 30 feet on deck with moderate overhangs — enjoyed a widespread popularity undiminished until the First World War.

"Knockabout" was the name given to most of these craft, whether or not they were designed to officially qualify as 15-foot, 18-foot, or 21-foot WL knockabouts as defined by the Massachusetts Bay Yacht Association. For their day, and compared to some of the freaks that preceded them, they were sensible craft, easily handled by one or two persons and fun to sail. They were simple to build and inexpensive to buy (boats from the first batch of 17½-footers featured here cost but $500 in 1909).

In 1908, B.B. Crowninshield, who was a well-connected Boston yacht designer with blueblood ancestry seeming to go back to God Himself, was asked to draw up a one-design class of knockabouts, which became known initially as the Manchester 17½-foot class. In the spring of 1909 a dozen boats emerged from the Rice Brothers building sheds at East Boothbay, Maine — all of them for members of the Manchester (Massachusetts) Yacht Club — initiating what was to become the most popular and long-lived class of their type in the history of yachting. Records indicate that another seven boats were ordered the following year and that before the building of new boats ceased in the mid-'30s, about 200 boats had been launched.

Not long after the early boats were built, the center of interest moved from Massachusetts Bay to the coast of Maine, between Penobscot Bay and Frenchman's Bay, and the name of the class was altered in a variety of ways depending on the particular yacht club affiliation. There is a group of a dozen or so boats still rac-

ing from the Buck's Harbor Yacht Club, and occasionally one finds a 17½-footer still sailing from other New England harbors as well.

There's good reason for their longevity: they're planked with cedar, have ballast keels of lead, and are fastened with copper rivets and bronze bolts. The simple deck layout and canvas over cedar or pine deck discourages freshwater leaks — the bane of all wooden boats. Their continued popularity is understandable, for they are still fun to sail. They'll move along in light air without extra sails, they spin on a dime, and they can take more rough weather as a rule than their owners can, although at times they are wet since the freeboard is low.

The most common name for this design nowadays is Dark Harbor 17½, named after the summertime watering hole at Islesboro, Maine, that once had the largest number of these boats. There was also a smaller, equally exciting version known as the Dark Harbor 12½, which was without a cabin and which sold in 1915, their first year, for a contract price of $300. It is also still an active class.

Across the bay in Camden, "Bodie" Crowninshield came up that year with a longer-ended (and to our eyes, better-looking) day boat for a few members of the Camden Yacht Club. According to the records, there were only four boats built: those by Hodgdon Bros., a shop that was only a stone's throw away from the Rice yard in East Boothbay. But at least one of these boats survives as perhaps the finest combination of performance and beauty ever developed within the definitions.

It may be that Mr. Crowninshield himself had little to do with the design of any of these boats and simply passed on their general requirements to his man Friday of the drafting stool, R.N. Burbank, whose

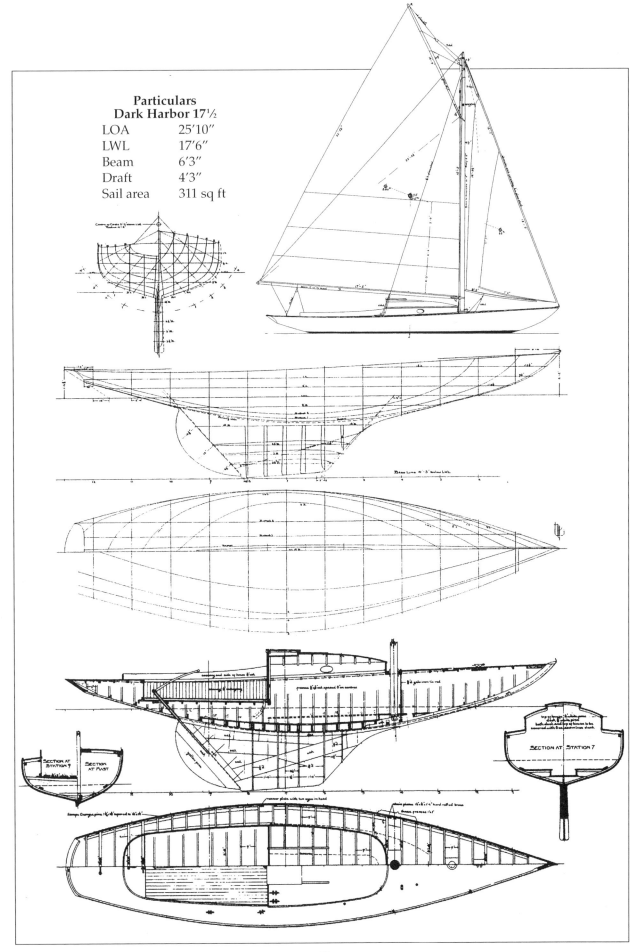

**Particulars**
**Dark Harbor 17½**

| | |
|---|---|
| LOA | 25'10" |
| LWL | 17'6" |
| Beam | 6'3" |
| Draft | 4'3" |
| Sail area | 311 sq ft |

initials are on all of the drawings and in whose hand all the calculations appear. In any event, the owners of all three one-design classes appeared to be pleased with their boats. Office log entries read: "...these boats have proved absolutely satisfactory...all owners are pleased...boats proved satisfactory in every way." "Boat handled and sailed well and seemed quite stiff. Sails set well. Boat trims and measures almost exactly like plan."

*Plans for the Dark Harbor 17½, Dark Harbor 12½, and the Camden Class can be ordered from The WoodenBoat Store, P.O. Box 78, Brooklin, ME 04616; 800–273–7447.*

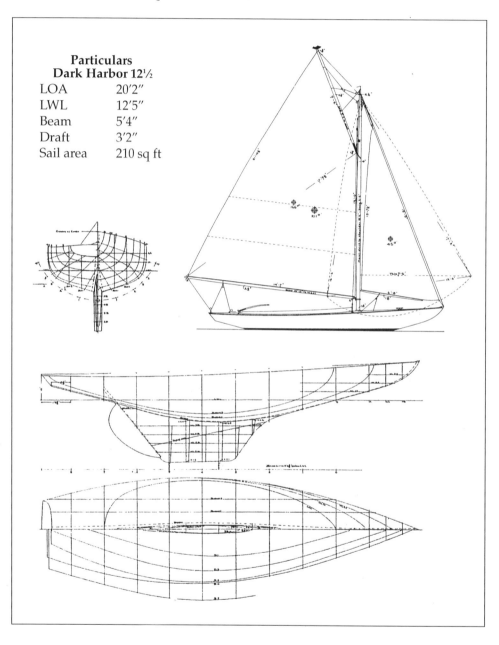

**Particulars**
**Dark Harbor 12½**

| | |
|---|---|
| LOA | 20'2" |
| LWL | 12'5" |
| Beam | 5'4" |
| Draft | 3'2" |
| Sail area | 210 sq ft |

**Particulars**
**Camden Class**

LOA      28'3"
LWL      17'0"
Beam     6'9"
Draft     4'3"
Sail area   350 sq ft

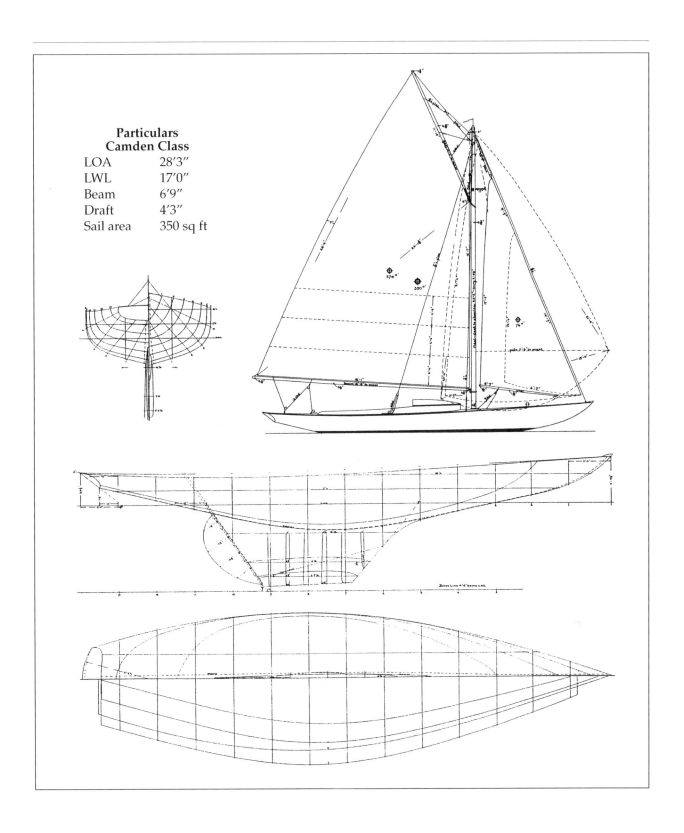

# An Ultralight Cruiser

Design by Robert W. Stephens
Commentary by Mike O'Brien

ere we have something different: an easily trailered beach cruiser that should provide the thrills of high-performance sailing during the day and, yet, offer reasonably comfortable accommodations after the sea breeze fades.

The fully battened mainsail catches our notice at first glance. This configuration might be common on catamarans and trimarans, but we don't often find small monohulls rigged in this manner. Designer Robert W. Stephens drew full-length battens because they can support substantial roach and, therefore, carry adequate sail area on a relatively short mast (desirable for ease of trailering and rigging).

Fully battened sails provide another benefit: silence. These sails don't flog wildly when luffing, but they do take some getting used to. They will not telegraph word of improper sail trim in the immediate fashion of unsupported sailcloth. Until we're accustomed to handling this rig, we'll want to stitch a forest of yarn telltales to the sails.

To a reasonable extent, fully battened sails offer positive control of their shape. We can fuss with the compression and thickness of the battens to alter the amount and location of draft (camber) in the mainsail. To throw more curve into the sail at a particular height, we simply tighten the line that secures a batten's after end to the leech (thereby forcing more of the batten into its pocket). For more precise and permanent control of shape, we can thin down the batten stock selectively along its length, or replace a batten with one of different flexibility.

When sailing beach catamarans during the 1970s, I habitually kept the battens slightly too long — for no particular reason. Now, it seems there might be sound logic in letting battens extend an inch, or two, beyond a sail's leech. Writing in *Natural Aerodynamics* (Amateur

Yacht Research Society, Publication No. 117, 1995), Ian Hannay discusses vortices and drag. He explains that a sail fitted with battens that protrude from the leech generates a series of separate trailing vortices, similar to those formed behind the feathers on a bird's wings. These vortices eventually combine to form one large, but ill-defined, vortex well behind the leech. This vortex, Hannay says, causes less drag than the more tightly wound vortices that tend to form close behind conventional sails with smooth, uninterrupted trailing edges.

Theories of shape and flow aside, typical short battens make sails difficult to handle when setting and furling; in a minor (but pleasant) paradox, full-length battens lie neatly parallel to the boom for efficient reefing, furling, and transport.

Given the above advantages, why — except for reasons of prejudice and inertia — haven't all monohull sailors switched to full-length battens? There are items on the debit side of the ledger: Short batten pockets cost money; long batten pockets cost more money. Of course, battens can be lashed to a sail that has no pockets. As may be, full-length battens tend to be heavy. Their weight can make a small, initially tender monohull feel tiddly even in a slick calm. But, all said, perhaps more single-hulled boats should be fitted with fully battened sails.

Aboard this light cruiser, the midship location of the mast will allow us to hoist and lower sail from the safety of the cockpit, and it results in a big headsail that will generate plenty of lift. Keeping the headstay from sagging might prove difficult, but Stephens has given the shrouds considerable drift — that is, the chainplates are located well abaft the mast — which should help us crank more tension into the headstay. In any case, if a sailmaker knows that the stay won't

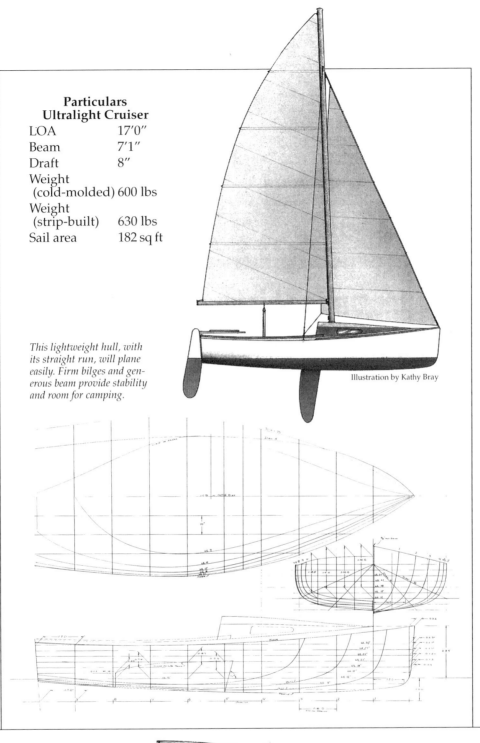

**Particulars**
**Ultralight Cruiser**

| | |
|---|---|
| LOA | 17'0" |
| Beam | 7'1" |
| Draft | 8" |
| Weight (cold-molded) | 600 lbs |
| Weight (strip-built) | 630 lbs |
| Sail area | 182 sq ft |

*This lightweight hull, with its straight run, will plane easily. Firm bilges and generous beam provide stability and room for camping.*

Illustration by Kathy Bray

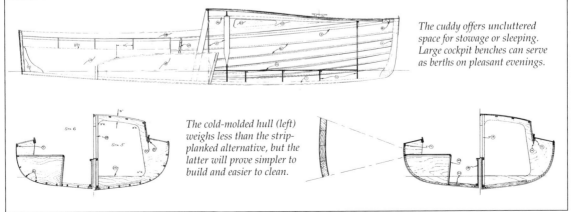

*The cuddy offers uncluttered space for stowage or sleeping. Large cockpit benches can serve as berths on pleasant evenings.*

*The cold-molded hull (left) weighs less than the strip-planked alternative, but the latter will prove simpler to build and easier to clean.*

form a perfect straight edge, he can compensate, to a degree, on the sail-loft floor.

A word of caution: Unless we actively control fully battened rigs, they want to keep sailing — because the sails tend to retain their airfoil shape even with the sheets let go. We should remember this as we approach the ramp, lest we wind up in the parking lot.

The designer shows two hull construction options: cold-molding, and strip-planking. Both methods call for the liberal application of epoxy resins. For the cold-molded hull, four layers of $\frac{1}{16}$-inch Western red cedar veneers go together over $\frac{5}{8}$-inch by 1-inch ash, spruce, or mahogany stringers. The stringers remain in the hull, not on the molds, after completion of the boat. Bulkheads and frames must be notched to accept the stringers.

If we don't have the requisite patience to accomplish that tedious job with neatness and accuracy, we might consider strip-planking the hull. Cedar strips ($\frac{3}{8}$ inch by 1 inch), sheathed with 12-ounce fiberglass cloth, offer a cleaner interior at the expense of slightly greater hull weight.

We'll build the decks from plywood: $\frac{1}{2}$ inch for the washboards and two layers of $\frac{1}{4}$ inch for the foredeck and house top, all covered with 4-ounce fiberglass set in epoxy.

The plans specify that we get the spars from stock aluminum extrusions. Although I can think of few technical arguments against metal tubes, I'd be inclined to glue up a nice wooden stick. A builder who chooses the aluminum mast will, perhaps, paint it the best buff color he can mix — and, then, ignore the noise, cold feel, and clumsy untapered shape.

Stephens has drawn a hull with firm bilges and generous beam. This boat should have no trouble sailing on its feet — particularly if we don't mind hiking out on the weather rail. If we're careful about weight — building materials and cargo — we'll be able to break onto a plane without too much provocation.

The centerboard and rudder swing up to permit sailing in shallow water. As the board and blade are raised, however, the lateral centers of both appendages move quite far aft; we might find ourselves dealing with some lee helm when we're sailing in 10-inch-deep water. Perhaps the important point is that we can sail in 10-inch-deep water.

The open accommodations aboard this cruiser are flexible, indeed. We can sleep in the cuddy or in the tented cockpit. The galley probably will be set up in the cockpit. In public situations, at least, the toilet can be positioned just abaft the main bulkhead under a dodger. Owners who install fixed furniture might later regret the clutter and the loss of performance under sail. This boat is essentially a big sailing dinghy fitted with a cabin. To work as planned, it must be kept light.

The cruising range of the 17-foot Ultralight Cruiser will depend largely upon the dedication of its crew. Weekend adventures ought to be pleasant and easy. To get some idea of the outer limits, you might want to read Frank and Margaret Dye's account of sailing an open 16-foot Wayfarer dinghy across parts of the North Atlantic, among other places (*Ocean-Crossing Wayfarer*, David & Charles, North Pomfret, VT, 1977).

*Plans from Robert W. Stephens Boat Design, P.O. Box 166, Brooklin, ME 04616.*

# XIX

# Two Small Cruisers

———— Designs by Jay R. Benford and Iain Oughtred ————
Commentary by Mike O'Brien

*B*ack in 1976, Jay Benford sat down at his drawing table to design a small cruiser for Dick Wagner, creator and driving force behind The Center for Wooden Boats in Seattle. The result of Benford's labor, a preliminary study for an 18-foot centerboard canoe yawl, was published in the young designer's catalog. Its evocative sail plan soon was pinned to the walls of more than one boatshop along the coast. But, for various reasons, the little packet never was built.

Fortunately for posterity, the designer himself was taken with the personality of his proposed double-ender, and he set to work on plans for a similar boat drawn to his own parameters. He increased the draft and the freeboard in an effort to provide sitting headroom below and to make "a better all-around cruiser."

Fooling with designs that were right the first time can be a tricky business, but Benford seasoned the broth without spoiling the flavor. He kept the house that he had worked into the staved coaming on the original drawings. Today we tend to associate this arrangement with catboats, but the device was altogether common on a variety of types during the last century. It provides a continuity of line that seems to permit greater cabin heights without causing visual offense. Hiding the coaming behind substantial bulwarks helps — as does keeping the house out of the bows. (Sleeping crew members don't require full sitting headroom over their feet.) Iota's relatively great beam and bold sheer also allow her to carry the increased height with dignity.

The first boats built to this design were constructed of ferrocement. Those of us who have been around the waterfront for more than a few years can remember when this late, and unlamented, medium was hailed

by a number of promoters as being something akin to the Second Coming. Ferrocement boats were said to require meager skills from their builders, to cost little, and to be virtually impervious to any harm contemplated by man or nature. But usually they didn't, they didn't, and they weren't. Benford, to his credit, raised one of the few voices of reason from the "concrete boat" community. He detailed realistic expenses and expectations. As a result, his ferrocement canoe yawls were well faired and fared well.

In 1987, Benford redrew Iota for cold-molded wood/epoxy construction. The new drawings specify an inner layer of ⅜-inch by ⅝-inch red cedar strip planking covered by two layers of diagonally laid ⅛-inch red cedar veneer. In yet another revision, not shown here, the rudder stock was moved to a vertical position just forward of Station 7. This change simplifies the arrangement of the mizzen maststep.

In addition to these modifications, the designer has experimented with different sail plans for this hull: a 260-square-foot cat rig (shown with a small headsail, and sometimes referred to as a "cat-sloop" nowadays); a gaff cutter (260 square feet); and a ketch boasting 280 square feet of Dacron. That's a lot of horsepower for a boat only 18 feet on deck, but she's a big 18 feet: 4,200 pounds big.

By the way, the ketch rig is shown atop a short-keeled version of the hull. The original 233-square-foot yawl rig would be my choice both aesthetically and technically, as it offers superior control and ease of handling.

Many boats have come from Jay Benford's board since Iota was conceived, yet she remains one of his favorites. Considering the love/hate relationship that most artists have with their early work, her designer's loyalty constitutes high praise for this likable yawl.

While Iain Oughtred was in residence at *WoodenBoat* magazine, discussions developed about creating plans for an able cruising boat that would be suitable for trailering and amateur construction. The transplanted Australian designer began working up some preliminary studies. As the sketches evolved, they displayed his admiration for Norwegian small craft. Well aware of the dangers involved in tampering with respected traditional types, Oughtred forged ahead, admitting simply, "I can't help it!"

Gray Seal represents a subtle, and we think successful, blend of Scandinavian characteristics. The designer sees this boat not as a miniature of a larger yacht, but rather as "what a faering builder might do if he wanted cruising accommodations." At any rate, the little cruiser shows a strong sheer and buoyant hull. She'll not be overwhelmed easily.

The plans call for epoxy-glued plywood lapstrake construction — a method that Oughtred has specified for several smaller pulling boats and canoes. Gray Seal's hull will be light, strong, and handsome, but only the very highest-quality plywood ought to be used. Common construction grades should be dismissed out of hand, and ordinary fir marine plywood won't be satisfactory — unless you find panels superior to any I've seen during the last two decades. Bruynzeel or an equivalent, if it has an equivalent, would be the way to go. This method of building pushes plywood to its limits in terms of potential exposure to damage, and it demands the best.

Having satisfied the original design criteria with a shoal-draft keel/centerboard hull powered by a snug gunter rig, Oughtred set out to draw a full-keeled version of Gray Seal driven by a fractional marconi rig. The deeper hull will be quite striking. In the designer's words, "She'll look rather like a small, double-ended Folkboat; not at all, as I first feared, like a shallow hull with a keel stuck on."

The gunter rig can be used with either hull, but the designer suggests that the tall marconi rig not be mated with the keel/centerboard hull. My choice would be for the simplicity of the full-keeled hull under the security (short mast) of the gunter rig. Certainly, the full keel will render Gray Seal less roadworthy, but I have difficulty considering any boat of this size (displacement, that is) truly trailerable. As may be, people are out there on the Interstate every weekend dragging heavier packages. And the merits of trailering your boat home for the winter, or on an occasional overland sojourn, are pleasant to contemplate.

Oughtred has drawn several interior arrangements for Gray Seal. Some of the accommodations include quarter berths, and one arrangement shows an enclosed head. (I trust nobody expects anything resembling real privacy aboard a pocket cruiser.) The simple, traditional two-berth-forward plan will be the easiest to build, and the friendliest to use. Perhaps that explains why it is traditional.

*Iota's plans are available from Jay R. Benford, P.O. Box 447, St. Michaels, MD 21663.*

*Gray Seal's plans can be ordered from The WoodenBoat Store, P.O. Box 78, Brooklin, ME 04616; 800–273–7447.*

*Iain Oughtred can be contacted at Altyre Stables, Forres, Moray IV36 0SH, Scotland.*

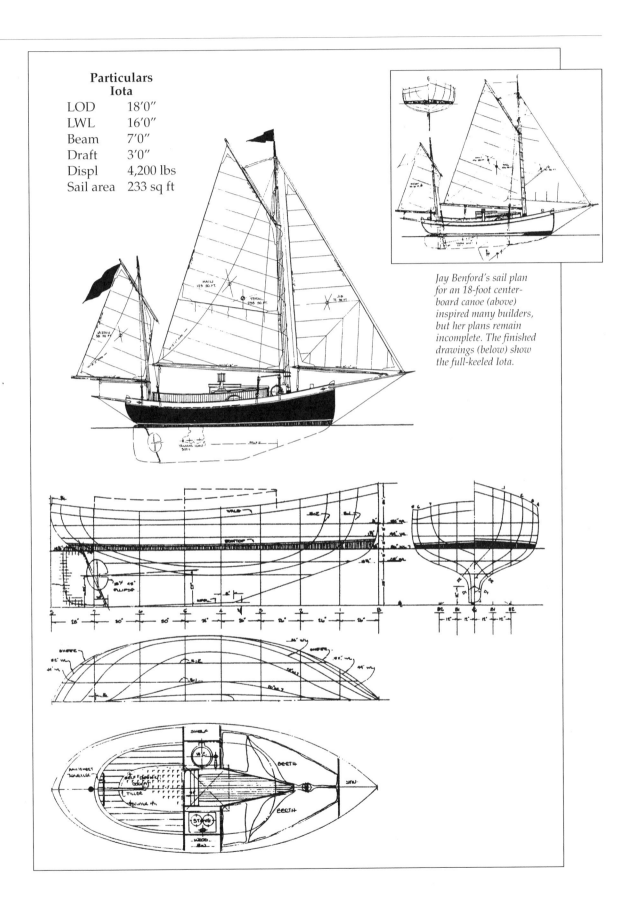

**Particulars**
**Iota**

| | |
|---|---|
| LOD | 18'0" |
| LWL | 16'0" |
| Beam | 7'0" |
| Draft | 3'0" |
| Displ | 4,200 lbs |
| Sail area | 233 sq ft |

*Jay Benford's sail plan for an 18-foot center-board canoe (above) inspired many builders, but her plans remain incomplete. The finished drawings (below) show the full-keeled Iota.*

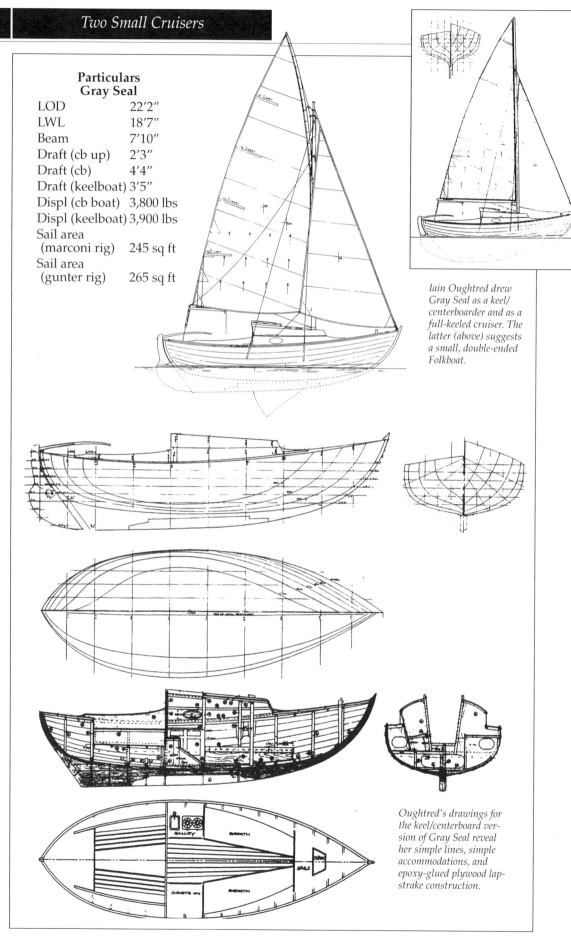

**Particulars
Gray Seal**

| | |
|---|---|
| LOD | 22'2" |
| LWL | 18'7" |
| Beam | 7'10" |
| Draft (cb up) | 2'3" |
| Draft (cb) | 4'4" |
| Draft (keelboat) | 3'5" |
| Displ (cb boat) | 3,800 lbs |
| Displ (keelboat) | 3,900 lbs |
| Sail area (marconi rig) | 245 sq ft |
| Sail area (gunter rig) | 265 sq ft |

*Iain Oughtred drew
Gray Seal as a keel/
centerboarder and as a
full-keeled cruiser. The
latter (above) suggests
a small, double-ended
Folkboat.*

*Oughtred's drawings for
the keel/centerboard ver-
sion of Gray Seal reveal
her simple lines, simple
accommodations, and
epoxy-glued plywood lap-
strake construction.*

# XX

# *A Simple Pocket Cruiser*

Design by S.S. Crocker ————
Commentary by Joel White

*I* have a theory, difficult to prove but intriguing to think about, that the best yacht designers are able to instill some of their character traits into their designs. Nat Herreshoff, genius designer, workaholic, a demon for speed, turned out a huge body of work, meticulously designed and crafted, fast and long-lived. His son, L. Francis, was inventive, eccentric, a lover of beauty and simplicity; he produced a number of beautiful and simple yachts as well as some that were more inventive than beautiful. John Alden, ardent racer and deepwater sailor, took the fisherman-type schooner and modified the design into offshore yachts that were simple, strong, and economically appealing to the yachtsmen of the Depression years.

I am sorry that I never knew S.S. (Sam) Crocker, but over the years I have come to know a number of his boats. I have built two boats to his design, and have stored and maintained several others in my boatyard. If my theory is correct, Sam Crocker must have been a practical, sensible man, one who enjoyed comfort and rugged good looks, a man who preferred simplicity to extravagance. He was a cruiser rather than a racer, a man well versed in practical yacht construction with a good knowledge of what makes a boat look "right."

In 1967, I was privileged to build the little sloop shown here for a rather special client. I had a great deal of enjoyment with the project, and the client enjoyed a great little boat for many years.

If you have studied Sam Manning's fine drawings for the "Anatomy of a Wooden Boat" in the tenth anniversary issue of *WoodenBoat* magazine (WB No. 60), you were looking at perspectives of this boat, Sallee Rover. Crocker designed her as a yawl in 1953; later, in 1955, a sloop-rigged version was drawn. It was this sloop-rigged design that I built in 1967.

Perhaps more than any other boat in my harbor, she is admired for her good looks; people are always inquiring about the origins of this sloop named *Martha*. I can see her now out of my drafting-room window, looking extremely jaunty with her dark green topsides, red bottom, white top strake and cabin sides. Her spars and deck are painted a fisherman buff, and her trailboards have three leaping dolphins picked out in gold leaf. The only varnished item on the boat is her oak tiller.

As you can see from her lines plan, the hull is of shallow draft and wide beam, sort of a cross between a catboat and a Muscongus Bay sloop. To me, she is prettier than either one, more delicate than the chunky cat, more graceful than the Muscongus sloop. The large outboard rudder hangs on a well-raked transom, and the deadwood just forward of the rudder is cut away for the propeller of the 8-hp single-cylinder Palmer Baby Husky engine installed under the big hatch in the cockpit floor. This power plant is perfectly suited to the character of the boat, driving her easily and economically, and producing a wonderful, old-fashioned "putt-putt" exhaust out the stern. The round-fronted cabin trunk goes well with the clipper bow profile and the strong sheerline. The general appearance is of huskiness and grace, an eyecatching little boat. Only a naval architect knows how difficult this is to achieve on such a small boat. Crocker deserves high marks for this design.

I might as well confess right away that we made a few changes when we built her. To give a wider deck and make it easier to go forward to gaff the mooring or to furl the jib, the cabin sides were moved inboard about 3 inches. The top of the stern was given a high arch above the deck crown, the tiller brought through it above the deck, and the coamings carried aft to join the stern as in a Herreshoff 12½-footer. I think this made her even prettier. A boom gallows was added to eliminate the need for a boom crutch and to give a good handhold aft.

Rugged is the best description of her construction. For example, the keel is 7-inch by 9-inch oak! The stem is sided 4½ inches and molded about 8 inches — all this on a boat only 20 feet overall. What Crocker has done has been to incorporate much of the ballast needed into the backbone structure of the boat. A keel entirely of oak is cheaper than one having a specially cast chunk of lead or iron ballast attached to it. This boat has no outside ballast at all, which simplifies the building.

The heavy construction continues with 1-inch cedar planking over 1¼-inch-square bent-oak frames on 9-inch centers and 1½-inch-thick oak floor timbers. All of this weight is pretty low in the boat where it will improve stability as well as strength. The deck, of ½-inch plywood covered with Dynel and epoxy over oak beams, is of normal weight. She is tremendously strong and should last a long, long time. About 700 pounds of lead ballast stored under the floorboards abreast the centerboard trunk brings her down to her lines, and together with the heavy backbone and wide beam makes her a stiff boat in a breeze.

Below, the cabin is split in two by the centerboard trunk, which runs from the cockpit almost to the mast. A low seat/bunk on each side allows the boat to he used for overnight cruising for two. Forward of the mast, a raised platform permits stowage, both under it and on top. There are no toilet or galley facilities.

The rig, a low marconi mainsail with self-tending jib, and a total area of 218 square feet looks a bit stumpy on paper, but to my eye appears just right on the actual boat. She is certainly no light-air flyer, but sails well in moderate and strong winds, giving one the feeling of being on a boat much longer than 20 feet.

For the owner's convenience, we arranged to lead the halyards aft so they can be handled from the cockpit. Her original sails were tanbarked canvas, which looked wonderful, but her second suit of white Dacron proved easier to handle and longer lasting.

I have another theory, one which I think can be proved, that good-looking boats last longer than plain ones. The boat that gives one pleasure merely to look at it is a great joy, evoking favorable comment from others. This fills the owner with pride, causing him to take extra care with the boat's appearance. More attention is paid to a handsome craft by everyone involved in her care, whether owner or paid professional; her paint and varnish are better kept, dirt and grime are washed away, problems are dealt with as soon as they appear. Such a boat will last much longer than the homely and less-loved craft on the next mooring. I suspect Mr. Crocker knew this to be true; certainly he designed attractive boats, and many of them have aged gracefully.

*Plans for the 19-foot 9-inch Sallee/Rover are available from The WoodenBoat Store, P.O. Box 78, Brooklin, ME 04616; 800–273–7447.*

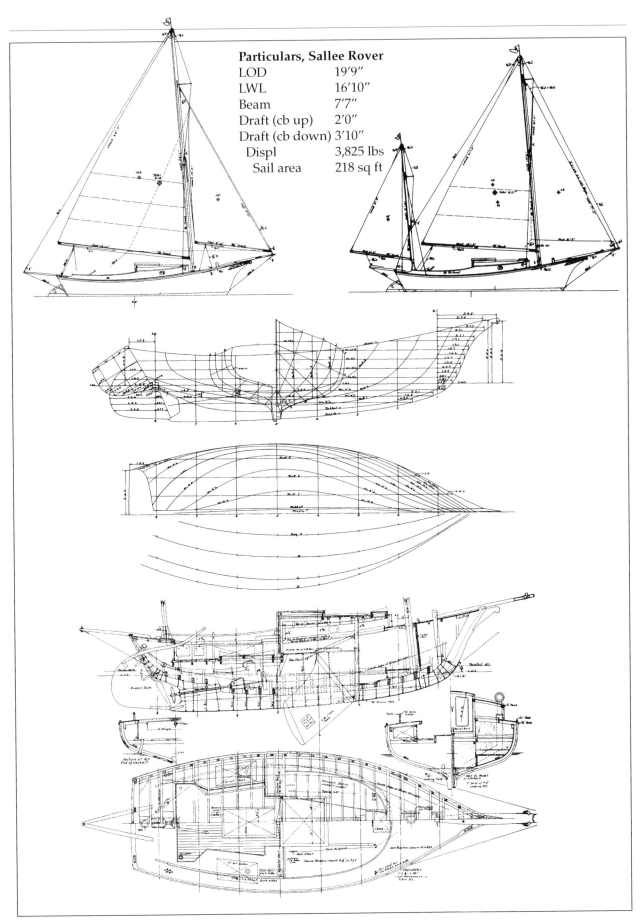

**Particulars, Sallee Rover**

| | |
|---|---|
| LOD | 19'9" |
| LWL | 16'10" |
| Beam | 7'7" |
| Draft (cb up) | 2'0" |
| Draft (cb down) | 3'10" |
| Displ | 3,825 lbs |
| Sail area | 218 sq ft |

# A Little Sloop

—————— Design by Nelson Zimmer ——————
Commentary by Joel White

This little sloop by Nelson Zimmer has the feel of a real deepwater vessel, yet she is only 21 feet overall. A strong, springy sheer, a bold stem profile that just suits the V-bottom shape, a well-proportioned cabin trunk, and a good-looking, highpeaked gaff sail plan all contribute to this feeling.

According to Mr. Zimmer, this design, which was drawn back in 1946, has continued to draw inquiries through the years, an indication of her wide appeal. She certainly appeals to me. I built a boat for my dad a number of years ago that was very similar in size and type, and she has given great pleasure and good service — as would the Zimmer sloop.

The lines show a beamy, husky centerboard hull with considerable reverse curve worked into the bottom, aft. The buttock lines are flat and fair, and she should be stiff and reasonably fast. The chine line rises well out of the water at both the stem and the stern, and there is a very short aft overhang ending in a counter stern — certainly better-looking than a transom stern and outboard rudder would be on this design. The displacement is 3,110 pounds, and Zimmer recommends about 750 pounds of inside ballast.

All the plan sheets for this boat are carefully detailed, and the construction plan is particularly complete. She has sawn frames on each station, spaced 2 feet apart. The topsides are batten-seam construction, while the bottom has two intermediate frames between the sawn frames. Planking is to be finished ⅞ inch, of mahogany, cedar, or pine. The backbone is oak, and there is plenty of it — it will weigh nearly as much as the ballast, and really serves as such. Decks are specificed to be ¾-inch tongue-and-groove pine, canvas-covered, as is the cabintop. She has a full set of lodging and hanging knees, unusual to see in so small a boat. I would not call her easy to build in terms of man-hours

needed, but her construction is straightforward and well thought out.

I like the gaff-sloop rig, with the large main and small jib. Both sails are self-tending. There is much to be said for a gaff rig in a small boat, where the gaff is light enough to be easily hoisted and won't become a lethal weapon in a hard chance. The mast can be much shorter and more easily stayed, while still allowing an ample sail area. Best of all, the gaff rig looks right on this sloop — much prettier than if she were marconi-rigged.

Mr. Zimmer has detailed a complete rigging and block list of some 60 items, not usually seen on sail plans these impatient days. There is also an entire sheet entitled "Spar and Fitting Details" available to the builder of this little sloop. Goosenecks, boom travelers, sheet horse, masthead truck, gammon iron, and belaying pins are all carefully dimensioned and detailed, as are the spar sizes and tapers, spreader details, and gaff jaws. How nice it is to see such attention and care given to rigging a little boat correctly.

Below, simplicity is the theme. There are settees about 6 feet long to port and starboard, with the centerboard trunk splitting the cabin down the middle. Forward of the mast is a large slatted platform for gear stowage, and a single, small, built-in locker. A nice large hatch in the foredeck allows access to the storage area without having to traverse the cabin.

I suspect this little sloop would be used mostly for daysailing, or camping-out cruising. She has no engine installation shown, so I assume it was intended that outboard power could be used. I would prefer to keep her a pure sailer, counting on the large rig to get me home in light airs.

Were I to build this boat, I would be tempted to fool around with the cockpit seats — widening and slanting them a bit, and making the cockpit coaming smooth on the inside for a more comfortable backrest. What a joy she would be!

*Plans for this boat are available from The WoodenBoat Store, P.O. Box 78, Brooklin, ME 04616; 800–273–7447.*

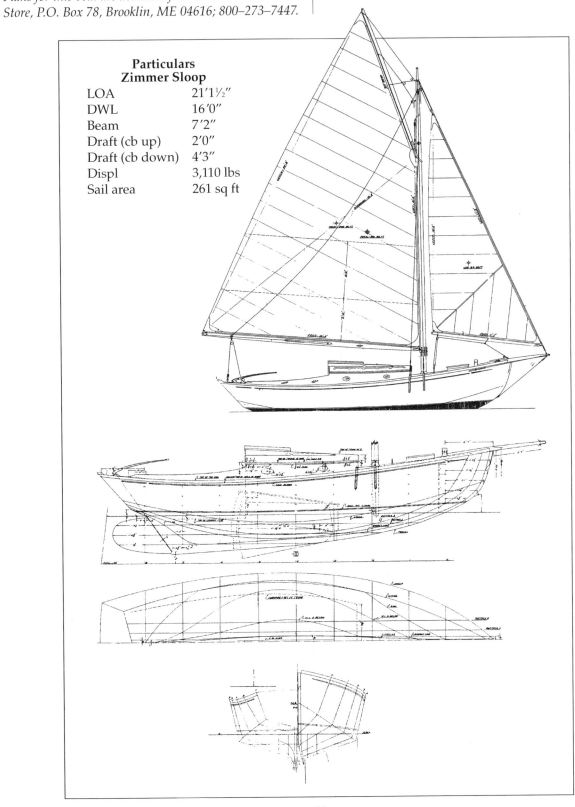

**Particulars**
**Zimmer Sloop**

| | |
|---|---|
| LOA | 21'1½" |
| DWL | 16'0" |
| Beam | 7'2" |
| Draft (cb up) | 2'0" |
| Draft (cb down) | 4'3" |
| Displ | 3,110 lbs |
| Sail area | 261 sq ft |

**Zimmer Sloop**

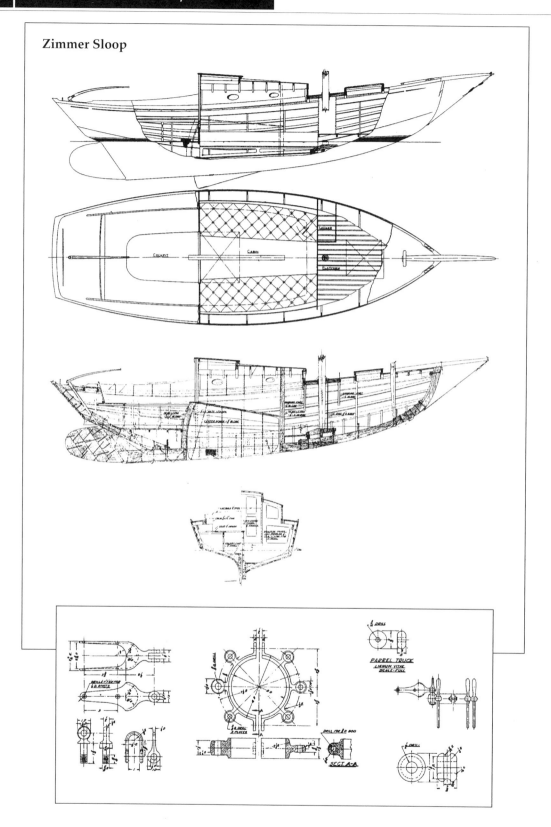

# A Double-Ended Sloop

————— Design by John G. Alden —————
Plans and specifications by Fenwick Williams
Commentary by the editors of *WoodenBoat*

Double-enders, from Viking longships to Pinky schooners and North Sea pilot cutters, have long been held in high esteem as seakeepers. It shouldn't be surprising, then, to see this remarkably small variation on a theme. If you're familiar with Fenwick Williams's 24-foot gaff yawl, you'll recognize the similarities to this fascinating little boat. And if the similarities carry through, there is considerably more boat here than meets the eye, for Williams's 24-footer is not only fast and weatherly, but also remarkably spacious below.

Five of these 21-footers were built in 1929, after which the Depression must have caused many to forget about such things. But we can't bear to see the design forgotten, for here could be a wonderfully versatile cruising boat.

Two rigs are offered — a high-peaked gaff and a marconi — and both provide nearly equal amounts of sail area. The taller mast of the marconi rig, of course, requires more stays (eight as opposed to three), but it also requires one less spar (the gaff) and one less halyard. Like the gunter rig, the nearly vertical gaff presents a complication in reefing, since the peak halyard must be seized or clipped all the way out on the gaff in order for the sail to set properly with reefs tucked in. On the other hand, the running backstay arrangement in the marconi rig presents its own complications (which will surely occur with more frequency) and we tend to favor the gaff.

Whatever the rig, this is a wonderfully simple boat. Her construction is rugged and straightforward, yet she is a finely modeled hull (see those hollow waterlines and that finely chiseled forefoot). Tiller steering, outboard rudder, a very simple cockpit arrangement, and spliced eyes for the standing rigging instead of tangs contribute to the simplicity.

Her layout below is simple but comfortable, with two berths, a stove, an ice chest, a dish locker, a hanging locker, and stowage beneath platforms. Indeed, she is very charming and cozy.

Having been designed in 1928, this boat's engine access hatch and bridge deck configuration were designed for a contemporary auxiliary. A modern auxiliary might require some alteration to the plan. The engine compartment is separated from the cabin by a watertight bulkhead.

This is a fine little boat.

*Plans for this 21-foot double-ended sloop are available from The WoodenBoat Store, P.O. Box 78, Brooklin, ME 04616; 800–273–7447.*

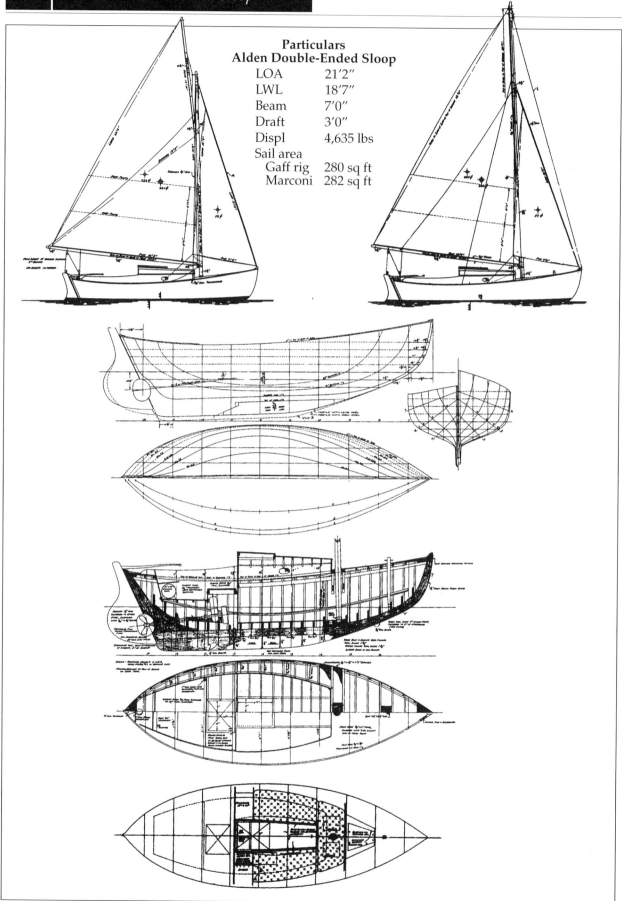

**Particulars**
**Alden Double-Ended Sloop**

| | |
|---|---|
| LOA | 21'2" |
| LWL | 18'7" |
| Beam | 7'0" |
| Draft | 3'0" |
| Displ | 4,635 lbs |
| Sail area | |
| Gaff rig | 280 sq ft |
| Marconi | 282 sq ft |

# Two Plywood
# Pocket Cruisers

—————— Designs by Karl Stambaugh and Philip C. Bolger ——————
Commentary by Mike O'Brien

*B*oth Karl Stambaugh and Phil Bolger started with similar stacks of plywood and a drawer full of traditional ideas. Both came up with trailerable pocket cruisers that measure 19 feet 6 inches on deck. There the similarity ends.

Stambaugh's Mist awakens memories of plywood sloops that filled the pages of Popular Whatever magazines in the years following World War II. But, in some ways, she's quite different. Many of the early-1950s hulls were designed aggressively for sheet construction. That is to say, every ounce of twist had been wrung out of their carefully developed developable shapes. Stems and rails were faired into the hulls to the extent that they virtually disappeared.

In order for strongly flared hull sides to mate well with a nearly plumb stem, some twist should be worked into the plywood sheets up forward. Alternatives include increasing the rake and/or curve of the stem (particularly near its heel) and/or tolerating less flare. Stambaugh chose to twist the plywood. As a reward, Mist has a hull shape that probably will appeal to most sailors. It is stiffer structurally, and the entry is a touch finer. Twist isn't all bad — although if you ever try to hang the bottom panels on a sheet-plywood catboat, you might think it is.

Stambaugh has gone out of his way to ensure that this plywood boat doesn't look like a plywood boat. He insists that the stem stand proud, as it would on a conventionally planked hull. Solid, coved sheerstrakes add to the illusion, as does the severe rounding-over specified for the chines back aft. And the curved, raked transom isn't exactly standard fare for sheet-plywood

boats. In all, this is a handsome little cruiser.

Down below, there has been no attempt to cram in coffin-style quarter berths or an enclosed head. The arrangement is simple and traditional, and it should work fine. Mist's relatively wide cabin sole survives the intrusion of the long centerboard trunk, part of which hides under the bridge deck.

The cockpit offers good lounging space, but the motor well intrudes. I can understand the designer's reluctance to desecrate Mist's transom with a bracket. Perhaps we should eliminate the well and investigate the mysteries of the yuloh, the over-the-stern sculling oar of Eastern origin.

The gaff-sloop rig suits Mist, and sailmakers who have experience sewing four-sided sails seem to be easier to find than they were a decade ago. Although standing rigging can become a time-consuming nuisance when a boat lives on and off a trailer, Stambaugh has kept it simple here. If he were to draw a free-standing arrangement, the mast would likely be heavier and/or more expensive in an attempt to support tension in the jib's luff — and the tabernacle would have to be altered.

*I*n the early 1980s, Phil Bolger drew the Micro pocket cruiser for sailor and plans promoter Elrow LaRowe. The 15-foot 4-inch plywood cat-yawl has proven to be a popular and capable sailer. Long Micro, as the name implies, is a stretched (19-foot 6-inch) version on the same 6-foot beam.

This boat's hull consists of a rigid plywood box, with free-flooding ends and watertight accommodations amidships. The curve of the sides, in plan view, more or less matches the profile of the bottom's rocker. Cross-flow is reduced, and performance is improved.

The most controversial feature of this hull is certain to be the complete lack of flare. Its sides stand dead perpendicular to the water. Long Micro's designer writes that the deck is a "necessary parasite weighing down the bottom, so the smaller it is relative to the bottom, the better the boat will run." Like thinkers will point out that, for hulls of this type, vertical sides can result in nicely drawn-out waterlines, maximum initial stability, easier construction, and slightly reduced materials cost.

The opposition will claim that this reasoning makes sense only if the boat is to be built in a particularly narrow shop or kept in a 6-foot-wide box. Why not increase Long Micro's beam at the rail to, say, 8 feet (to match Mist's), and let the crew hike out to take advantage of the increased lever arm? The Bolger camp will shoot back that, indeed, a flared side acts as an outrigger supporting an alert, athletic crew — it demands caution for that very reason. In a plumb-sided hull, the bottom extends out under any point on which someone can stand, and the boat tends to roll less as the crew moves. Detractors might respond with the unanswerable point that they simply don't like the looks of vertical sides. So the debate rages, and it won't be settled here.

Be that as it might, plumb-sided boats really can sail, and they can demonstrate friendly stability curves. The reputation for treachery this type holds in some quarters stems from the bad behavior of similar canoes and skiffs when they are overloaded. If the depths of immersed rectangular sections become too great relative to their widths, these unballasted boats can turn

unfriendly in a hurry. Long Micro, with external ballast and predictably lighter relative loading, will maintain her composure.

We've talked before about the self-vanging properties and other advantages of sprit-boomed leg-o'-mutton sails. The cat-yawl arrangement adds merits of its own. The masts are stepped in the ends of the boat, they're clear of the accommodations, and they put the sail area where it's useful for maneuvering. With no headsail luff to support, the spars can be light and unstayed. When it breezes up, only the mainsail need be reefed. The main's center of effort moves forward as it's shortened down, but, because its size relative to the mizzen is reduced, the helm remains balanced.

Either of these boats would make a fine end for a stack of plywood.

*Plans for Mist are available from The WoodenBoat Store, P.O. Box 78, Brooklin, ME 04616; 800–273–7447.*

*Plans for Long Micro can be obtained from Common Sense Designs, 11765 S.W. Ebberts Ct., Beaverton, OR 97008.*

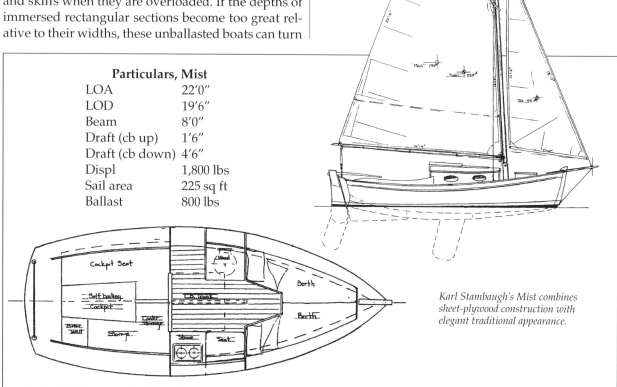

**Particulars, Mist**

| | |
|---|---|
| LOA | 22'0" |
| LOD | 19'6" |
| Beam | 8'0" |
| Draft (cb up) | 1'6" |
| Draft (cb down) | 4'6" |
| Displ | 1,800 lbs |
| Sail area | 225 sq ft |
| Ballast | 800 lbs |

*Karl Stambaugh's Mist combines sheet-plywood construction with elegant traditional appearance.*

# Mist

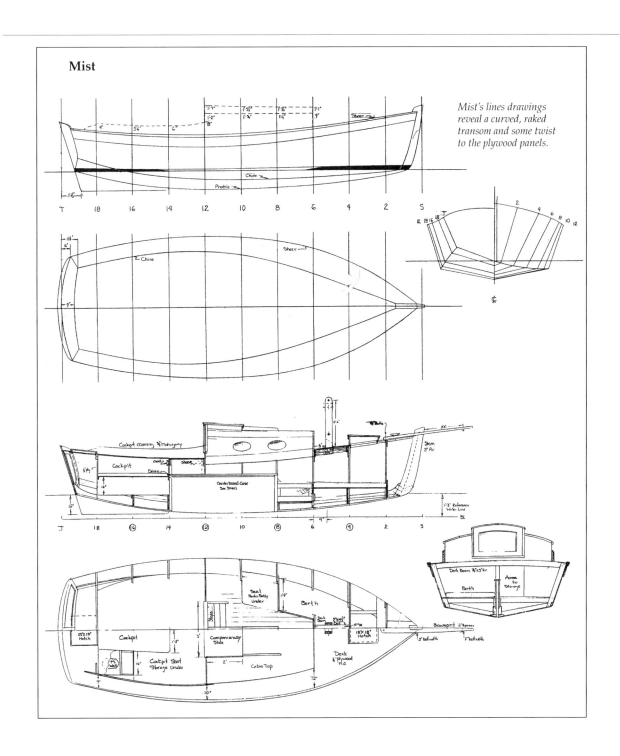

*Mist's lines drawings reveal a curved, raked transom and some twist to the plywood panels.*

**Particulars, Long Micro**

| | |
|---|---|
| LOD | 19'6" |
| Beam | 6'0" |
| Draft | 1'9" |
| Displ | 2,400 lbs |
| Sail area | 263 sq ft |
| Ballast | 532 lbs |

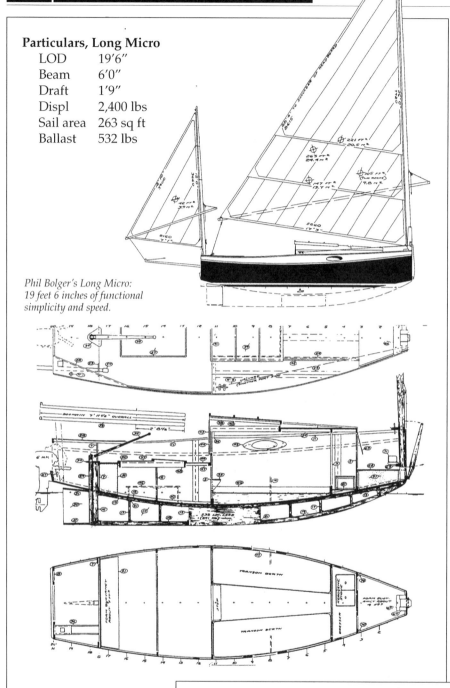

*Phil Bolger's Long Micro:
19 feet 6 inches of functional
simplicity and speed.*

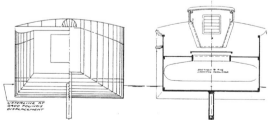

*Long Micro's body plan (left) illustrates the cat-yawl's absolutely
plumb sides and adequate rocker. A view looking forward from the
cockpit (center) shows the cover for the open standing room, the
afterdeck or seats, and the arrangement at the companionway.
The main bulkhead (right) speaks of ultra-simple construction.*

# An Electric Auxiliary Cutter

Design by Antonio Dias
Commentary by Joel White

Antonio Dias designed this little cutter, *Annabelle Two*, for a customer who lives in Indiana and who sails on the medium-sized lakes in that area. The boat will be used for daysailing and occasional weekend cruising. Concern for the pollution of these lakes led the owner to consider an unusual auxiliary propulsion system for the boat.

This handsome little vessel shows an interesting contrast between the new and the old: She's old-fashioned looking, with plumb stem, round-fronted cabin, and gaff-cutter rig; new thinking is reflected in her modern construction methods (strip-planked and fiberglassed hull) and her electric-drive auxiliary power plant.

It is high time that we begin to see more use of modern electric technology in powering boats. The auto industry is reluctant to face up to demands for a cleaner power source. Dragging its feet into the twenty-first century, Detroit has still only a smattering of experimental electric cars on the roads. Why shouldn't the marine industry step up boldly to seize the initiative in the electric-drive field? There may be a lot of potential customers out there waiting to back an environmentally clean marine power plant.

There is one tremendous advantage we have in the marine industry compared to automotive designers when planning an electric drive unit. In an automobile, the considerable weight of the batteries required to power the car is a pure loss — a dead weight that has to be moved up hills, adding to the amount of horsepower required to propel the automobile. In a boat, the road is basically level at all times, and weight (displacement) is less of a drag factor. In fact, we deliberately attach large hunks of heavy stuff to the bottoms of most sailboats (in the form of ballast keels) to improve the stability of the boat and her ability to stand up to sail. Why not utilize the weight of the propulsion batteries as ballast?

Dias has done just that in designing *Annabelle Two*. The batteries are as low in the boat as possible with this sort of shallow-draft hull and are located close to the longitudinal center of buoyancy. In addition, the boat has an external lead ballast keel of 477 pounds, and a heavy centerboard weighing 538 pounds. Dias calls for 12 batteries, each weighing 48 pounds for a total battery weight of 576 lbs. Adding these three components together, we get 1,591 lbs of total ballast. This gives a ballast/displacement ratio a bit in excess of 50 percent, which is very good for a small cruiser of this type.

A couple of quick calculations indicate that the center of gravity of the total ballast will be 15 inches below the designed waterline with the centerboard lowered, and the center of gravity of the entire boat, including ballast, will be only a few inches above the waterline. With her firm, high bilges and generous beam, the boat's stability should be quite good for her type. Remember, too, that one-third of the ballast weight carried is serving as the auxiliary power source.

The lines plan shows a burdensome, shallow-draft hull, with a cutaway forefoot sloping down to a long, straight keel, which draws only 18 inches of water with the board raised. This feature will allow the boat to be run up on a beach for picnicking, and will make her easy to load onto a trailer. Her firm bilges and wide stern will improve stability and give good room aft.

The designed displacement of only 3,000 pounds puts *Annabelle Two* in the light-displacement category; her long waterline gives her a low displacement/length ratio, 152.3. Her 298 square feet of sail yields good horsepower numbers: A sail area/displacement ratio of 22.9 will ensure that she performs very well under canvas.

The rig is a low-aspect gaff cutter, with the jib set flying on a long bowsprit. This jib is tacked to a big ring, which encircles the bowsprit and can be hauled in and out — a rig much used by English cutters a hundred years ago. This boat is so small that both the jib and the forestaysail are quite tiny (63 square feet and 52 square feet, respectively), and I wonder if it wouldn't be handier to have a single, loose-footed headsail. The forestaysail with its boom and traveler is self-tending, but the foredeck is badly cluttered by its gear, an impediment to picking up the mooring or lowering the anchor. I like the look of the double-headsail rig, but it will be less efficient than a single jib and requires a lot more hardware — sheets, sheet blocks, boom, boom gooseneck, and traveler. Either way, the center of effort of the rig is low — a desirable feature in a shoal-draft boat.

Hull construction calls for the boat to be strip-planked of ¾-inch bead-and-cove cedar strips laid over seven structural plywood bulkheads. After planking and fairing, the hull is to be fiberglassed inside and out with 24-ounce biaxial cloth set in epoxy. Deck and cabintop are cold-molded from three layers of cedar covered with Dynel and epoxy. The cockpit and coamings are constructed of plywood. The area under the cockpit is cut up into several compartments, and it is not clear from the plans what access there is to these spaces.

I had some concerns with the construction details of the boat, particularly the strength of the centerboard trunk, and the hoisting mechanism for lifting the heavy board. I have spoken with Mr. Dias about these points and believe that he is making some minor revisions in these areas.

The layout of the boat is very simple, as it should be for such a small vessel. The cockpit is nearly 8 feet long, with wide seats all around and a small, self-bailing footwell. The companionway to the cabin is offset to port because of the centerboard trunk. Below, there is a flat counter on either side of the companionway, and there is a V-berth forward under the deck. The mast steps on deck in a tabernacle, with a compression post underneath, from deck to keel.

The banks of propulsion batteries are grouped around the after end of the centerboard trunk — four on either side of it, and four more just abaft the trunk. The propulsion motor is shown behind the batteries. It turns the propeller shaft through a belt-drive. The motor controls are located in the cockpit, within easy reach of the helmsman.

While electric drive is an option I firmly believe should be explored, the prospective owner ought to be aware that certain facilities must be available in order to take advantage of battery power: There must be a convenient place to bring the boat in close proximity to 110-volt shore-power and a suitable battery charger. After the 12 boat batteries are discharged to the point where they need recharging, it will require a stretch of time hooked up to a powerful battery charger to bring them back to full charge. It would be well to determine the power and time requirements for charging up the batteries before deciding that an electric power plant is compatible with your boating needs. If it is feasible for your situation, you can be content knowing that turning on the auxiliary aboard *Annabelle Two* will have minimum impact on our increasingly vulnerable marine environment.

*You can reach designer Antonio Dias at 193 Tillson Lake Rd., Wallkill, NY 12589.*

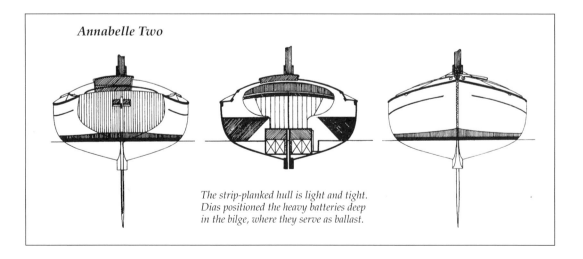

*Annabelle Two*

*The strip-planked hull is light and tight. Dias positioned the heavy batteries deep in the bilge, where they serve as ballast.*

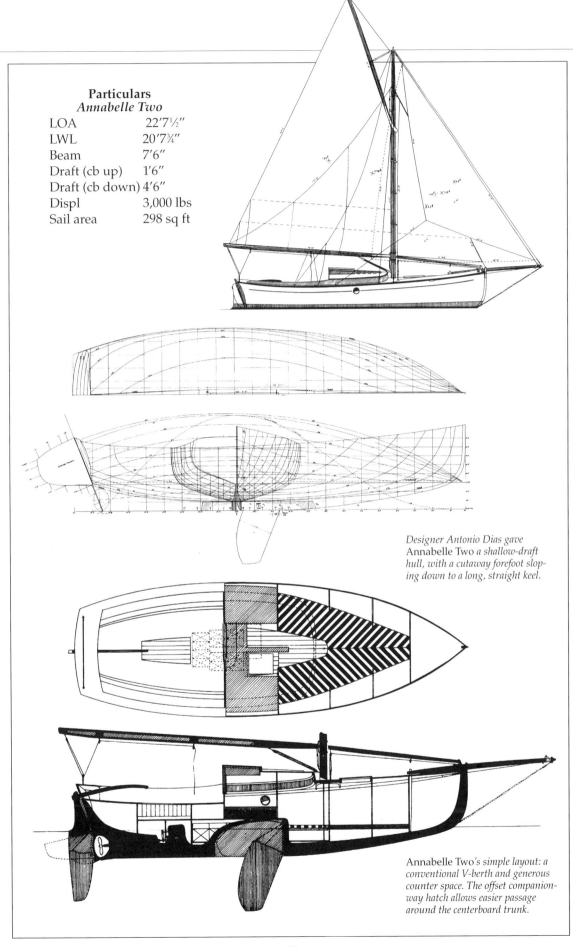

## Particulars
### Annabelle Two

| | |
|---|---|
| LOA | 22′7½″ |
| LWL | 20′7¾″ |
| Beam | 7′6″ |
| Draft (cb up) | 1′6″ |
| Draft (cb down) | 4′6″ |
| Displ | 3,000 lbs |
| Sail area | 298 sq ft |

*Designer Antonio Dias gave*
Annabelle Two *a shallow-draft hull, with a cutaway forefoot sloping down to a long, straight keel.*

Annabelle Two's *simple layout: a conventional V-berth and generous counter space. The offset companionway hatch allows easier passage around the centerboard trunk.*

# Two Double-Enders

Designs by Paul Gartside and Joel White
Commentary by Maynard Bray

It has always seemed to me that the world of wooden boating is full of happy coincidences. Here's one I feel is important enough to share. It involves two of my favorite designers, one of whom is set up in Sidney, British Columbia, and the other right here where I live in Brooklin, Maine. Without knowing what the other was up to and working at drawing boards that were some 3,000 miles apart, Paul Gartside and Joel White created preliminary plans at almost the same time for double-ended, keel/centerboard sloops, nearly identical in size.

The boats are within a foot of being the same length overall, and have almost exactly the same 6-foot beam. Paul's, however, being a cruiser with a small trunk cabin and deeper hull, is expected to weigh about twice as much. For this reason, it should come as no surprise that he has given her considerably more sail area.

Paul's design was conceived to respond to what his client asked for, which was a canoe yawl. Beyond that, the inspiration came partly from a book on Albert Strange's wonderful work in designing boats of this type and partly on boats from Paul's country of origin. Paul grew up among the gaff-rigged working craft of England's Cornish coast, and you'll find other boats of his design carrying a mainsail of the same long-gaff, short-boom proportions. He prefers a single mast for its simplicity rather than adding the clutter of a tiny mizzen, with which most of the turn-of-the-century canoe yawls were fitted.

This boat's hull will be of conventional plank-on-steambent-frame construction, but with double planking — both layers running fore-and-aft with their seams offset from each other, Herreshoff and Nevins style. In West Coast fashion — Gartside now lives and works in the Pacific northwest — the deck is to be in two layers

of red cedar. The lower layer is to run fore-and-aft and have the corners of its strakes chamfered on the underside for appearance; the upper layer is to be glued diagonally over the first, then sheathed with Dynel or fiberglass cloth laid in epoxy. The ballast is specified to be cast lead, located entirely outside where it will be needed for stability on this narrow hull. The centerboard will be of wood with enough lead cast into its lower edge to make it sink. Its L-shaped trunk will be out of the way and hidden from view below the floorboards in the cabin. The small portion that projects into the cockpit, although higher, will essentially be concealed under the seat platform.

Paul points out that the boat's Folkboat-sized cabin is intended for weekending, and, although quite usable, may seem cramped in light of today's expectations. There are two berths, stove and pantry flats, a bucket head between the berths, and storage forward for sails and the anchor rode.

The lines plan shows a lovely shape. Even before all the construction drawings are complete, it is apparent that this will be an unusually beautiful craft well able to carry on the canoe yawl tradition, albeit with a sloop rig.

Now let's look at Joel White's daysailer. Refreshingly handsome from all angles, the indicators point to its being super-swift as well. The lines plan shows her to have the firm bilges that centerboarders require for stability, and because much of her bilge shows above the water, the resulting narrow waterplane and low wetted surface will be helpful for speed in light weather. The buttocks and diagonals show no trace of a pot belly; they're straight enough to ensure minimum wave-making resistance, so the boat should easily reach her hull speed in moderate winds. As a relentless proponent of hollow waterlines, I am happy

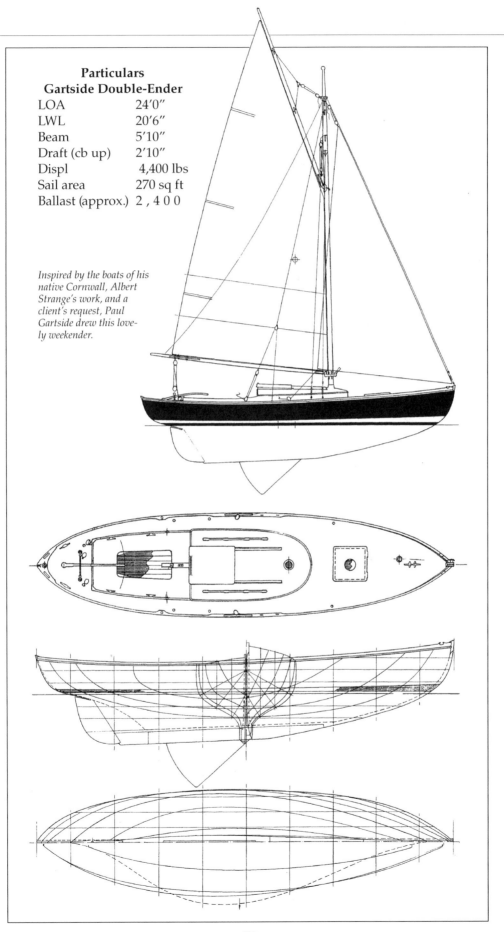

**Particulars**
**Gartside Double-Ender**

| | |
|---|---|
| LOA | 24'0" |
| LWL | 20'6" |
| Beam | 5'10" |
| Draft (cb up) | 2'10" |
| Displ | 4,400 lbs |
| Sail area | 270 sq ft |
| Ballast (approx.) | 2 , 4 0 0 |

*Inspired by the boats of his native Cornwall, Albert Strange's work, and a client's request, Paul Gartside drew this lovely weekender.*

to see that Joel has accomplished this at the stern as well as at the bow.

This boat's ballast also is all outside as a lead casting. Her centerboard, although made of wood to a foil shape, will be ballasted with a big piece of lead cast into its lower end. Not much of the centerboard trunk will show above the floorboards — really only a raised portion forward where the board's operating arm will be housed, and even some of that part will be under the deck.

As for construction, Joel recommends a cold-molded, or possibly DuraKore, hull to keep the weight down and to avoid plank shrinkage and leaks if the boat is dry-sailed. Her shallow draft and straight keel make trailering a real possibility. Joel plans to work out a tabernacle for the mast so it can be raised and lowered without too much trouble.

The rig is tall and efficient, and there's plenty of it. At first glance, in fact, the shallow and narrow hull's ability to carry this much sail might be questioned. But, fear not. Joel has had a good deal of experience with rig size vs. stability, and this boat, which carries about half her displacement as a ballast keel, will not be especially tender. But I'll wager she'll be especially fast.

*Paul Gartside, 10305 W. Saanich Rd., RR #1, Sidney, BC, V8L 3R9, Canada.*

*Plans for Joel White's 23-foot centerboard sloop are available from The WoodenBoat Store, P.O. Box 78, Brooklin, ME 04616; 800–273–7447.*

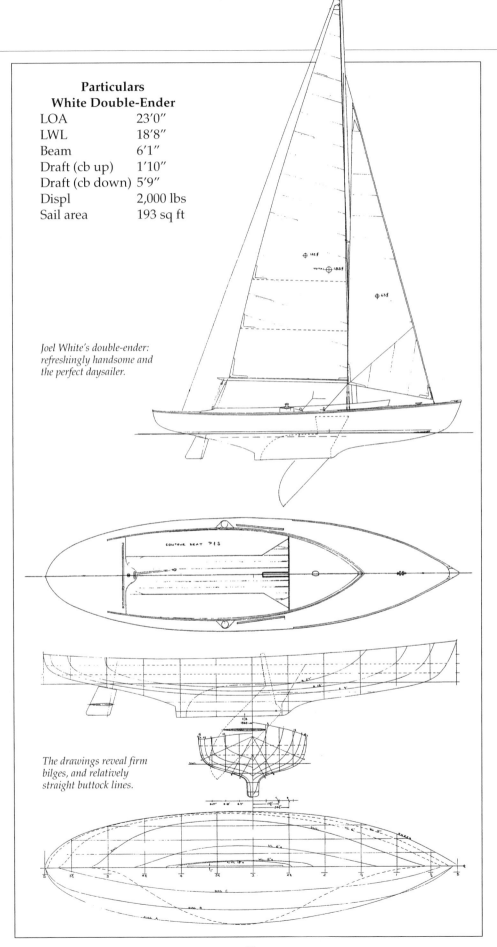

**Particulars**
**White Double-Ender**

| | |
|---|---|
| LOA | 23'0" |
| LWL | 18'8" |
| Beam | 6'1" |
| Draft (cb up) | 1'10" |
| Draft (cb down) | 5'9" |
| Displ | 2,000 lbs |
| Sail area | 193 sq ft |

*Joel White's double-ender: refreshingly handsome and the perfect daysailer.*

*The drawings reveal firm bilges, and relatively straight buttock lines.*

**XXVI**

# *Two Shoal-Draft Yawls*

———— Designs by Albert Strange and Philip C. Bolger ————
Commentary by Mike O'Brien

Nearly 100 years and 3,000 miles of Atlantic Ocean separate the canoe yawl *Wenda* from the leeboard sharpie *Martha Jane*. As might be expected, these shoal-draft cruisers differ considerably in construction and style, but they share similar purpose and a certain quality of independence.

Implications of the name notwithstanding, canoe yawls are not canoes and need not be yawl rigged. Essentially, they are small centerboard cruisers with canoe sterns. The type evolved on the estuaries of nineteenth-century England as a logical, more able, development of light sailing canoes. Capable of substantial coastwise passages and displaying a spirit that transcends functional definition, these compact cruisers stir deep passions in many romantically inclined sailors.

*Wenda*, possibly the prettiest of her breed, was drawn by artist Albert Strange to meet the following criteria: "...as light a displacement as possible consistent with immunity from capsizing...fair accommodation for two persons...but within the power of one to work a passage singlehanded...speed to be kept in view, but...the extent of sail area to be very moderate." Though expressed nearly a century ago, these desires are not foreign to contemporary cruisers.

In drawing *Wenda*'s lines, Strange carefully combined art and function. He skated along a thin edge — giving her enough bottom to carry sail while keeping her sections easy but not too soft. Her hull reveals a pervasive curvature with no hard spots or awkward transitions; she would be a joy to cold-mold. Her forefoot seems severely cut away by current standards, but her stem forms an interesting curve of changing radius. A nicely crafted canoe stern balances her profile.

*Wenda*'s cutaway but buoyant ends, combined with relatively symmetrical waterlines and a fair amount of drag to the keel, should ensure polite behavior. It's difficult to imagine her rooting or becoming hard-mouthed. The shallow but powerful rudder will have no problem keeping things under control. Old-fashioned to many eyes, its low-aspect-ratio blade won't be inclined to pick up pot warp and eelgrass. This little yawl will scull along quite well if the tiller is wiggled properly (her skipper won't care about frowning race committees).

None of *Wenda*'s interior arrangement drawings has survived, but we suspect two people could be quite comfortable aboard her. A sleeping flat might be worked in around her low centerboard trunk and leave enough room for a small galley and head. At any rate, there's no excess volume in these boats. In order to save space, the old British canoe yawls often had centerboards that were badly shaped, too small, and hung too far forward. *Wenda* fares tolerably well in this area because she is more drawn out than some of her cousins, and her accommodations are carried farther aft.

*Wenda*'s low divided rig deserves close inspection, and perhaps some imitation. It's well suited to her slender hull. Long, light, narrow boats must keep on just the right amount of sail — a simple task aboard Strange's yawl, as a deep reef in the main would have little effect on her balance. The tiny mizzen certainly isn't a powerful device, but it provides razor-sharp control. Underway, it can fine-tune the helm or kick the boat's stern in the desired direction during tight maneuvering. Successful tacking in difficult situations can be guaranteed by sheeting or shoving the mizzen to the inside of the turn — easier and more positive than backing a jib. Speaking of headsails, *Wenda*'s testifies that roller-furling isn't a recent invention.

The simple sophistication of the standing-lug main is most persuasive. Considerable changes in sail shape can be accomplished by varying outhaul and halyard tensions in conjunction with sliding the halyard's rolling hitch up or down the yard. The short masts will mitigate desperation when the breeze is building and you have lowered everything that will come down without using an axe.

Built with contemporary materials to her original displacement, Strange's old design has the makings of a strong and able estuarine cruiser. Wherever *Wenda* drops her hook, she'll improve the scenery.

Sharpies, in their simplest flat-bottomed form, hold a strong fascination for sailors and architects. They offer, perhaps, the most performance for the least investment. *Martha Jane* is a recent thin-water cruiser from the board of Philip C. Bolger — an acknowledged master of modern sharpie design.

Don't be misled by this little yawl's radical appearance. Almost every detail of rigging and hull design has been proven in her designer's earlier work. Bolger's sharpies always show adequate rocker in their bottoms, and the heels of their stems are carried well clear of the water. This configuration reduces crossflow at the chines, resulting in better performance — particularly in light air. The docile steering demonstrated by these shoal-draft cruisers will be appreciated by anyone who has wrestled with sharp-ended flat-bottomed boats in heavy weather.

You'll notice that this new sharpie has rectangular sections. Her sides stand perfectly perpendicular to the water's surface. Weren't we brought up to respect flare as one of nature's absolutes? We might have argued about how much was appropriate, but that there would be some flare was never in doubt. Be that as it may, arguments can be presented in favor of rectangular sections. For boats with *Martha Jane*'s proportions, vertical sides can result in nicely drawn-out waterlines, maximum initial stability, easier construction, and slightly reduced materials cost.

Some plumb-sided skiffs and canoes have earned reputations as ugly, bad-tempered monsters. These very small craft are usually unballasted, and the crew often weighs much more than the boat. If, as the load increases, the depth of the immersed rectangular section becomes too great compared to its width, there are problems. When the boat is heeled, the center of buoyancy can slip to the wrong side of the center of gravity with alarming suddenness, causing almost instantaneous inversion. With her predictably lighter relative loading and greater beam producing shallow immersed rectangular sections, *Martha Jane*, carrying 500 pounds of seawater ballast, should display a reasonably friendly stability curve.

You might object to vertical sides on aesthetic grounds; perhaps they — along with painfully dry white wine, black olives, and your favorite music — represent acquired taste. Bolger summed up his feelings about this controversial matter in a letter to a British boatbuilder: "I'm convinced that these rectangular-sectioned boats are functionally superior as well as highly economical of time and material, but it's hard to get the point across...as most people can't grasp that the behavior they like is due to the looks they don't like."

*Martha Jane*'s construction plan shows Bolger's usual clean and clever way of working with plywood. A few bulkheads combine with stringers to produce great rigidity without the clutter of extensive transverse framing. Virtually every element in the design adds to the boat's strength — sliding hatch rails serve as supporting girders for the deck, and supporting guards strengthen the sides. Assembly is "instant boat" fashion, a refinement of traditional skiff-building methods. Bolger provides drawings showing the real or expanded shape of the sides. These are recreated at full scale directly on the plywood, cut out, and wrapped around the molds. True lofting and building jigs aren't needed. This is easy work for rank amateurs and fast work for experienced hands.

Leeboards have become a trademark of Bolger sharpies. Because they live outside the hull, the boards don't intrude on the accommodations. The boat need not be holed for their installation, and the single biggest maintenance problem for shoal-draft wooden boats — the centerboard trunk — is eliminated. A leeboard need work on only one tack, and it can be oriented for maximum efficiency on port or starboard. The working board angles away from the hull, presenting a perpendicular face to the water as the boat heels. A small amount of toe-in relative to the boat's centerline increases lift (some designers specify asymmetrical foils for the same reason), but Bolger cautions against overdoing it. In extremely shallow water, leeboards will remain effective long after centerboards must be fully retracted.

Because they are ballasted only enough to make them sink readily the immersed working leeboard "weighs" virtually nothing. At the same time, the other board rides completely clear of the water; its full weight in the air helps keep the boat on her feet. In effect, you have an uncomplaining crew member who is willing to hang 6 inches outboard of the weather rail forever.

For this sharpie, Bolger specifies traditional Flemish leeboard "hardware," consisting of stout rope. As the boards are lowered the loops tighten, holding them firmly in position. Yet the weather board can "broken-wing" (swing away from the boat) if it's left lowered. For shorthanded short tacking, both boards can remain down. They're quite happy that way, and — because the rig is self-tending — the skipper need only point the tiller properly.

The kick-up inboard rudder is a new Bolger creation. Unlike blades that retract into trunks, this arrangement should permit steering even when it's partially lifted. The designer describes its geometry as being the outcome of "excruciating mental effort."

*Martha Jane* shares the virtues of *Wenda*'s sail plan, and adds a few of her own. Her unstayed rig can be struck in minutes — handy for trailering and comforting in a blow. The mainmast stands in a tabernacle; with proper counterbalancing (about 90 pounds of lead), swinging it should be a one-handed operation. Measuring just 16 feet in height and 3 inches square at its partner, the mizzenmast will present no

problems. Both the sprit-boomed mizzen and the balanced lug mainsail are more or less self-vanging and reduce concern about sheeting angles.

Built as drawn, *Martha Jane* should be self-bailing, self-righting, unsinkable, easily trailerable, and fast under sail. She's a most significant sharpie.

*Wenda's plans are available from The WoodenBoat Store, P.O. Box 78, Brooklin, ME 04616; 800–273–7447.*

*Martha Jane's plans are available from Elrow LaRowe, 11765 S.W. Ebberts Ct., Beaverton, OR 97008.*

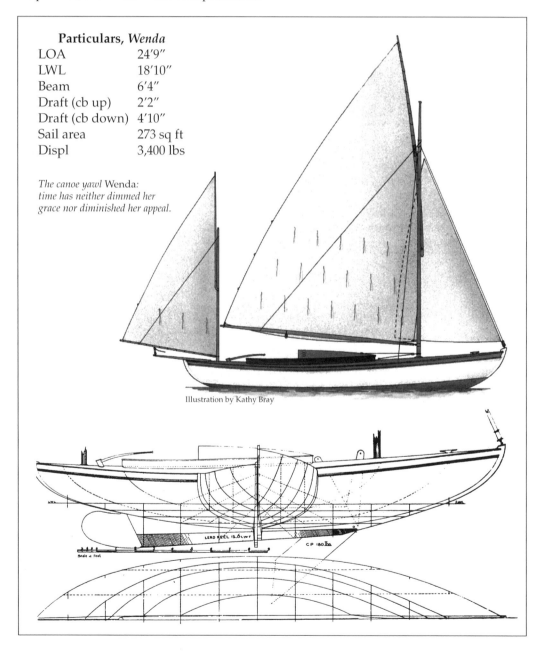

**Particulars, *Wenda***
| | |
|---|---|
| LOA | 24'9" |
| LWL | 18'10" |
| Beam | 6'4" |
| Draft (cb up) | 2'2" |
| Draft (cb down) | 4'10" |
| Sail area | 273 sq ft |
| Displ | 3,400 lbs |

*The canoe yawl* Wenda: *time has neither dimmed her grace nor diminished her appeal.*

Illustration by Kathy Bray

**Particulars, *Martha Jane***

| | |
|---|---|
| LOD | 23'6" |
| Beam | 6'0" |
| Displ | 2,350 lbs |
| Empty (trailer) weight | 1,400 lbs |
| Sail area | 247 sq ft |

*Simple and reliable Flemish leeboard "hardware"— viewed from above (left) and from back aft (right). Note how the line will tighten as the board is lowered.*

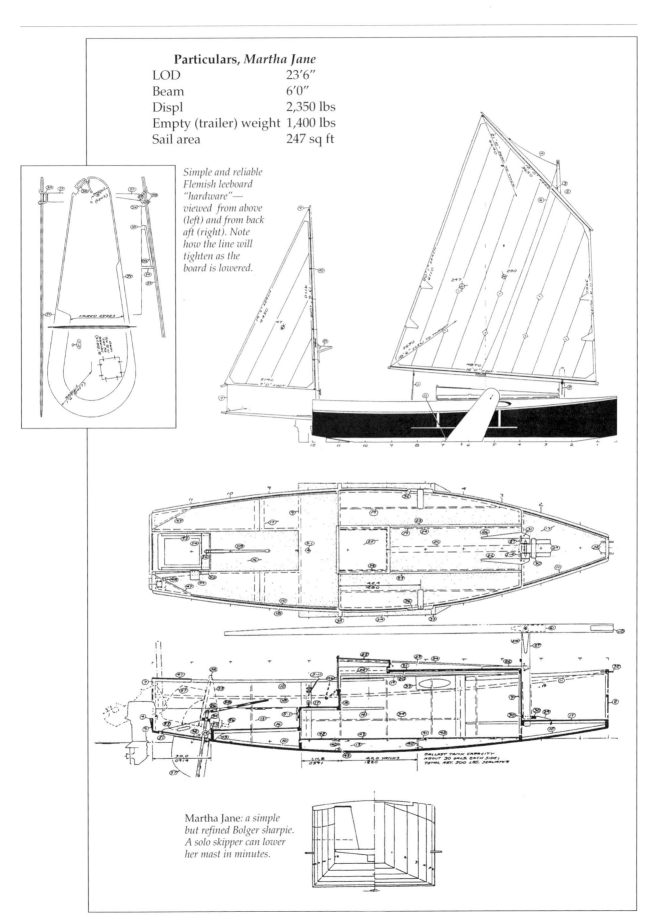

Martha Jane: *a simple but refined Bolger sharpie. A solo skipper can lower her mast in minutes.*

# XXVII

# A Keel/Centerboard Sloop

—————— Design by John G. Alden ——————
Commentary by the editors of *WoodenBoat*

Although John G. Alden company records indicate that no boats were built to this 1929 design, we are quite fascinated by its potential as a fast and able cruiser. We're also impressed with the rather elaborate construction details, which are well worth a careful study.

It's very easy to speculate on the influences that have governed the design of different boats, but the roots of this one are most assuredly the Cape Cod catboat. The differences are less beam, a stretched-out forebody, and, of course, the gaff sloop rig. The rig is quite simple despite its power, with only three stays supporting the mast and with the forestay tension coming from the bobstay and shroud turnbuckles. The self-tending jib is rigged with lazyjacks, and the main would be somewhat easier to handle while lowering if it were similarly rigged.

This sloop has a number of distinctive details about her, beginning with the beautiful steam-bent house sides and coamings, the latter being bent around vertical staving. She has wheel-steering, but an alternate tiller-steering arrangement is provided for. The after end of the bowsprit is fashioned and pinned to form a mooring cleat so that neither a conventional cleat nor a mooring bitt are required.

There are several interesting details in her construction, including the slotted cast-iron keel (1,500 pounds), the numerous lodging knees, the maststep/partners tie rod, the simple but strong centerboard case, and the built-up rudder. As we mentioned, here is a construction plan worth studying.

Accommodations are very simple, with two berths in the main cabin, and a single berth and head up forward. The galley stove is located just aft of the forward bulkhead, and the drop-leaf table on the centerboard case is the working surface. Interestingly, the forward third of the case is cut down to the level of the cabin sole, which provides considerably more freedom of movement in that area. The bridge deck at the after end of the cabin provides the additional room needed below as well as increased transverse strength (always desirable in a sailing hull). Beneath the bridge deck are a stowage box and an ice box, both of which are removable for cleaning or painting. A 25-gallon freshwater tank supplies the boat through a simple gravity-feed line.

A watertight bulkhead separates the cabin from the engine compartment, and access to the engine is through a hatch in the cockpit sole designed to accommodate the engine selected.

We note provisions for running backstays with a marconi rig configuration, but it is assumed that the rig was never developed. (We'd probably recommend the gaff, anyway.)

This is quite a fine little boat.

*Plans for the Keel/Centerboard Sloop are available from The WoodenBoat Store, P.O. Box 78, Brooklin, ME 04616; 800–273–7447.*

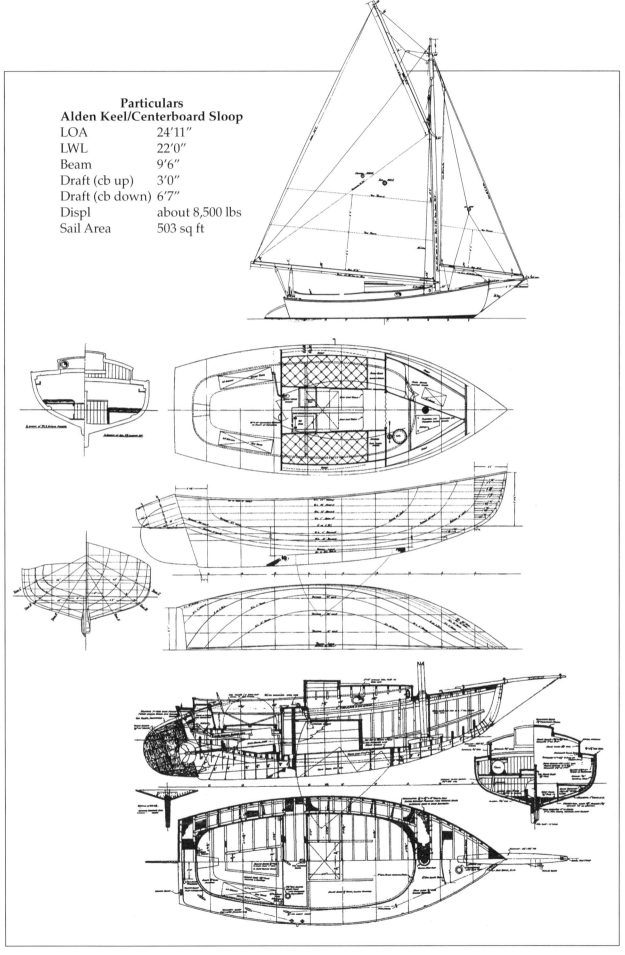

**Particulars**
**Alden Keel/Centerboard Sloop**
| | |
|---|---|
| LOA | 24'11" |
| LWL | 22'0" |
| Beam | 9'6" |
| Draft (cb up) | 3'0" |
| Draft (cb down) | 6'7" |
| Displ | about 8,500 lbs |
| Sail Area | 503 sq ft |

# A Pilothouse Sloop

———— Design by Scott Sprague ————
Commentary by Joel White

This 26-foot cruising sloop, known as Al's 26, by Scott Sprague of Poulsbo, Washington, is a boat that shows the effect a particular locale can have on design. The Pacific Northwest will be her home, and the special weather patterns of that part of the world — cool, with wet spells that might last a week or more — are the reason for her large pilothouse and dual steering stations. The pilothouse also allows full headroom in at least part of the accommodations — an unusual feature on a boat this small with a normal cabin configuration.

The drawings show a perky hull, with lots of sheer, a canoe stern, high bulwarks, and a short bowsprit. The rig, a conventional masthead sloop, has a foretriangle larger in area than the mainsail: 210 compared to 183 square feet.

I have always thought it would be interesting to take two identical hulls, and vary the proportions of the sail plan of one, then sail the two boats against each other to determine which combination of areas is best for different points of sail. My guess would be that larger mains and smaller foretriangles would win out to windward, while less difference would be noted when reaching. Running before the wind, the large mainsail would again be best, unless provision were made to wing out the jib.

There is also some point at which a sloop with too much foretriangle and not enough main loses her ability to handle easily and surely under mainsail alone. This ability is a very useful trait. With no jibsheets to handle, the skipper has only to steer and plot his moves, whether making a mooring, landing alongside the dock, or dropping anchor, while regulating speed with the mainsheet.

This boat was designed to be built by the owner using laminated wood as the hull material. For that reason, the lines show sections that lend themselves to this sort of construction — easy curves without any reverse. The short ends and good beam make for a roomy hull, which is exactly what is needed to provide cruising accommodations for three in the 26 feet of overall length. The nearly circular sections give the most volume with the least wetted surface, and should make an easily driven hull at low to moderate speeds. There is a trapezoidal fin keel, about two-thirds of which is lead ballast, and a big rudder hung on a large fixed fin. Designed displacement is given as 7,100 pounds, with 2,665 pounds of ballast.

Her interior is planned to make the best use of the full headroom under the pilothouse. The galley, the enclosed head, a quarter berth, and the below-deck steering station are aft, where headroom is 6 feet 1 inch. Forward of the pilothouse, under a low cabin trunk, there is a large storage locker to starboard, and V-berths with sitting headroom. The V-berth insert, when raised, makes a dinette table, and a good-sized double berth when it is lowered. It is difficult to imagine how better to allot available space in a 26-footer. Granted, the head enclosure is quite small, and one must use the quarter berth as the seat for the lower steering station; but, all in all, it is impressive how much room there is in this little boat.

Up three steps from the pilothouse, one steps aft onto the engine box and then down into the self-bailing cockpit. The afterdeck itself serves as seating for the cockpit, with lockers under hinged covers. There is tiller steering in the cockpit, with a radial quadrant under the short stern deck and cables leading forward to the wheel in the pilothouse. When the weather is damp and chilly the forward steering station will be a nice place from which to handle the boat under either sail or power. A clear panel in the pilothouse roof would

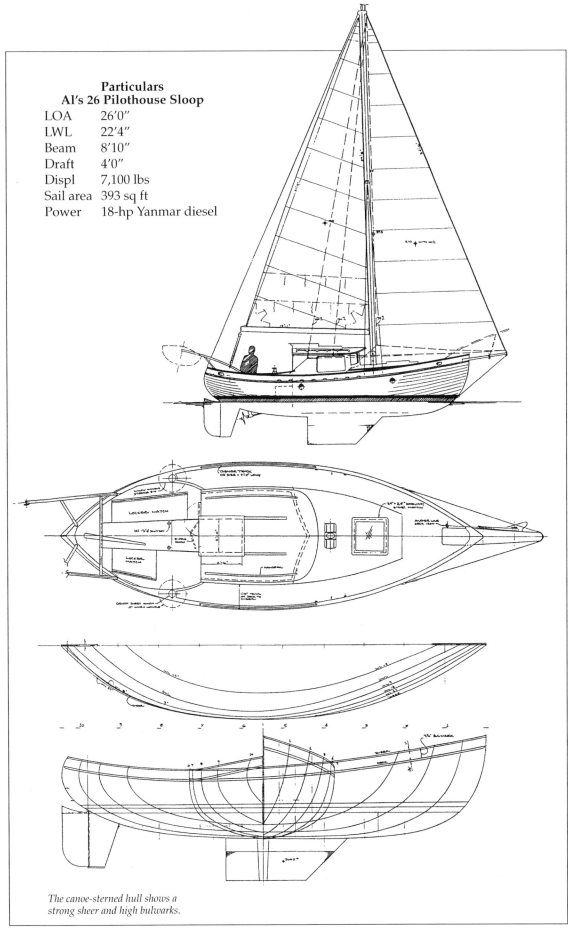

**Particulars**
**Al's 26 Pilothouse Sloop**

| | |
|---|---|
| LOA | 26'0" |
| LWL | 22'4" |
| Beam | 8'10" |
| Draft | 4'0" |
| Displ | 7,100 lbs |
| Sail area | 393 sq ft |
| Power | 18-hp Yanmar diesel |

*The canoe-sterned hull shows a
strong sheer and high bulwarks.*

be useful for checking sail trim.

The dinghy davits astern are unusual in a boat this size. These are made from pipe, with a cross brace forming the mainsheet traveler. As long as the dinghy is small enough to be in proportion to the mother craft, this is probably a good solution for dealing with the tender, getting it out of the water and out of the way. The hoisted dinghy also makes a great place to stow extraneous stuff.

The hull is ⅝-inch fore-and-aft strip planking with two layers of ⅛-inch veneers glued on the outside. The cabin bulkheads, plus a few laminated frames and floor timbers, provide the necessary inside stiffeners. The deck is two layers of ¼-inch plywood over a very simple deck frame. The cabin and pilothouse are plywood, epoxy-and-glass covered, as is the deck. The mast is stepped on a laminated arch in the cabin trunk, supported by bulkheads. Chainplates are bolted to the inside of the hull. This is certainly a hull that could be built by a reasonably skilled amateur craftsman with ordinary woodworking tools and enough available time.

The plans include a sheet on spars and rigging details. The spars are spruce box sections with simple hardware. The bowsprit is a Douglas-fir plank bolted through the deck.

You will notice that there are two round portlights in the topsides to let in light and allow the crew to have a look about without leaving the bunk. Having built a couple of boats with topside ports, my advice is this: If you use such portlights, paint the hull a dark color — black or dark green. If you don't, your boat will look as though Captain Hornblower put a couple of broadsides straight through your timbers!

*Plans for Al's 26 are available from Accumar Corp., 1180 Finn Hill Rd. NW, Poulsbo, WA 98370.*

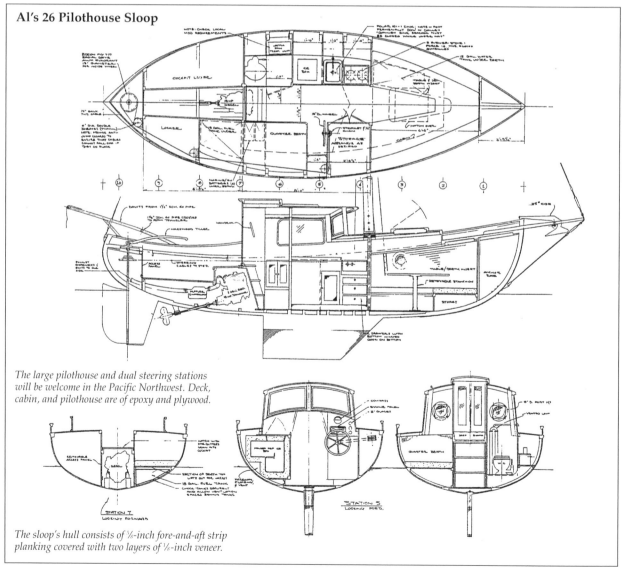

**Al's 26 Pilothouse Sloop**

*The large pilothouse and dual steering stations will be welcome in the Pacific Northwest. Deck, cabin, and pilothouse are of epoxy and plywood.*

*The sloop's hull consists of ⅝-inch fore-and-aft strip planking covered with two layers of ⅛-inch veneer.*

# Three Concordia Cruisers

———— Designs by Concordia Company ————
Commentary by Maynard Bray

Waldo Howland has always liked practical things, so when there was a forced reawakening to things practical in the depressed mid-1930s, he was probably a jump or two ahead when it came to boats.

Waldo was running the Concordia Company then, but that was before it became a boatyard. In 1938, Concordia was a struggling little brokerage and design office on the Fairhaven, Massachusetts, waterfront with only one or two people besides Waldo in it. But one of them was an exceptionally talented designer named Wilder B. Harris, and that fall he and Waldo had been working up plans for an inexpensive four-berth family cruiser — a practical boat — to be built, they hoped, in quantity. Before their design was complete, there was a customer, the Sawyer brothers, giving Howland and Harris an opportunity to finish things up and then go on and prove their contention that their design was a good one.

Finishing up meant "more conferences, more letters, and more detail sketches than would be needed to construct an ocean liner," Waldo recalls, "but in those days we had the time, and the interest, and urgently needed the business."

That their design was a good one was proven in a way when, before the first boat was finished, a second had been ordered. Bud McIntosh of Dover, New Hampshire — also a practical man — along with his brother, Ned, built *Star Dust* and *Lauan*, the first two Concordia "31s" ("25s" they were called back then because of their waterline length), and the only ones built before World War II. Both boats were launched in 1939 and are still looking lovely and going strong today (1982).

But before these "31s," there was the design that they were based on — the "28." And after the Concordia "31" came the bigger "33." So to keep the boats in chronological sequence and in the order of their size — and to avoid confusion — let's first examine how the "28" came into being.

There was only one Concordia 28, *Shawnee II*. In 1937 — the year before the "31s" were designed — Arthur Morse came to Concordia seeking a "big" little boat for himself, his wife, and their teenage son to go cruising in. Neither full headroom nor an auxiliary engine were important, and a three-berth arrangement was just fine. Bill Harris drew up her plans, and she was built in 1938 by Bert Briggs at the Pierce and Kilburn yard in Fairhaven, Massachusetts — and all the while watched over by Waldo and his old friend Major William Smyth, who was foreman at P&K.

Of the the boat's conception, Waldo says: "Waterline length, beam, and depth of hull really determine the size of a boat. In order to attain a usable cockpit, a simple galley with a quarter berth opposite, full length berths for a tall man, plus a fo'c's'le for storage and installation of a head, we were led quite directly to a waterline length of 22½ feet and a (moderate) beam of 8½ feet. By going to short ends, it is always easier to attain a little extra useful freeboard. On a long-ended boat, raised freeboard looks just terrible and usually with the extra windage, acts that way, too. *Shawnee*'s freeboard was not excessive in any way, but was of sufficient height so that by making the cabin seats low and sloping outboard, one could sit comfortably without constant head-banging on the deck above. *Shawnee*'s cabin, being substantially open from end to end, gave a generous feeling of space and an actuality of ventilation — both true and blessed luxuries. Too much furniture, too many lockers, an overabundance of shelves all can crowd living quarters and collect nonessential gear.

"The flat transom stern with outboard rudder was strong, uncomplicated to build, and easy to maintain. It matches up in harmony with the short, rounded bow. With fairly hard bilge and wide keel, displacement evolved at a moderate 9,900 pounds. This is neither heavy nor light. The shape happily resulted in good floor space. Unless needed for some special reason, I find myself opposed to extremes in any boat. The moderate approach just seems to make for a more useful, better performing, and better looking cruising boat. Too much displacement requires extra sail area; too little limits the cabin space and ability to cope with added cruising equipment and weight."

The "28" led to the "31s." As already mentioned two were built before World War II and seven more were built after the war ended; McIntosh built one (his third of this design), and the others were built by the Concordia yard in South Dartmouth, Massachusetts. Most of these later boats had their sheers slightly raised and straightened for more interior space. Our favorites, however, are the originals as Bill Harris drew them, and that's the boat whose plans are included here.

The Concordia "31s" are exceedingly well-thought-out boats, and a great many of their features showed up later on in the famous Concordia yawls. The "31s" were never intended to be fancy, though, and experience has shown that workboat construction standards and paint schemes look right at home on these craft.

Here's what Waldo had to say about these boats when they first came out:

"From bitter experience, I have learned that 'modest comfort' on a coastal cruise cannot be obtained for four adults on a waterline length of less than 25 feet.

"There are many possible rigs for such a boat. Mainsail and single jib, however, are efficient, simple, and relatively inexpensive.

"Such a boat should have good working deck space and a comfortable, watertight cockpit with seats below deck level.

"The fewer deck fittings and gadgets, the better.

"A good, small engine, carefully installed, and so located that it can easily be gotten at, is an essential for most owners.

"The best place for the gas tank is under a seat in the watertight cockpit, with a proper shutoff near the tank.

"A really wide companionway hatch is a delight; if it is made longer than it is wide, it will slide easily and not jam; if it is canvas covered, it will not leak.

"A forward hatch is essential.

"A coal stove is the most foolproof, serves for heating and drying as well as for cooking, and is best located aft on the starboard side under the companionway where there is light, air, and headroom; the working part of the galley is best located opposite the stove.

"Comfortable seats to sit on, and dry and comfortable bunks to sleep on are most essential; we install special Concordia berths, which in the daytime form backs for the seats and which at night fold down to form canvas berths — the most comfortable ones possible when equipped with a light mattress.

"An underseat location for the toilet has been chosen in the forward cabin, where privacy comes from shutting the doors between the two cabins.

"Locker space has been planned very carefully: In the forward cabin two transom seat lockers, one on each side, give storage space for two people's clothes. Back in the main cabin, the shelved locker to starboard gives clothes stowage for two with a hanging locker to port for the going-ashore clothes. Linens and extra blankets are kept in the bureau to port, with a place on its top for books. A raingear locker is aft of the galley to starboard, where it is handy to the companionway.

"The outside finish is almost entirely paint; there is no varnish whatsoever, and certain things like rails and rubbing strakes are oiled for easy care."

Only three "33s" have been built — at least so far — and they are lovely boats, enough bigger than the "31s" to appear a little more graceful and to sail a bit faster. Waldo tells the story of how the design came into being:

"Shortly after we had lost our Norwegian pilot boat *Escape* in the 1938 hurricane, my father began considering different plans for a new boat. At the time, Bill Harris and I were working with real enthusiasm on drawings for the Concordia "31s", but these were not quite big enough for Father's needs. Bill therefore drew a preliminary study of a slightly larger "31" type which could comfortably include a good cockpit, headroom, two cabins, and an enclosed toilet. Attractive as the plans were, Father had his mind set on a different type of boat, and the Concordia "33" proposals were set aside for the time being.

"In 1947 a family project developed with our neighbors, the Fergusons, whereby Bob's son, Ricketson Ferguson, was to build a boat on speculation. They rented space from Palmer Scott in one of the old New Bedford cotton mill weavesheds. As Scott had his boatbuilding operation there at the time, all necessary equipment was on hand, as well as a boatbuilder by the name of Ollie Bowen. He advised and helped young Ferguson, who had a number of willing but inexperienced friends as crew.

"The boat they decided to build was the Concordia '33,' having had some earlier experience with the type by chartering a '31.' As the original designer Bill Harris

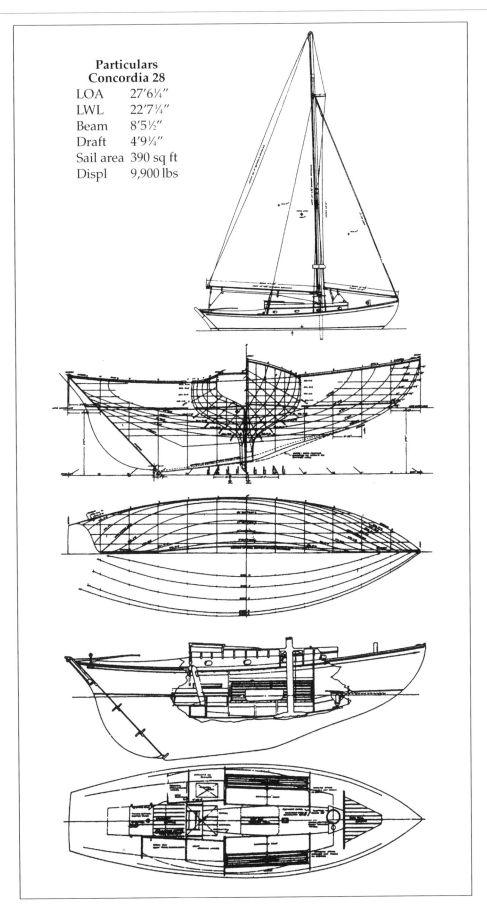

**Particulars**
**Concordia 28**

| | |
|---|---|
| LOA | 27'6¼" |
| LWL | 22'7¼" |
| Beam | 8'5½" |
| Draft | 4'9¼" |
| Sail area | 390 sq ft |
| Displ | 9,900 lbs |

was now in Alabama, Concordia's part-time drafts-man (and a very good one) Miller Nichols finished up the design work necessary for complete plans. The boat, *Mitty*, was finished during the winter of 1948, with Bob Ferguson as the owner.

"I have always had a special liking for the Concordia '33s.' They had ample room for a two-cabin boat. With added length, their freeboard with nice sheer was in pleasing proportion to their bow and stern. With a roller jib and well-proportioned mainsail, Mitty was as easy to handle as the '31s.' And although she would normally cost a bit more than her 31-foot sisters, I have often wondered just how much. The labor would be about the same."

A second "33" was built in 1959, and a third only a few years ago. It's such a timeless design, perhaps there will be more.

*Plans for the Concordia 33 are available from The WoodenBoat Store, P.O. Box 78, Brooklin, ME 04616; 800–273–7447.*

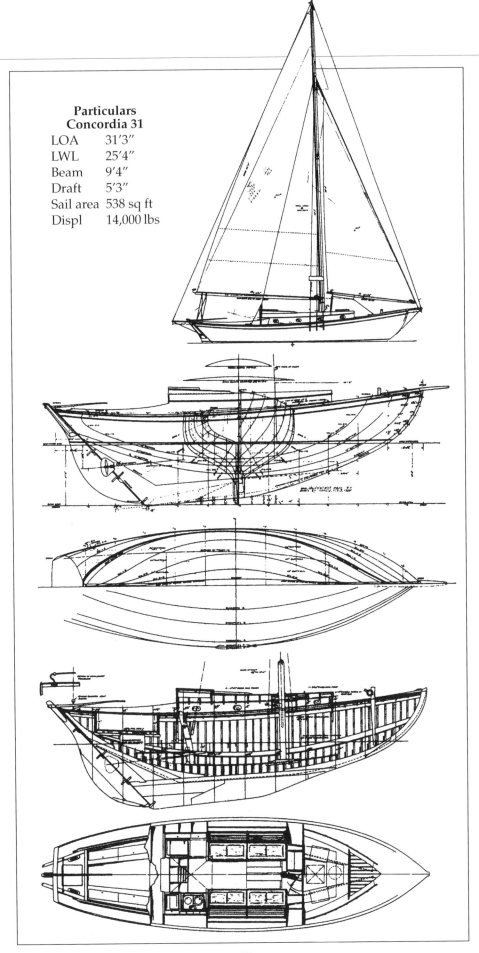

**Particulars**
**Concordia 31**

| | |
|---|---|
| LOA | 31′3″ |
| LWL | 25′4″ |
| Beam | 9′4″ |
| Draft | 5′3″ |
| Sail area | 538 sq ft |
| Displ | 14,000 lbs |

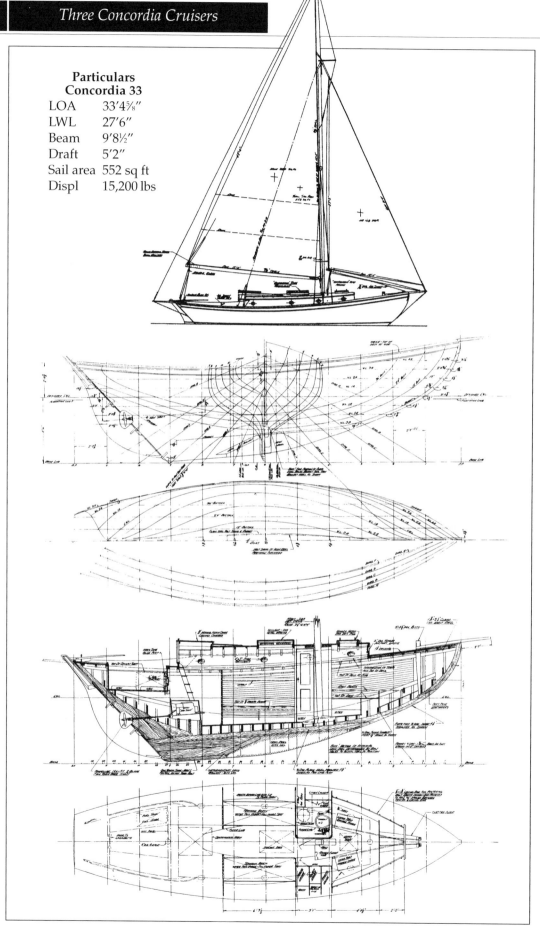

**Particulars**
**Concordia 33**

| | |
|---|---|
| LOA | 33'4⅝" |
| LWL | 27'6" |
| Beam | 9'8½" |
| Draft | 5'2" |
| Sail area | 552 sq ft |
| Displ | 15,200 lbs |

# A Double-Ended Sloop

Design by Joel White
Commentary by William Garden

*I*should qualify this design review at the start by confessing that I am a certifiable boat nut. I love all boats.

Joel White's neat little double-ender that we're reviewing here reminds me of the term "vice free," an expression I've come across in New Zealand and one that brings to mind a lovely, docile sort of yacht.

Vice free is a great term; its opposite (vice riddled?) brings to mind some vicious sort of down-by-the-head thing — probably manned by a crew of ruffians crouched along the weather rail, badmouthing the competition. The vice-riddled boat embodies all sorts of nasty spinnaker broaches, heavy weather helm, poor sail-carrying power, and a steady leak over my bunk. All this vice requires as a cure some sort of detoxification tank full of riggers and carpenters. The rudder must be shifted, ballast added, winglets attached to the keel, and perhaps a set of ballast tanks implanted. The mast will be moved and cosmetic surgery performed on the diving forebody, (and the crew's mouths will be washed out with soap) — all this in order to eliminate nightmares of death-roll broaches, sinkings, broken rudder stocks, or sudden by-the-lee uncontrolled goosewinged runs off towards disaster.

Vice free is a great term for my kind of boat.

Let's get into an evaluation of Joel's sloop. A quick look brings out some endearing features that will bear thought and study. First off, she has a nice canoe stern, which I always find appealing. With that as a hook, we're well into it. Further study turns up many good features in a thoughtfully presented and highly professional set of drawings.

A full-bodied hull form of 23 to 24 feet on the waterline is a nice size, since it allows standing headroom plus good internal volume with enough space available for several possible variations in interior layouts.

Let's climb down below and look around. The basic, simple layout has a pleasant saloon, good seating, and reasonable stowage — particularly so since the forward berth will accept stowage overflow when she's doing any offshore voyaging. Canvas berths are always appealing, and they will be a great boon to a tired crew. One's clothes can be folded on the day settee then stowed between settee and canvas berth above. This, plus the lockers, will do much toward keeping a tidy ship on long cruises.

At sea in rough weather, my choice of an off-watch berth would probably be the cabin sole, well chocked off with a sail bag. Now, shipmates, Joel has developed a vessel to suit his clients' needs, a plan that works out very well and that can be followed on the drawings. But let's digress from an account of her as drawn and ease off into what I would ask for if Joel were designing her for my own use.

A voyage aboard this sturdy double-ender is pleasant to contemplate. I've already bunked down on the cabin sole, it's blowing fresh, and down here there's no lower spot on which to be thrown. Temperature is foggy damp and a gas stove wouldn't do. My solid fuel heater has the cabin warm and dry, the lid is secured, and a closed pot of stew is chocked off in the corner fiddle. As wet weather morale boosters, a snug cabin and dry socks are difficult to beat. The heating stove, incidentally, fits nicely into the forward starboard locker space. The galley range, or Primus, is relegated to major cooking tasks.

For my galley, Joel has reversed the positions of hanging locker and ice box from those shown in the drawings. This allows engine heat to keep the locker dry, and gives better access to the icebox top when it's used as a galley sideboard or chart table. I also asked him to put a bridge deck in my ship in order to fit an athwartships galley counter under it. This is a nice area for dish and galley lockers.

Let's go back to the main cabin. The weather has eased off, and we're ready to eat a proper meal. The centerline table is a mixed blessing. (I was going to say a pain in the ass.) So I've jettisoned the beautiful teak table and replaced it with a sturdy folding one. It has concave edges fore and aft, and it's fitted port or starboard at mid-length of the settees. We're eating partly sidesaddle with the passageway clear for transit. With this arrangement, the cabin looks half again as large. But for those of you who prefer centerline tables, the neat details in Joel's drawings here are well worth studying.

The minor below-deck items noted above were requested of the architect prior to my placing the order, so we have remained on excellent terms — although I'm suspicious of a little black book that seems to be used for adding up dollar signs.

Now we've wandered around below looking at things, so let's get on up and look over her deck layout. The bridge deck provides a nice spot on which to stretch out athwartships — particularly so since I've also spent some money on a dodger over the forward end of the cockpit. This is a great shelter when the spray is flying.

Joel has just written down some more numbers with dollar signs attached, but we'll continue.

I like the plank bulwarks and the good shipshape stanchion details. We've agreed to put the mainsheet horse and traveler aft on the gallows, and we'll add small weather cloths port and starboard from the gallows forward to the first stanchion.

As for the rigging, forward we must have a strong roller furling system, and on the main an equally good jiffy reef. Maybe we'll use the seven-eighths rig with the headboard coming to jibstay terminal height when one reef is down. And maybe we'll add another pair of winches in the cockpit while we're spending all this money. Nice deep seats in the cockpit. We've made the coamings a couple of inches higher for my bad back.

We'll fit double anchor rollers forward and use a good heavy plow. For singlehanding, the rode will lead aft via snatch blocks to the cockpit winch — handy to the helmsman when getting underway. Pulpits look well made and extra strong. Full marks for a good pulpit aft and a good lazarette that accommodates fenders, warps, and other cruising gear.

Let's talk about the lines. There is a spidsgatter look to the waterlines — nicely formed, good freeboard, ends well balanced, and a lovely body plan. There is a good deck line and a pleasing run to the trunk cabin. The body plan is downright Junoesque.

For my ship, I'd have Joel plumb up the rudder stock and move it back to the waterline. Also, I'd like him to scoop out some deadwood aft to trim wetted surface and add some leading edge — and, I'd like a steering vane swivel bearing on the sternpost. When we're plunging along cold, wet, and tired, and wondering why we left home, we'll have some shelter behind the dodger while the vane keeps her charging along.

So we come to the construction plan — well thought out, showing Joel's wealth of experience as a naval architect and as a boatbuilder. Lots of good detail delineated in a clear style.

Strip construction is a practical method for an amateur builder, because a couple of strakes can be put on during an evening, and the material is relatively light and easy to handle. Epoxy or resorcinol glue can be used with nonferrous or galvanized common nails as the edge fasteners. The strips are slightly hollowed concave and convex to match, or bevels can be taken and a few plane cuts will trim the strip for a fair glue line. A skin of epoxy and Dynel will seal her off for a tight, dry hull. The sheathing should be done while she's still upside down, prior to fitting the deadwood.

In summary, this is a really fine little ship. She is well within the capabilities of handy backyard builders, and she won't prove to be too small after the first season's cruise. We'll give her a "10."

*Joel White can be reached at the Brooklin Boat Yard, P.O. Box 143, Brooklin, ME 04616.*

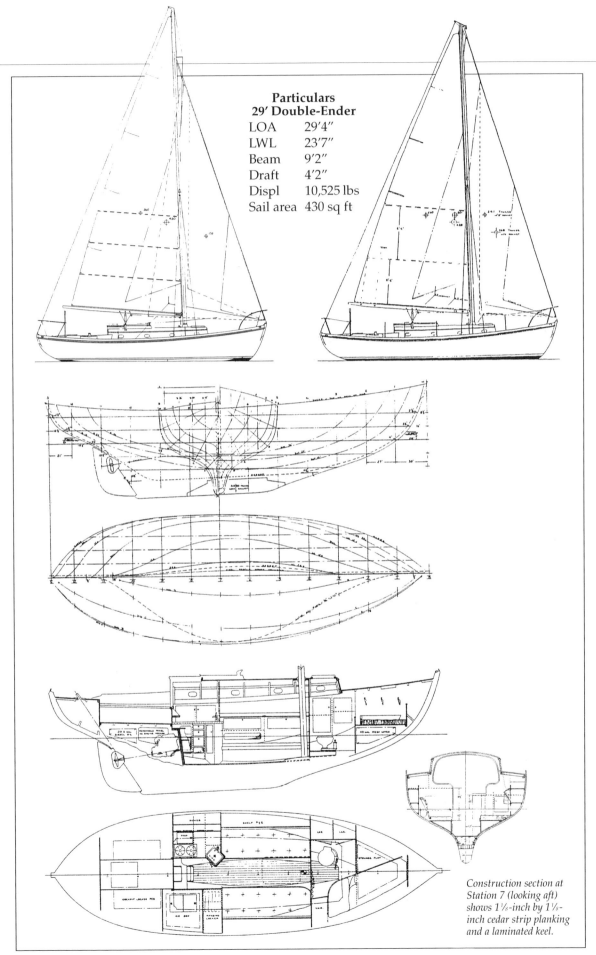

**Particulars**
**29′ Double-Ender**

| | |
|---|---|
| LOA | 29′4″ |
| LWL | 23′7″ |
| Beam | 9′2″ |
| Draft | 4′2″ |
| Displ | 10,525 lbs |
| Sail area | 430 sq ft |

*Construction section at Station 7 (looking aft) shows 1 1/8-inch by 1 1/8-inch cedar strip planking and a laminated keel.*

# XXXI

# A Shoal-Draft Plywood Ketch

Design by Karl Stambaugh
Commentary by Joel White

Over the past few years, America has experienced a rebirth of wooden boat building. There is no question that this is true, but much of the coverage in the yachting press might lead one to think that this renaissance is limited to a few extremely elegant and expensive yachts built for those with unlimited funds and time to indulge in such hobbies. The glitz and glitter have always received more media attention than the simple and mundane — yet the news is perhaps more interesting if one digs a little deeper for the facts.

A healthy amateur boatbuilding effort is turning out dozens and dozens of small, good-looking, useful boats made from forest products. One has only to turn to the "Launchings" column in each issue of *WoodenBoat* magazine to find the evidence. There are, in addition, many professional shops building a variety of boats on custom order, and employing a surprising number of craftsmen. It would be a mistake to fall into the trap of thinking that only the rich and famous are having wooden boats built.

As a result of all this activity, there are now a number of designers turning out boat plans that cater to this somewhat invisible market — boats that can be easily built of non-exotic materials, boats that will not break the family budget.

Designing such boats is neither easier, nor does it require less skill than designing the gold-plater. It is, in fact, probably more difficult. In addition to creating a safe and useful boat, the designer must give constant attention to construction that properly utilizes low-cost materials while minimizing the hours needed to complete the project. Bahama Mama is a perfect example of such an effort.

This little cruising ketch is built from sheet plywood, using multiple-chine construction, and fiberglass tape and epoxy to join the various sheets of plywood together at the edges: tack-and-tape is a good description of the process. Bulkheads are part of the construction setup, and are integral with the structure.

Karl Stambaugh designed Bahama Mama in collaboration with Gary Clements of G.F.C. Boats. The designer describes her as "a capable coastal cruiser to voyage beyond local waters and explore the backwaters when she arrives. All in a package within the means of time and dollars of most with the desire to live the cruising lifestyle." There, doesn't that thought get your blood moving?

Let's start by looking at the sail plan. The simple ketch rig is of moderate size, and is in no way unusual except in how well it seems to fit the hull below. The mizzen, as with most ketches, lands smack in the middle of the cockpit, passing through the bridge deck. Yet, Stambaugh has made the bridge deck wide enough to give easy access to the companionway forward of the mizzen, and to allow the on-deck crew to stretch out in comfort. The 380 square feet of sail is divided in such a way that the center of effort does not change much under various sail combinations. A large genoa on a roller-furler is offered as an option to increase sail area when the wind is light. The simple box-section spars are well stayed, and the stay between the mastheads ensures that the mizzen will remain in column when sheeted in tightly. All working sails show reef

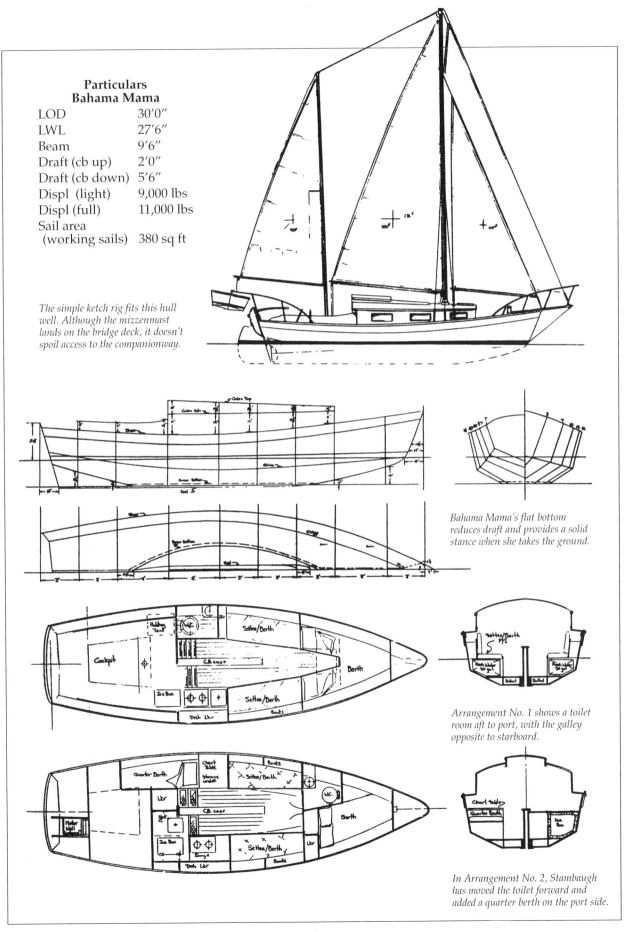

## Particulars
## Bahama Mama

| | |
|---|---|
| LOD | 30'0" |
| LWL | 27'6" |
| Beam | 9'6" |
| Draft (cb up) | 2'0" |
| Draft (cb down) | 5'6" |
| Displ (light) | 9,000 lbs |
| Displ (full) | 11,000 lbs |
| Sail area (working sails) | 380 sq ft |

*The simple ketch rig fits this hull well. Although the mizzenmast lands on the bridge deck, it doesn't spoil access to the companionway.*

*Bahama Mama's flat bottom reduces draft and provides a solid stance when she takes the ground.*

*Arrangement No. 1 shows a toilet room aft to port, with the galley opposite to starboard.*

*In Arrangement No. 2, Stambaugh has moved the toilet forward and added a quarter berth on the port side.*

points, one set in the mizzen and the jib, and two for the mainsail. Shoal-draft centerboard boats need to reef more often than those with deep ballast keels.

Notice what an attractive profile Bahama Mama makes, with her strong sheer, low freeboard, and cleverly proportioned house. Stambaugh has a very good eye.

The lines plan shows the unusual shape of this little boat. Let's imagine that she had been designed as a single-chine hull with quite a lot of deadrise, and much rocker to the keel. Then, imagine that 2 feet below the waterline we drew a horizontal line, cutting off the deep center V-section, and producing a flat bottom parallel to the waterline. Forward and aft of this flat bottom, the V shape continues upward to meet the stem and stern. This one stroke of the pencil changed her from deep-draft to shoal, keel to centerboard. The straight section lines are dictated, of course, by the sheet-plywood planking. Stambaugh has managed to keep most of the twist out the forward and after sections for ease of planking.

The boat's displacement is given as 9,000 pounds light and 11,000 pounds loaded with cruising gear and stores. With her long waterline length of 27 feet 6 inches, this gives a displacement/length ratio of 193 light and 236 loaded, surprisingly light for so small a cruising boat. This hull should be seakindly, buoyant, and, because of her long waterline and moderate displacement, reasonably fast.

Bahama Mama is what I would call a unified design. By that, I mean all elements of the design contribute to the overall purpose of the boat, and work towards the desired end result. For example: the straight, flat bottom allows the boat to have shallow draft. It also allows the boat to take the ground and remain completely upright while doing so. One of the problems with such boats is how to hang the necessary ballast keel. Stambaugh has solved that in the most simple and direct way — by pouring a mixture of cement and scrap iron on top of the flat bottom to a height of about 4 inches, using rebar through the floors to lock it all in place, then laying the cabin sole over all. Marvelous! He recommends a minimum of 5,500 pounds of ballast, which will give a 50 percent ballast ratio in the loaded condition. A stability curve that came with the plans shows Bahama Mama having positive righting arm to more than 120 degrees of heel, unusually good for a shoal-draft centerboarder.

Two interior layouts are included with the very complete plans package of 11 sheets. Both are simple and well thought out. Arrangement No. 1 has a toilet room aft to port, with the galley opposite to starboard, settee/berths each side amidships, and a pair of V-berths forward. In Arrangement No. 2, the toilet is forward to port with a larger berth to starboard, settee/berths

amidships again, and a quarter berth aft to port in place of the toilet room.

The centerboard trunk starts at the bulkhead at the after end of the cabin and runs forward about 7 feet into the cabin, dividing it along the centerline to a height of 28 inches off the sole. This gives the cook something to lean against or sit upon, yet is low enough that it does not visually interrupt the cabin space. The single centerline companionway opens onto matching port and starboard ladders, offering a choice of routes when going below.

Cabin headroom varies from 5 feet 4 inches forward to about 6 feet aft under the companionway hatch — pretty darn good for a small shoal-draft cruiser. The toilet space is quite limited in either layout. In Arrangement No. 1, I would be tempted to sacrifice some width on the port ladder and add it to the toilet room. Except for the V-berths, the bunks are a bit short for my taste (about 6 feet). But both arrangements make the most of the available space, and when cruising Bahamian waters, most of one's time would be spent in the large cockpit, under a big awning when not underway.

Bahama Mama's construction is mostly sheet plywood of various thicknesses, easily obtainable from the local lumberyard. The flat bottom is two thicknesses of ¾-inch ply, glued together. The lower planking strake is two layers of ½-inch ply, glued together. The upper planking strake is ¾-inch plywood, with a 1½-inch fir or mahogany sheerstrake glued on top. The deck is ½-inch plywood covered with Dynel and epoxy. Plywood bulkheads are lofted and shaped before setting them up on the bottom plank, and the remainder of the planking is wrapped around these bulkheads, which act as construction molds — all simple and very strong.

The box-section spars are wood: spruce glued with epoxy. The mainmast steps on the cabintop, and the mizzen passes through the bridge deck to the cockpit floor. Standing rigging is specified as 1 x 19 stainless-steel wire, and the running rigging is Dacron rope. No skimping on materials here, and properly so, the integrity of one's rig being crucial to safe and enjoyable cruising.

Auxiliary power can be either an outboard in a well, or, for those desiring a more efficient inboard unit, a small diesel is shown under the bridge deck. There is room for 50 gallons of fuel in two tanks under the cockpit seats. Stambaugh also calls for 60 gallons of fresh water in plywood tanks under the main cabin berths.

By now you probably realize that I like this design a lot. I think it fills a need for a simple, inexpensive cruising boat that can be built by a handy amateur, or put together quite reasonably by a professional shop.

Stambaugh estimates that 2,000 hours of labor would be required to complete Bahama Mama, and $10,000 to $12,000 [1994] would do it for basic materials (I think he might be a bit low on material prices). In any case, these figures add up to a very affordable boat.

*Plans for Bahama Mama are available from G.F.C. Boats, 490 Hagan Rd., Cape May Court House, NJ 08210.*

*Karl Stambaugh can be reached at 794 Creek View Rd., Severna Park, MD 21146.*

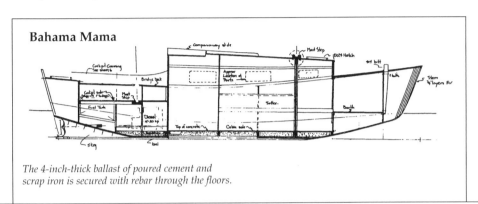

**Bahama Mama**

*The 4-inch-thick ballast of poured cement and scrap iron is secured with rebar through the floors.*

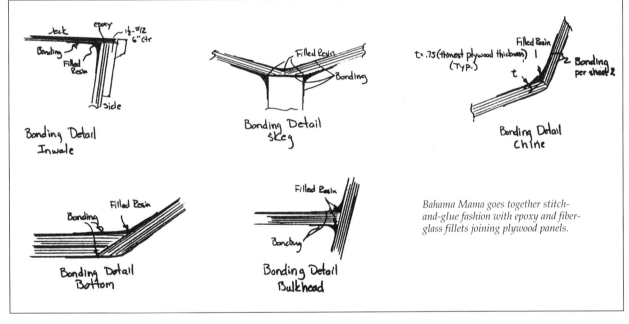

Bonding Detail Inwale

Bonding Detail Skeg

Bonding Detail Chine

Bonding Detail Bottom

Bonding Detail Bulkhead

*Bahama Mama goes together stitch-and-glue fashion with epoxy and fiber-glass fillets joining plywood panels.*

# A New
# Old-Fashioned Yawl

Design by Nat Benjamin
Commentary by Joel White

Gannon & Benjamin of Vineyard Haven, Massachusetts, is a boatyard of the old school — dedicated to wooden vessels. Their business includes a bit of new construction, always some repair work, and the care and maintenance of a variety of wooden boats. Over the past few years there has emerged from their boatshop doors a small but steady rivulet of handsome new wooden sailing vessels, most of them designed by Nat Benjamin, one of the firm's partners. This 30-foot yawl is a fine example of the quality of design and craftsmanship that has made Gannon & Benjamin well known to a small but discerning circle of admirers.

*Candle in the Wind* was commissioned by an Englishman who has a summer home in Marion, Massachusetts. He wanted a sailing boat with a large cockpit for daysailing, yet capable of occasional overnight cruises. Hoping to keep his two growing teenagers busy and involved in the sailing of the boat, he specified a two-masted gaff rig without self-tending jib as having the maximum number of strings to pull. Having owned racing boats in the past, he also wanted a responsive, easily driven hull of traditional shape for use as a family boat.

"I couldn't have hoped for a better set of design requirements," says Benjamin, "as I am convinced that performance, comfort, and looks are all very compatible, and to design and build a boat for a family to enjoy is the most reasonable request. I had to cast into the waters of my English ancestors to catch the muse that provides a gaff yawl, and with a few ideas from Albert Strange — and the expert eye of my partner

Ross Gannon — all went well."

Snapshots of the new boat indicate that it worked out very well indeed. To my eye, at least, the boat is very good-looking, and a study of the plans indicates delicate lines, a well-proportioned rig, and a large, comfortable cockpit. Let's look more closely at this old-fashioned boat that I believe has implications for the future.

The greatest fun in boating usually comes in the simplest boats. The main thing that so attracted me to sailing and particularly to cruising more than 50 years ago was the total change in lifestyle — no hot baths, an icebox with real ice rather than the refrigerator, oil lamps, the isolation from the daily affairs on shore, the good smell of tarred marline and manila rope mixed with the aroma of cedar and bilgewater — all combined to make even an overnight cruise an adventure. Curled up in the red Hudson's Bay blanket on the kapok bunk cushion, listening to the water moving against the hull, I felt transported to a different world. And I still feel that way about cruising.

Most modern boats are simply too complicated. They are so full of systems, which all too often fail to work, that the feeling of self-reliance — that wonderful ingredient in the pleasures of cruising — is now missing. The modern cruising boat makes the owner a slave to the systems and to the chore of keeping them all working. The Loran isn't working? — well, we can't sail without that. Call the electronics man. While waiting for him, we discover that the refrigeration has quit. Another expert to call. On my dad's old cutter *Astrid*, the only "system" was the 1932 four-cylinder Palmer,

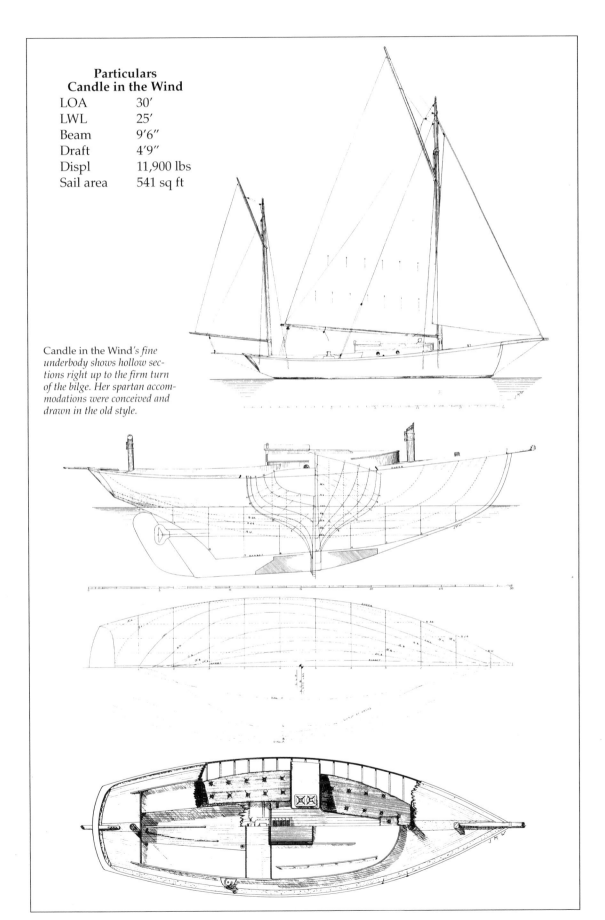

**Particulars
Candle in the Wind**

| | |
|---|---|
| LOA | 30' |
| LWL | 25' |
| Beam | 9'6" |
| Draft | 4'9" |
| Displ | 11,900 lbs |
| Sail area | 541 sq ft |

*Candle in the Wind's fine underbody shows hollow sections right up to the firm turn of the bilge. Her spartan accommodations were conceived and drawn in the old style.*

and I don't recall that it ever failed to start. We never missed an expedition, whether for mackerel fishing, or for a weekend cruise, due to system failure. Keep it simple and have more fun.

*Candle in the Wind* is about as simple as a 30-foot boat can be. It would be difficult to imagine a boat that would be more fun to own. Her plans show a three-cylinder Yanmar diesel to move her in a calm, a stove, a sink, a portable cooler, and as a concession to pollution abatement, a Porta Potti. The simple rig with wooden spars and laced-on sails is about as foolproof as possible — nothing there to go wrong or keep one ashore because of breakdown.

The hull reminds me a bit of small English cruising designs of the 1930s — perhaps a touch of Fred Shepherd and Albert Strange. But I think it is mostly Nat Benjamin, distilling a lot of random ideas into a consistent whole that will fulfill the design requirements for good looks, speed, comfort, and sufficient volume to allow limited cruising accommodations on a 30-foot boat. Of necessity, the ends are short so that the waterline length will be long enough to contain the accommodations, an engine, and allow for a large cockpit for daysailing. What catches my eye when looking at the lines is how fine the underbody really is, with the sections showing a marked hollow from the garboard right up to the firm turn of the bilge just below the waterline. The shape of these reminds me most of the sections on Tim and Pauline Carr's old Falmouth quay punt *Curlew*, a very swift and well-traveled gaff-rigger. These hollow sections in turn produce relatively flat buttocks and slim lower diagonals, both of which undoubtedly contribute to the boat's speed. I like the way the basic shape of the 'midship section carries on into both the forward and after sections. This continuity of shape from end to end, I think, makes for a much more handsome hull than one in which there are abrupt changes of section.

The designed displacement of *Candle in the Wind* is only 11,900 pounds on a waterline length of 25 feet, for a displacement/length ratio of 340 — less than that of a Concordia yawl, for instance, at 355. The designed waterline is fairly fine forward, with a nice hollow at the entrance. The forefoot is moderately cutaway and the sternpost raked; the draft of 4 feet 9 inches allows the 4,000-pound lead ballast keel to be low enough to give good stability. Nothing revolutionary in the lines plan, but a very nice combination of elements to produce a fast, shapely hull that looks right under its old-fashioned gaff-yawl rig.

The proportions of the rig are perfect. It is not easy to draw a gaff rig that looks right when built — the angles of the gaffs, the lift of the booms, the taper of the spars, and the shape of the quadrilateral sails comprise an art nearly lost in this marconi generation.

Benjamin has drawn a large mainsail, knowing that this sail will have to provide most of the drive, the mizzen being more of a balance sail. The loose-footed jib gives a nice slot effect for the mainsail, and helps keep the teenagers busy during windward legs. The mizzen sheets to a longish boomkin, which complements the nicely curved bowsprit forward. So many new boats built today with gaff rigs suffer from ill-proportioned spars, clumsy rigging details, and a lack of knowledge of how things were done a century ago. *Candle in the Wind*, with her eye-spliced shrouds and wooden blocks, would not have looked out of place in a turn-of-the-century regatta.

We do not have a construction plan to show you, as, like most builder-designers, Benjamin did not draw one. In an old-fashioned wooden boatshop, once the lines are laid down, construction proceeds along traditional paths with very little need for plans. In his letter to me about the boat, Benjamin describes her construction. I will quote from it verbatim, as it not only indicates the materials used but the sequence of events, and gives a feeling of how straightforward traditional construction can be when done with understanding and practice.

"The keel," writes Benjamin, "is longleaf yellow pine sided 5 inches with a maximum width of 10 inches, tapering at the ends as shown on the lines drawing. Hurricane Hugo live oak provided a one-piece horn timber/sternpost, as well as the stem. Locust and purpleheart floor timbers were then through-bolted to the backbone on 9-inch centers and the ballast keel attached with ¾-inch bronze bolts between the floors. White oak frames 1½-inch square were steamed into place and bolted to each floor. White cedar was used for planking, except for the bottom four strakes, which were cypress, and the sheerstrake and one below, which were vertical-grain Douglas-fir. The planks are ¹¹⁄₁₆-inch thick, fastened with bronze screws. After installing bilge stringers and sheer clamps, the deck was framed with locust, and the carlins let in on the flat. Framing the cockpit was challenging, as the seats are 4 inches below the deck, giving a snug feeling when aboard. Three layers of ⅜-inch mahogany were bent and laminated for the round-fronted house. A three-cylinder 27-hp Yanmar diesel lives under the bridge deck, with the fuel tank under the cockpit sole. After installation of the spartan interior, a 1⅛-inch teak deck was laid, which dresses her up a bit. The cabintop is canvas over plywood — grooved inside to take the curse off the overhead. Gretchen Snyder, who owns and operates the sail loft above the Gannon & Benjamin shop, made the beautiful set of Dacron sails."

Sounds simple, doesn't it? Well, it is.

Again, quoting from Benjamin's letter: "I am very pleased with the performance of this boat — she stiffens up dramatically as the rail gets close to the water, steers easily, and is quite fast."

I think this little boat is very close to perfect. Her appearance would make any owner proud, and her simplicity has tremendous appeal for me. Both owner and designer speak highly of her speed and handling qualities. When Nick Verey, the owner, heard that I was writing about the boat, he called me up to extol her virtues. Even more, he wanted to tell me how satisfying the entire experience of having a boat designed and built at Gannon & Benjamin had been. The right people coming together in pursuit of a mutually perceived goal can often strike sparks of great brilliance.

*Author's note about the drawings:*

*The moment I saw the plans for this lovely little cruiser, I was reminded of the beautiful drawings of late-nineteenth-century sailing craft in C.P. Kunhardt's book* Small Yachts. *Kunhardt was the yachting editor of the sporting journal* Forest and Stream, *and a magnificent draftsman as well. The first edition of* Small Yachts *was published in 1885. In 1985,* WoodenBoat *published an edited and abridged version of* Forest and Stream's *1891 edition. The 1985 edition is now (1997) out of print.*

*When asked, Nat Benjamin was gracious enough to let me attempt to copy Kunhardt's style in redrawing these plans. I am uncertain how successful I have been in recapturing the style, but I had a grand time trying.*

*Gannon & Benjamin can be reached at P.O. Box 1095, Beach Rd., Vineyard Haven, MA 02568.*

# Two Chesapeake-Style Deadrise Yachts

Designs by Joe Gregory
Commentary by Mike O'Brien

Drawn by Joe Gregory in the early 1970s, these 30-foot deadrise yachts, a schooner and a ketch, share essentially the same hull design. Both of these cruising boats stem from traditional Chesapeake bateaux.

The working bateaux appeared on the Bay during the late nineteenth century. Typical examples had shallow V bottoms with deadrise (the "V" shape) increasing forward to a sharp forefoot. Low sides swept aft from extraordinarily long longheads to substantial outboard rudders hung on flat, raked transom sterns. Masts, no matter whether a boat carried one or two, were always strongly raked. The sails' aspect ratios (length of the luff compared to length of the foot) often approached toy-boat proportions of little more than 1 to 1 — strange to contemporary eyes, perhaps, but powerful in the extreme.

These bateaux ranged in length from about 22 to 60 feet on deck. The smaller boats worked at tonging oysters and crabbing. Larger bateaux were (and in Maryland still are) used for dragging dredges across the oyster beds. Virtually all bateaux in honest employ were painted white above their waterlines. This color (or lack of color) kindly kept the wood orders of magnitude cooler during the Chesapeake's rot-friendly, hot and humid summers. Be that as it may, dark-painted bateaux invited suspicions of less-than-legal nocturnal activities.

As with many traditional craft, scores of yachts have been derived from the original working bateaux. Apparently, the type does not lend itself easily to the conversion process. More than one talented designer has succumbed to the lure of providing full headroom in too short a hull. The resulting monstrously tall deckhouses probably contribute more to aesthetic discomfort than technical disaster, but....

A potentially serious functional problem lurks in another temptation — drawing a hull with too much, far too much, deadrise amidships. The attractions are clear. Increasing the deadrise permits: greater displacement (compared to a flat bottom) on the same waterline length without degrading performance; a lower cabin sole, thereby increasing headroom without driving the house still farther into the sky; reduced volume of deadwood; and reducing wetted surface (for a full-keeled hull if LWL, draft, and waterline beam remain more or less unchanged). Also, by specifying more deadrise, the designer addresses some clients' objections to chined hulls — especially, it seems, to hulls that show any hint of flat-bottomed origins. Indeed, deadrise can be a worthwhile commodity (the Ann Boats, as these design of Gregory's are known, show about 12½ degrees amidships). But, if we crank too much of it into one of these boats, we'll manage to combine a remarkable lack of initial stability (and inability to carry sail) with impressive leeway when sailing anything above a broad reach.

Joe Gregory has sailed the Chesapeake and studied its boats for a long time. His rules of thumb for capturing the essence of the bateaux, without compromising their performance under sail, evolved from averaging measurements of some 45 workboats. Of course, he applies his own good judgment to the standards when he's designing yachts.

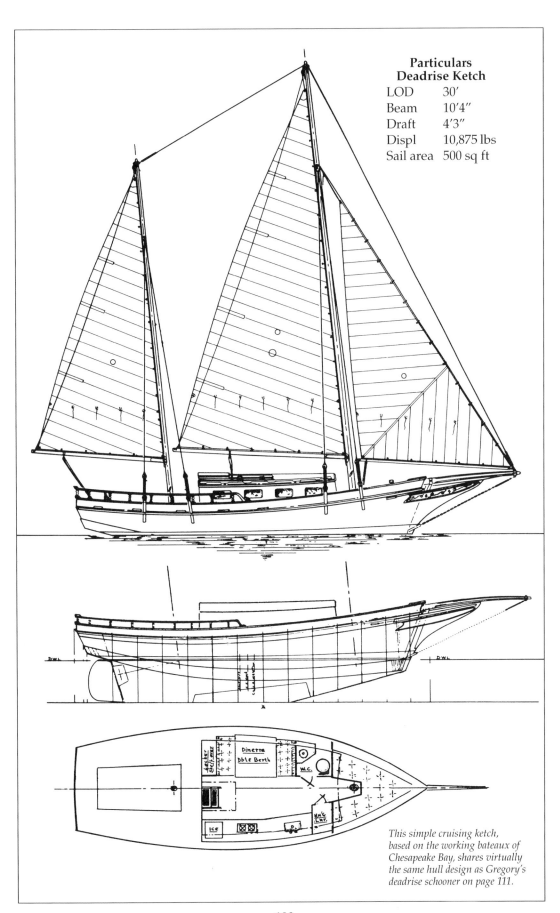

**Particulars
Deadrise Ketch**

| | |
|---|---|
| LOD | 30' |
| Beam | 10'4" |
| Draft | 4'3" |
| Displ | 10,875 lbs |
| Sail area | 500 sq ft |

*This simple cruising ketch, based on the working bateaux of Chesapeake Bay, shares virtually the same hull design as Gregory's deadrise schooner on page 111.*

The working bateaux hull-design parameters delineated by Gregory are as follows: maximum beam on deck equals 33 percent LOD; beam at transom equals 65 percent maximum beam on deck; deadrise amidships equals 10 to 12 degrees; sides flare 3½ feet for each foot of height (usually more near the stern); minimum freeboard equals 6 percent LOA; freeboard at stem equals 14 percent LOA; forward one-third of the chine runs in a straight rise to the stem and terminates just below the waterline.

Unlike the old bateaux, most of Gregory's variants display counter sterns. I suppose this device helps to balance the longhead visually. Also unlike the working boats, which virtually always had centerboards, the schooner and ketch shown here were given full keels. The increased draft will require that they stand clear of some pleasant anchorages, but the traditional cabin-cleaving centerboard trunk won't be missed. Offshore, the ballast keel's righting moment might be comforting. Centerboard bateaux can, and sometimes do, capsize — and they're not known for being self-righting.

Because neither tongs nor dredges would have to be hauled over the Ann Boats' rails, Gregory drew a hull with substantial freeboard. No need for skyscraper houses here.

The hull goes together Chesapeake fashion with the bottom cross-planked in a herringbone pattern. Up forward, staves (short, thick, vertical planks worked to shape) ease the transition from the sharp forefoot to the shallow-deadrise bottom. (Some of the older boats used hewn blocks to the same end.) This is a fast method for those accustomed to it, and it produces a cleaner interior than do most building techniques.

Gregory specifies 1⅛-inch white cedar for the Ann Boats' sides; 1¼-inch white cedar or spruce pine for the bottom; 1¾- by 2¾-inch yellow pine for the frames; and 4- by 10-inch yellow pine for the keel.

So long as we're not after the ultimate-gloss finish, annual maintenance should prove easy and inexpensive. Twenty years on the Bay taught me to be happy with white latex house paint (over an oil-based primer) for the topsides. It lasts well, covers better than any marine enamel of my acquaintance, and costs relatively little. Pay no heed to the derision of spectators. We're in the fine company of many working watermen, at least two well-known yacht designers, and one contributing editor of *WoodenBoat* magazine (Peter Spectre) who apply house paint to their own boats.

Choosing whether to build the Ann schooner or the Ann ketch comes down, of course, to preference and prejudice. I'm inclined to think that both rigs suit the aesthetics of the hull. Gregory considers the ketch easier to get underway. Once we're sailing, both rigs will be self-tending.

The bald-headed schooner makes do with a mainmast that is some 6 feet shorter than the jibheaded ketch's. Because low-slung electric-power lines guard the entrance to many a Chesapeake cove, this feature ought to be considered for Ann's home waters.

Arrangement plans for both boats are dead simple. The Ann Ketch has more room below because her house has been lengthened and moved aft slightly. Both cockpits, or at least the cockpits and the surrounding deck areas, measure little short of huge.

Because the first Ann schooner lives in a shallow river, she was built to draw 3 feet 6 inches. The designer tells us that the Ann ketch needs 4 feet 3 inches of water to float her ballast clear of the bottom. Neither boat is extremely shoal draft by Chesapeake standards, but — given good tenders — their skippers won't be excluded from too many tidal creeks.

Pure coincidence created the "Ann" class name. Owners of the first four cruisers built to these lines christened their boats, respectively, *Julie Ann*, *Barbara Ann*, *Darcy Ann*, and *Carol Ann*. Gregory, not inclined to fight the momentum, bestowed the title on the drawings after the fact. By whatever designation, this design seems to be a personal favorite in his fleet of bateaux that range from an 18-foot two-sail daysailer to a 46-foot three-sail offshore cruiser.

*Joe Gregory can be reached at 301 Janis Dr., Yorktown, VA 23692.*

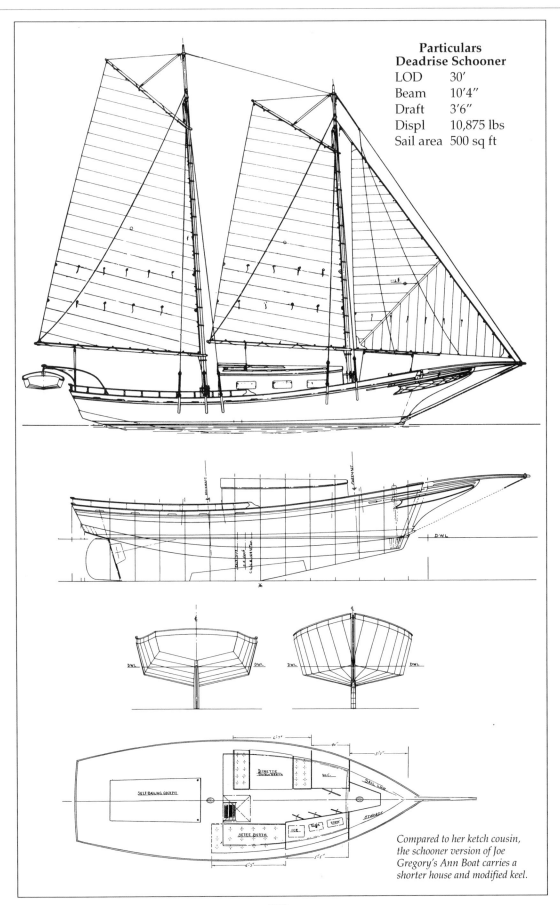

**Particulars**
**Deadrise Schooner**
LOD 30'
Beam 10'4"
Draft 3'6"
Displ 10,875 lbs
Sail area 500 sq ft

*Compared to her ketch cousin, the schooner version of Joe Gregory's Ann Boat carries a shorter house and modified keel.*

# A Sloop or a Yawl

——— Design by John G. Alden ———
Commentary by the editors of *WoodenBoat*

Several different versions of this design, the Malabar Jr., emerged from the offices of John Alden. The first, a 29½-footer available as either a gaff or marconi sloop, came out in 1924. By that time, there was considerable interest in small, wholesome cruisers that could be cheaply built, and Alden responded to that interest. It is not well known, however, that the inspiration for this boat was the renowned and able Friendship sloop. A careful study of the Malabar Jr.'s lines will show a marked resemblance to the form of its forebears, differing primarily in the spoon bow and outside ballast/underbody profile. When studied in this light, it must be seen as quite remarkable that the accommodations to the needs of cruising were so beautifully handled.

The version shown here is a combination of the second and third stages in the evolution of the type, produced during the years 1926–28. Though there were numerous other versions as the years progressed, this example appeals to us as representing the best combination of the old and the new, and the most versatility in rig. It's no wonder that the type became so popular.

The sloop rig is lofty, indeed, with double spreaders, and sports both a permanent backstay and lower runners. The jib is self-tending for ease of handling, and the deck layout is clean and simple. The yawl rig carries more sail area, though that of the main is reduced by the presence of the mizzen. With a single set of spreaders, the shrouds are more simply arranged. It's interesting that Aage Nielsen, who drew up the sail plan, included lazyjacks for all the sails. It was obviously a well-thought-out rig for the singlehander yet designed to achieve good performance.

Construction is sturdy and straightforward, designed to make the best use of materials, and go together with-out complications. Two different cabin trunk configurations (with the forward end either bent round or squared off) are provided, as are two different layout plans. The first is a three-berth arrangement with galley amidships, the second, a four-berth arrangement with galley forward. Both offer simple, spacious treatments, and would be difficult to improve on.

This version of the Malabar Jr. series represents one of the earliest efforts at combining the best attributes of traditional working craft with the state of the art (at the time) in rig design and cruising accommodations. For us, it is a timeless example that ought to grace our waters again.

*Plans are available from The WoodenBoat Store, P.O. Box 78, Brooklin, ME 04616; 800–273–7447.*

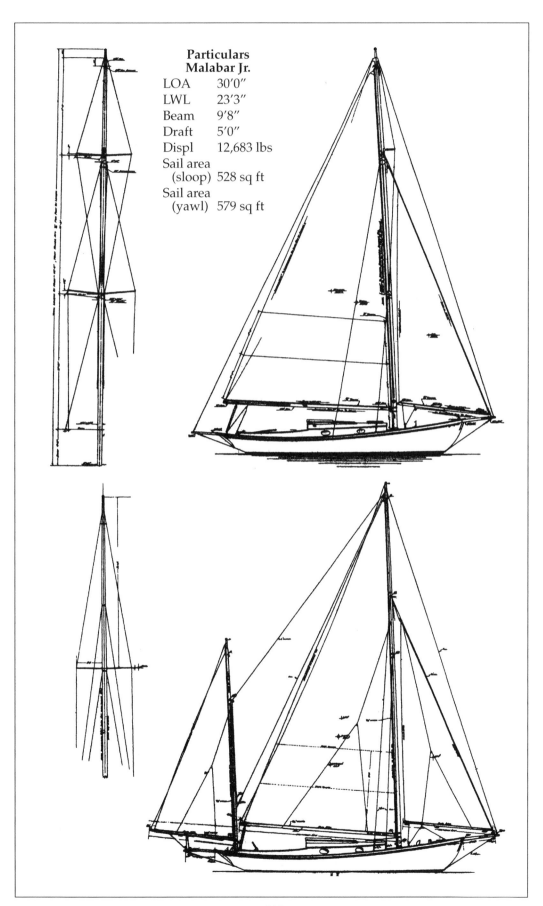

**Particulars
Malabar Jr.**

| | |
|---|---|
| LOA | 30'0" |
| LWL | 23'3" |
| Beam | 9'8" |
| Draft | 5'0" |
| Displ | 12,683 lbs |
| Sail area (sloop) | 528 sq ft |
| Sail area (yawl) | 579 sq ft |

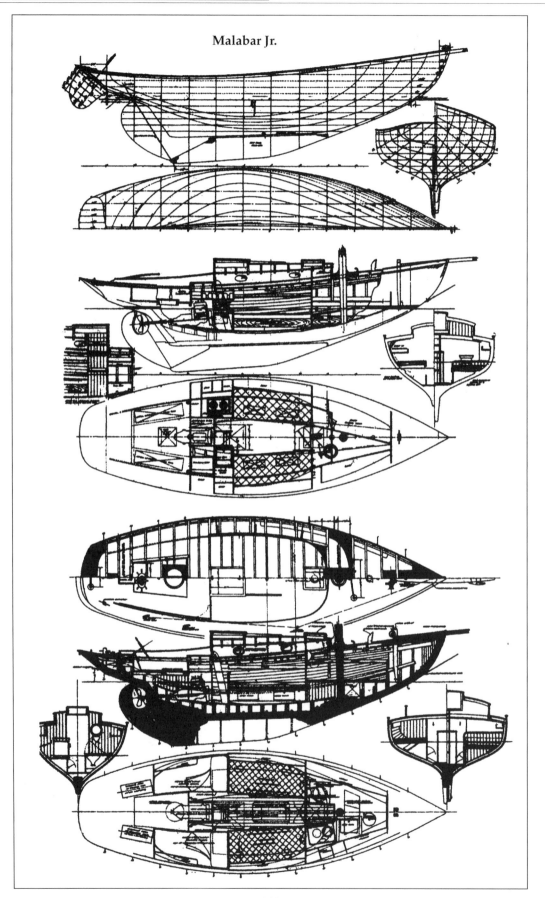

Malabar Jr.

# A Keel/Centerboard Sloop

———— Design by John G. Alden ————
Commentary by the editors of *WoodenBoat*

When this auxiliary cruiser was designed in 1926, the contemporary yachting press was busy publishing letters and essays on the pros and cons of keel vs. centerboard cruising boats. Though the discussion raged on for months, and though the remarkable performance of centerboard craft at sea was well documented by a number of men of tremendous experience, there was always the sense that the lovers of deep-keel craft were simply greater in number. And in those days there was plenty of deep water to go around.

Times have changed in this last half century. The crowded harbors have caused the modern cruiser to search for thinner water, where fewer boats can go. So, if you like the look and feel of the Malabar Jr. but require a board-up draft of no more than three feet, this design deserves a very close look. She is a wholesome boat with a simple rig, simple accommodations, and a wonderfully traditional look.

Though her sail plan is tall, it is not as tall as it would have to be were it marconi-rigged, and not as complicated either, as it would be with the additional shrouds and stays required. In fact, she would make a fine little singlehander with her self-tending jib, aft-leading upper and lower shrouds (no running backstays), and main and jib lazyjacks.

The lines of this sloop provide an interesting combination of elements: hollow entrance, slowly rising run to the buttocks, and very firm bilges. Those elements should combine to make her weatherly, fast, and stiff. In addition, she is a most pleasing shape to behold in profile and plan. (But what else would we expect from Fenwick Williams, who drew her while employed in the John Alden offices?)

Accommodations are limited in this plan to three, although other layouts could be devised without much trouble. The forward cabin is separate from the main cabin, and it contains the head. The offset companionway ladder gives the cook plenty of room, and the layout of the compartments and lockers is simple and straightforward. It has to be, for this is a cruiser with under five feet of headroom. The two hatch openings will provide good ventilation, however, as well as two means of escape in case of a fire below decks.

This sloop's construction is rugged and simple, and though there isn't a considerable amount of detail in the plan, there is plenty for a builder with experience. In any case, the scantlings present no problem as far as materials go, and a fine boat would result. A 3,200-pound cast iron ballast keel is specified, and some inside trimming ballast in the form of lead pigs would be required as well. The self-draining cockpit is really a large foot-well, in that the seating is on the bridge deck and the after deck, and therefore no cockpit seats are drawn in.

The more one studies this little craft, the more one realizes that she embodies the whole spirit of yachting as it was once meant to be, and perhaps should be again.

*Plans of the Alden 30-foot Keel/Centerboard Sloop are available from The WoodenBoat Store, P.O. Box 78, Brooklin, ME 04616; 800–273–7447.*

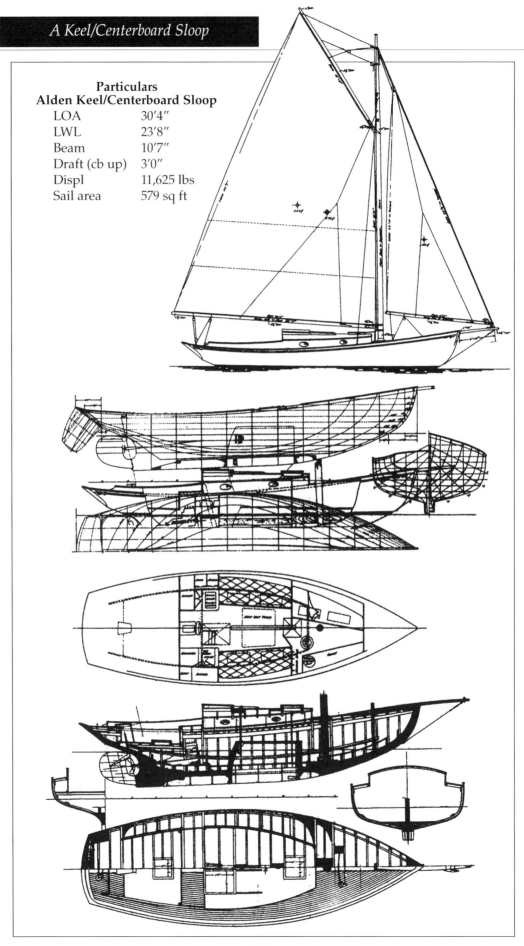

**Particulars**
**Alden Keel/Centerboard Sloop**

| | |
|---|---|
| LOA | 30'4" |
| LWL | 23'8" |
| Beam | 10'7" |
| Draft (cb up) | 3'0" |
| Displ | 11,625 lbs |
| Sail area | 579 sq ft |

# A Chesapeake Skipjack

—— Design by Joe Gregory ——
Commentary by Mike O'Brien

Records indicate that the skipjack appeared on Chesapeake Bay in the late nineteenth century. A type of bateaux (see Chapter 33), it is used commercially as an oyster dredger under sail. It has also been adapted to pleasure use. *Calico Jack*, among the best of those adaptations, was designed by Joe Gregory of Yorktown, Virginia, after he had completed a detailed study of 45 working bateaux and developed a set of rules for designing and building these traditional craft (see sidebar on page 118).

Drawings of some early skipjacks show differences from Gregory's not-so-rigid rules, including a higher chine forward and less deadrise amidships. Apparently, the Chesapeake watermen concluded that the lower chines produced more speed and that greater deadrise allowed the bateaux to hang on better when tacking. The boats studied by Gregory reflected that reasoning. Careful inspection reveals that *Calico Jack* herself strays from these parameters in some areas: the designer incorporated a few favorite "fudge factors." Be that as it may, one should deviate from these guidelines with respect and care. They are measures of evolution, and evolution encourages proper design.

Gregory notes that some designers have resorted to raising the chines forward to reduce pounding in a chop. Agreeing with most Bay builders, he considers the lower chines faster and draws them for all his boats. To mitigate pounding in his bateaux, *Calico Jack*'s creator establishes the "proper deadrise at an X-dimension" abaft the stem and uses this in conjunction with the "correct configuration of the...keel in the area of the forefoot." Although he reveals neither the length of the X-dimension nor the "proper" angle of deadrise at that point, the hull lines shown here might yield that information.

If you're searching for speed, some areas of bateau design deserve special consideration. Howard Chapelle and Joe Gregory concur that a boat's quarter-beam buttocks should be fair and easy while still sweeping up sufficiently to clear the run. Both warn that building a bateau too full forward will degrade her windward performance. Experience with unsuccessful bateau-yachts has shown that excessive deadrise amidships produces boats that can't stand up to their sails.

The skipjack rig seems strange to most modern eyes. Its almost comically low aspect ratio looks to have been pulled out of a bathtub toy or a cartoon in the Sunday paper, but it does provide a lot of power for a minimum of heeling force. It is forgiving of inattention and won't stall if slightly mis-trimmed. The mast's extreme rake helps keep the boom clear of the water when reaching or running in a sea and results in a main halyard location that is most convenient for lifting cargo. On the negative side, raked masts tend to make heavy booms self-centering in light air, and they need to be rigged to keep them outboard.

By any standard, skipjack booms are truly impressive and command respect. Gregory tells of sailing aboard the oyster bateau *Howard* in Tangier Sound: "I really learned to duck a boom, a boom that was 45 feet long with a diameter that would shame many power company poles. When that hunk of lumber was winged out, and the captain decided to jibe without warning, you had better hug the deck." During one unannounced jibe, an unfortunate crew member stood too tall. As the mighty boom came across, it struck him at his belt buckle, folded him over, and continued on its way — carrying him some 20 feet outboard. Surveying his dangling crew, Captain Taylor spit tobacco juice and ordered simply, "Sheet 'im in."

*Calico Jack* was built in Deltaville, Virginia, for her designer's own use. She went together in a mostly traditional manner, with her bottom cross-planked herringbone fashion. Her sharp forefoot was staved — that is, shaped from short, thick, vertical planks. Although *Jack* was built upright, many of her cousins have had their bottoms planked while inverted on dirt floors. Their stems often protrude into pits, leaving the work at comfortable waist-high levels. After the bottoms are planked, the boats are righted and finished off in a more-or-less conventional way.

Typical bateau construction makes good use of local materials and results in clean boats, as relatively little framing is needed. Builders accustomed to the method can make quick work of it, but a beginner will find that staving a forefoot requires considerable skill and a good eye. As an alternative, the forefoot can be hewn from a solid block — as it was in some of the older bateaux. The block forefoot was prone to rot, however, and fell from favor, but with the new compounds and adhesives it might work. Still, there's something elegant about a workmanlike job of staving. With some changes, *Calico Jack* could be built of plywood; her forefoot likely would be cold-molded. As may be, traditional bateau construction and design have evolved to complement each other — and they stand somewhere just short of perfection. Why not build *Calico Jack* as she's drawn?

In designing his two-sail bateau, Gregory had in mind a big daysailer/weekender. By today's standards she's large for those assignments, but she can handle loads and conditions that would overwhelm lesser boats of similar accommodation. Her layout is simple and traditional. Going below, you'll pass between the head and the galley; just forward sit two good-sized berths. That's it. This arrangement isn't bristling with new ideas, but it is pleasant and open. As you lie on one of the berths contemplating the nature of the universe, or what you're going to eat for lunch, plainly visible structural members (knees, deckbeams, etc.) lend a feeling of security. They seem more comforting than molded surfaces that have no obvious means of support.

Whatever this little skipjack's merits below decks, the preferred berth for a night on Chesapeake is on deck. A boom tent is rigged for protection from evening showers or morning dew, and the skipper is obliged to find a bug-free anchorage.

*Calico Jack* is rock stable. She seldom needs her working jib, as the genoa can be carried in a 20-knot breeze. She seems at her best sailed a little free and heeled so that her lee bottom is parallel to the water's surface. Gregory sold the original *Jack* some time ago, but he recalls, "When the water boiled aboard through the forward scupper, raced along the bulwarks and out the after scupper — then she was moving out!"

When driving to windward in a steep chop, *Calico Jack* could bury her bowsprit — but she always came up for more. "When the Bay kicked up," her designer observes, "my theory was that if she made it over the first sea, she would make it over the next...and probably the next. I was never disappointed, and rarely did I have to reef."

Gregory's skipjack was as far from being drawn to a rating rule as a boat can be, but he campaigned her actively. During her first year afloat, they'd leave her anchorage off the York River on Friday evenings and sail the 20 miles up to Fishing Bay Yacht Club. En route, if light winds were predicted, some of the "cruising ballast" would be dumped for the weekend on the secluded beach at New Point Comfort. Reportedly, *Jack* was defeated by no boats less than 30 feet LOD that season.

Since the original *Calico Jack* was launched, more than 30 sisters have been built — well, perhaps some of her descendants are better described as cousins. As a series of *Jacks* emerged from a well-known Lower Bay shop during the early 1960s, each succeeding boat wandered

## *Rules of Thumb for Skipjack Design*    (Based on Joe Gregory's study of 45 working bateaux)

Maximum beam on deck equals 33 percent LOD.

Beam at transom equals 65 percent maximum beam on deck.

Deadrise amidships equals 10 to 12 degrees.

Side's rake (flare) equals 3.5 inches per foot (more near stern).

Minimum freeboard equals 6 percent LOA.

Freeboard at stem equals 14 percent LOA.

Forward one-third of the chine runs in a straight rise to the stern and terminates just below waterline.

Centerboard length equals 33 percent LOD.

Mast length equals LOD plus beam.

Boom length equals LOD.

Bowsprit length equals beam.

Sail area equals 55 times immersed midship section area.

Area of mainsail equals 70 percent total sail area.

Lateral plane area equals 14 percent sail area.

Maststep on keel equals 17 percent length of keel abaft stem.

Mast rakes to let main halyard fall amidships.

Lead (geometric center of sail ahead of center of lateral plane) equals 11 percent LWL.

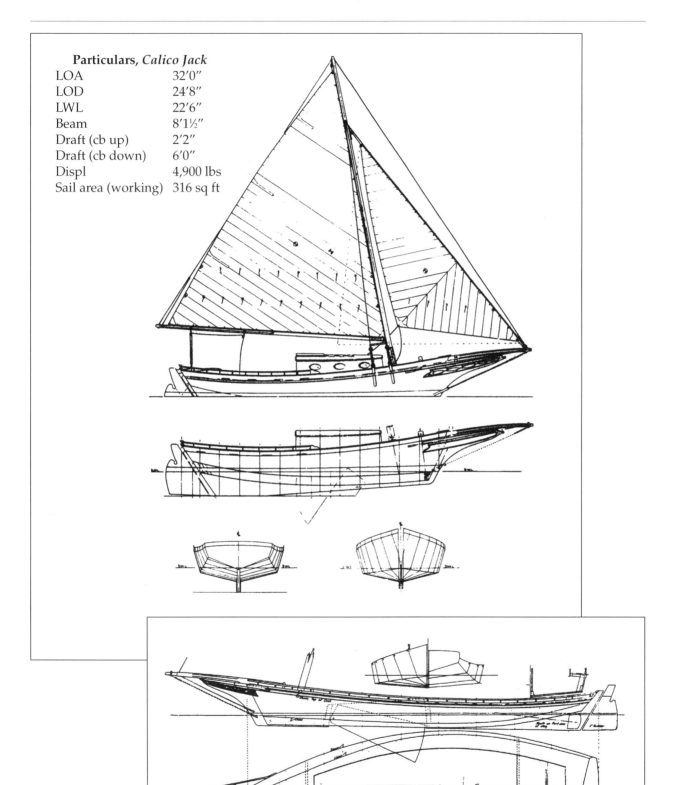

**Particulars,** *Calico Jack*

| | |
|---|---|
| LOA | 32'0" |
| LOD | 24'8" |
| LWL | 22'6" |
| Beam | 8'1½" |
| Draft (cb up) | 2'2" |
| Draft (cb down) | 6'0" |
| Displ | 4,900 lbs |
| Sail area (working) | 316 sq ft |

*The two-sail bateau* Rosa Lee *influenced* Calico Jack's *design. Shown here in a weathered Howard Chapelle drawing from Joe Gregory's collection, the Deal Island workboat clearly had less deadrise and freeboard than her descendant.*

farther from Gregory's drawings and intent — freeboard was increased in the search for greater headroom, and some of the boats had rigs that were inappropriate for their hulls. At least one bastard bateau was fitted with a keel/centerboard; it proved to be slow and poorly balanced under sail and sluggish in stays. The original design's easy grace had been lost to awkwardness and affectation. According to local legend, a frustrated Gregory stormed into the shop, ripped *Calico Jack*'s sail plan from the wall, and tossed it into an old woodstove.

Deriving yachts from workboat origins involves a delicate balance. History has raised a select group of the resulting boats above their near sisters. Alden's Malabars, Stadel's Pilot Boats, Bolger's Light Dories, and a few others come to mind. Isolated technical arguments might be thrown at them, but taken as a whole they approach aesthetic perfection. Perhaps, in her own simple way, *Calico Jack* is the same — among the best of her breed.

*Plans for* Calico Jack *are available from The WoodenBoat Store, P.O. Box 78, Brooklin, ME 04616; 800–273–7447.*

# A Cutter and a Sloop with Regional Roots

Designs by William Garden and Murray Peterson
Commentary by Joel White

Just as a painting is influenced by the artist's environment and early training, so is the naval architect's design affected by the area in which he lives and the local traditions of boatbuilding. It would be difficult to imagine a South Seas proa being developed in our cold northern waters; while all sailors like to go fast, most dislike being sprayed by cold water while doing it.

The two designs shown here are good examples of these influences. Both are drawn by masters of their trade, both designs are aimed at providing a handsome, traditional, small sailing craft for coastal cruising. Both designs are strongly rooted in the workboats of their region.

The smaller boat, a 27-foot-overall gaff sloop, was designed by the late Murray Peterson, who grew up in New England, worked for the John Alden office, and opened his own office — first in Marblehead, Massachusetts, and later in South Bristol, Maine. He became famous for designing a number of lovely small traditional schooners based on the coaster type.

The larger boat, a 32-foot-overall gaff cutter, is from the board of William Garden, who lives and works in the Pacific Northwest. He has practiced his trade long and well, turning out hundreds of handsome designs for both commercial and pleasure craft.

Let us compare these two boats, designed in and for opposite sides of the country; let us observe their similarities and their differences, and indulge ourselves in a little armchair speculation as to what made them the way they are.

An examination of their lines reveals instantly two distinct differences. The Peterson sloop has considerably more beam in relation to draft than does the Garden cutter: $B/D = 2.176$ for the Peterson, compared to $B/D = 1.853$ for the Garden. This is perfectly in keeping with our regional-influence argument. In the early days, East Coast working craft were usually of the beamy, shallow type (including the larger coasting schooners), while the West Coast designers turned out deeper, narrower vessels. My guess is that the nature of the two coasts had much to do with this. New England has many harbors and coves that are used for shelter and trade (particularly in southern New England, where these harbors are often shallow), whereas the West Coast has far fewer shelters. There, much of the coast is unbroken by harbors or inlets; the boats tend to be good seakeeping types that can, if necessary, stay offshore and handle a blow.

The full bilges and low deadrise on the Peterson sloop are in interesting contrast to the steep deadrise and heavily hollowed garboards of the Garden cutter. (There is a special reason for the deep, hollow garboards on the cutter; we will discuss this later.)

Another difference we notice immediately in the lines of the two boats is in the shape of the two sterns. The smaller Peterson boat has a very traditional, broad counter-stern with a small amount of crown and considerable rake — strongly influenced by the eastern coasting schooners and other small working craft. The Garden cutter, on the other hand, has a handsome round stern with a knuckle above the waterline. I don't know why, but this type of stern is seldom seen on New England small craft, whereas it is common on the western side of the continent; there seems to be more Scandinavian influence on western small craft. This stern shape is prevalent in parts of Scandinavia and also in the Mediterranean. There is no doubt that it makes a handsome and seakindly after end for a small vessel.

Otherwise, the lines show two boats similar in purpose: each has a generous freeboard, a long keel, and short overhangs aimed at providing as much volume as possible within the hull to contain the accommodations desired, yet both hulls are graceful in spite of their fullness. The Peterson sloop has a displacement/length ratio of 478; that of Garden's cutter is 463 — definitely on the heavy-displacement end of the scale.

The sail plans of both boats show a traditional gaff rig, the major concession to modernity being the roller furling jibs of both boats. The larger Garden boat has the foretriangle split between a boomed forestaysail of 145 square feet and a large Yankee jib of 245 square feet. By going to the cutter rig, Garden is able to keep the area of the mainsail to a manageable 371 square feet, only a little bigger than the mainsail on the Peterson sloop. The mast of the sloop is well forward, resulting in a small foretriangle and a large mainsail. This is a more efficient rig to windward than that of the cutter, but it is less versatile when the time comes to shorten down. Both boats show lazyjacks on the main to keep the sail up off the deck when lowering and furling.

Now let's look at the accommodation plans. They are totally different in arrangement, yet the basic elements provided are quite similar.

Garden, in a somewhat larger hull, had more space to work with and thus was able to separate the seating space from the two principal bunks. In fact, by raising the cabin sole in the fore part of the boat and forgetting about standing headroom, he is able to create a little saloon forward with a settee on each side and a table between, an unusual concept in so small a craft. He also specifies Root berths port and starboard over the settees forward, but I suspect these would be used only rarely. I still regard this design as basically sleeping two, using the generous built-in berths on either side of the pilothouse aft.

Between the forward saloon and the aft pilothouse, Garden gives us a good-sized galley to port plus an oil heating stove, while to starboard there is a hanging locker, an enclosed toilet room, and a couple of steps up to the pilothouse. Right in the middle of this space is the mainmast, where the cook can brace himself in a seaway. The pilothouse, besides containing two berths, has a raised seat with a footrest built against the after bulkhead, and the steering wheel with controls in front of this — a grand spot from which to con the ship on a calm and wet Puget Sound afternoon while one's shipmate snoozes within toe-poke reach.

Pilothouses have just recently come into vogue in production sailing craft, but Garden has been using them for many years.

The engine is under the pilothouse floor, flanked by two 50-gallon fuel tanks, one under each bunk. It is hoped that the tanks are heavily baffled both fore and aft and athwartships, as there is nothing more annoying than liquid bumping and gurgling around your pillow in a seaway. Aft of the pilothouse is a 6-foot-long hold extending the full width of the vessel, accessible through a large (3-foot by 3-foot) hatch on deck with a high (18 inches) fisherman-type coaming and hatch cover.

Mr. Garden, in his notes accompanying the design, states that the boat was developed from an earlier design built in 1952 as a combination fishing and sailing boat. This dandy little hold, so useful for stowing everything from scuba tanks to bicycles, apparently was one of the features retained from the original design. Right aft, framed by the horseshoe of the stern, is a half-elliptical cockpit with matching seat, and a tiller to get you out of the pilothouse on nice days. The aft deck weatherboards curl around the cockpit to form a comfortable backrest.

All in all, this is a most unusual, yet I believe workable, arrangement plan. Notice, too, that the deck amidships is raised right up to the sheer height with a low cabinhouse and the high pilothouse for headroom. This puts her cabin sole on three different levels below, also unusual. Fore and aft, the deck level is sunk below the sheer to give good, high bulwarks for security while working the anchors or fishing.

The interior arrangement of the Peterson sloop is simple, straightforward, and very traditional. It also offers the most comfort possible in such a small boat. (She is small — only 27 feet overall — and we must remember this when comparing the layouts of the two boats; we are comparing a grapefruit and an orange when it comes to interior volumes.) The two wide, comfortable berths located right amidships are used as the seats for the dropleaf table located on the centerline. Far aft on the port side is an enclosed toilet room, small but functional.

From the after end of the port berth there is a very ingenious alcove with two drawers beneath that extend into the toilet room. This gives a surprising amount of stowage space without overcrowding the head, typical of the care that Murray Peterson gave in designing the interiors of little boats. The galley is opposite the toilet at the aft end of the cabin on the starboard side, with the companionway ladder offset to starboard. The galley is only 3 feet long, fore and aft, yet it contains a two-burner stove on the countertop, icebox with trap through the counter, a small sink with a locker under, and a large locker outboard under the

**Particulars**
**Garden cutter**

| | |
|---|---|
| LOA | 32'4" |
| LWL | 28'0" |
| Beam | 10'6" |
| Draft | 5'8" |

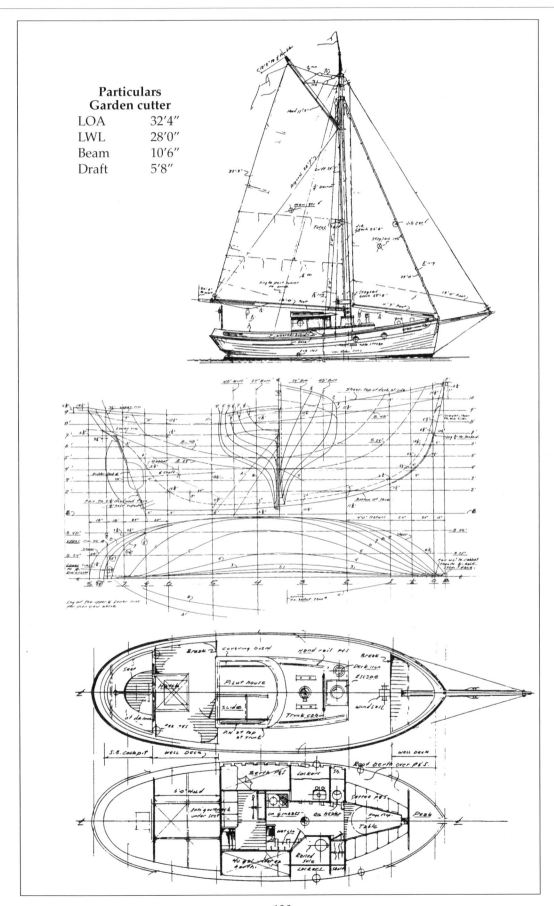

deck. The two-step ladder lands on the top of a storage drawer, which makes the third step. Neat, and very compact. At the forward end of the cabin, just aft of the mast, is a Tiny Tot solid-fuel heater, nice for foggy summer days and crisp autumn nights.

To port and starboard of the mast are hanging lockers and shelves. The forepeak, occupying the forward 6 feet of the boat, has stowage for sails, anchor rodes, spare anchors, and all the other stuff you can't leave the mooring without. This space can be reached through an off-center hatch in the forward deck (off center because of the anchor windlass) or through the main cabin. The bulkhead at the after end of the cabinhouse has a 24- by 33-inch removable section in the toilet room for access to the port side of the engine. A flush hatch in the bridge deck will allow the engineer to cozy up to the Universal Utility Four gas engine for maintenance and communion. While there, he can check the gas and water tanks, one of each, both port and starboard, for a total of 40 gallons of gas and 20 gallons of water. (Some might prefer to reverse the amount of fluids carried.)

The little sloop has a nifty, big cockpit, wheel steering, and a traditional wooden compass binnacle with a sloping, hinged viewing panel. She has no coamings or backrests, but a raised box over the steerer provides, under some conditions, a seat for the helmsman. Doors in the cockpit sides allow some limited access to the space under the deck on each side, but it is poor storage at best. Perhaps a couple of movable deck boxes could be used to give some on-deck storage for docklines, fenders, and such. Both boats have a gallows frame aft to catch the main boom, and more importantly, to provide a fine handrail across the after end of the boat.

If we can forget the difference in size between the two boats, my impression is that the Garden cutter is laid out with emphasis on shelter from the elements with a place to steer that is under cover, while the crew of the Peterson sloop will relish a day outdoors with wind and sea, and only retire to the cabin when the sun is gone and the bunk calls. Isn't this perhaps because of climatic differences between the Pacific Northwest and New England? (Not that New England doesn't have its share of drips and drizzle, and the Northwest sparkling sunshine, but overall, I think the difference is there.) The Northwest is blessed with a longer sailing season than we have in New England (almost year-round, in fact), while around here, the onset of winter abruptly ends the sailing season. The Garden cutter can be used at any time of the year, with its sheltered steering station in the pilothouse and the oil heater chasing the chill away. By the time the autumn leaves are on the ground in New England, the little sloop will be there as well, resting on her cradle, covered against the snow.

The construction plans of the two boats make a most interesting contrast. The little sloop is pure East Coast construction — oak backbone and bent frames, 1-inch cedar planking, laid teak decks, and 3,585 pounds of cast-iron ballast keel, bolted on the bottom of all. At the joint between hull and deck frame, the traditional clamp and shelf, bolted to each other and to the frame heads, make a strong and handsome "angle iron" in wood the entire length of the boat.

By contrast, the Garden cutter has a hefty keel timber, $9\frac{1}{2}$ inches by $11\frac{1}{2}$ inches by 21 feet long, with a $2\frac{1}{2}$-inch gum wormshoe on the bottom, and her ballast all inside; the latter consists of lead pigs in cement, poured in place after the hull is completed. Bent oak frames with $1\frac{5}{16}$-inch planking form the hull skin.

The Garden cutter's deck and deck edge structure are quite different from those of the Peterson sloop — the raised deck through the middle portion of the boat is built of two diagonal layers of red-cedar glued together over deckbeams, with a harpin at the juncture with the hull.

A harpin is almost never seen in East Coast construction, while Garden and others use it frequently in the West. It is similar to a shelf, except that its outer edge lies against the planking with notches for the frame heads to pass through, and its upper edge lies against the decking with the ends of the deckbeams notched under it. The only East Coast boat that used this construction regularly was the Friendship sloop. This design has the advantage of putting a heavy, continuous timber where it is most needed for fastening guardrails, toerails, covering boards, lifeline stanchions, jibsheet leads, and all the other assorted hardware that follows the rail of a boat.

The Garden cutter also has a sheer clamp lower down, into which the well-deck frame (at the bow and the stern) is notched and bolted. At these well decks, the frames come through the covering board and, together with the topside planking, form the bulwarks.

On the Peterson sloop, the covering boards are not pierced by any frames or stanchions, and the bulwarks are built up on top of them, using a vertical rail drifted on and then covered by a horizontal caprail. Aft, the quarter rail and cap are piled up on top of the lower bulwark. I am always a little worried about having frames or stanchions that penetrate through the covering board, for these can be potential leak and rot areas, as on the Garden boat, but the modern flexible sealants available to builders now have done much to alleviate this problem.

The Garden boat's handsome round stern is framed with two "horseshoes"; tapered staving makes the vertical planks. The cockpit sole is $\frac{3}{4}$-inch plywood, and lands on top of the lower rim, or "horseshoe," while the semi-elliptical seat sits on the upper rim. This is most interesting and highly unusual to my eastern eye.

Let's think about cement and lead pigs as ballast, another item somewhat rare to the East Coast, at least for small boats. This type of ballast certainly has the advantage of lower cost and easier installation, compared with cast-iron or cast-lead keels. It allows a certain amount of adjustment of fore-and-aft trim, especially if (as Garden recommends) the fore and after sections are not poured until after launching. The disadvantages would seem to be: less protection to the boat structure in case of a severe grounding, and lower bilges that are inaccessible to inspection or repair without a great deal of jackhammer work. My understanding is that this poured inside ballast works well if the boat is to be left in the water most of the time, but less well if the boat is to be hauled out for lengthy periods, especially in frosty climates. Again, this fits our theory that regional and climatic influences dictate different design and construction practices. When looking at her lines, we can understand why the Garden boat has those deep, hollow garboards that we noted earlier. That shape was necessary to get considerable volume down as low as possible in order to contain the lead pigs and cement.

Even the methods of setting up the two boats for construction are different. The Peterson sloop was built by the late Elmer Collemer, of Camden, Maine. I am dead certain that the molds were set up, ribbanded out, the frames steamed and bent inside the ribbands, and, as the planking progressed, the ribbands were removed as they got in the way. All of Elmer's boats were built that way, as are most traditional wooden boats in this part of the world.

Garden, on the other hand, shows the setup for building his boat right on the drawings, using the harpin system. The molds and ribbands are set up to the inside of the frames, the harpin is placed in position on top of the molds, which are cut to the finished sheerline and deck crown; the laminated clamp is notched into the molds lower down, then the frames are bent outside the ribbands and let into the notches already cut in the harpin. Using this method, the deck can be built prior to bending the hull frames, if desired. The ribbands are left in place until after planking is completed. In fact, Garden states that the upper ribbands may be incorporated into the structure of the boat. This is a totally different approach to that used on the East Coast, due mostly, to the use of the harpin.

So, what conclusion can we draw from the study of the two boats? First, that there is no "right" way or "wrong" way in construction and design. What works well, is good. Also, that all boat designs are based on a long series of choices and compromises having to do with shape, materials, and methods. Many of these choices seem to be influenced by the region in which the designer lives and works, as well as the boat-building traditions that have developed there. The designer of a boat for service in a different part of the world with differing climatic conditions might very well use other materials and methods appropriate to the area in which the boat would be used. And lastly, that the diversity and imagination of our talented designers is what makes the study of small boats so endlessly fascinating.

*Plans for the Peterson sloop are available from Murray Peterson Associates, Jones Cove, South Bristol, ME 04568.*

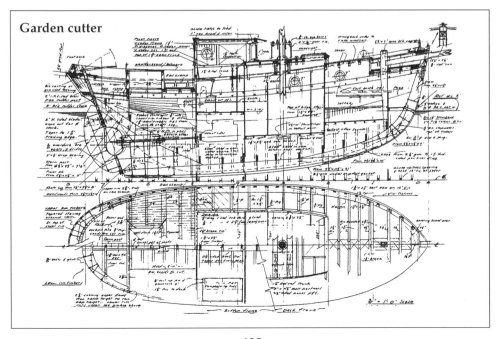

Garden cutter

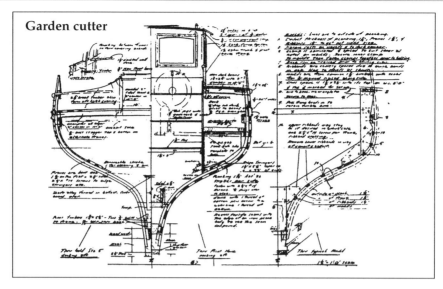

Garden cutter

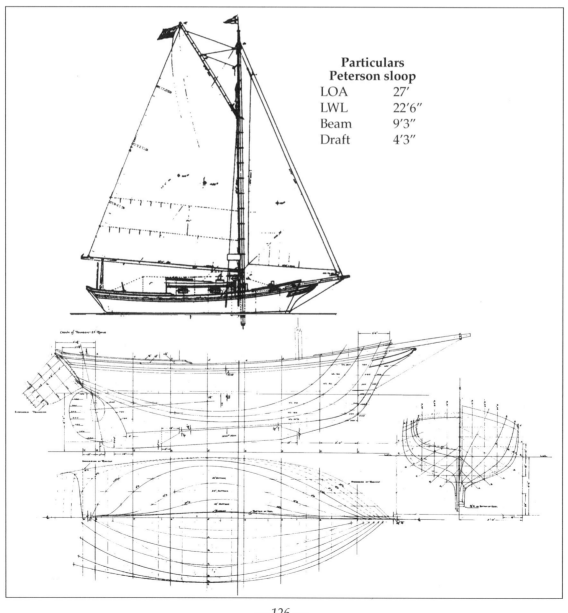

**Particulars
Peterson sloop**

| | |
|---|---|
| LOA | 27' |
| LWL | 22'6" |
| Beam | 9'3" |
| Draft | 4'3" |

# Peterson sloop

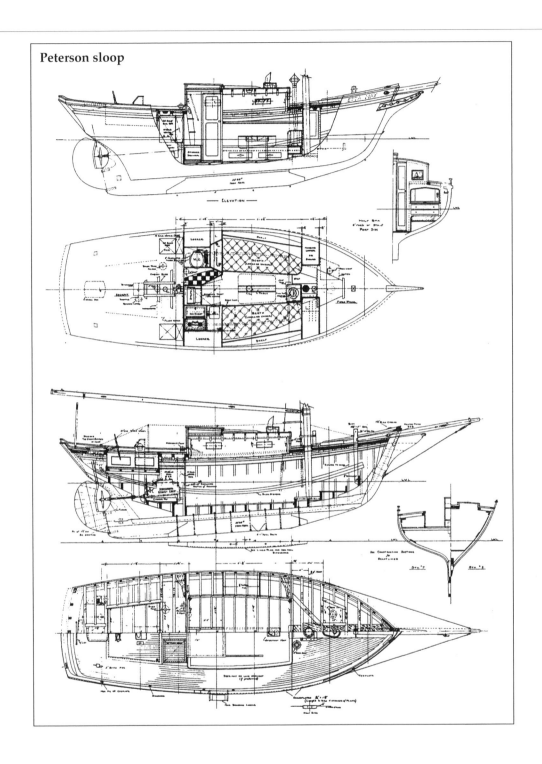

# A Scottish Yawl

Design by David Raeburn
Commentary by Joel White

The west coast of Scotland, particularly the Firth of Clyde, was once the northern center for yachting in the British Isles. Such famous designers as Fife, Watson, and Mylne lived and worked here, and most of their designs were built by the excellent boatshops of the region. A fine, friendly rivalry developed between the Scottish boats and their southern cousins from the Channel coast, where equally fine designers — Nicholson, Giles, and Fox — created wonderful wooden vessels for both racing and cruising.

It is interesting, and fitting, that a new class of wooden boat should be developed in Lanarkshire, in the Clydeside region of Scotland. The Tarbert Yawl was designed by David Raeburn and built by the firm of Clyde Classics Limited of Wishaw. Even more interesting is the choice of a basically old design, now executed in a thoroughly up-to-date construction method, making the best possible use of modern materials and adhesives.

Based on an existing boat designed and built by Dickes of Tarbert, the new Tarbert Yawl is a double-ender with a canoe stern, a long keel with a conventional rudder, moderate overhangs, and a strong, pretty sheer. The rig is a gaff yawl, with bowsprit and boomkin, double headsails, and topsail. (Albert Strange designed a number of boats similar to this one, and indeed, the designer and builders freely admit that inspiration for the Tarbert Yawl is derived from Strange designs.) For more interior space and greater stability, beam has been increased. In a move made possible by the new lighter, stronger construction methods, displacement has been reduced to improve performance under sail. Clyde Classics is betting that a handsome, traditional design coupled with modern wooden construction, increased performance, and larger interior accommodations will prove to be a winning combination.

Comparing the new lines with older Strange designs, we see that David Raeburn has lengthened the forward overhang, cut away the forefoot considerably, moved the center of buoyancy aft, and reduced displacement by 25 to 30 percent. The sweet sections still have a lot of deadrise, and because of her balanced ends and clean underbody, the boat will undoubtedly be able and fast. The sharp sections in both the bow and stern ensure that the boat will be comfortable at sea in rough weather, with none of the pounding that occurs in boats with long, flattish overhangs. The bottom of the keel is straight and parallel to the waterline, making her easy to haul on a railway or ground out alongside a dock.

The designer has made no major changes in the rig, staying with the gaff-yawl sail plan of the original boat. At 742 square feet, including topsail, the rig is a large one for a boat of this size. If the builders can indeed hold the displacement to 6 tons as advertised, the yawl's sail-area-to-displacement ratio works out at 20.9 — right up there with the racers. Clyde Classics says the topsail is regarded as a working sail up to about 20 knots of wind, at which point it will be handed as the first step in reefing down. I must say the rig looks right on the boat — it is difficult to imagine that her appearance would be improved with marconi sails. But I would like to see both the main and mizzen booms cocked up more aft, and I deplore the looks of the down-turned boomkin. The curve in it is nice, but please, steeve it upward like the bowsprit! Running backstays are fitted, but it is hoped that they need only be used in heavy going.

The lack of frames in the construction shows up as additional room below, and Raeburn has packed a lot of interior into a boat of only 34 feet overall length. I believe there is really only one layout that works well

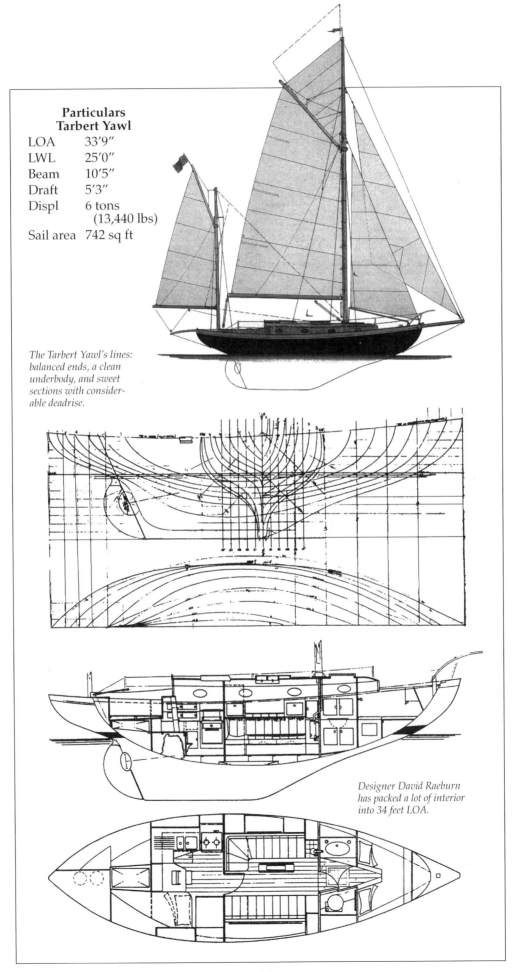

**Particulars
Tarbert Yawl**

LOA      33'9"
LWL      25'0"
Beam     10'5"
Draft    5'3"
Displ    6 tons
         (13,440 lbs)
Sail area  742 sq ft

*The Tarbert Yawl's lines: balanced ends, a clean underbody, and sweet sections with considerable deadrise.*

*Designer David Raeburn has packed a lot of interior into 34 feet LOA.*

in a boat this size: V-berths forward, followed by toilet room, main cabin with settees port and starboard and dropleaf table between, galley aft on the port side, and quarter berth and navigation area to starboard. (In British yachting nomenclature, including the Clyde Classics brochure, the navigation space is called a "navigatorium." What a horrible term — it sounds like a padded cell for round-the-bend navigators!) The icebox is under the forward end of the quarter berth, and can be fitted with refrigeration if desired. Tucked beneath the galley counter and the companionway ladder is the diesel engine. The plans also show a cabin heater mounted on the bulkhead at the forward end of the main saloon.

By sleeping two on the main-cabin settees, the boat will accommodate five. This will appeal to many, particularly families with growing children, but others like myself would prefer fewer bunks and a less crowded cabin with more and larger lockers. The V-berths forward appear to be very narrow at the foot, and there does not seem to be a hanging locker of any kind. By opening up the layout a bit, a nice arrangement could be developed that would let fewer people cruise in more comfort. With the V-berths drawn so far forward, the cabin trunk must be extended well forward of the mast, resulting in a very short foredeck.

Aft of the cabin trunk and abbreviated bridge deck is a small, self-draining cockpit. The boat steers with a tiller, the rudderpost piercing the deck just forward of the mizzenmast. The Clyde Classics brochure calls for a 25-(Imperial?) gallon fuel tank under the cockpit, feeding the 20-hp Yanmar or Volvo diesel. A freshwater tank of 30 gallons is fitted under the cabin sole amidships. This is a good place for the water tank, as the weight is low and trim is not affected by the amount of water in the tank. I wish it were bigger, as 30 gallons, even if they are the larger Imperial ones, will not last very long with a full crew aboard, and the specified shower will deplete the supply quickly if used.

The cabin trunk (what our friends across the sea call the coachroof) has a handsome rounded front, an opening hatch forward of the mast over the toilet room, a traditional opening skylight over the main saloon, and, of course, a sliding companionway hatch aft. The portlights in the cabinsides appear to be fixed.

While the shape, the rig, and the interior are all based on boats of traditional form, the construction of the Tarbert Yawl is thoroughly modern, using the concept of laminated wood with epoxy glue as the adhesive. The hull skin is composed of approximately ¾-inch-thick cedar strip planking overlaid with two outer diagonal skins of khaya (African mahogany) veneers about ⅛-inch thick, and a biaxial fiberglass surface sheathing. After the boat is turned right-side up and the interior smoothed, another diagonal layer of khaya is glued on the inside from the sheer down to the level of the cabin sole, while the bilge area is glassed to strengthen and protect it from spills. The laminated backbone is glued up from iroko.

I have great faith in the strength and longevity of this type of construction. We have built several large boats here at the Brooklin Boat Yard using these techniques, with excellent results. The strength-to-weight ratio is very good, the hulls go together quickly, and the smooth, frameless interior is pleasant to look at and gives more interior volume than does traditional plank-on-frame construction.

After the interior sheathing is complete, the builders at Clyde Classics install the main bulkheads and stainless-steel strap floors through which the ballast keelbolts pass. Clamps and deck framing follow, then the ⅝-inch plywood underdeck and the overlaid ⅜-inch teak decking.

Spars are varnished spruce made by Noble Masts of Bristol, England. The mainmast steps on deck, supported below by the main bulkhead at the after end of the toilet room. Standing rigging is stainless-steel wire with bronze turnbuckles. Most of the deck hardware appears to be bronze, in keeping with the traditional look of the boat.

The people at Clyde Classics have turned out a fine job, from initial concept to finished product. These are wooden boats of the new type, easy to maintain through the years, offering much improved performance over their older but heavier forebears, and generating great pride of ownership — a quality that cannot be measured in dollars or pounds sterling, but which will be a source of great satisfaction to the future master of a Tarbert Yawl.

*For more information about the Tarbert Yawl: Clyde Classics Ltd., 648–656 Glasgow Rd., Wishaw ML2 7SL, Lanarkshire, Scotland.*

# XXXIX

# A Scandinavian-Inspired Cutter

— Design by K. Aage Nielsen —
Commentary by Joel White

Many years ago, I bought a boat. While I had owned boats since childhood, this was my first large boat, a 35-foot cruising cutter named *Northern Crown*.

The story of this purchase actually goes further back. In 1957, I saw the plans for *Northern Crown* in *Yachting* magazine. She had just been built in Denmark by A. Walsted's yard and shipped to this country for delivery to her American owner. In addition to the cutter's plans, the *Yachting* article contained a couple of pictures of her under sail. Because there was such immediate attraction on my part, I saved the copy of the magazine for future reference.

In 1972, while thumbing through the *National Fisherman*, I found *Northern Crown* listed for sale, and located in nearby Camden, Maine. While I had no plans at the time to buy a boat, I could not resist going to see her. After a trial sail, a condition survey, and a trip to the local bank, she was mine.

It is not often that a design reviewer gets a chance to write about a boat that he knows so intimately. I am not at all sure that such familiarity will make the task any easier or more reliable. Boat ownership is such a subjective thing — a love affair, in effect — that I may find it more difficult to be objective.

*Northern Crown* was designed by K. Aage Nielsen, a distinguished Danish-born American designer. Everything about her appearance speaks of Scandinavian ancestry. I believe she would be called a spidsgatter. The beautifully sculptured round stern comes to us directly from Danish fishing craft and has been heavily imitated in recent years by designers of modern fiberglass cruising boats, but not one copy has come even close to the grace and power of *Northern Crown*'s stern.

Let's consider her lines first: *Northern Crown* is a very large boat for being only 35 feet overall; her waterline length of 30 feet 9 inches is a much better indicator of her size. With her long waterline and beam of 11 feet 5 inches, I would estimate that she has half again more interior volume than a Concordia yawl, whose dimensions are about 40 feet overall and 28 feet 6 inches on the waterline. She has full sections and a relatively shallow draft of 5 feet. Her underwater profile shows a forefoot sloping downward to a long keel with little drag, and a nearly upright rudderpost. This profile makes her steady at sea, with little tendency to yaw. The waterline forward has a nice bit of hollow, while aft it is relatively full because of the broadness of her stern sections. The buttock lines are fair and easy, and she is a notably good sailer for so husky a boat.

But feast your eyes on that stern! It is such a logical, yet graceful ending for a sailing yacht hull. While the hull aft is very full on deck, there is a lot of deadrise in the after section, with a rather hard turn to the bilge — a shape that echoes the hull sections farther forward. Another reason the stern looks so handsome is the large amount of exterior sternpost showing beyond the rabbet line, a detail that the fiberglass builders simply do not undertake. This form of stern is not easy to plank in wood, as the curves are quite severe, but when properly designed and built, the result is glorious. (Those last few sentences are perfectly unbiased and objective, right?)

This hull form has proved to be eminently seaworthy, well tested on offshore trips to Cape Breton and Bermuda. We have only once filled her cockpit with water, while running before a gale across the Strait of Canso. But, because her cockpit holds about as much water as a wheelbarrow, it was merely a short-lived inconvenience.

*Northern Crown* is cutter rigged. In boats of this size, single sticks make the most sense, as the sails are still small enough to be easy to manage; there is not the clutter of a mizzenmast in or abaft the cockpit, and the number of sheets and halyards to be handled is reduced. The mainsail is only 350 square feet, well within the capabilities of a small crew. The divided foretriangle, with self-tending boomed forestaysail and larger overlapping yankee jib, makes for light work on the foredeck. There is only the yankee sheet to trim when tacking. When the wind pipes up, lowering the yankee (in combination with one or more reefs in the main) makes a significant reduction in sail area. I keep the yankee bent on all the time and stopped down to the bowsprit with permanent rope ties, so the manhandling of heavy jibs forward is pretty much eliminated. In practice, the small jib, while a nice alternative sail in a blow, is not often used.

When I first purchased *Northern Crown*, one of the changes I made was to lengthen the bowsprit about a foot and a half. This was done to make it possible to hang a 50-pound kedge anchor on the roller chock at the end of the sprit with the fluke end housed in a bronze hook back near the stem. But an unforeseen advantage to the longer sprit was the increased space between the jibstay and forestay, which makes tacking the yankee much easier. A genoa is never used because of the difficulty in tacking such a big, low-cut sail between the stays, and because it would reduce visibility forward.

One disadvantage of the cutter rig, at least on *Northern Crown*, is the relatively poor performance of the boat under mainsail alone. While she will sail slowly this way, I have never felt that I had full control in a tight maneuvering situation — there simply is not enough sail area, and it is placed too far aft. My little sloop-rigged daysailer, on the other hand, is completely reliable and as handy as a cow pony under just her mainsail.

*Northern Crown* came to me with roller reefing on the mainsail. The system proved to be so slow and unhandy that I soon fitted her with jiffy reefing with permanently rove lines for both reefs. With the second reef down, the area of the main is reduced by one-half. This has turned out to be very satisfactory, and with the help of the bottom-action winch on the boom just abaft the gooseneck, one person can reef her in a minute or two. And reefing is something we do often. *Northern*

*Crown* has a large sail plan for her size, 708 square feet, and because she was built with a relatively small iron ballast keel and quite a lot of inside ballast, she needs to be reefed earlier than many boats.

One thing I always planned to do — but never got around to — was to remove both the inside ballast and the iron keel, and cast a new ballast keel of lead. This would significantly lower her center of gravity and make her considerably stiffer. The large sail area is great in light conditions, and I am a believer in designs that have high sail area/displacement ratios, and easy reefing systems. It makes sailing much more fun and satisfies my competitive instincts.

*Northern Crown*'s accommodations are grand. The layout is basically traditional, but there are a number of unusual features that make the cabin special and functional. The galley is aft and entirely on the starboard side. It includes a large wood- and coal-burning range (for use in warm weather, we carry a two-burner pressure kerosene stove that sits atop the wood range), a sink near the centerline, a good-sized icebox, and much stowage space tucked under the large bridge deck. Opposite the galley is a wide quarter berth. This is the captain's bunk. It has two large shelves outboard on which all one's gear for a two-week cruise can be stowed. A shelf built over the foot of the bunk stows the sextant box and other navigational gear in complete safety. Under this large bunk, there is room for two big, shallow chart drawers, each about 3 feet by 2 feet and 3 inches deep. While I have never counted them, there must be close to 100 charts stowed here, with the ones currently used on top.

Nielsen, with great ingenuity, conceived the idea of a chart table that stows above the top chart drawer. When needed, this is withdrawn and placed over the forward end of the quarter berth, providing a large, flat work area for the navigator. The recording fathometer is at hand on its mount, which allows it to be swung out into the companionway for viewing from the cockpit, or in the stowed position is available to the navigator at the chart table. The recently installed Loran is directly below the fathometer, so that the navigator is surrounded with all his tools, yet no space has to be dedicated to a navigation area. The only disadvantage is that the navigator must stand — which at least keeps him on his toes!

The forward cabin is unusual in having only one berth, not the usual V-berths. This allows the toilet room on the port side to be large, while the space forward of the toilet room and opposite this berth is used for stowage. The main cabin has a high pilot berth to port, with an extension berth below it that makes a narrow seat, or, when extended, a reasonably comfortable bunk. A previous owner modified the pilot berth so that it converts to a double. *Northern Crown*

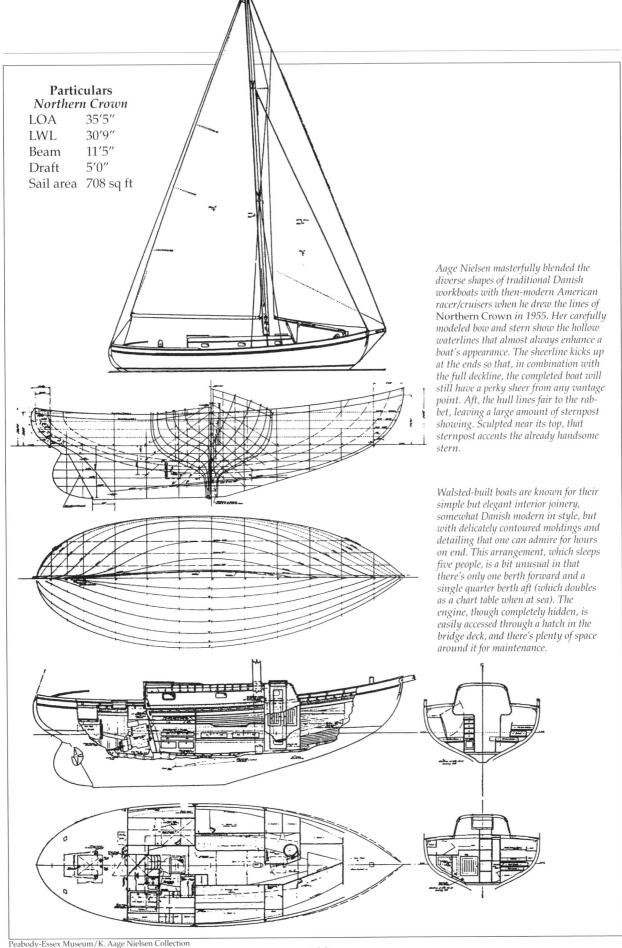

**Particulars**
*Northern Crown*

| | |
|---|---|
| LOA | 35'5" |
| LWL | 30'9" |
| Beam | 11'5" |
| Draft | 5'0" |
| Sail area | 708 sq ft |

*Aage Nielsen masterfully blended the diverse shapes of traditional Danish workboats with then-modern American racer/cruisers when he drew the lines of* Northern Crown *in 1955. Her carefully modeled bow and stern show the hollow waterlines that almost always enhance a boat's appearance. The sheerline kicks up at the ends so that, in combination with the full deckline, the completed boat will still have a perky sheer from any vantage point. Aft, the hull lines fair to the rabbet, leaving a large amount of sternpost showing. Sculpted near its top, that sternpost accents the already handsome stern.*

*Walsted-built boats are known for their simple but elegant interior joinery, somewhat Danish modern in style, but with delicately contoured moldings and detailing that one can admire for hours on end. This arrangement, which sleeps five people, is a bit unusual in that there's only one berth forward and a single quarter berth aft (which doubles as a chart table when at sea). The engine, though completely hidden, is easily accessed through a hatch in the bridge deck, and there's plenty of space around it for maintenance.*

can sleep five, no matter which configuration is used. Some cruising couples seem to like the double, others do not. I like the versatility of the arrangement.

When I bought *Northern Crown* I discovered that she had no fixed cabin table, but instead relied on a folding one similar to a card table that stowed on the after bulkhead in the toilet room. My first thought was to add a dropleaf table, but after the first summer of cruising, I realized that the uncluttered space in the main cabin was far more valuable and useful than a fixed table. We use the folding table for sit-down meals, and relish the open space the rest of the time.

The 50-gallon water tank is located under the cabin sole. This is a marvelous arrangement because it keeps the weight of the water as low as possible, and it frees up the space under main cabin berths for food stowage. The floor timbers in way of the water tank are wrought iron rather than wood. We pulled these out a couple of years ago, and found them in surprisingly good shape after 30-plus years of being hidden under the stainless-steel tank. The floors were sandblasted, epoxy coated, painted, and reinstalled; we also renewed the keelbolts in this area.

Walsted's yard did a beautiful job of cabinetwork below, with the overhead and bulkheads painted white, furniture and trim of varnished walnut, and galley counters and cabin sole of bare teak. The feeling is of beauty, comfort, and fine craftsmanship without being fussy or ornate.

On deck, *Northern Crown* feels as well as looks like a much larger boat. The wide side decks and narrow cabinhouse, and the tiny cockpit aft all combine to give great expanses of flat deck surface. Sail handling, sunbathing, napping, and even an occasional deck dance are possible and easy. The high bulwarks, 8 inches or more, supported by heavy oak top timbers and topped with a nice oval railcap, give a wonderful feeling of security.

The engine has a room of its own, accessed through the large raised hatch just aft of the companionway. The whole after part of the boat is taken up with the diesel engine, its 35-gallon fuel tank under the cockpit, battery bank, stowage space for life jackets, fuel for the galley stove, spare parts, bilge pumps, and fenders. Being able to work on the engine in relative comfort and with full access to all sides of the machinery is a tremendous luxury in such a small boat. Under these circumstances engines receive much better care and maintenance, and are consequently more reliable. The original 35-horsepower Mercedes diesel gave good service for 30 years, after which time it was replaced by a Westerbeke 58, which to date has been equally reliable. At cruising speed of 6 knots, each engine used less than half a gallon per hour. This works out to roughly 15 miles per gallon, numbers quite similar to

larger automobiles! I seldom fill the fuel tank more often than every other summer, and once went two years without a refill.

*Northern Crown*'s construction is heavy, with 1¼-inch African mahogany planking on laminated oak frames, fastened with large copper rivets. It is fortunate that the rivets were used, as the glue in the frame laminations has given up. The rivets, spaced every 3 inches or so, hold the frames tightly together, and I have never worried about them, glue or no glue. Forward of the mast, the frame spacing was cut in half, and looking at her from inside it would appear that she could break ice! When slamming into heavy head seas, I have always appreciated the tightly spaced frames. The deck framing is heavy, and so is the mahogany plywood deck, originally covered with canvas and painted. When I bought the boat, the canvas was bad, and one of the first tasks was to rip it off and cover the deck with two layers of Dynel and epoxy. The cabintop recently received the same treatment.

What of the intangibles that one learns about a boat from sailing her for 20 years? This is more difficult ground. First, let me say that most boats have a character, or ambiance, that is felt by their crews. *Northern Crown*'s always comes through as one of competence, sturdiness, and unquestioned ability. I've never felt nervous aboard her, except perhaps one wild night in the Gulf Stream when I had doubts about my own stamina, not hers. Her seaworthiness is supreme. I find her beautiful, in a rugged sort of way — not delicate or dainty, but beautiful nonetheless. She provides great comfort below, and I love cruising on her. She sails very well — about equal to a Concordia yawl, I would estimate. In light airs, she has enough sail area to keep moving, and in heavy going and reefed down, she is superb.

*Northern Crown* is no longer mine, and I miss her. I sold her because more of my sailing was done in a 24-foot daysailer, and I was feeling guilty about *Northern Crown*'s lack of use. And I was beginning not to enjoy the inevitable work that goes with owning a larger boat. Even with one's own boatyard to care for her, there is a heavy load of chores that go with keeping such a vessel. Now she is in the best of hands, and her new owners are aware of what a gem she is and will keep her looking trim.

I couldn't ask for more. But after 20 years, it is a strange feeling to look out the window and find her mooring empty.

*This review was first published in 1992. —Ed.*

*The plans of* Northern Crown *are in the K. Aage Nielsen Collection at the Peabody-Essex Museum, East India Square, Salem, MA 01970.*

# A Designer's Choice

Design by Joseph H. Hack
Commentary by Joel White

*A* boat created by a designer for his own use is always very interesting and instructive. The designer is dealing with the most demanding client of all — himself — but also the ideal customer from the point of view of similar personal taste and design philosophy, and one with whom communication could hardly be better. If the designer in question is the president of a firm that deals almost exclusively with producing designs for tugboats and barges for use all over the world, then we must indeed be curious about the sort of yacht he has personally designed, and built, for himself.

Joseph H. Hack, president of Marine Design, Inc. (formerly Tams, Inc.) drew the plans shown here in 1960. His letter accompanying the drawings states:

"I guess it's quite common for yacht owners to feel something special about their boat, and I find myself no exception. Having designed and built the boat myself only reinforces this feeling. This boat was built in 1965 with four others following, so ample time has elapsed for the boats to prove themselves.

"Living on the South Shore of Long Island and cruising eastward in the summer months, we need a boat that is shoal-draft, has a strong bottom for grounding, is capable of running inlets, and is a satisfactory deep-water sailer as well. In addition to this, I wanted to go to a shoal-draft keel and get rid of the centerboard. Centerboards work well in deep water, but if you are constantly grounding on them, between the twisting and stones, they can sure be troublesome. I also wanted a simple backbone structure; after all, I am really a naval architect and not a boat builder."

A photograph of the finished boat indicates that Mr. Hack is being modest about his abilities as a boatbuilder. The 36-foot sloop in the picture looks very handsome and well finished.

To accomplish his stated purpose of designing a shoal-draft yacht without a centerboard, Mr. Hack has drawn an underwater profile with a maximum draft of 3 feet 6 inches, a keel with very little drag (the bottom nearly parallel to the waterline), a rather deep forefoot, and a sternpost with moderate rake. This gives a lot of lateral plane underwater, which is the justification for eliminating the centerboard.

It is certainly true that eliminating the centerboard makes the boat much easier and less costly to build, avoids a prime source of potential leaks, and does away with all the nuisances of having a board-jammed slot, noises at anchor and at sea, and loss of inside space to the trunk and lifting mechanism. But it is also true that a well-designed centerboard is a more efficient device for reducing leeway than is a long, straight keel profile. This is the sort of compromise that designers are always wrestling with — will the good points more than offset the bad? I imagine that the boat does well to windward, but would surely do better with a centerboard, less forefoot, and less wetted surface. Still, I think the tradeoff is a good one. Her interior would be more cluttered if the centerboard trunk intruded into the cabin, and even if it did not, there would be potential jamming and noise problems, as well as the inevitable ones of cost and difficulty in construction.

The lines plan shows an overall hull length of 36 feet, 25 feet on the load waterline, beam of 8 feet 10 inches, and draft of 3 feet 6 inches. The only surprise in this set of numbers is the beam, which is considerably less than is usual in a shoal-draft vessel of this length. At a time when length-to-beam ratios of three are normal, even for deep-keeled craft, here is a shallow boat with a length-to-beam ratio of more than four. It is true that her waterline beam is nearly equal to her beam on deck, which gives her wide, firm bilges. I imagine that Mr. Hack wanted to keep beam down to improve her windward ability, especially in a seaway, where a beamy boat tends to be slowed by wave action. The argument for a beamy boat, of course, is much greater interior volume for accommodations, more spacious decks and cockpit, and — other things being equal — improved stability. We will see in a minute how this narrow beam affects accommodations.

This design has very nice, easy buttock lines, and fair, flowing diagonals, both of which indicate a boat that should sail well. Her bow and stern overhang, combined with a generous-sized counter stern, make for a boat whose sailing length will get longer, and thus faster, as she heels. To me, her bow sections look a little full, and I wish her forefoot and the forward end of her keel were a little more streamlined. But, all in all, she's a handsome hull, nicely drawn.

I am surprised that the ballast keel shown on the construction plan is so small — only 3,430 pounds of lead. The designed displacement of the boat is 11,900 pounds in salt water. The 3,430 divided by 11,900 gives a ballast ratio of about 29 percent, a bit lower than is usual in this type of boat (33 to 37 percent would be the normal range). However, a call to Mr. Hack elicited the information that there was no additional inside ballast, and that the boat had sufficient stability. The sail area of 530 square feet is modest for a boat of her size, and Long Island, New York—her area of intended use—has relatively gentle summertime breezes.

The boat's construction is conventional, but well thought out and with many nice touches, such as a bronze knee aft where the sternpost meets the keel, bronze fish plates instead of tenons connecting the sternpost to the keel and horn timber, and a good chainplate arrangement with Monel straps running down the insides of the frames and tying into the floor timbers. Planking is $7/8$-inch Port Orford cedar over $1\frac{3}{8}$-inch-square white oak frames. The deck calls for $5/8$-inch teak over $1/4$-inch marine plywood.

I admit to a prejudice against this type of deck construction, having seen so many cases where water penetrated to the plywood, where it just sits and festers until real rot problems develop. Repair is very difficult and expensive, and usually the problem isn't discovered until rot is quite advanced and widespread. I really think that if teak decks are wanted, they should be solid teak with no underlays, so that a leak is immediately noticeable (nine times out of ten it will be directly over your pillow) and can be fixed before disease spreads into the deck framing. The solid teak also gives sufficient thickness to the deck so that the inevitable wearing away of the wood due to traffic and cleaning shouldn't be a problem for many years. Personally, I like a deck of high-grade mahogany plywood covered with Dynel and epoxy; it is watertight,

long lasting, and except for painting, maintenance free. End of lecture.

The cabin trunk sides are $1\frac{1}{8}$-inch Spanish cedar, raked inboard for appearance and more deck space. The cabintop is three layers of $1/4$-inch plywood molded to the crown without beams. Headroom under the doghouse aft is 6 feet, while going forward, it becomes progressively less until at the forward end of the cabin trunk it is just over 5 feet. If cabintop beams were used, these figures would be reduced by about 2 inches. I am glad that Mr. Hack gave precedence to moderate freeboard and a good-looking profile rather than full headroom throughout. The insistence on full headroom has done more to spoil the appearance of modern yachts than any other factor. You hardly ever see a cruising boat now under 45 feet that doesn't look like a high-rise apartment building.

Mr. Hack has drawn a conventional arrangement plan, with two berths forward, then a toilet room the full width of the boat, the main cabin with two berths and drop-leaf table, a smallish galley to port, and to starboard a hanging locker, chart table, and electronics area. The hanging locker has an unusual feature in that the top swings to one side so that it is easier to see into and get at the contents. There is a nice hinged backrest that makes the main cabin berths comfortable for sitting and dining, and that swings up under the cabin lockers out of the way for sleeping.

The toilet room is a bit unusual in that there are two doors that hide the toilet to port and the lavatory sink to starboard and create a corridor to the forward stateroom. In order to use the facilities, these doors must be opened (or is it closed?) athwartships, thus making a full-width room. But it must take a skinny contortionist to close both doors. The first door would be easy, but it doesn't look to me as though there would be much space left for the person closing the second door. (Mr. Hack tells me that the forward door was changed to a sliding curtain to cure this problem.) This arrangement also forces the toilet itself far off the centerline, and mostly out under the deck, rather than under the cabin trunk. Another foot of beam would have opened up the accommodations considerably, giving those few extra inches that often make a big difference. But again, every design is a balancing act. Performance against space, beauty against headroom.

My other minor quibble is with the cockpit. As drawn, the seats are quite narrow (about 12 inches) and the vertical coaming that makes the seat backs looks cramping and uncomfortable. My inclination would be to narrow up the side decks aft a bit, widen the seats, and cant the coamings outboard to form a slanted backrest. The drawings also show access to the stowage space under the cockpit seats through five rather small lifting doors. I would rather have the entire

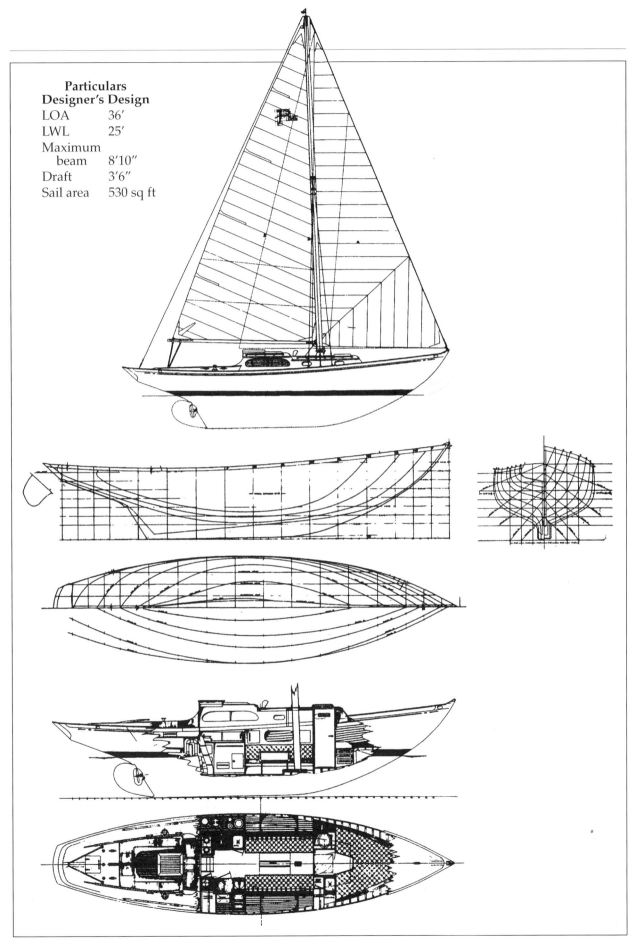

**Particulars**
**Designer's Design**

| | |
|---|---|
| LOA | 36' |
| LWL | 25' |
| Maximum beam | 8'10" |
| Draft | 3'6" |
| Sail area | 530 sq ft |

seat hinge up, with gutters to carry off water leakage.

Mr. Hack states that one of the very few changes made to his boat is the addition of wheel steering. A wheel takes up less space than a tiller, and in most cases enlarges the amount of seating space available.

There are a couple of unusual features: a built-in icebox under the galley counter to port, and a portable-type refrigerator under the navigation area to starboard. And the gasoline tank is forward, under the V-berths. Other than having a long supply line running aft through the cabin, there is nothing wrong with this arrangement; it is just not often seen. (It should also have the psychological effect of inhibiting smoking in the forward berths.)

A great deal of attention has been given to ventilation of the below-deck spaces. The high lockers outboard of the main-cabin berths have slatted bottoms, the outboard portions of the galley and navigation counters are gratings, and the cockpit lockers under the deck also have slat bottoms. All these efforts will pay off in keeping the wooden yacht sweet-smelling and long-lived. A moving supply of fresh air below is one of the best rot preventers known.

The sail plan is a simple masthead sloop rig, but with the mast placed a little farther aft than usual, giv-

ing a relatively larger foretriangle and a smaller mainsail. I suspect that access in and out of the toilet room may have had an influence on the mast position. Because of the boat's shoal draft and narrow beam, the sail plan is not large, but it should be efficient. The spars are wood, and the mast scantlings show ¾-inch walls throughout, which give a fairly light stick. This will improve sail-carrying power, for a few pounds saved aloft can make a big difference in stability. A large genoa is shown for light weather, and a smallish heavy-weather jib whose luff reaches only two-thirds of the way to the masthead. For offshore work, one would also want a trysail, and a very small storm jib.

So here we have a naval architect's own dream ship — his answer to his own personal needs and desires in a boat. The fact that four more were built after the original boat is a strong indication that the design is successful and appeals to others. I find her very attractive, and I'll bet Mr. Hack's tugboat designs are good looking, too.

*Further inquiries should be addressed to: Joseph F. Hack, Marine Design, Inc., 5418 Tradewinds Rd., Fairfield Harbour, New Bern, NC 28560.*

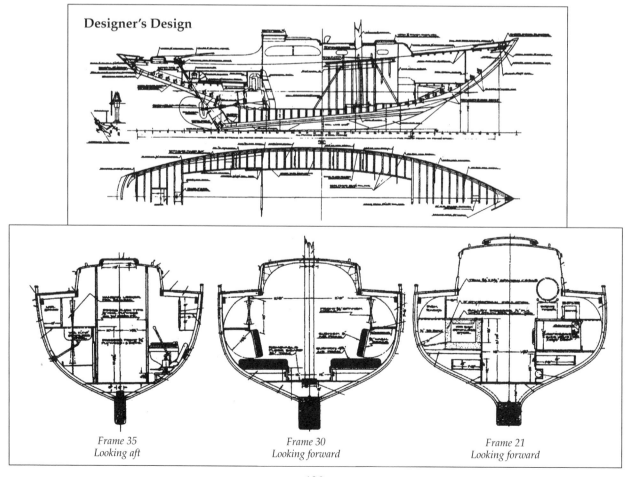

**Designer's Design**

| Frame 35 | Frame 30 | Frame 21 |
| *Looking aft* | *Looking forward* | *Looking forward* |

# A Stout Cruising Ketch

—— Design by Tom Tucker ——
Commentary by Mike O'Brien

*Alegria* swings to her mooring off Hadlock, Washington. If we were to ghost past this ketch one foggy morning, we might guess her to be the full-keeled, 40-year-old work of Winthrop Warner or, perhaps, John Alden. We would be wrong. Launched in 1995, after seven years building, this robust cruiser came from Tom Tucker's drawing table — and, despite her traditional topsides, she carries a fin keel and separate rudder.

Owner Denis Dignan describes the creation of the 40-foot ketch as a "Port Townsend [Washington] collaboration." Dignan, designer Tucker, and Roger Nisbet built the boat. Kit Africa rigged her, and Julia Maynard did the finish work.

This is one strong boat — just as well, as she sails in a part of the world where any driftwood smaller than a house isn't thought worthy of mention. The hull went together upside down on a timber-girder strongback. Tucker and Nisbet laminated the Douglas-fir keel over frames (also glued up of Douglas-fir, on 40-inch centers) and temporary molds. Then, they worked a meranti sheer clamp into notches in the molds.

The skeleton was sheathed as follows: 7/8-inch fir strip planks (running fore-and-aft), fastened with bronze ring nails and epoxy; two diagonal layers of 1/8-inch red cedar; one diagonal layer of 1/8-inch meranti. All veneers were secured with bronze staples and epoxy. Finally, the exterior was covered with fiberglass cloth set in epoxy. The resulting hull measures more than 1 1/4 inches thick; it is reported to be extraordinarily stiff.

After turning the hull rightside up, the builders laminated in place two or three leaf-spring floor timbers between each pair of frames. (That is, each layer of a typical laminated floor is slightly shorter than the layer below it.) A 1 3/4-inch-thick keelson was laminated over

all this to make the keel structure effectively an I-sectioned girder. They fastened the foil-shaped lead ballast and wooden fin to every appropriate frame and floor with staggered bolts.

The skeg and rudder consist of brutally strong stainless-steel fabrications sheathed with wood and epoxy. They are secured by bolts running through the hull's backbone to stainless-steel backing plates. Substantial deadwood runs forward from the skeg to the trailing edge of the keel. The idea was to reduce cross-flow and delay separation as the water passes by the run. Tucker reckoned that the relatively long, straight-bottomed, fin keel would combine handy performance with ease of hauling on the builder's railway.

*Alegria's* hull sections show more deadrise than we usually see on contemporary canoe-bodied hulls. The designer was looking to ensure an easy motion at sea, and early reports suggest that he succeeded. He also wanted to provide full headroom below without having to erect a three-story house on deck. As built, the house is about 1 1/2-inch lower than indicated by the drawings. It hides nicely behind the bulwarks and, yet, offers 6-foot 2-inch headroom in the main cabin.

Down below, *Alegria* seems to be arranged more for inshore cruising than for life at sea. For privacy and comfort, the double berth in the forward cabin will be the place to bed down when in port. Occasional guests can sleep in the dinette, which converts to a double berth. Offshore, the settee and the quarter berth would seem to be the beds to grab first. Perhaps unfortunately, they're both on the same side of the boat — precluding our choice of weather or lee berths.

The U-shaped galley rests near the point of least motion, and it is convenient to the cockpit. There appears to be sufficient room for the cook to hide from the wet traffic, which will pass through the slightly-off-center companionway. We're told that half of the workbench might be sacrificed to provide space for a hanging locker.

Tucker and Dignan chose the ketch rig for ease of handling by one or two people. The jib, at 335 square feet, constitutes the largest single spread of Dacron. The other sails measure as follows: forestaysail 135 square feet, mainsail 300 square feet, and mizzen 139 square feet. The forestaysail sets on a club. Roller-furling gear for the jib might be added somewhere down the road.

The stoutly stayed spars should be cause for great joy among riggers and purveyors of wire rope — and

will provide peace of mind for *Alegria's* crew. Tucker shows the mizzenmast stayed independently from the main. Mizzenmast shrouds that are secured far forward obviate the need for a springstay (which could have run from the head of the mainmast to the hounds of the mizzen). A springstay might have provided somewhat better support for the mizzen — at the expense of near total disaster should one of the masts fail. In any case, few circumstances, short of a full Eskimo roll, will press this rig to its limits.

*Plans for* Alegria *are available from Tucker Yacht Design, P.O. Box 328, Port Townsend, WA 98368.*

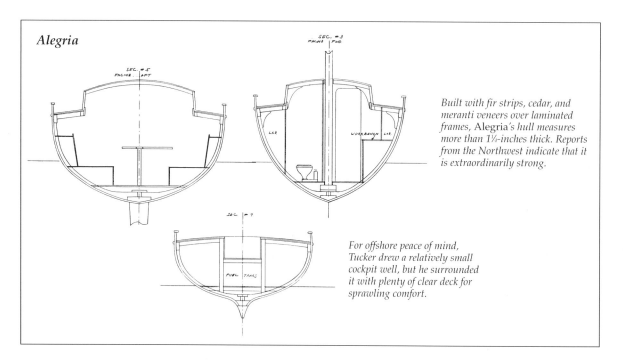

**Alegria**

Built with fir strips, cedar, and meranti veneers over laminated frames, Alegria's hull measures more than 1¼-inches thick. Reports from the Northwest indicate that it is extraordinarily strong.

For offshore peace of mind, Tucker drew a relatively small cockpit well, but he surrounded it with plenty of clear deck for sprawling comfort.

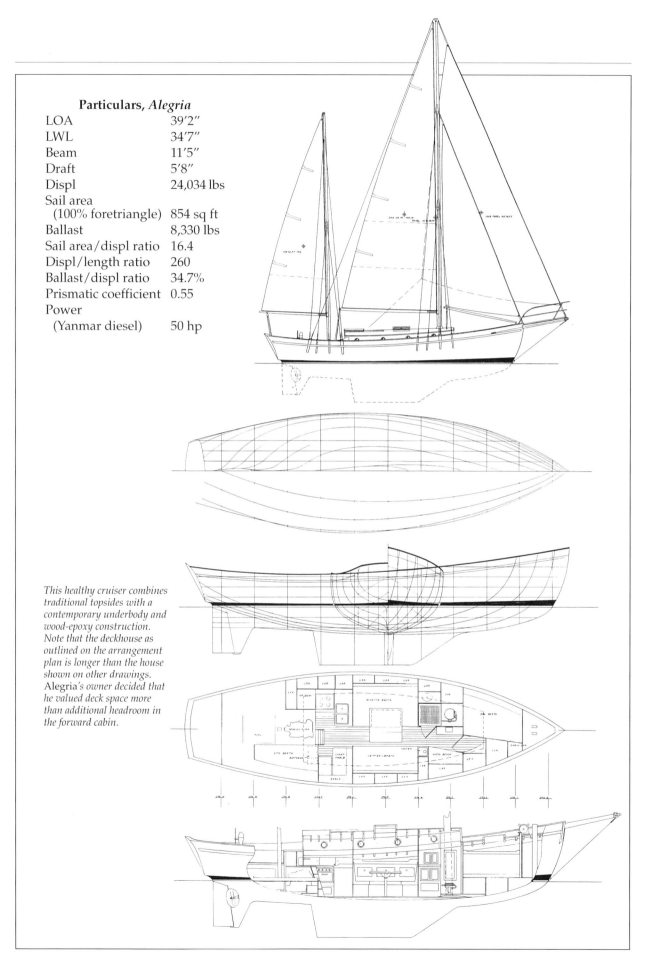

**Particulars, *Alegria***

| | |
|---|---|
| LOA | 39'2" |
| LWL | 34'7" |
| Beam | 11'5" |
| Draft | 5'8" |
| Displ | 24,034 lbs |
| Sail area | |
|   (100% foretriangle) | 854 sq ft |
| Ballast | 8,330 lbs |
| Sail area/displ ratio | 16.4 |
| Displ/length ratio | 260 |
| Ballast/displ ratio | 34.7% |
| Prismatic coefficient | 0.55 |
| Power | |
|   (Yanmar diesel) | 50 hp |

*This healthy cruiser combines traditional topsides with a contemporary underbody and wood-epoxy construction. Note that the deckhouse as outlined on the arrangement plan is longer than the house shown on other drawings. Alegria's owner decided that he valued deck space more than additional headroom in the forward cabin.*

# A Cold-Molded Cutter

Design by McCurdy & Rhodes
Commentary by Joel White

*A*eriel is a McCurdy-designed, cold-molded cutter built in British Columbia by Bent Jespersen. This boat is a nice blend of modern design, precise craftsmanship, and attention to traditional details and aesthetics. By all accounts, she is also extremely fast and well-mannered.

Once again, we have a chance to examine a design executed by a professional naval architect for his own use. Such designs are always of special interest, for the designer is free from the restraints, conditions, and prejudices of any client but himself. With no input except his own, he has a chance to dream. I find that such designs are often very good ones.

Jim McCurdy (of the design firm of McCurdy and Rhodes) executed this design for his own use and had a boat named *Selkie* built using composite construction. The boat was intended both for offshore and coastal cruising, and to race under the IMS Rule. McCurdy points out that the design has less beam and more draft than most contemporary boats, with a relatively high displacement/length ratio of 301. These characteristics produce a hull with a high range of stability (130 degrees), which is so necessary for safety and comfort offshore.

This design, with a few minor modifications and built in wood, was the basis for *Aeriel*. She was built for Bill Malone of Nanaimo, British Columbia, and launched in 1989. Her builder, Bent Jespersen, is one of Canada's premier wooden boat builders. His shop on the waterfront at Sidney, on Vancouver Island, has become known for expertise in cold-molded wooden construction, and for quality craftsmanship.

There are several differences between *Selkie* and *Aeriel*, the most noticeable being the change to an aft-raked stern on *Aeriel*. A look at the sail plan will show this, as well as the tall, modern cutter rig with short main boom and large foretriangle (the base of which is 2 feet longer than the foot of the mainsail). Hall Spars supplied the mast and boom. The mast is supported by two spreaders and three forestays, one of them a baby stay from the cabintop to the lower spreaders, giving plenty of strength and support for offshore sailing. Total sail area is 747 square feet when figured with 100 percent foretriangle. By my calculation, this works out to a sail area/displacement ratio of 17.25, indicating that she has plenty of wind horsepower to move her.

The sail plan also shows us a modern-looking hull profile, with relatively high, flat sheer; straight, raking stem; and short stern overhang, with the upper part of the rudder showing above the waterline. The straight-sheered house profile fits the hull shape well. The window arrangement on *Aeriel* has been changed a bit from that in *Selkie*. The new boat has two large windows aft, rather than one, and two smaller portlights forward.

Let's next look at the perspective lines drawings kindly furnished by McCurdy. *Aeriel* has a modern underbody with a small fin keel amidships, and a large skeg/rudder right at the after end of the waterline. Notice how her belly abaft the fin bulges out a little to increase displacement aft and to allow the engine to be installed farther aft and lower in order to free up the accommodations a bit. The sections are basically semicircular, with no reverse to them (it's a pity reverse is so seldom seen in modern lines plans, if only for aesthetic reasons).

*Aeriel*'s cold-molded hull skin consists of three diagonal layers of 1/4-inch red cedar followed by the final outer skin of 3/8-inch mahogany running fore-and-aft, all glued with epoxy. The outer surface is sheathed with epoxy and fiberglass cloth. A monocoque structure such

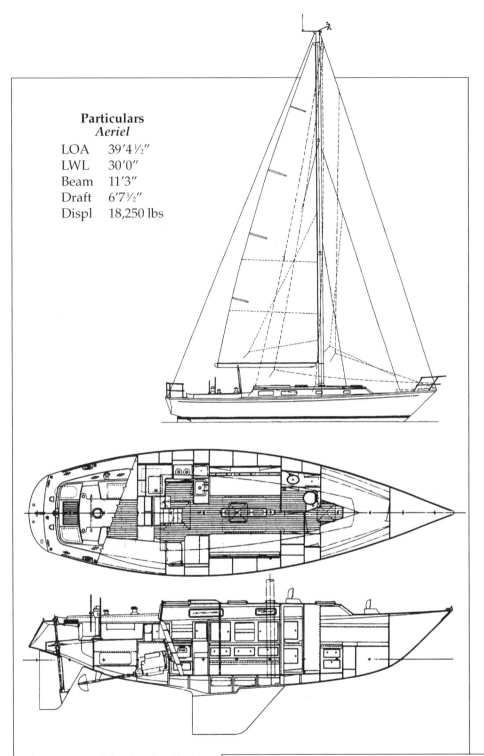

**Particulars**
*Aeriel*

| | |
|---|---|
| LOA | 39′4½″ |
| LWL | 30′0″ |
| Beam | 11′3″ |
| Draft | 6′7½″ |
| Displ | 18,250 lbs |

*These arrangement drawings show the interior of Aeriel's sister, Selkie. The accommodations differ only in detail, but note Selkie's reverse transom. The perspective hull lines drawing (right) reveals the shape that has helped Aeriel succeed on the racecourse.*

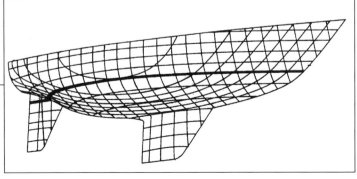

as this is immensely strong for its weight, as well as being leak-free. After smoothing up the inside surface of the hull, laminated oak frames were installed on all bulkhead locations and spaced on approximately 16-inch centers through the middle of the boat, with greater spacing toward the ends. The plywood deck is fiberglass covered, while the cockpit sole and the seats are teak. The trim both outside and below is varnished Honduras mahogany. The lead ballast keel weighs 8,700 pounds and is attached with bronze bolts. The resulting ballast/displacement ratio of 48 percent is high, contributing to the excellent range of stability and enabling *Aeriel* to stand up to her rig in all weather.

The accommodation plan shown here belongs to *Selkie. Aeriel*'s differs from it only in detail, not general arrangement. On *Aeriel*, a double sink replaces the single one shown; there is no pillar at the after end of the cabin table; she has a Yanmar diesel instead of the Westerbeke shown on the *Selkie* plan.

The layout is unusual only in that it is so much copied — it seems to be the most practical and popular arrangement for boats around 40 feet in length. The centerline companionway steps serve to separate the port-side galley from the main traffic flow, providing a nook in which the cook can brace himself while plying his art during the bumpy going of offshore racing. The chart table and seat opposite the galley are big enough for serious chart work. Around it are concentrated the switchboard and electronic components in one protected area. Abaft the navigation station is a quarter berth, with most of its length under the starboard cockpit seat.

Moving forward, the main saloon with extension berths on each side and big lockers outboard is a standard and well-proven arrangement. A dropleaf table attached to the after side of the mast will allow the whole crew to take a meal together.

*Aeriel*'s beam of 11 feet 3 inches is somewhat on the narrow side to accept pilot berths with settees inboard. The big advantage of pilot berths is that someone can be in the bunk, asleep or reading, and there is still a place to sit down in the main cabin; nevertheless, not everyone likes them.

A toilet room to port, hanging locker and bureau to starboard, and two V-berths forward complete the accommodations. There is a door to the forward stateroom for privacy. If the quarter berth is used, *Aeriel* will sleep five.

*Aeriel*'s cockpit is large and comfortable. The pedestal steerer with large-diameter wheel is located aft, with a seat across the after end of the cockpit. Forward of the wheel, seat lockers on each side give seating for the crew with easy access to the sheet and backstay winches on top of the cockpit coamings. While the boat is set up with serious racing in mind, she is not rendered uninhabitable for leisurely cruising, as is the case with so many flat-out modern racing designs.

*Aeriel*, to me, is the perfect example of why wood should be seriously considered as an option for yacht construction. Her cold-molded hull must be equal to or better than composite in strength-to-weight ratio. I'll bet the cold-molded hull is cheaper to build one-off, and it certainly wins hands-down in appearance and warmth. If the hull is properly cared for, its durability should be outstanding. With a lovely wooden yacht such as this, pride of ownership (so difficult to measure but which means so much to most boat owners) will get the highest marks. Jim McCurdy's handsome modern design, coupled with Bent Jespersen's craftsmanship and good taste, has resulted in one of the nicest wooden sailing craft in Northwest waters.

*You can reach McCurdy & Rhodes at P.O. Box 206, Cold Spring Harbor, NY 11724.*

# A High-Performance Cruising Sloop

—————— Design by Rodger Martin ——————
Commentary by Joel White

*Gray Wolf* is one of a new breed — a design that utilizes new technology and new thinking, yet is built of that oldest of boatbuilding materials, wood. Granted, the strip-planked cedar hull is strengthened and stiffened by the use of fiberglass overlays, on both the inner and outer surfaces (she is built much like a stripper canoe), but the panel design is carefully engineered for minimum weight and was proof-tested at the Gougeon Brothers Material Test Laboratory. Eight different panels were tested, including one glass-composite panel used as a control. The final choice for hull skin construction was 1-inch Western red-cedar strip-planking with light, biased fiberglass cloth set in epoxy running at 90 degrees to the plank seams.

One look at the sail plan tells us that this boat was designed for speed. The fractional sloop rig is huge (1,110 square feet) for a 40-foot light-displacement hull. The spar is of carbon fiber and has no shrouds — although there are forestays and running backstays. The enormous mainsail is fully battened, and lazy-jacks help contain the battens and sail when lowered. The forestay hits the mast at about three-quarter height, thus keeping the roller-furled jib to a reasonable size. This large rig, in conjunction with the light (13,500 pounds) displacement hull, gives a sail area/displacement ratio of 31.2 — truly horsepower with a capital H, sending a shiver of anticipation through all of us who like to sail really fast.

As a platform on which to mount this Ferrari of a rig, Martin has designed a big dinghy hull having a nearly plumb stem profile and a very short stern over-hang to maximize waterline length. The hull sections aft are close to semicircular, becoming elliptical as they go forward. Notice that maximum beam is well abaft amidships, and the stern is broad, giving lots of hull-form power to carry sail. Looking at the lines, the plan view showing the waterlines is drawn on both sides of the centerline, giving a graphic visual presentation of the hull shape, which is quite reminiscent of a flatiron. This shape is ideal for an all-out sailing machine such as this. The hull sections minimize wetted surface, and the buttock lines are shallow and straight, with a bit of up-curve aft to keep the stern from dragging — all in all, a powerful, easily driven shape.

I like the looks of this boat, both in plans and in the photographs I have seen. While she could never be described as traditional in looks, there is a grace about her that suits her intended purpose. The sheer is springy, and the rather high freeboard is reduced in appearance by a well-proportioned top strake painted a contrasting color. The cabinhouse is handsome and sits nicely on the hull. She has a 7-foot-long bowsprit from which to fly enormous reaching sails, and this complements the straight stem.

Owner Eric Urbahn, who is an architect by trade, was apparently a major part of the design team. He has a wealth of sailing experience, both in oceangoing craft and in round-the-buoys racers. His aims for the boat were daysailing, occasional racing, and the ability to cruise with a relatively small crew.

The interior is simple, modern, and comfortable. It is influenced by the engine placement — the Yanmar diesel Saildrive unit is placed amidships, with the propeller just abaft the fin keel. This keeps the weight of the engine over the center of buoyancy for maximum efficiency. The engine is hidden under a table between the settee bunks in the main cabin. At the forward end of these bunks, a structural bulkhead transmits the heeling moment of the mast to the hull. The head is just forward of this to port, while the passageway leading to a double berth and hanging locker is to starboard.

The large galley is aft and to port, with the quarter berth and navigation area to starboard. The centerline companionway ladder leads directly out to the big cockpit, the nerve center of a boat such as this. All sheets, halyards, and control lines are led aft from the mast through line stoppers to a pair of winches on the after end of the cabin. A pair of sheet winches are bolted to large winch platforms on each side, outboard of the cockpit coamings. The after winches are for the double-ended mainsheet, while the forward pair handle the jibsheets. Even farther aft, a pair of winches is dedicated to the running backstays. The boat is tiller steered.

*Gray Wolf* is very fast, as one would expect. According to her designer, she has sailed at over 12 knots in 16 knots of wind. As one also would expect from such a thoroughbred, this boat is fussy about how she is sailed. Martin mentions that she likes to be sailed upright — 20 degrees, or less, of heel — and if this angle is exceeded, she begins to drag her transom corner and will slow down, just as a dinghy hull will act when overpowered. Much of the fun in sailing high-performance boats lies in understanding how to go the fastest under varying conditions.

The boat was nicely built by Lyman-Morse Boatbuilding Co. of Thomaston, Maine. I was particularly interested in her construction details, as it is not easy to design a 40-foot cruising boat that will weigh less than 7 tons. As mentioned before, the hull skin is red-cedar strip-planking covered with double-bias fiberglass fabric inside and out, and weighs less than 2½ pounds per square ft. Bulkheads and laminated mahogany frames set on 3½-foot centers stiffen the hull, and laminated floor timbers with carbon-fiber tops spread the strain of the deep fin keel and lead bulb.

The fin keel itself is a clever bit of work, built of 316 stainless steel, and the 4,100-pound lead bulb is poured around the lower end of the fin, thus eliminating the need for bolts or other fastenings to hold it in place. Nitronic 50 stainless-steel keelbolts attach the fin assembly to a heavy fiberglass sump built onto the bottom of the hull. The deck is fiberglass-covered plywood over wooden beams.

Ballast tanks of plywood, glassed into the outboard bilges of the boat, can carry 2,200 pounds (about 260 gallons) of water ballast to help keep the boat upright and sailing fast. The water can be transferred from side to side with electric pumps in three to four minutes. To achieve the designed displacement of 13,500 pounds, Martin had to use a fin keel weighing only 4,500 pounds, giving a ballast ratio of but 33 percent.

Obtaining decent ballast ratios is a chronic problem in very light-displacement boats. The use of water ballast is one solution, allowing considerable improvement in stability when needed in stronger winds, without carrying excess weight in light airs. The effect of adding 2,240 pounds of water ballast is the equivalent of having eleven 200-pound crew members perched on your weather rail. In many ways water ballast is preferable to live ballast — it doesn't have to be fed or rested. But the big advantage of the eleven people is their natural instinct to stay on the high side, while water naturally prefers the low side!

Rodger Martin, who has created a number of innovative designs for really fast boats, including *Coyote* and *Duracell*, has again come up with a very modern solution to that rather old set of criteria — how to look good, go fast, and derive maximum enjoyment from sailing. I think *Gray Wolf* is a steppingstone design from which other designs will develop. Not all of them will go in exactly the same direction, but they will use the latest in technology to achieve lightweight construction and enough stability to carry large sail plans. And — who knows? — perhaps some of the boats may be built of that finest of materials, wood.

*You can reach designer Rodger Martin at P.O. Box 242, Newport, RI 02840.*

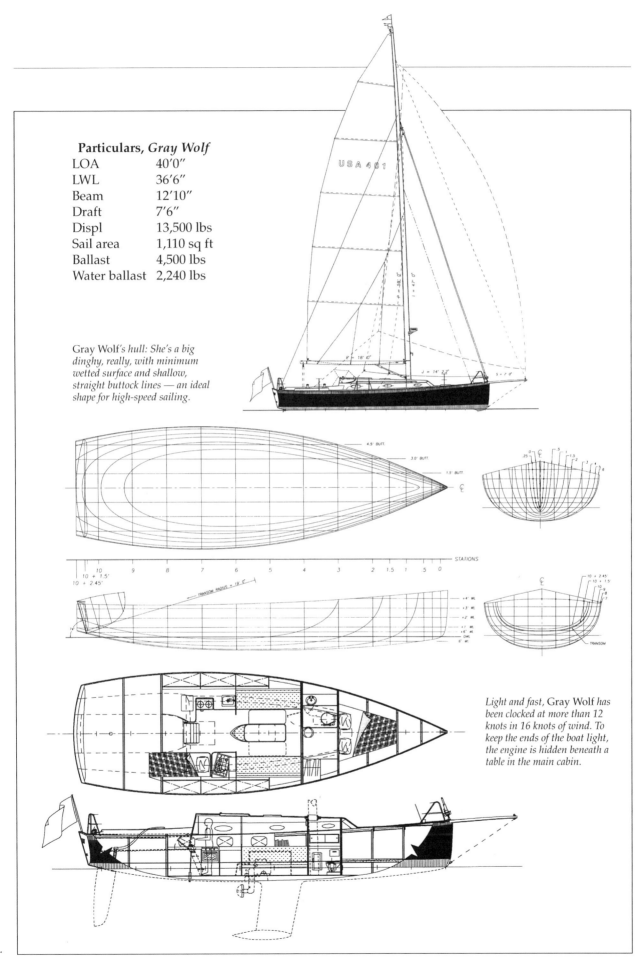

**Particulars, *Gray Wolf***

| | |
|---|---|
| LOA | 40'0" |
| LWL | 36'6" |
| Beam | 12'10" |
| Draft | 7'6" |
| Displ | 13,500 lbs |
| Sail area | 1,110 sq ft |
| Ballast | 4,500 lbs |
| Water ballast | 2,240 lbs |

*Gray Wolf's hull: She's a big dinghy, really, with minimum wetted surface and shallow, straight buttock lines — an ideal shape for high-speed sailing.*

*Light and fast, Gray Wolf has been clocked at more than 12 knots in 16 knots of wind. To keep the ends of the boat light, the engine is hidden beneath a table in the main cabin.*

# XLIV

# A Modern Traditional Yawl

—— Design by Tim Evans ——
Commentary by Joel White

This 40-foot yacht, the St. Lawrence Yawl, drawn by Canadian Tim Evans, represents an example of a growing trend in wooden boat design. She's a new design based on an old boat — but with changes that allow more modern construction techniques, more efficient rigs, larger accommodations, and faster shapes. I don't have any philosophical argument with this idea, and it is always interesting to study the criteria used and the compromises made in drawing such a design.

Most of the designs falling into this category try to exploit some of the so-called advantages of modern technology while retaining the basic character of the original type from which they are derived. Many owners like and want the aesthetic feel of an earlier boat while hoping to sail faster, to have a boat requiring less maintenance, and to be able to cruise in luxury rather than in the cramped quarters found in the original vessels. One can hardly argue with the validity of these aspirations, but achieving them is not always easy.

The original St. Lawrence yawls were common in the 1800s along the shores of the lower St. Lawrence River, where they were used by pilots, fishermen, and rivermen for a variety of waterborne tasks. The boats ranged in size from 25 to 50 feet overall, and they had perfectly plumb stems, overhanging sterns, and gaff-headed yawl rigs. They had cabin trunks, were fully decked, and had varying degrees of interior accommodations.

Alan Evans, the man who commissioned this modern version of the St. Lawrence yawl, stipulated that certain features must be retained for aesthetic reasons — the gaff rig, the plumb stem with bowsprit, the traditional cabin trunk, and the long aft overhang. In other words, he wanted the original above-water profile retained.

The client and designer decided to use modern cold-molded construction techniques, and to have a ballasted fin keel and skeg-mounted rudder. To make the cold-molded hull easy to build, all reverse curve in the sections has been eliminated. Thus, a totally different shape of underwater hull results. The old model had a long, straight keel with a fairly deep, sharp forefoot, but the new hull has a shallow, dinghy-like hull with a shoal, U-shaped forefoot, flat floors, and semi-circular sections throughout her length. To this shallow hull are added a fin keel with ballast at the bottom, and a skeg and rudder aft. The lateral plane of the new boat is concentrated amidships, and she will turn and maneuver more quickly than the original boats could.

The flat-floored hull and the lack of internal framing permitted by the cold-molded construction provide a lot of extra interior volume for accommodations, and the designer has taken full advantage of this when drawing the layout. The new boat has a stateroom with double berth both forward and aft, a roomy toilet room with shower, and a really large galley aft on the port side. Amidships there is a three-sided dinette with a table to port, and a settee/berth and navigation station to starboard. A generous amount of locker space is shown. For auxiliary propulsion, a Perkins 4-108 diesel is mounted under the forward end of the cockpit. The plans I have do not indicate the placement of water and fuel tanks, but I presume they are located under the bunks and cockpit, respectively.

If I look at the accommodation plan in profile and section, all is modern. With a glance at the sail plan, however, I am transported back a century. The gaff-rigged yawl with high topsail, plumb stem, trailboards, long bowsprit, and the slightly sheered cabin trunk with square ends and round ports — these features put me in a nineteenth-century frame of mind.

All the elements of a boat must come together into an integrated whole, and must work in a functional way. In this design, the contrast between aloft and alow is so abrupt that blending all the pieces must have been difficult at best.

**Particulars**
**St. Lawrence Yawl**

| | |
|---|---|
| LOD | 40'10" |
| LWL | 34'0" |
| Beam | 12'6" |
| Draft | 6'0" |
| Displ | 24,000 lbs |
| Sail area | 1,128 sq ft |

# A Fast and Able Cruising Schooner

—————— Design by John G. Alden ——————
Commentary by the editors of *WoodenBoat*

**F**ew rigs charm the hearts of sailors as much as the schooner, and John Alden knew how to design cruising schooners that were fast and able, dry and comfortable. In the first three Malabars Alden was striving not only for these qualities, but also for a simplicity of rig that would allow the small schooners to be singlehanded by none other than himself, for the boats of that name were all designed and built for himself. Yet, it is *Malabar II* that appeals to us most — both in outward appearance, with her single, small deckhouse, and in accommodation, which is simple and symmetrical. The later Malabars were bigger and much more sophisticated boats, which in turn required considerably more money to keep them going.

What the designer wanted was a cruising boat in which he could go anywhere — onshore or offshore — which would stay at sea in almost any weather, and yet which would not be too much to handle alone. Although the Malabars performed remarkably well under racing conditions, Alden wanted anything but a racing machine, with its high angle of heel, and constantly straining hull and rig. *Malabar II*'s generous freeboard and high sheer forward made her as dry a boat as a sailor could want.

As for the rig of *Malabar II*, it was very simple. The sails were sheeted to travelers, making them all self-tending when tacking. Lazyjacks were rigged on all the sails, and the foremast was stepped well forward so as to keep the jib small enough to handle comfortably. John Alden noted that *Malabar II* would beat to weather under foresail alone, and would "move along well in light weather." It was the efficiency of this rig,

in combination with the carefully worked out lines, that made *Malabar II* unique.

The construction of the schooner is stout but simple, worked out, we feel certain, in collaboration with Charles Morse of Thomaston, Maine, her builder. She was said to have endured extremely well, and failed to show any signs of weakening under the stresses of considerable sailing. She embodied, in fact, a remarkable combination of wisdom and experience on the part of both designer and builder. She is still going strong, having had a new hull built for her in the mid-1950s. Shortly afterward she made a successful transatlantic passage.

*Plans for* Malabar II *are available from The WoodenBoat Store, P.O. Box 78, Brooklin, ME 04616; 800–273–7447.*

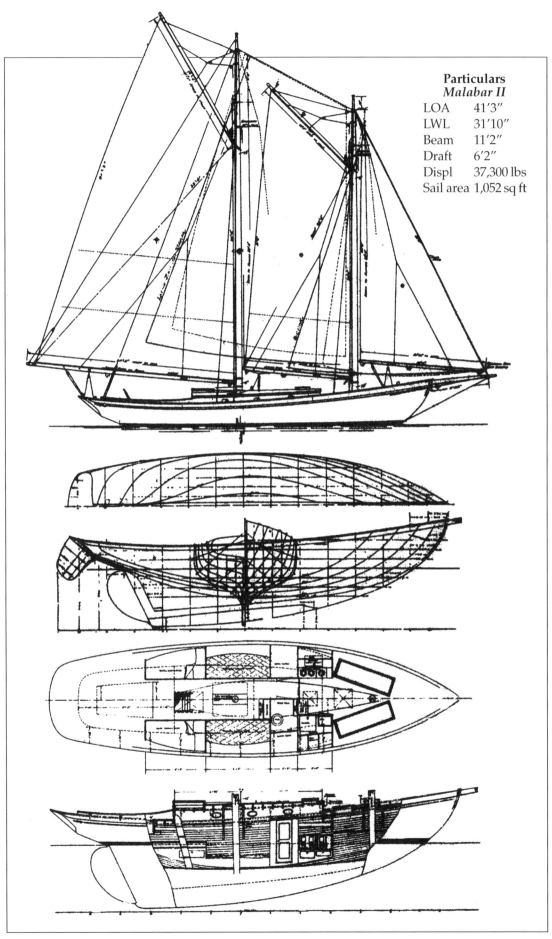

**Particulars**
*Malabar II*

| | |
|---|---|
| LOA | 41'3" |
| LWL | 31'10" |
| Beam | 11'2" |
| Draft | 6'2" |
| Displ | 37,300 lbs |
| Sail area | 1,052 sq ft |

# XLVI

# *A Pilothouse Cutter*

——— Design by Paul Gartside ———
Commentary by Joel White

*I*was immediately intrigued when the plans for this cutter came across my desk — here was a boat that is a bit outside the usual in shape, layout, and construction. Before commencing to write about her, I asked Paul Gartside, her designer, to send me more information about her purpose and conception. His reply confirmed her unusual genesis.

This pilothouse cutter was designed for a couple with two very young children. They live in Bamfield, British Columbia, a lovely isolated town on the west coast of Vancouver Island. A couple of years ago, while cruising in that delightful part of the world, I spent an afternoon exploring the town. Bamfield is divided in two by an inlet from Barkley Sound; the houses on the western edge of this inlet are connected by a wooden sidewalk built on pilings out over the water. It would be difficult to find a more beautiful setting for shoreside habitation.

The realities of life in Bamfield are such that when the children finish elementary school, they must either go to boarding school, or the family must leave to be near a high school. This boat is a solution to the problem — a floating home in which the family can live (in Victoria) during the school terms, then return to Bamfield for the summer. It also provides a vehicle for the owners' future dream of long-distance cruising with the family.

With these facts in mind, the unusual features of this design all fall into place as a cohesive whole. While the hull has a lot of displacement for a 43-foot yacht, almost 31,000 pounds, her moderate beam of 12 feet 3 inches and long waterline of 36 feet 9 inches translate to a displacement/length ratio of only 277, definitely on the moderate side.

The lines plan shows a double-ended hull of great power and grace, with firm, high bilges, a bit of flare in the topside sections both forward and aft, and a lovely overhanging stern. Gartside carefully modeled the stern; my only criticism is that the profile of the stem doesn't quite seem to quite blend with the handsome shape of the stern. There is a whisper of hollow in the waterline forward, and the underwater lines are easy and fair.

The hull has a long keel profile, with a scoop taken out aft at the bottom of the nearly vertical rudderpost. This cutter will track easily and be steady on her helm. Almost 12,000 pounds of lead ballast are bolted to the bottom of the keel, which, combined with the powerful hull, will ensure good stability. The hull is quite full on deck at each end. A liveaboard boat needs a maximum of hull volume and walking-about space, and full ends contribute toward this goal.

Let's look below as we continue to explore the rationale behind this unusual boat. Upon first looking at the arrangement plan, I was struck by the number and variety of lockers and stowage space — just what is needed, whether long-distance cruising or living aboard at the city dock. Starting right forward comes fo'c's'le stowage with chain locker underneath, followed by a large double bunk flanked by big lockers on each side, with a 100-gallon water tank underneath. A 6-inch round port on each side lets in light, air, and a bit of view.

Next aft, in the main saloon, is a settee with padded backrest on each side of the centerline cabin table. A transparent hatch overhead provides extra light and air. Behind the seatbacks are more large lockers and bookshelves. To starboard is a diesel-fired heater, an indispensable item in the Pacific Northwest. Right amidships to port is a well-laid-out galley with a gimbaled stove, an icebox, and a sink close to the centerline. Drawers and lockers abound. Opposite the galley is a large head with the ultimate of yachting luxuries,

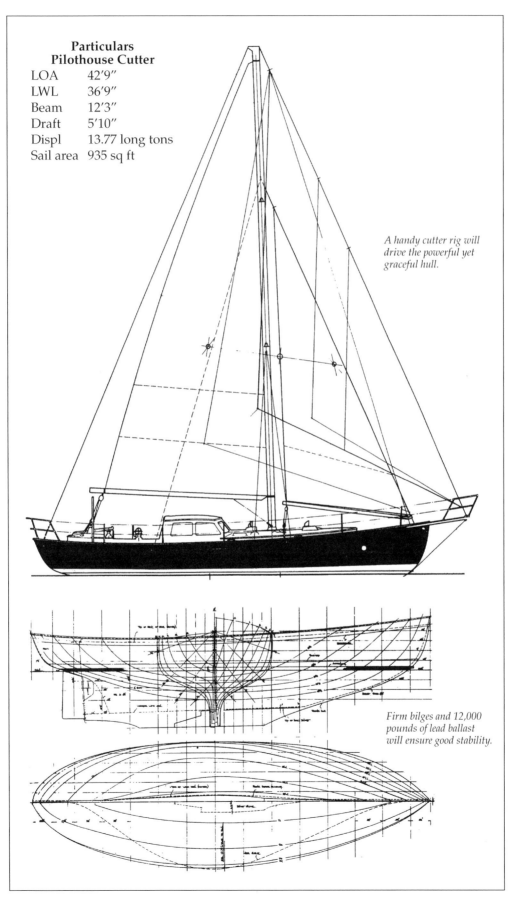

**Particulars**
**Pilothouse Cutter**

| | |
|---|---|
| LOA | 42'9" |
| LWL | 36'9" |
| Beam | 12'3" |
| Draft | 5'10" |
| Displ | 13.77 long tons |
| Sail area | 935 sq ft |

*A handy cutter rig will drive the powerful yet graceful hull.*

*Firm bilges and 12,000 pounds of lead ballast will ensure good stability.*

a combination shower/tub. The oilskin locker is shown outboard in the head, an unusual but sensible placement. Small, transparent hatches over both galley and head will admit light and air as needed.

You will have noticed by now on the plans that this vessel has a center cockpit. Flanking the cockpit to port, just abaft the galley, is a single berth. There is not full headroom here, as the overhead space is made by the seat in the cockpit. But as a sleeping area it should serve well for the occasional guest or extra crew member. The space on the starboard side of the cockpit is given over entirely to a huge cockpit locker, where everything from sails to docklines and fenders can be stowed.

The diesel engine is directly under the cockpit, with access panels on three sides. Under the after end of the cockpit is a space dedicated to batteries, with 50-gallon water tanks outboard on either side. (Thus she will carry 200 gallons of water total, a great boon for a liveaboard craft, especially one with a bathtub!)

The after cabin is only 6 feet 4 inches long, and it contains two berths, four lockers, and its access ladder. This looks to me like the children's sleeping area. The rudder quadrant is beneath the foot of the berths. It would be nice if there had been room for a toilet, but none is shown.

One cannot help noticing the large pilothouse over the forward end of the cockpit, or as Paul Gartside calls it, the fixed dodger. The Pacific Northwest gets its share of rain, mist, and fog, and the dodger helps to make life aboard habitable under such conditions. On a liveaboard boat, it can serve as an extension of the below-decks space. You can poke your head out for a look around without the need for oilskins; a dodger will also keep the crew out of the brutal sun of the tropics, if and when they get there. As Gartside comments, the trick with these dodgers is to get the heights just right for headroom as well as the helmsman's view forward.

Gartside has drawn a cutter-rigged sail plan with a large foretriangle ending on an A-frame bowsprit of moderate length. This type of bowsprit, which is a real platform from which to handle headsails and anchors, is much safer and stronger than the old single-pole type with whisker stays. The large forestaysail is shown fitted with a boom to make it self-tending, although the decision on whether or not to use it is still open. A variety of jib sizes is shown, and the mainsail has two deep reefs. Spars appear to be aluminum. The mast is strongly stayed with double spreaders, which will give confidence to the crew when offshore.

I have saved for last a discussion of the construction of this vessel. Gartside chose glued construction because of the extremely damp climate of that part of the world, a temperate rain forest. The hull is cold-molded, while the cored deck structure will be fiberglassed after construction, an attempt to reduce moisture penetration to zero. The hull skin is four layers of red cedar, the inner three laid diagonally, the outer laid fore-and-aft, with a final thickness of 1¼ inches. After the hull has been righted and the inside surface cleaned up, 2½- inch by 2¼-inch laminated oak frames will be built and fitted to the hull, spaced on average about 20 inches. The backbone is glued up from 2-inch lifts of hard Douglas-fir stock before it is cut to shape and bolted together. All this will produce a tremendously strong hull without seams, and one that is easy to maintain. The hull planking is carried right up to the caprail to form bulwarks. Many of these details are shown on the accompanying construction plan.

The decks are a cored structure of cedar and Airex foam, as is the cabintop. The deck is laid up over beams, while the cabintop has no framing. Wherever hardware or deck fittings are located, the foam is replaced with a solid wood core. The fiberglass covering runs from railcap to railcap, to ensure seamless decks and complete watertightness. The foam-core construction is not only strong and light, but also has good insulating properties that will help to make the boat more comfortable to live aboard.

You will note that the cabin house has round ends both forward and aft, an idea I really like. The cabin sides, at least at the ends, will no doubt be laminated from thin stock to make these rounds. The clean, flowing lines of the cabin sides and coamings running from bow to stern without corners or breaks should produce an exceedingly handsome appearance to the entire deck layout.

This type of fully glued construction has several advantages — no seams and great strength, and it eliminates the need for large, clear pieces of lumber, which are increasingly difficult to find for boatbuilding. Compared to traditional methods, it has the disadvantage of requiring more man-hours of labor in building, and a higher degree of skill. It also requires a certain amount of temperature and humidity control during construction in order to ensure sound glue joints.

I think these plans show how a good designer, with clear, innovative thinking at the drawing board, can meet the special needs of a client. Should I ever return to Bamfield, as I hope to do, I will be looking for a handsome pilothouse cutter tied to one of the docks in that fascinating town. Perhaps I'll even get a tour below.

*Designer Paul Gartside can be reached at 10305 W. Saanich Rd., RR #1, Sidney, BC, V8L 3R9, Canada.*

**Pilothouse Cutter**

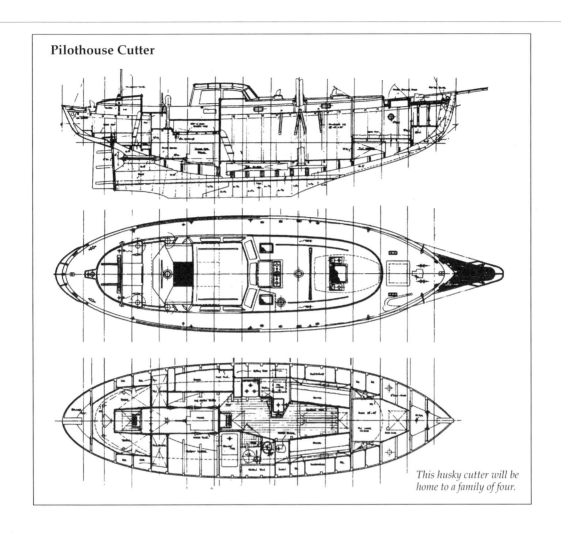

*This husky cutter will be home to a family of four.*

# A Cutter of the Colin Archer Type

Design by Nelson Zimmer

Commentary by the editors of *WoodenBoat*

This 45-foot LOA cutter by Nelson Zimmer is a development of an earlier design of his, a derivative of the Colin Archer type, which in turn was based on traditional Norwegian workboats.

Colin Archer, after whom the type is named, was born and brought up in Norway, though his family was Scottish. He was a boatbuilder and designer from 1865 to his retirement in 1911, specializing in craft that he developed from the centuries-old double-ended Norwegian fishing boats. These mostly open rowing and sailing craft had evolved over the years in response to the unique sea conditions along the Norwegian coast and were noted for their beauty, utility, and seakeeping ability. Archer incorporated these characteristics into his designs for fishing boats, pilot boats, yachts, rescue boats, even polar-exploration ships, adding his own improvements and innovations to achieve superior designs with a deserved reputation for seaworthiness.

Archer's ketch-rigged rescue boats (redningskoites), through their exploits in some of the worst possible sea conditions, became known beyond Norway as an excellent type, and serious cruising yachtsmen became enamored of them for long-distance voyaging. Some of the most notable ocean voyages of the first half of the twentieth century were undertaken in boats that were either converted redningskoites or derivations of the type by contemporary naval architects.

There is still strong interest today in the Colin Archer type, even though by modern standards such boats are relatively slow and unhandy. The appeal is easy to understand, especially for cruising: the boats have the seakeeping ability to go anywhere at any time, are strong and substantial, and are both comfortable sailers and comfortable homes.

This Zimmer design is a refinement of a 42-foot ketch, which was shorter, beamier, much heavier, and consequently a closer approximation of the true Colin Archer type. It was produced for a client who found appeal in the ketch's purpose — comfortable "home-like" accommodations for two, plus two guests — but wanted more length, and much less displacement. The result is a yachtier version of the Colin Archer type, a boat that is handsome, strong, and seaworthy. Contruction is plank on bent frame, rather than the sawn frames of the original Colin Archer redningskoites.

Regarding the rig, Zimmer says: "The long nose pole is bound to appall most of today's sailors, but the sailplan is arranged to set the jib flying on its own luff and set on an outhaul. The alternative, of course, is roller furling or a combination of both."

*For more information about this cutter, write Nelson Zimmer, N.A., 505 Maple St., Marine City, MI 48039.*

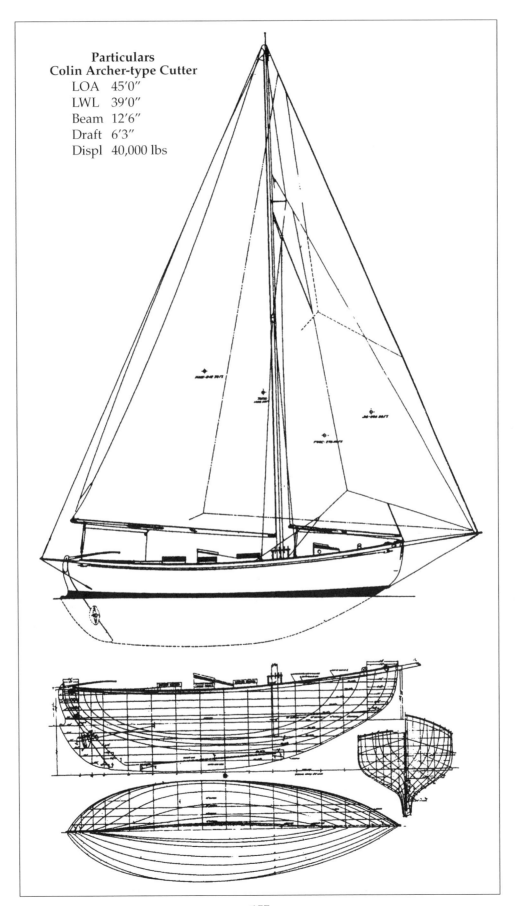

**Particulars**
**Colin Archer-type Cutter**
LOA   45'0"
LWL   39'0"
Beam   12'6"
Draft   6'3"
Displ   40,000 lbs

# A Masthead Yawl

—— Design by Cyrus Hamlin ——
Commentary by Joel White

Wanderer is a design that was ahead of its time when drawn several decades ago, and it remains one whose time has never come, for no boat has ever been built to the plans. Cyrus Hamlin, N.A., drew the design for a prominent sailor as a boat that could race under the CCA (Cruising Club of America) rule with some hope of success, yet be a comfortable, seakindly, safe, and good-looking cruiser. The hull was extensively tank tested, which indicated that the boat should do well racing with her calculated CCA rating. As sometimes happens, plans change and the boat was never built, so her potential as a fast and handy cruiser is still waiting to be proven.

Hidden away behind the conventional sail plan and outboard profile of this 48-foot yawl are a number of quite unconventional features, particularly when it is understood that the design was drawn in 1959. For instance, her displacement is only 23,000 pounds, some 15 percent lighter than my 35-foot LOA cruising cutter. The draft with the centerboard up is only 4 feet 3 inches, which makes most shoal-water cruising areas available to this good-sized yacht. What makes the light displacement of this design possible is her construction, which is light yet extremely strong.

Cy Hamlin and Farnham Butler started developing light-displacement cruising boats using glued strip-planked cedar construction back in the 1950s, and perfected the system for the line of Controversys and Amphibi-Cons built and marketed by Mt. Desert Yacht Yard. As an independent naval architect, Cy continued to use and develop the glued-strip construction with laminated backbone members, which are almost a trademark of his boats. Continuous contact with some of his designs over a period of years, as both a builder and a maintainer, has convinced me that the system works, and works well. The boats are strong and light, and require less maintenance than those of more conventional plank-on-frame construction.

Let's examine in more detail the unusual features of this design. Her construction, which can only be viewed as cold-molded, calls for 1¼-inch by 1¼-inch glued-strip cedar planking (resorcinol-glued with bronze Anchorfast edge-nailing), covered on the outside with a fore-and-aft layer of ⁵⁄₁₆-inch by 2-inch Honduras mahogany strips, glued and nailed to the cedar. There are no sawn or bent frames, but rather plywood bulkheads with oak and mahogany margin pieces to which the planking is glued and screwed. All interior joinerwork — shelves, bunk tops, cabinets, counters, etc. — is to be considered structural, and is securely glued and fastened to the planking as stiffening members. The backbone is of laminated oak, which makes a virtually one-piece centerline structure to which all planking and floor timbers are glued. The result is a monocoque hull of great strength, rigidity, and watertightness. This construction is much less labor-intensive than today's typical cold-molded construction that often calls for four to six layers of veneer planking, plus a substructure of longitudinal stringers. The interior of this hull is smooth and clear between bulkheads, and thus easier to keep dry and clean. Cy writes that the only change he would make in the construction today is to build the centerboard trunk of fiberglass, rather than of laminated wood as shown.

Perhaps the most unusual — and best — aspect of this design, however, is the way in which the interior volume of the hull is used to provide comfortable quarters for living and sailing. Look at the cockpit — it's huge. More than one-third of the length of the boat is given over to the cockpit and after deck.

The cockpit has a centerline island that contains the worm gear steering unit and the engine exhaust

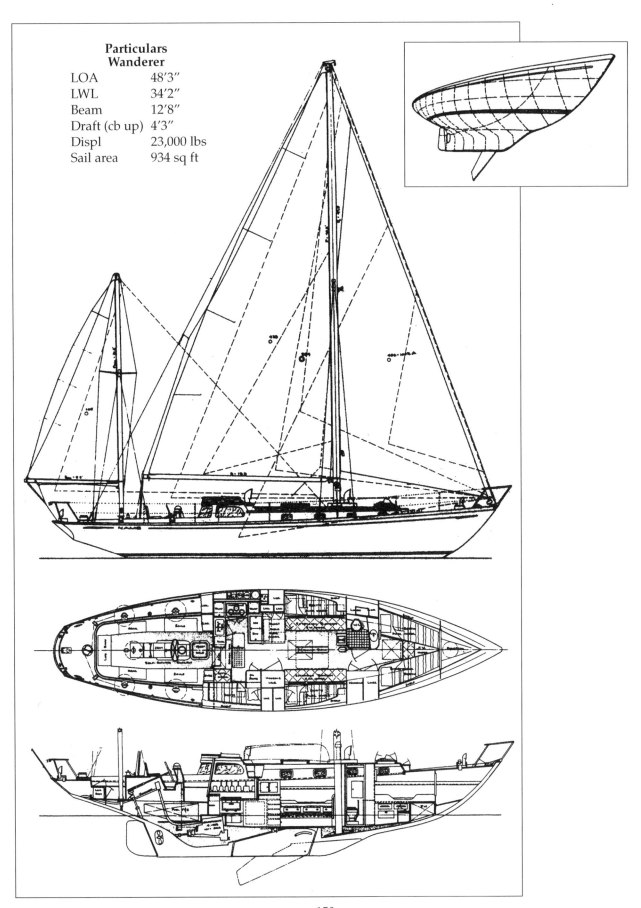

**Particulars**
**Wanderer**
LOA        48'3"
LWL        34'2"
Beam       12'8"
Draft (cb up)  4'3"
Displ      23,000 lbs
Sail area  934 sq ft

system, and provides a binnacle for the compass and engine controls. There is a comfortable seat with footrests for the helmsman; the mainsheet traveler and winch are aft of the helmsman. The steering seat is raised so forward vision is excellent, and the helmsman is removed from the hurly-burly of the racing crew at the winches. Yet everything needed to sail the boat is near at hand. A man and wife could easily handle the boat.

Indeed, Wanderer was designed for just that. There is a coffee-grinder winch located on the after deck, plus a pair of sheet winches on each side of the cockpit coaming. The life raft has its own locker under the seat across the after end of the cockpit. The doghouse roof extends aft over the forward cockpit seats, giving protection from wind and weather, and the slanted main bulkhead provides a comfortable backrest. I can't imagine a nicer spot to enjoy the scenery, or a good book, than the forward corner of this cockpit, protected by the doghouse roof and side glass, yet available instantly to trim a sheet or spot a buoy. Because of the center island, however, this giant cockpit conforms to CCA volume requirements for offshore boats.

One might think that Cy Hamlin had given away too much of the boat to the cockpit, and that the below-deck accommodations would suffer as a consequence. Yet it would be hard to improve upon the cabin arrangement shown. Spaciousness is the theme, with comfort for a moderate-sized cruising crew, and enough capacity to accommodate a larger gang for racing. There are five fixed berths, plus two extension transoms. The layout has the great virtue of considerable symmetry about the centerline — a pair of V-berths forward, a matched pair of pilot berths, and extension transoms amidships.

There is an incredible amount of walking-around floor space. The cabin sole is all on one level, which is certainly preferable to the split-level ranch-style arrangements often seen with doghouses. The cook has a truly bounteous U-shaped galley to port, clear of fore-and-aft traffic to and from the cockpit. The forward leg of the U is a large icebox (which today would undoubtedly be a freezer-refrigerator), the after leg is a counter with double sink, with drawers underneath, while the base of the U is formed by the gimbaled stove on the outboard side. Across from the galley, there is an ample quarter berth, an oilskin locker, and a seat.

A large chart table to port and a hanging locker to starboard separate the galley area from the main saloon amidships. The navigator is given lots of space, both flat surface for chart work and stowage for the necessary gear and equipment. My only complaint about the accommodations is that the toilet faces athwartships — a fore-and-aft orientation is preferable on a boat headed offshore. Hamlin gives credit

to the owner for much of the basic arrangement, which was based on several previous boats. Both parties deserve high marks on the layout.

A Graymarine 4-162 gasoline engine of 63 horsepower is specified. This tucks away nicely under a removable box that forms the first step up to the cockpit. The access to the engine for service and repairs should be excellent — more than can be said of the engine access on many modern boats, where it is often difficult to even get a glimpse of the engine, let alone work on it. Fifty-six gallons of gasoline are contained in two tall, narrow tanks under the cockpit. This arrangement allows for a big stowage lazarette in between the tanks, reached through a manhole in the cockpit floor forward of the helmsman's seat. There are large sail and gear lockers under the cockpit seats on each side.

The Wanderer is rigged as a conventional masthead yawl. Because of her light displacement, the rig is small for her length — only 934 square feet. Yet her sail-area-to-displacement of 18.49 predicts good performance. The aspect ratio of the rig is quite low; to my eyes she would look better with taller spars and shorter booms. The drawback to such a change is a slightly higher center of effort, which would affect her stability, so heightening the aspect ratio would have to be done carefully and the stability recalculated. But the taller rig would certainly improve the overall appearance of the boat.

The lines are not shown, although I have a perspective drawing showing a bow view of the hull. The shape is pretty much what you would expect — cutaway forefoot, long, straight keel with a narrow centerboard dropping through the ballast keel, and the rudder hung on the after end. There is a total of 14 feet of overhang in the bow and the counter stern, giving her a waterline length of 34 feet 2 inches.

As you have gathered by now, I like this design a lot. It offers truly outstanding accommodations and cockpit comfort, and excellent sailing qualities in a boat of considerable length, but very modest weight. Since construction costs vary almost directly with displacement, this design when built should prove to be a lot of boat for the money.

Cy Hamlin writes: "It always disappointed me that Wanderer was never built. She was one of those salubrious designs when everything comes together nicely; not only did no large problems arise, but when the design was completed, I was well satisfied with the results. Usually, by the time I have finished a design, I have a long list of ways in which I would improve it 'next time.' This has not happened with this design."

Perhaps someday the first Wanderer will slip into Center Harbor at sunset. The owners, friendly folk, will invite me aboard, and sitting below at the cabin table, I will look around and it will all be just as I imagine it — the feeling of space and comfort, soft highlights glinting off the varnished trim, the combination of aromas that emanate from the interior of a choice wooden vessel — cedar, teak, and tar, supper and rum,

and the accumulated wind and sunshine of a good day's run.

*Further inquiries about Wanderer should be addressed to: Cyrus Hamlin, N.A., Ocean Research Corp., P.O. Box 67, Kennebunk, ME 04043.*

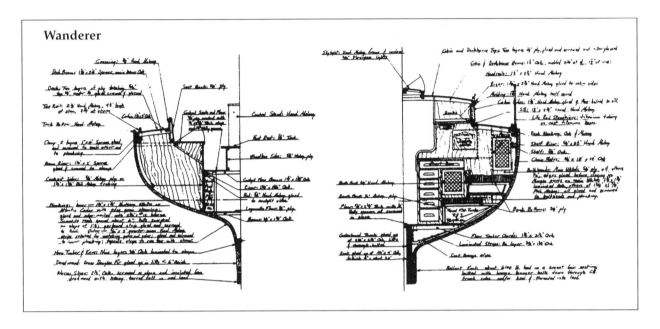

**Wanderer**

# A Shoal-Draft Ketch

Design by Craig V. Walters ————
Commentary by Joel White

This 49-foot ketch is an interesting blend of old ideas and modern materials and technology. The old ideas were formulated nearly a century ago for developing seaworthy, shoal-draft cruising boats. Modern materials and technology help make the concept workable.

This design is frankly based on Commodore Munroe's famous *Presto* design, but a number of recent developments have been incorporated — both in materials and engineering — that simply were not available to Munroe. The idea of lightweight but strong hull construction using thin skins and a core material had not been thought of in Munroe's time, nor were heavily ballasted swing keels in general use when *Presto* was built.

The lightweight hull and the lowered center of gravity, produced by dropping 2,500 pounds of weighted centerboard, combine to give greatly improved stability in this boat as compared to *Presto*, and this allows the rather lofty, large sail plan shown. *Presto's* low gaff-ketch rig was dictated by her modest stability and by the fact that she had none of today's sophisticated equipment that adds so much to the convenience and safety of our present-day yachts — auxiliary engines, electronic navigational aids, or VHF radio. When *Presto* put to sea, she was there for better or worse, until the gods of the weather carried her to her destination. There was little chance to turn and run away, or call for help.

The owner's objectives for this shoal-draft ketch were to produce: a cruising yacht, initially for use along the eastern U.S. coastline, and later for extended offshore passages; economy of construction; low maintenance costs; and charter accommodations for four guests and two crew.

*Salt*, as this vessel is called, has much in common with *Presto*. She is about the same size and draft; both

have ketch rigs, though the rig on *Salt* is marconi and greater in height and sail area. Those familiar with Commodore Munroe's work will remember that *Presto's* hull was plumb-stemmed, with low, slack bilges and considerable flare to the topsides. Her initial stability would have been low, but would have increased as she heeled and the topsides immersed. Walters has used higher and harder bilges on his design, with a sort of low-slung pot belly amidships in the area of the ballasted centerboard and 3,100 pounds fixed ballast. Notice how the profile of the hull at the centerline dips sharply to the low point amidships, thus concentrating displacement there, while keeping the ballast as low as possible. Walters writes that the original lines plan had a tumblehome bow and longer waterline, but this was changed to a shorter waterline with longer overhangs, thus reducing wetted surface for light-air speed. Walters also states that the longer overhangs improve the boat's appearance.

I think the boat looks fine in the plans, and photographs bear this out. I do think the bow might have been more handsome without the modern stem profile with a knuckle just above the waterline. I like the old spoon-bow shape when it is well drawn and don't understand why it is so seldom seen anymore. The forward sections are quite U-shaped. Aft, the sections are more flattened as they fair into the rather large stern.

When the centerboard/drop keel (I don't know which term to use) is raised, the deepest point on the hull is the small skeg that protects the propeller and the shaft. The rudder is a couple of inches shoaler than this — I suppose, on the theory that it is better that the skeg take the ground than the rudder. The rudder is interesting in that it has an end plate on the lower edge, and has a small balance forward of the vertical post, even

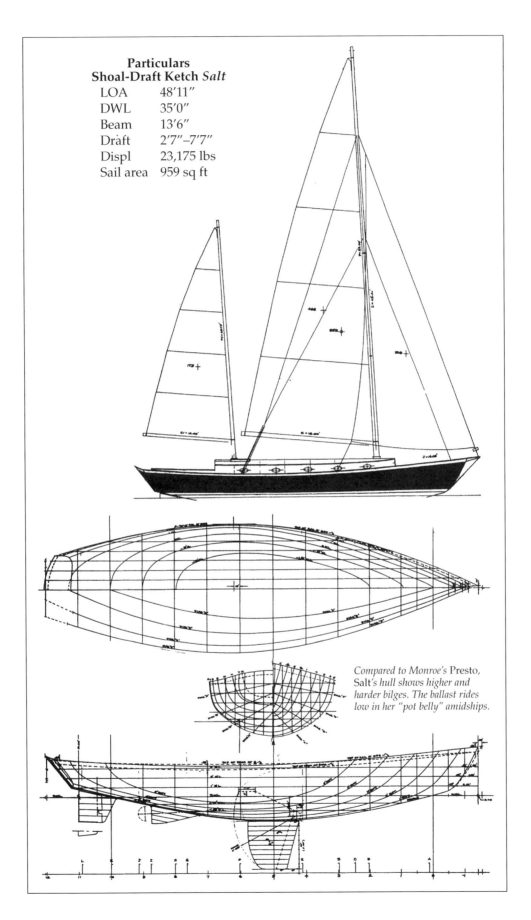

**Particulars**
**Shoal-Draft Ketch** *Salt*

| | |
|---|---|
| LOA | 48'11" |
| DWL | 35'0" |
| Beam | 13'6" |
| Draft | 2'7"–7'7" |
| Displ | 23,175 lbs |
| Sail area | 959 sq ft |

*Compared to Monroe's Presto, Salt's hull shows higher and harder bilges. The ballast rides low in her "pot belly" amidships.*

though the whole rudder is behind a fixed skeg. It is not clear from the plans exactly how the geometry of this works. Shallow rudders suffer from problems of loss of "bite," and the end plate is one way to reduce rudder ventilation and the resultant loss of control.

While we are on the subject of appendages, let's have a look at the centerboard. Its shape is most interesting, for when lowered, the exposed portion looks very much like a modern fin keel — with its raked, straight leading edge, straight horizontal bottom, and an elliptical trailing edge. The large notch in the back edge is designed to fill the entire centerboard slot when the board is fully down. If the board is raised just a little, there will be a big open portion of the slot that will ·cause considerable drag. But raise the board some more, until it is about half retracted, and it again fills the slot nicely. It appears that the board was designed to have two working positions — one fully down, and the other half up, for sailing in shallow waters where draft needs to be as little as possible (but where we still need to have enough fin down to reduce leeway, and enough ballast down to maintain good stability). The best way to see this is to make an outline of the centerboard shape on tracing paper, cut it out, then rotate it on the plan, using a pin as the pivot.

The forward edge of the centerboard (shall we settle on that name rather than drop keel?) consists of a 1,340-pound lead casting bolted to a steel reinforcing frame inside the glass-and-epoxy board. The complete board weighs about 2,500 pounds. The board is raised and lowered with a block-and-tackle arrangement using ½-inch Dacron braid led to a winch. When up, the board is flush with the bottom of the hull, and it provides an adjunct to the fixed inside ballast, also located at the lowest point of the hull. When the board is lowered, its center of gravity drops about 3½ feet. Making a couple of simple assumptions, I estimate that this will lower the center of gravity of the whole boat as much as 5 inches, which will have a very positive effect on stability. With the board fully raised, the boat will float in less than 3 feet of water. There are several wonderful cruising grounds (the Bahamas is one of them) where really shoal draft makes the difference between having fun, or being aground much of the time.

The sail plan shows a tall ketch rig on unstayed spars, with fully battened sails on both the main and the mizzen. The fractional roller jib has a small overlap. There were some initial problems with the unstayed spars, and double diamond stays later were added to the mainmast, along with an intermediate headstay and backstays. The sail plan is a tall one for so shoal a boat, and her sail area of 959 square feet is ample in relation to the designed displacement of 23,715 pounds. (This works out to a sail area/displacement ratio of 18.5 — quite respectable.) That the boat can carry such a generous sail plan indicates the efficacy of a heavily ballasted centerboard in providing stability. The minimum amount of standing rigging helps fulfill the objective of low construction and maintenance costs.

A look at the plans show us a very long cabin trunk (more than 25 feet) in relation to the overall length of the boat. The cabin ends 3 feet aft of the mizzenmast, and the companionway is by necessity offset, to starboard in this case. The forward end of the cabin is rounded, reminiscent of *Presto*.

The arrangement below is most interesting, being geared around that dominant presence, the centerboard trunk. This trunk extends about 8 feet fore-and-aft, and rises from the keel to the cabin overhead. The auxiliary engine, a Westerbeke 40, is located just aft of the trunk. It is enclosed in a large box, which forms part of the galley counter and contains the double sink. The propeller shaft is skewed off the centerline slightly to allow the shaft to be removed without hitting the rudder. The remainder of the galley is located to starboard, with a three-burner stove and refrigerator across from the engine box, and lockers under the side deck. Opposite the galley on the port side is a small dinette with more lockers outboard. The boat has two heads (always a good idea for a charter boat), the after one being tucked into the end of the cabin trunk behind the mizzenmast. Within this head there are a large hanging locker, which I expect will be used for oilskin stowage, more lockers, and an access door leading to the space under the cockpit.

Amidships is an upper and lower berth unit on either side of the centerboard trunk. A portion of the upper bunk hinges down to make a nice backrest for comfortable seating during the day. The centerboard trunk rising between these berths gives a degree of privacy between the port and the starboard berths, and I expect that these berths will be used by guests when the boat is on charter.

Moving forward again, we find the second head located to port, with two doors providing access from either forward or aft. Opposite, to starboard, is a large workbench with storage for tools. The whole forward end of the cabin can be closed off with a door on the starboard side. There is a dandy double berth in the bow, where V-berths are more usually found. Between the double berth and the head, there is a large hanging locker on each side and more lockers with a cushioned seat on either side of the mast. This private stateroom, with such ample storage space, is surely for the captain — a nice sanctuary clear of the general living and dining area.

I like the layout of this boat. The after part, I believe, will have a spacious feeling to it, despite the tall centerboard trunk, while the forward quarters are unusually good for a boat this size, and should allow the owner/captain to live aboard in comfort and reasonable privacy.

Walters's description of the construction methods is as follows: "To meet objectives for a yacht with considerable strength, a hybrid composite was developed. The hull laminate has a core of Baltek DuraKore (balsa) with double-diagonal skins (Douglas-fir and Sitka spruce) and biaxial fiberglass — all are set in WEST System Brand epoxies. The topsides are just over 2 inches in thickness yet weigh less than 3 pounds per square foot. Deck and cabin construction, and much of the interior joinery, are of Baltek Decolite panel. Scantlings were designed to meet American Bureau of Shipping rules."

I expect that *Presto*'s plank-on-frame construction weighed closer to 6 pounds per square foot. Every pound saved in hull construction is a pound that can be added in low-down ballast, with the end result being enough stability to stand up to the sail plan. It is not generally recognized, but the greatly improved stability of modern yachts is the single biggest advance made possible by technology and new lightweight materials.

Shoal draft adds a whole other dimension to a cruising boat's versatility. *Salt* can float in 3 feet of water, and she has the ability to explore areas where other boats cannot penetrate. Commodore Munroe firmly believed that it was possible to design a seaworthy and safe cruising boat of minimum draft. Walters appears to have followed Munroe's lead and, by the use of new materials and techniques, to have achieved a most interesting modern *Presto*.

*Designer Craig V. Walters can be reached at 17 Palmer Ln., Riverside, CT 06878.*

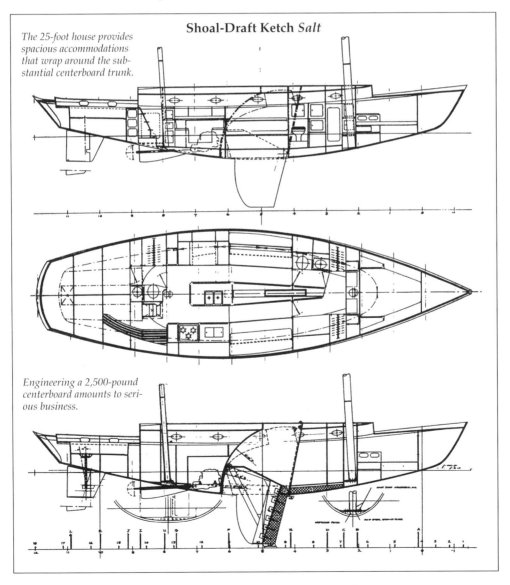

**Shoal-Draft Ketch *Salt***

*The 25-foot house provides spacious accommodations that wrap around the substantial centerboard trunk.*

*Engineering a 2,500-pound centerboard amounts to serious business.*

# A Big, Fast, Modern Cutter

—————— Design by Bruce King ——————
Commentary by Joel White

*Saskianna* is a 50-foot LOD auxiliary cutter, designed by Bruce King for an overseas client. Photographs show her to be big, fast, and modern.

I can hear you saying, "Isn't she a modern boat that was designed to look traditional?" I don't think so. She looks fine — her hull appeals to me and, I expect, to many others. But I wouldn't describe her as traditional. Certainly she has many features that have appeared on older designs — designs that are now labeled "traditional." She has a clipper bow, trailboards, a bowsprit, an elliptical stern with a raised taffrail, and a pleasant conventional sheer. These features are nicely blended together and produce a harmonious and attractive appearance. But traditional? The sheer is straighter and higher than it would have been 50 years ago, the clipper bow has less curve to it, and the bowsprit is shorter than the traditional length. *Saskianna* is a modern design that happens to have a clipper bow with a bowsprit and a conventional sheer with a taffrail.

There are reasons for using traditional elements in this design. You will notice that the boat has a center cockpit, something not found on older traditional designs. King explains that, while the layout below requires having the center cockpit, he is not happy with the idea visually. The taffrail masks the appearance of the center cockpit. The rounded stern and taffrail look better in conjunction with a clipper bow than with a typical modern straight-raked stem. That is the reason for having the clipper bow, but a clipper bow without a bowsprit seems unfinished or incomplete. Add a bowsprit for appearance, and you get a great place to house the anchor. The roller-furling drum can be mounted out of the way, and the furling line can be led aft without tripping up the foredeck crew.

All these "traditional" features have real reasons for being there — not just that King was trying to make the boat look like an L. Francis Herreshoff design. King can design good-looking boats on his own, without having to imitate anyone.

The arrangement below can only be described as sumptuous. The large after cabin is entirely given over to the owner's stateroom, containing a double bunk and a single, and an unusual head layout. The toilet and shower are to starboard in their own enclosure while to port is a large vanity with washbowl and seat. There is room for a good-sized hanging locker. A companionway ladder leads up to the afterdeck, and you can get forward by going through the engineroom, which is under the center cockpit.

Entrance to the forward cabin is by ladder down from the cockpit. At the foot of the ladder, the galley is to starboard — entirely out of the flow of traffic. It has a four-burner stove outboard, and a large counter aft, with a refrigerator underneath. A smaller counter forward contains a double sink and a trash bin. There appears to be a considerable amount of storage space in lockers above and behind the stove and the refrigerator.

On the port side, opposite the galley, there is a wet locker and a navigator's desk with a seat; electronics and a bookshelf are readily at hand. Moving forward, to starboard, you'll find a large, U-shaped settee with a table opposite a big, cushioned lounge area. I am not sure whether or not to call the latter a bunk; I imagine that it will be used for leisure activities such as reading, but it is certainly big enough to sleep one or two when needed.

Going forward again we come to a two-bunk stateroom that houses upper and lower bunks to port, and a head to starboard. Forward of the head, there is a

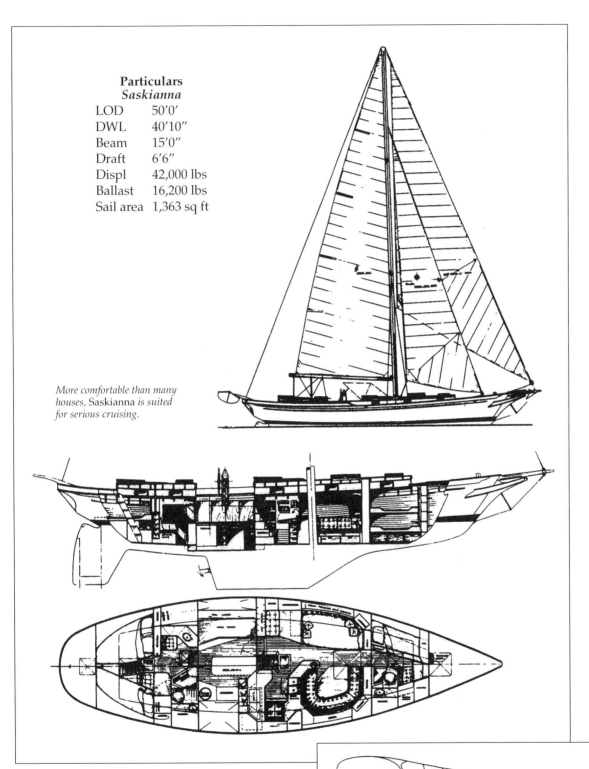

**Particulars**
*Saskianna*

| | |
|---|---|
| LOD | 50'0" |
| DWL | 40'10" |
| Beam | 15'0" |
| Draft | 6'6" |
| Displ | 42,000 lbs |
| Ballast | 16,200 lbs |
| Sail area | 1,363 sq ft |

*More comfortable than many houses,* Saskianna *is suited for serious cruising.*

*King planned to give* Saskianna *twin bilge keels, but tests at the Davidson Laboratory predicted disappointing windward ability (a 12 percent reduction of VMG in moderate wind). The designer decided on a shoal fin with a substantial flat to its bottom, which permits the boat "to sit safely on her keel with lateral support only."*

seat and a vanity, with lockers and hanging lockers to port and starboard. A watertight bulkhead forms the forward end of the cabin, and a hatch in the forward deck and some bulkhead steps give access to the large forepeak.

Between the two cabins, under the center cockpit, a large engineroom contains a Volvo MD-40A main engine that drives a Hundsted variable-pitch three-blade propeller through a V-drive. On the starboard side of the engineroom there is a generator set and a hot-water heater, while to port is the passageway between cabins. Outboard of the passageway is a large workbench and good stowage for tools and spare parts.

While the arrangement is typical of a center-cockpit layout, it is unusually well done. It would certainly be livable for coastal cruising, providing excellent privacy for two couples. The only problem I see with the layout for offshore sailing is that there are no single berths amidships, where there is the least motion. Wide double bunks can be a problem when it is rough, because it is difficult to wedge oneself in tightly enough to prevent rolling around. The forward ends of the bunks in the after cabin splay outboard because of the shape of the hull. When the boat is heeled over, the forward end of the leeward bunk will be lower than the after ends, and you'll have to sleep head-aft.

The perspective lines drawing indicates that the hull is of modern configuration, having full sections without much deadrise, and a long fin keel. The rudder and its skeg are well aft, with the rudderpost located right at the after end of the waterline. The area of the rudder and skeg is quite large, which should give good control and directional stability, even in rough conditions.

*Saskianna* was cold-molded using epoxy and four layers of planking. The inner layer is ⅝-inch Alaska yellow cedar running fore-and-aft, followed by two diagonal layers of ¼-inch Maine cedar. The outer layer is ⅜-inch Honduras mahogany, again running fore-and-aft. The deck is of ⅝-inch sprung teak over a plywood-and-foam subdeck.

A look at the sail plan shows us a tall, modern cutter rig with a very large foretriangle and a relatively small mainsail. This rig is efficient and powerful, yet not too difficult to handle with a small crew. I think the appearance of the rig suits the hull very well, and it should provide plenty of horsepower to move her under all conditions. Many boats of this size are ketch-rigged, but the added weight and windage of another spar and its rigging, plus the reduced efficiency of the divided rig, are not always good tradeoffs for the benefit of having smaller sails to handle. However, I am a cutter man of long standing, and others may think differently.

*Saskianna* is large enough to provide a truly comfortable home afloat for extended periods of time. Self-sufficient, seaworthy, and capable of fast passages, she should make an ideal cruiser for those who want — and can afford — to travel first class.

*Inquiries should be directed to the designer, Bruce King, P.O. Box 599, Newcastle, ME 04553.*

# A Modified Pungy

—— Design by Bruce Northrup ——
Commentary by Joel White

Chesapeake Bay is the source for many unusual names used to differentiate boat types. Bugeye, skipjack, tuck-up, deadrise, pungy — all of these names come to us from the Chesapeake.

Here is a yacht of some size whose design is based on the Chesapeake pungy schooners. Bruce Northrup, who designed her, indicates that she is not intended to be a faithful reproduction of a pungy, but rather a cruising vessel derived from the pungies, modified to suit special conditions.

Northrup, by the way, is no newcomer to large schooners. A few years back, he had Pete Culler design the 54-foot Baltimore clipper schooner *Lizard King*, and proceeded to build her on the West Coast. When I opened the package of plans from Northrup for this schooner, I was startled by the similarity to Culler's drafting style and design philosophy. It is good to have someone come along to carry on Captain Pete's ideas.

If you haven't been reading up on pungies lately, you may be saying, "What is a pungy, exactly?" Well, it isn't anything, exactly. Some pungies were deep models, with lots of drag to the keel, known as "he-pungies." Some were centerboarders, known as "she-pungies." (The "he" and "she" definitions are from John Burke.) The characteristics that all pungies seem to have are fine ends compared to the usual bulky schooner models of the 1800s: low freeboard, lots of beam, lack of interior volume caused by the sharp model, and a reputation for speed under sail that spread far beyond Chesapeake Bay.

Maritime historian Howard I. Chapelle says that the pungy was the last Baltimore clipper type built on the Bay, and that they finally disappeared about 1940. He also states that by 1850, many shoal Chesapeake schooners had been bought by New Englanders for use in various fishing and coastal trade ventures. The speed of these boats was a big attraction, but their low freeboard and lack of hull depth tended to make them wet in a sea, and the shoal-draft fishing schooners proved to be unsafe in the winter fisheries of the North Atlantic. But the type was very popular for vessels that needed to make quick passages coastwise, where a large carrying capacity was not necessary.

Keeping in mind this brief look at the origins of the pungy, let's examine Bruce Northrup's schooner and how the pungy was used for inspiration.

This schooner, named *Ruben de Cloux*, has a length on deck of about 53 feet and a waterline length of 47 feet. Beam is nearly 16 feet. This is a big schooner-yacht by present-day standards. The rig is very traditional, with a main topmast, and a topsail and a single jib. The jib, 326 square feet in area, is loose-footed, with a 12-foot club. ("Club" is an apt name for this spar when attached to such a sail. I have always suspected that these old-fashioned schooners had extra-tall bitts so that one could take cover by lying on the deck beneath their protection when things weren't going well on the foredeck.)

The lines plan shows that Northrup has drawn a hull with rather slack bilges, fine ends, and nice, easy buttock lines. The hull has the double stern, which was once quite common, with the rudder coming through its lower section. She also has the long Chesapeake Bay billethead with large trailboards. The midsection shows much deadrise without any reverse in the garboard area. Displacement is given at 55,510 pounds, about normal for a schooner of this size. This works out to a displacement/length ratio of 241 — a very moderate displacement for a boat of this type.

Northrup has this to say about pungies: "They can be dainty and pretty in appearance...their low freeboard, elaborate head, and wide, round tuck transom make them receptive to much decoration and elaborate paint schemes. Reducing some of the more extreme hull characteristics, while retaining the pungy form, would, I reasoned, result in a handy sea boat, albeit a bit wet, and capable of fast passages under sail in some degree of comfort. To this end, she is a bit deeper and less beamy than the classic pungy. I've kept the flared topsides and shallow run of the original, while fining the bow down somewhat to move the center of buoyancy aft, in keeping with more modern ideas of displacement distribution."

The fine ends, low freeboard, and heavy sawn-frame construction all conspire against there being much usable interior space, considering the size of the vessel. The space below is wide but not very high. The cabin sole has to be high enough to allow room below it for the inside ballast; standing headroom is achieved only under the rather high houses.

The arrangement of the interior is unusual and, I think, quite good, making the most of the space available. Under the 15-foot cabin trunk, there are three bunks to port and what appears to be a small dressing room. To starboard in the after cabin is a large chart table with stowage under, an electronics area, with batteries under, and a large hanging locker. Right in the middle is the engine, a Lugger 4-276 diesel of 77 horsepower. The forward cabin contains a big galley to port, 72-gallon freshwater tanks outboard on each side, and a good-sized stateroom with lockers, drawers, and a double bunk, also to port. To starboard is a large toilet room.

The space amidships under the flush deck between the two houses has only 4 feet of headroom. This is used rather nicely as a sleeping and dining area by arranging for low seating (in this case, a bunk to port and a transom seat to starboard), on either side of a centerline table. Outboard is a pilot berth each side. (We used a similar arrangement on a small flush-decked ketch a few years back, and it proved to be very satisfactory.) Way forward, there is a separate hatch and ladder leading to a forepeak and paint locker.

I get a bunk count of seven, one of which could serve as a double. Except for the toilet room and the forepeak, *Ruben de Cloux* is open from end to end along the centerline, which I think gives a feeling of space and size that is lost when interiors are cut up into compartments.

*Ruben de Cloux*'s construction is typical of double sawn-frame practice for a heavy vessel. Floors and lower futtocks are built of 4-inch stock; upper futtocks, 3-inch. Frame spacing is 16 inches. Planking is 1¾ inches thick; garboards and wale strakes are 2¼ inches; the ceiling is 1¼ inches. Fastenings are galvanized iron drifts, bolts, and nails as directed. Her deck frame has 5¼-inch by 5-inch heavy beams, and 2¾-inch by 5-inch light beams. The house sides are 2½ inches. Because she was built on the West Coast, by Siletz Boat Works in Kernville, Oregon, she is mostly of Douglas-fir. Rudderpost, bitts, and cabin trim are hardwood. Spars are Sitka spruce.

Lurking under the calm exterior of many sensible modern sailors lies a primal urge to own a schooner. What is it about schooners that is so enticing? Is it the backwards time warp to an earlier era that makes the traditional rig so appealing? Is it contempt for the advance of modern technology that tempts us to hang great sheets of canvas to the winds, held up by solid spruce sticks and a flurry of wire, deadeyes, lanyards, and a bit of chain and hemp?

Every sailor knows that when he sails his schooner into a harbor, rounds up, and drops anchor, all eyes will be on him. There is a grace and jauntiness built into a well-proportioned schooner that perhaps cannot be found to such a degree in any other craft.

Bruce Northrup, commenting on this type of vessel, may have hit upon the answer when he said, "The first cost, of course, is pretty high, and schooners are beyond the capability of all but the most experienced and determined home builders. Perhaps this just-out-of-reach quality is what makes them so attractive."

*Inquiries should be directed to the designer, Bruce Northrup, 224110 N.W. Gilkison, Scappoose, OR 97056.*

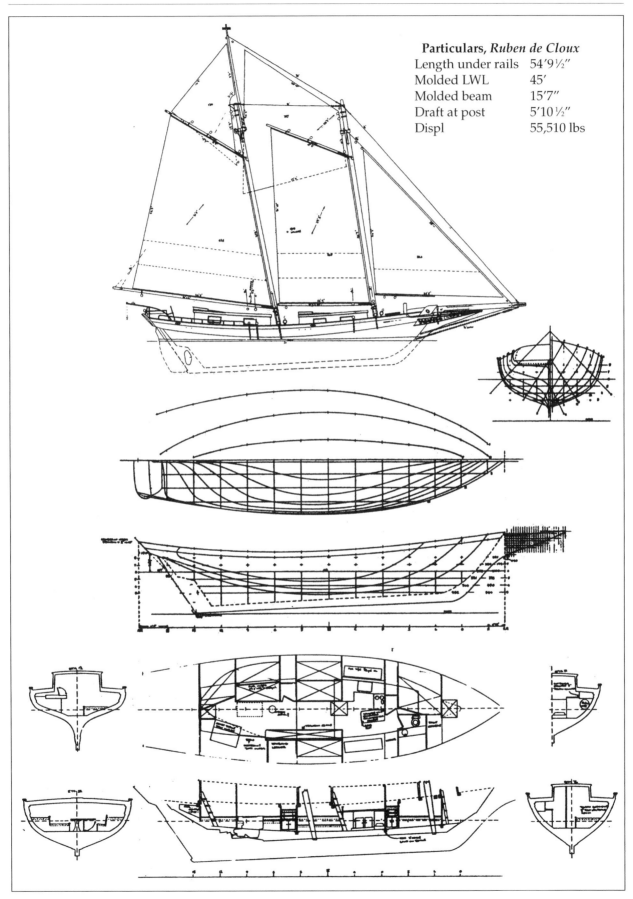

**Particulars,** *Ruben de Cloux*
Length under rails   54′9½″
Molded LWL   45′
Molded beam   15′7″
Draft at post   5′10½″
Displ   55,510 lbs

# A Heavy Cogge Ketch

Design by William Garden
Commentary by Joel White

Writing in *Yachting* magazine during the mid-1920s, Douglas P. Urry and F. Wavell Urry described three boats of their design called cogge ketches. These articles elicited a fair amount of interest among offshore cruising sailors, for the boats were handsome and oozed romance. All three boats (42 feet, 50 feet, and 65 feet LOA) had round spoon bows, exaggerated sheerlines, raised poop decks, and doubly curved transoms with stern windows surmounted by large, cast-bronze stern lights of eighteenth-century design. One could fairly smell the tar and watch the flying fish flop in the scuppers.

The appeal of the cogges has not diminished since the 1920s. William Garden, naval architect of Victoria, British Columbia, has produced his own version of the 50-foot ketch, drawn for a client who was unable to get plans for the original design. She is "all boat," being 43 feet 6 inches on the waterline, with a displacement of 67,500 pounds. This translates into a displacement/length ratio of 366, which places her firmly in the long-distance cruising category.

Bill Garden is no slouch in the romance department; as you would expect, his cogge is a temptress. He has retained most of the characteristics of the original boat while modernizing a few items and adding his own visions to those of the Urry brothers. The most noticeable difference between the two boats is in the sail plan, for the Garden boat has a jibheaded mizzen replacing the gaff-rigged original. The mainmast is now a pole mast, and the mainsail peak halyards lead right to the masthead to minimize sagging-off of the main gaff. The topsail sets underneath the peak halyards and is hoisted on a track. The large jib, which replaces the jib and the jib topsail of the original boat, is set on a roller-furling drum, which should make handling its 375-square-foot area easy for shorthanded crews. The forestaysail foot is on a boom, and its sheet becomes self-tending with the addition of a deck traveler. The forward end of this boom attaches to a fore-and-aft horse that allows draft adjustments and ease in lowering. All of these changes make good sense, as they simplify the rig and reduce windage; with perhaps the triangular mizzen being the only exception, they do not detract from the boat's appearance (I happen to think that ketches and yawls should be all gaff-rigged or all marconi).

Much is the same on deck, but a few things are different. Garden has drawn a real cockpit, surrounded by a high coaming/seat structure that raises and protects the crew from the water that sprays and fish that soar. The center of the cockpit is sunken, and the resulting well leads into the main companionway, which is sheltered by a pleasingly shaped booby hatch. The other major change on deck involves handling the dinghies. The Urry boat shows a dinghy in davits amidships on the port side. Garden has moved the davits aft to the stern. In addition, he has notched the forward, starboard corner of the deckhouse so that another boat may be carried on the foredeck. I don't think I would want to clutter my foredeck to this extent, but stowage for hard dinghies is a tough problem that every naval architect has grappled with, and all solutions are worth considering.

A hydraulic spool windlass shown on the inboard end of the bowsprit indicates that retrieving the anchors and stowing the anchor rodes has been provided for in good measure. Three large deck boxes are built flush into the deckhouse top, with drains through the house sides. These will provide a great deal of stowage without the clutter and wasted space of having separate boxes scattered about the deck. There is a 7½-inch break in the deck just abaft amidships, giving more space and

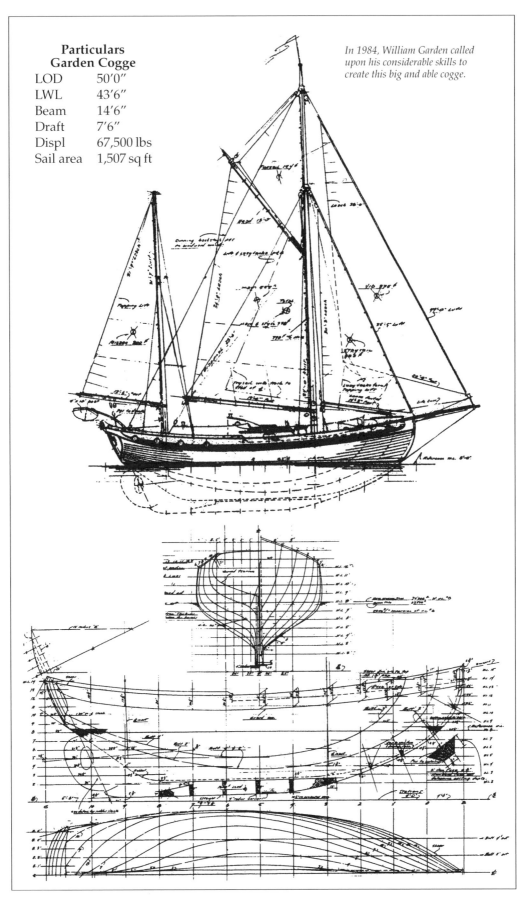

**Particulars**
**Garden Cogge**

LOD        50'0"
LWL        43'6"
Beam       14'6"
Draft      7'6"
Displ      67,500 lbs
Sail area  1,507 sq ft

*In 1984, William Garden called upon his considerable skills to create this big and able cogge.*

headroom below, and the raised poop keeps the romance level up there where it belongs. The disadvantage is a lack of bulwark height. Aft, only a 4-inch rail and the lifelines keep one aboard. Forward, there are built-up bulwarks, but their height is somewhat less than that shown on the plans of the Urry boat.

The lines plan shows a very husky boat of conventional shape that follows rather closely the look of the earlier boat. The same double crown is built into the stern, adding a bit of complication to its construction, but softening and enhancing the appearance of what is otherwise a massive stern. The three windows that illuminate the great cabin also help to relieve the expanse of stern planking. The only thing about the lines that surprises me somewhat is that the waterline beam amidships is greater than the beam on deck. This was done, I am sure, to give added stability to balance the large rig and provide as much space as possible below.

The construction section is included here because I find so much of interest contained in this drawing. William Garden has been designing wooden vessels for about 50 years, and there is always something to be learned from his construction plans. You will notice that this boat is conventionally framed and planked, with 1¾-inch cedar over 2-inch by 2¾-inch steam-bent white oak frames on 12-inch centers. What is not so conventional is the use of seven 1⅝-inch by 3-inch bilge stringers spaced out between the garboards and the sheer. At the sheer, a harpin is shown rather than the clamp/shelf construction we are used to here in the East. The frame heads extend upward through the covering boards and make the bulwark timbers; again, on this coast we would expect to see separate top timbers.

The cogge's fuel and water tanks are ideally located, being dead amidships and as low down as possible under the cabin sole. There are 200 gallons of fuel in two tanks and 280 gallons of water, also in two tanks. Virtually no change of trim would occur, whether the tanks were empty or full.

When we look at the accommodation of the Garden cogge, several changes from the original layout are apparent. The engineroom has been moved aft, directly under the cockpit. This has the unfortunate effects of making the great cabin less great and restricting the view into the forward part of the boat. Also, there is no access into the great cabin from on deck, whereas the Urry layout had an after companionway, as well as a forward one into the main cabin. On the Garden ketch, the galley runs for 16 feet along the port side amidships. To starboard is a huge master state-room (about 10 feet by 8 feet) with a double bunk, two bureaus, and a really large closet or wardrobe. The master stateroom has its own head, complete with toilet, wash basin, and large bathtub. When sitting in the bath, the mainmast is directly in front of you — better scenery than is around most tubs!

From the galley an angled corridor leads forward, with a single berth to port across from the master bathroom. Forward of this berth are two large hanging lockers. Then we reach the forward cabin, which is rather small, with two V-berths and its own small head without tub. This cabin is so far forward that there is almost no forepeak for storage — and, of course, the great cabin aft precludes having a lazarette.

Despite its reduction in size, the great cabin will be quite a pleasant place, with its long, semicircular settee and dropleaf table hung on the mizzenmast. The three stern windows, plus three portlights on each side, should ensure plenty of light and a view. To starboard is a hanging locker, and a fireplace to dispense cheer and dispel damp. Opposite, to port, is a good-sized chart table and navigator's station. I wish all this coziness didn't face the blank wall of the after engine-room bulkhead, but rather had a view forward to the rest of the accommodations.

My feeling is that the entire arrangement was designed around the idea of two people living aboard, mostly at the dock or on a mooring, and with the need for a lot of privacy. The layout will work well for this, but as a seagoing arrangement, it has several faults. All the bunks (there are five) are forward, and three of them are well forward, where there will be too much motion at sea. And there will not be the feeling of being on a large vessel, which she is, because the space is so cut up and partitioned off by bulkheads.

My own preference would be to open her up as much as possible below, removing all bulkheads that aren't essential. I'd do away with the double stateroom, having instead a main saloon with pilot berths each side and settees in front of them, and hope to find a spot for a bunk or two aft. In order to visually connect the great cabin with the rest of the interior, the cockpit would have to be eliminated, going back to the on-deck steering station of the original design. Different ships — different long splices.

I hope someone builds this ketch, completes her outfitting, and catches the tradewinds rolling around the earth's midsection. She will look even better anchored in the lee of a palm-fringed atoll.

# Garden Cogge

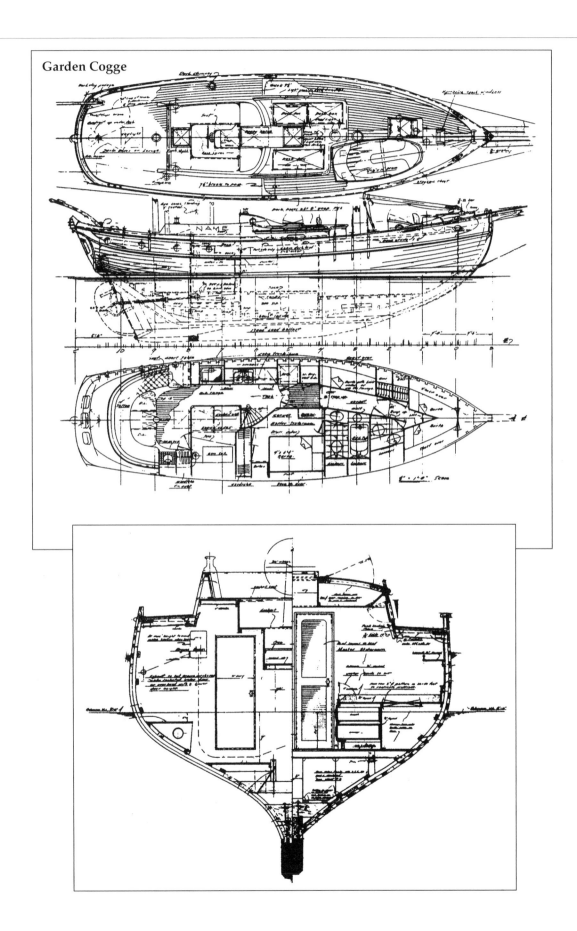

# Two Cruising Ketches

—— Designs by L. Francis Herreshoff and Jay E. Paris, Jr. ——
Commentary by Joel White

*A*lthough *Bounty* and *Lone Star* bear a superficial likeness to each other, they are very different vessels. Designed for widely different purposes, they vary in concept, construction, and character. *Bounty* was designed and built in the early 1930s, *Lone Star* was launched in 1982 after a four-year building period. Although 50 years separate their conception, both are products of an evolving tradition that is centuries old.

*Bounty* was designed by L. Francis Herreshoff as a full-keeled version of the centerboard ketch *Tioga*. She is an immediate ancestor of *Tioga II*, which later became *Ticonderoga*. In horse racing circles, this distinguished position would be equivalent to being the dam of Secretariat.

*Lone Star* was designed by Jay Paris for a Texas company as an offshore cruising boat of traditional looks, but with superior accommodations and more lasting construction techniques than were found in the Herreshoff ketches. Every advantage was to be taken of the past half-century of experience with wooden boat construction techniques — the past 50 years of development in materials, sealants, and adhesives. I believe Herreshoff would have approved.

Let us look first at the two designs in a general way. *Bounty* is 57 feet 6 inches on deck, and 50 feet on the waterline. *Lone Star* is 54 feet on deck and 45 feet on the waterline. Each has a similar underwater profile, with a shallow forefoot descending to a deep ballast keel amidships. The after deadwood is cut away to a rudderpost mounted far aft. Both boats are ketch rigged, but *Lone Star* has rig proportions more like a yawl — with a large main and a small mizzen.

A comparison of the two hulls shows that *Lone Star* is deeper in proportion to her length than *Bounty*, and that her hull sections are faired right down to her ballast keel. This filling out of the garboard area naturally increases the midship section, producing more room below. She also has a higher displacement/length ratio than *Bounty* — 241 versus 179 — and thus more volume for her length. Both hulls have lovely, easy lines and the potential for excellent speed under sail. *Bounty*, I believe, would be the faster of the two, not only because of her longer waterline, but also because her buttocks are flatter aft, and she looks to me to have less wetted surface for her length.

Though *Bounty* is longer than *Lone Star* she has considerably less in the way of accommodations. She might almost be called a giant daysailer. I rather like her simple, uncluttered arrangement plan, typical of yachts of her day, with separate quarters for the paid crew forward. The forward location of the galley and the limited storage space, however, make her unsuitable for offshore cruising. *Lone Star*, on the other hand, takes maximum advantage of the belowdecks volume, and has a great deal more comfort and stowage space for the long-distance cruiser.

Jay Paris has prepared an interesting sketch of the profiles of the two boats, showing the percentage of the interior of each used for accommodations. The drawing indicates how much more of *Lone Star* is given over to actual space for her crew. While this certainly improves her liveability, like all compromises it extracts a toll. *Bounty*'s engine and tanks are aft in a space of their own, where maintenance and repairs can be performed without interruption of other activities on board. On *Lone Star*, because the engine is in a box under the main companionway ladder in the center of the cabin, the work on her engine must take place in the galley and the main passageway, making disruption of traffic and meals inevitable. But the reward is *Lone Star*'s after cabin — a wonderful private space in the quietest part of the boat, where the motion is least. This cabin is connected to the rest of the accommodations by an ingenious tunnel under the centerline footrest that provides a passageway with full headroom. The construction section drawing through the cockpit shows how this tunnel is arranged.

The after cabin occupies the entire stern portion of the vessel and contains two large, comfortable berths, dressing room space with seats, and roomy lockers; a head and separate shower room are nearby. Moving forward through the tunnel, one emerges in the main cabin, and finds a large U-shaped galley to port, and a very complete navigator's station to starboard. Next forward comes the main saloon, with seating for the whole crew around a large table offset to port, much stowage space, and sleeping arrangements for two or four in a pinch.

Proceeding forward, through a door in the bulkhead at the mainmast, we find a head to port, hanging lockers to starboard, and two comfortable berths parallel to the centerline with lockers outboard. The forward portion of the boat is given over to stowage of those innumerable items of outfit that seem absolutely necessary

to long-distance voyagers. Under the cockpit, and to port and starboard of the centerline passageway to the after cabin, are machinery spaces for tanks and the myriad systems that make this cruiser function.

*Lone Star* was built in England, at Mashford Brothers Ltd. in Cornwall. Because of her complexity, she proved to be a bit more of a job than Mashford's had bargained for. But they stuck to it, and after four years of work, a real dazzler emerged from the humble sheds in Cremyll, Cornwall.

*Lone Star*'s garboard planks are rabbeted directly into the 16,000-pound lead keel. The forefoot and after keel are bolted to this lead casting. Much of the wood used in her construction is either teak or iroko; for instance, her single planking is teak $1\frac{3}{8}$ inches in thickness. Most of the hull frames are laminated iroko. Extensive use of cast-bronze floors throughout the length of the boat ties the framing to the centerline structure. The hull fastenings, for the most part, are copper and silicon bronze. The maststeps are stainless steel weldments. Silicon-bronze diagonal strapping ties the heavy chainplate structures to the rest of the

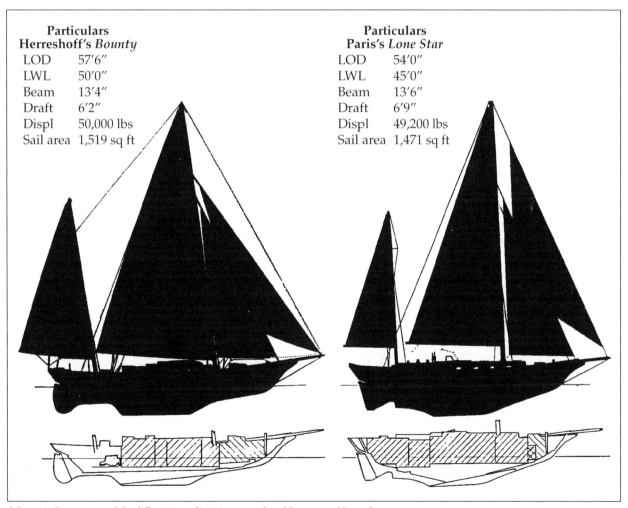

| Particulars Herreshoff's *Bounty* | | Particulars Paris's *Lone Star* | |
|---|---|---|---|
| LOD | 57'6" | LOD | 54'0" |
| LWL | 50'0" | LWL | 45'0" |
| Beam | 13'4" | Beam | 13'6" |
| Draft | 6'2" | Draft | 6'9" |
| Displ | 50,000 lbs | Displ | 49,200 lbs |
| Sail area | 1,519 sq ft | Sail area | 1,471 sq ft |

*Schematic diagrams reveal the different use of interior space aboard* Bounty *and* Lone Star.

## Herreshoff's *Bounty*

Bounty *carries the classic L. Francis Herreshoff ketch rig. She has less usable space below than* Lone Star, *but the author believes that — because of her longer waterline and flatter run — the older boat has greater speed potential. (*Bounty's *hull lines are superimposed on those of her near-sister, a centerboarder named* Tioga.*)*

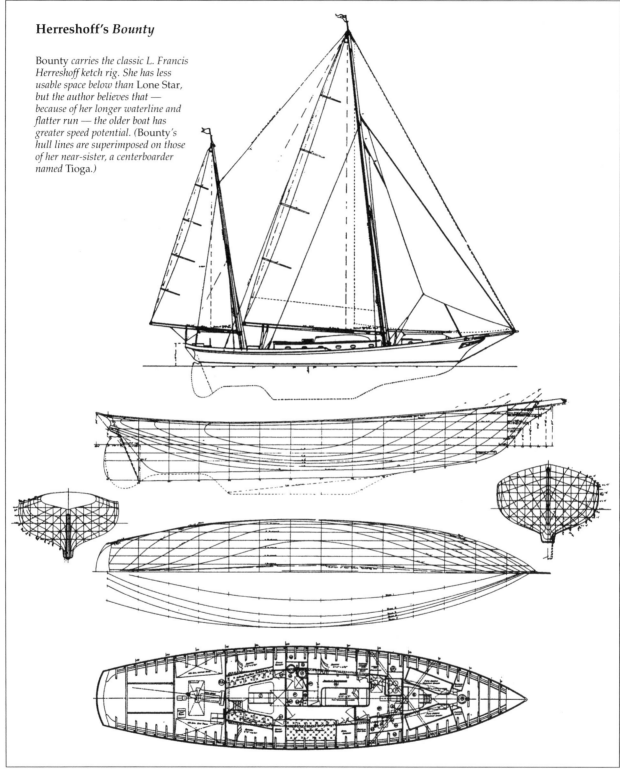

Bounty's hull lines from *Sensible Cruising Designs*, International Marine Publishing Co. Bounty's sail plan from *The Common Sense of Yacht Design*, Caravan-Maritime Books.

## Paris's *Lone Star*

*Connected only by a radio antenna,
Lone Star's masts are independently
stayed. In an attempt to avoid
unpleasant optical illusions, Paris
gave the boat a planar sheer. A relatively full run allows for standing
headroom in the after cabin.*

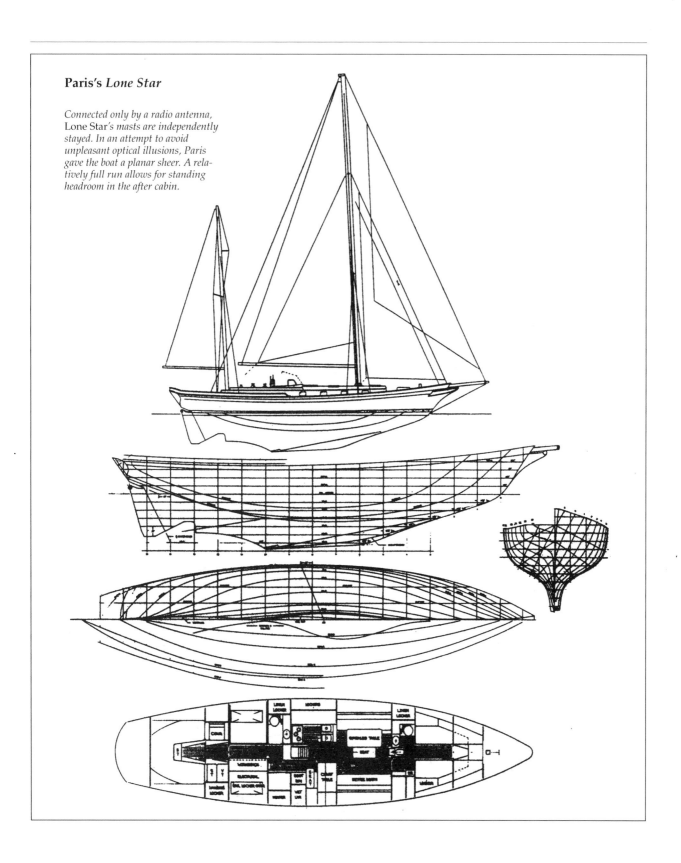

hull. All the planking butt blocks are ³⁄₁₆-inch silicon-bronze plates to which the plank ends are bolted.

The laid teak deck has a ½-inch mahogany plywood subdeck, all fastened to laminated iroko deckbeams. The cabin trunk is mostly teak, finished bright, with a laid teak housetop. There are multiple bilge stringers, and heavy iroko clamps and shelves at the deck edge. A great deal of time was lavished on the construction plans and specifications to ensure a strong and enduring hull structure.

There is a break in *Lone Star*'s deck at the forward end of the cockpit, and the entire afterdeck is raised in order to provide headroom in the stern cabin without the need for a house. Many people looking at this boat do not realize until going below that there is a large cabin tucked under the afterdeck. Because of the location of this cabin, the cockpit is farther forward than normal. This has the great advantage of putting the mizzenmast and all its clutter entirely abaft the cockpit. (To my mind, the biggest drawback of the ketch rig is that the mizzenmast and its rigging are so often directly in the middle of affairs in the cockpit.) Both the jib and the staysail are roller furling — a convenient arrangement, but one that usually does not make for the most efficient headsails.

The large mainsail and small mizzen mentioned earlier will ensure better windward performance than ketch rigs of more normal proportions. Off the wind, with her fair lines and good form stability, *Lone Star* is capable of making very good days' runs when the breeze is up and the crew is eager. She is also designed to keep that crew happy, comfortable, and well-fed on long passages.

I have a couple of minor quibbles: for one thing, *Lone Star* would look better to my eye if her sheer were raised 4 or 5 inches forward. And, I strongly suspect that if Jay Paris were to sit down today to design another boat to her specifications, he would enclose her in a slightly larger envelope — perhaps increasing her waterline length to 48 or 50 feet. A complex project such as this always grows a bit along the way, and more items get added to the inventory than were originally planned. Additional weight creeps aboard, and the designed waterline disappears below the surface. But these are minor problems — the overall result is magnificent.

*Lone Star* shows that careful design and engineering, combined with the best of materials shaped by master craftsmen in the old tradition of wooden boat building, can produce a truly superior vessel.

*Jay Paris can be reached at Designautics, P.O. Box 459, Brunswick, ME 04011.*

*Plans for* Bounty *are available from Elizabeth R. Vaughn, The Yacht Designs of L. Francis Herreshoff, 620 Galland St., Petaluma, CA 94952.*

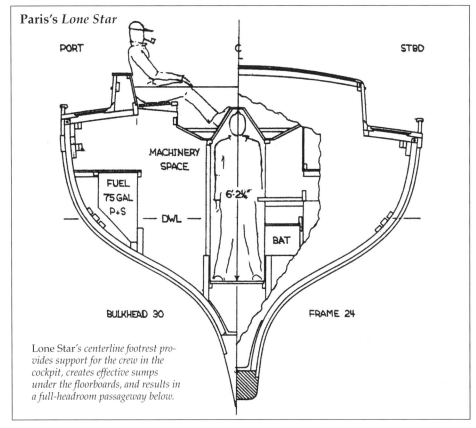

**Paris's *Lone Star***

PORT    STBD

MACHINERY SPACE

FUEL 75 GAL P+S

DWL

6'2½"

BAT

BULKHEAD 30    FRAME 24

*Lone Star's centerline footrest provides support for the crew in the cockpit, creates effective sumps under the floorboards, and results in a full-headroom passageway below.*

# LIV

# A Canoe-Sterned Sloop and Her Daughter

—————— Designs by William Garden ——————
Commentary by Joel White

William Garden has been designing boats for a long time. Through the years, he has drawn several craft for his own use — the most unusual and interesting of which is *Oceanus*, designed in 1954.

The usual approach to a new design is to pick a length — say, 40 feet overall — then draw the hull envelope, and pack in what accommodations can be fitted within the shell. If the resulting layout is insufficient, then a bigger boat is drawn — or one's expectations are reduced. The design approach to *Oceanus* was different.

Bill Garden wanted the most, and fastest, boat that could be handled by two people while cruising, and a boat that would perform equally well under sail or power. For him, this proved to be a boat 60 feet overall, with a waterline length of 48 feet, 12-foot beam, and 6-foot 8-inch draft. A sloop rig with 1,145 square feet of sail powers the 36,000-pound hull. A more timid man might have had a ketch rig, to divide up the sail area a little, but Bill stayed with the swifter sloop.

The numbers above give us a DL (displacement-to-length) ratio of 145, very much on the light side, and a sail-area-to-displacement ratio of 16.81 with a 100-percent foretriangle, and 23.8 with the 180-percent genoa. The sail ratio tells us how much power (sail area) a boat has in relation to her displacement. For *Oceanus*, it is ample with the 100-percent jib, and terrific with the 180-percent genoa. No wonder Bill says hoisting the jenny always felt like going into overdrive!

There is much to be said for this approach to a design. The amount of sail area that can be handled by the available crew is one of the first decisions to be made. From this, the approximate displacement is derived. It is an axiom of sailboat design that long waterlines and light displacements always produce speedy shapes; hence the long hull, narrow beam, and light weight.

Bill Garden has always liked double-enders, and *Oceanus* has a gorgeous stern — full on deck, a lot of hollow at the waterline, and a strongly knuckled profile. Easy, curving buttocks amidships that straighten out aft to form a long run indicate a hull shape that has proven to be a swift sailer. Because her hull was to be cold-molded, *Oceanus* was given slack bilges and lots of deadrise to aid in bending the $\frac{7}{16}$-inch veneers over the turn of the bilge. A 13,508-pound iron ballast casting forms the keel, with the rudder separated from it by a wedge-shaped skeg structure ending with the raked rudderpost. The propeller operates in an aperture between the skeg and the rudder — well protected from floating debris and drifting lines.

On top of this lean, lovely hull a low cabin trunk runs aft to a large streamlined deckhouse with big windows, a visored windshield, and an extension over the forward cockpit seats. In spite of its size, I have always liked the looks of this deckhouse — somehow, it fits the appearance of the boat. The cockpit is big and deep, with seats on each side and across the back; the steering wheel is mounted on a pedestal in the middle. The afterdeck is large enough that a small dinghy can be stowed there upside down.

A simple masthead sloop rig with single spreaders sits well forward on the hull. The jibstay is secured to the stemhead, and the backstay comes down to the deck at the after end of the cockpit about 8 feet forward of the stern. The mainsail is 550 square feet in area — a lot for one person or even two.

In spite of her length, *Oceanus*'s accommodations are simple — a pipe berth forward in the fo'c's'le reached from a hatch on deck, a toilet room the width of the ship, then a two-berth stateroom aft of that, followed by the galley to starboard and a dinette opposite to port. This brings us to the deckhouse, which contains a below-deck steering station, much prized in the Pacific Northwest, a fireplace, also indispensable in damp climates, a pullout berth, and a settee. A step or two leads up into the cockpit.

*Oceanus* is a big, simple, beautiful boat that will sail with the grace of a greyhound, and a boat that rivets one's attention as she passes by.

A couple of months ago, I received an envelope from Bill Garden containing some modified *Oceanus* plans, and a written description called "Oceanus Revisited" — giving whys and wherefores for the revisions. A client interested in the *Oceanus* concept had written for plans.

"A review of the original plans indicated a need for greater accommodations," Bill explains, "since a single private stateroom in a 60-footer isn't practical in view of resale. Development was in order. Plans for a longer deckhouse with toilet room looked to be closer to the ideal, allowing the saloon sleepers their own facilities. To supplement the larger saloon, we found an interesting sketch in the old *Oceanus* file showing an after cabin that looked practical as a bunkhouse for spry adults or kids, and that also seemed to be an improvement worth incorporating.

"Underwater she needed a lead keel because of the increasing cost of iron castings. In 1955 iron was 3.5 cents per pound, cast with cores to the owner's pattern. Lead was 7 cents per pound in those days of dollars with greater buying power. Today, the lead and iron castings are a close match to each other in cost, so lead is the logical choice.

"In my book *Yacht Designs* (International Marine Publishing Company, Camden, Maine, 1977) you will notice that the original boat's rudder was separated from the fin but raked, as a nod to then-conventional practice. With the new *Oceanus*, the rudder and skeg have been fitted farther aft for maximum directional stability, and the hull has been given slightly greater form stability with a fuller body plan. Old *Oceanus* was given fairly slack bilges, which we figured at the time to be about the safe limit to take the bone-dry Alaska yellow cedar triple-diagonal planking; however, we found in practice that the original $\frac{7}{16}$-inch stock was an easy bend, so a slightly firmer bilge looked best."

The new underbody configuration, with the rudder moved aft and separated entirely from the ballast keel, will improve directional stability and steering, at the expense of having less protection for the propeller. The rudder will be a lot more vulnerable to damage in the event of bad groundings. This is the sort of tradeoff designers wrestle with all the time, hoping to make an improvement without too much detriment to the boat.

The new deckhouse with after cabin and raised cockpit increases accommodations below. A careful comparison of the old and the new accommodations plans reveals what was attempted and the resulting gain. From the deckhouse forward, the layouts are virtually the same. Although there is some difference in detail, the space allotted and the arrangement of galley, dinette, double stateroom, toilet, and fo'c's'le are nearly identical. The deckhouse on the new boat is larger, and it has a toilet room worked into the port after corner. A chart table with two chairs to starboard sits just forward of the fireplace.

The similarity of the new layout to the old tells me that in 12 years of cruising, Bill must have found that the original arrangement worked pretty well. The big difference, of course, is the very small after cabin, with a bunk each side, that has been added abaft the cockpit. In order to accomplish this, Bill lifted the cockpit a couple of feet and shortened it — enclosing the seats within the extension of the deckhouse sides and forming a very short after house that gives a little standing-up room between the bunks. The feet of these bunks run forward under the cockpit seats in order to get enough length.

Does the new accommodations plan work? Well, yes — but I have some reservations. The addition of an extra toilet room on a 60-foot yacht seems entirely worthwhile. The addition of another private double stateroom (the after cabin) also seems worthwhile — although not every occupant will be happy with the cramped quarters and lack of adjoining head. I think the new cockpit suffers in comparison with the old, because it is too high out of the water, and one will feel he is sitting on the boat, not in it. Also, the jib sheets won't lead to the winches as naturally as they do in the older boat. Access to the after cabin is gained by swinging the center cockpit seat upwards to form a companionway — disrupting things in the cockpit. The cockpit is so high that three steps must be built into it for access to the deckhouse.

I guess what really bothers me about the new design is the appearance of the lengthened deckhouse. Its mass has shifted aft from amidships. This, combined with the very forward appearance of the rig, seems to make the boat's profile look unbalanced. (Bill Garden is very skilled at drawing deck structures that look terrific in three dimensions so I may be talking though my hat.)

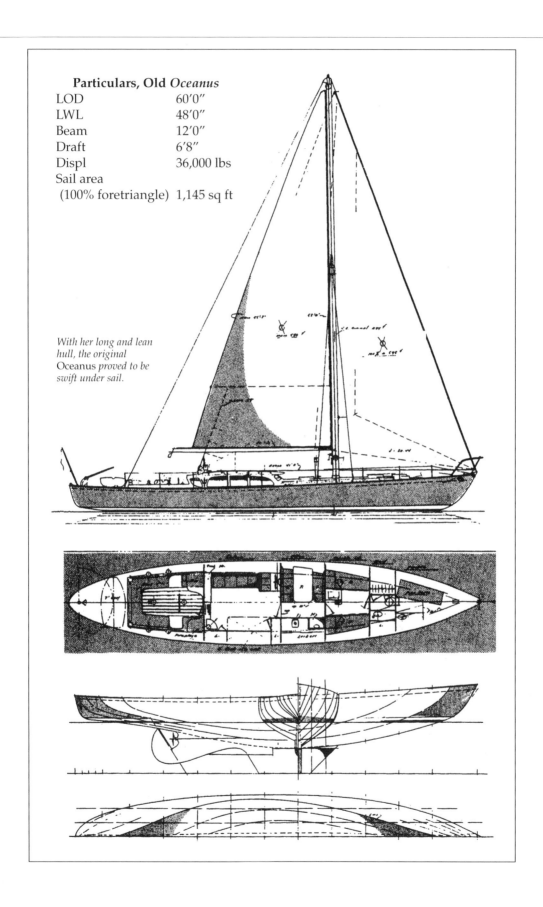

**Particulars, Old *Oceanus***

| | |
|---|---|
| LOD | 60'0" |
| LWL | 48'0" |
| Beam | 12'0" |
| Draft | 6'8" |
| Displ | 36,000 lbs |
| Sail area | |
| (100% foretriangle) | 1,145 sq ft |

*With her long and lean hull, the original* Oceanus *proved to be swift under sail.*

Back to Bill's "*Oceanus* Revisited": "The profile shown on the sail plan has slightly less spring to the sheer than *Oceanus*, but is otherwise about the same. If I were building her again for myself, I believe I would carry the curved stem out about 2 feet on deck for appearance and room around the jibstay."

I couldn't agree more. Appearance would certainly be improved, and the increase in space on deck around the jibstay would be a real plus. Being able to walk by the jibstay and stand forward of it would make handling large headsails much easier (although most people would probably have roller furling). Anchors, chains, windlasses, and all the other gear that accumulates on the forward deck would have more room.

The original *Oceanus* was cold-molded of three diagonal layers of $7/16$-inch Alaska yellow cedar over a laminated keel and longitudinal stringers let into the bulkheads. The stern was logged up of 6-inch stuff glued and bolted together, then sculptured to the finished shape. Decks were two layers of plywood, and everything above was fiberglassed. I see little or no change in the construction plans for the new *Oceanus*, so the system must have worked well.

Just looking at the plans for *Oceanus* old and new makes me envious of the owners of these great sloops. What fun they must be to cruise aboard — making great runs under either power or sail, passing everything in sight, then finishing the day anchored in some secluded cove, with the fireplace warming the deckhouse, and sunset coming on....

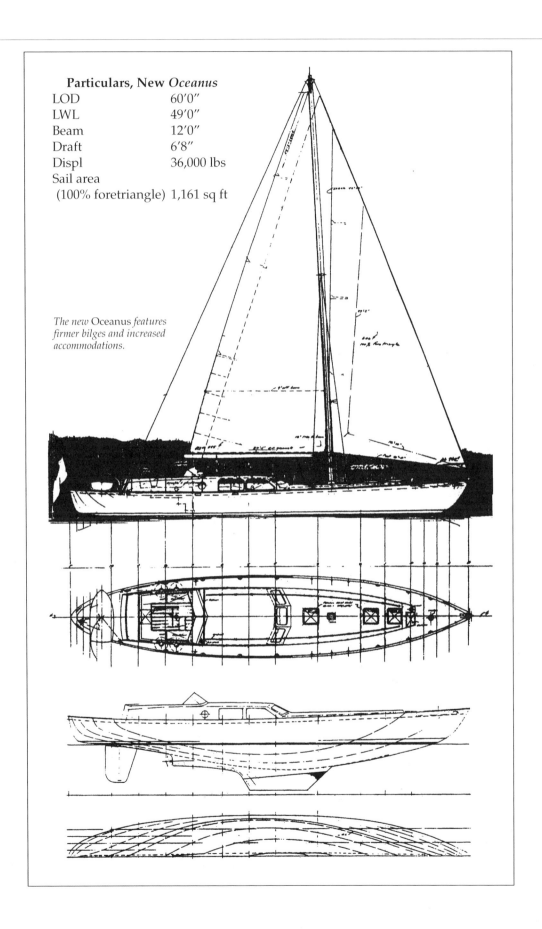

**Particulars, New *Oceanus***
LOD                   60'0"
LWL                   49'0"
Beam                  12'0"
Draft                 6'8"
Displ                 36,000 lbs
Sail area
 (100% foretriangle) 1,161 sq ft

*The new* Oceanus *features firmer bilges and increased accommodations.*

# A Fast Cruising Sloop

Design by Joel White ———
Commentary by Maynard Bray

Yachts designed these days for speed under sail invariably come out as a somewhat cigar-shaped hull atop a fin keel, and have a pendant-type rudder back near the after end of the waterline. They're reminiscent of the fin-keelers of 100 years ago, except they're far bigger and have a marconi instead of a gaff rig. Unquestionably, boats of this type have proven to be fast, but they're usually so damned ugly that they hold no interest for me. If I had to choose between one of those and a pretty boat that was slow, the nod would go to the latter. But this design is an exception — a modern yacht that could hold her own in about any company when it comes to performance, yet one that is very handsome as well.

She grew out of a two-year client-designer effort with numerous telephone calls, over 70 letters, and four iterations of drawings. She'll go upwind like a scalded cat with only her working sails, and by hoisting an asymmetrical, poleless spinnaker, she'll be no slouch downwind, either.

Long, skinny boats don't usually do very well unless there's a good breeze, but this one carries enough sail area to make her go in light weather, and, most unusual, has the stability to stand up to it when the wind begins to blow in earnest. She's geographically specific in that she was designed for the light average-wind velocities of Puget Sound, but still...if she were mine and I were to sail her anywhere else, I'd be inclined to use this same sail plan and keep her from being overpowered by reefing. You can always shorten sail, but with a given length of spars, it's difficult to add more if you find you need it.

As to the construction, she's to be built of glued-together ⅞-inch cedar strips over bulkheads and wide-spaced laminated frames. Three crisscrossed layers of ⅛-inch veneers are vacuum-bagged over the strips.

The hull is built upside down, then turned over to receive the interior, the deck and cockpit assemblies, the power plant, and the few, simple systems she'll have installed. The fin — with a bulging, five-ton chunk of lead at the bottom edge — and the rudder are installed last, just before launching.

How is a design like this created? Here's the story:

A reader of *WoodenBoat* magazine who happened to be a seasoned sailor and an experienced wooden-boat owner wanted a long, narrow boat similar to the Swede 55 *Vortex* but with some minor changes — a larger sail plan, a bit more sheer, and a traditional aft-raking transom. The 30-Square-Meter sloop *Bijou II*, with which he was familiar, also served as inspiration, as did the writings of Uffa Fox and L. Francis Herreshoff.

The client wrote to Joel White, who soon responded with a proposal based on his son Steve's boat *Vortex*. Both the designer and the client liked simplicity, performance, and good looks — so they went back and forth, letter after letter, fine-tuning the proposal until it satisfied them. Both parties agreed she'd be fast in all conditions.

*Vortex* has proven to be just about unbeatable except in light air, and the proposed boat was about the same length (56 feet) and shape but had 28 percent more sail area, a 4-inch deeper and 2,000-pounds heavier ballast keel, and 6 inches more beam. The numbers confirmed that she'd be fast. The sail area/displacement ratio was 22, compared to 16.36 for *Vortex*, and the plots of stability at various wind velocities and angles of heel suggested that she'd stand up to her rig within reason.

The designer and client agreed, too, not to count on a rule-beating genoa for speed, but to figure on using

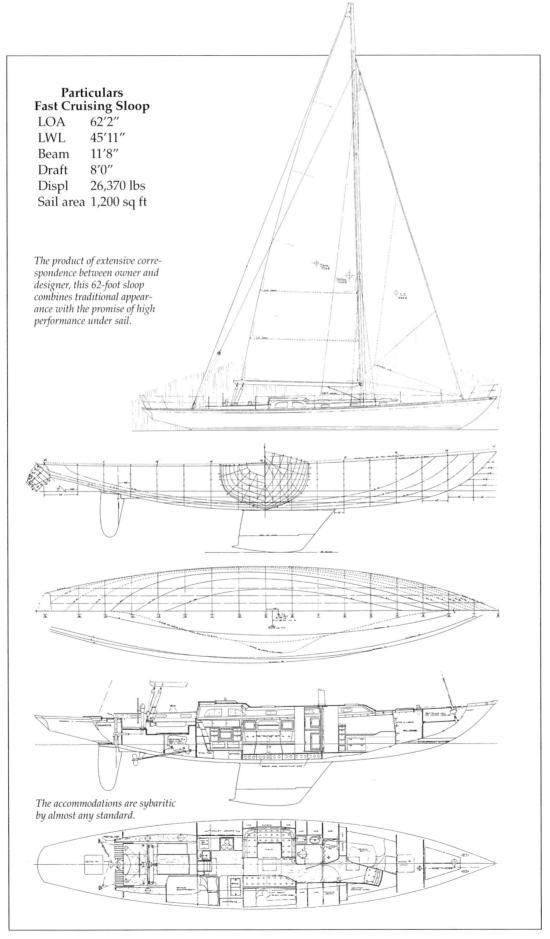

**Particulars**
**Fast Cruising Sloop**

| | |
|---|---|
| LOA | 62'2" |
| LWL | 45'11" |
| Beam | 11'8" |
| Draft | 8'0" |
| Displ | 26,370 lbs |
| Sail area | 1,200 sq ft |

*The product of extensive correspondence between owner and designer, this 62-foot sloop combines traditional appearance with the promise of high performance under sail.*

*The accommodations are sybaritic by almost any standard.*

a working jib. In fact, they agreed to ignore rating rules altogether and come up with a boat that would be fast, beautiful, and simple to sail. The thrill would come from boat-for-boat racing and from getting the first-to-finish gun from the committee boat.

Alternatives were considered along the way. A double-ended hull, Joel thought, wouldn't have the straighter sailing lines of a hull with a transom, and therefore would not be as fast. Tiller steering would be simple, but it would preclude having an after cabin.

Meanwhile, the client bought a fiberglass Swede 55 and cruised, raced, and otherwise studied it, for the purpose of refining the new design, especially the interior arrangement. But, exciting as the new design was, neither client nor designer felt quite comfortable with it. Their nearly simultaneous conclusion (reached independently after several months of reflection) was that there should be more usable interior space.

Joel's suggestion at this point was to scale down his 74-foot *Dragonera* design to 56 feet to match the overall length of the *Vortex* variant. This solved the interior space problem and showed great potential, but its stubby overhangs resulted in an unacceptable profile; the boat just wasn't sleek enough.

How to add sleekness to an otherwise right-on-the-money design? Simple, if you're as good at it as Joel is. You pull out the ends so there's more overhang at both the bow and the stern. The 62-foot 2-inch sloop was the result. It should be sleek enough for just about anyone, and will still be the same wolf in sheep's clothing when it comes to performance as the 56-foot *Vortex*. Compared to that design, this one is 14 percent wider, 32 percent heavier (and that much more costly), and has 19 percent more sail area. Because there's more freeboard, especially forward, she'll be drier when beating into a chop.

Let's go aboard and look around. At the bow, there's a self-bailing well for the anchor and its rode so they're out of the way when you're sailing. To get at them, you simply open up the hinged covers. Besides the anchor, the drum for the roller-furling jib also hides in this well, leaving the foredeck exceptionally clear.

Joel is an enthusiastic advocate of carbon-fiber masts on go-fast boats, and planned on specifying one from the very beginning. The difference in stability, compared to this design fitted with a heavier aluminum mast, is the same as lowering the ballast keel 18 inches, so it's not difficult to understand his reasoning.

The shrouds are set in from the deck edge so as not to interfere with flat-sheeting the jib, so the best route going forward may be outside, rather than inside the shrouds.

Moving aft, there's a big, deep cockpit where the passengers and/or crew will feel secure — they will feel as if they're sitting in, rather than on, the boat. The slanted cabin back provides a comfortable backrest if you want to sit facing aft and straighten your legs. All sheets lead to the forward two-thirds of the cockpit. The after one-third, separated by the mainsheet track assembly, is for the helmsman, and here he can choose either to stand or to sit on the pullout, camel-back seat. Either way, he'll have good visibility thanks to the low doghouse and the relatively small, high-cut headsail. There's a low bridge deck — it really amounts to a step — that makes climbing up out of the cockpit, over the sill, and down onto the companionway ladder very easy.

The coamings are like curved, hollow boxes with tops wide enough for the winch bases, and for sitting on; while winch handles, sunglasses, cameras, sail stops, and other small gear can be stored within. Access is through the oval cutouts along their inboard sides.

Heavy weights are always best kept out of the extreme ends of a boat, so there's a big storage compartment both at the bow and at the stern in which sails and other relatively light items can be kept. Access to each is through watertight deck hatches.

Running backstays terminate on the after deck where there's a dedicated winch, near which a crew member will be stationed during a race. At other times, the hauling parts of the backstays can be led forward and operated from the cockpit.

Now for the accommodations. First, because the engine is a V-drive, it can be totally separated from the living quarters and completely contained in its own soundproofed space, which very effectively cuts down on the noise and smell. Its air supply comes in through the ingenious Dorade-type vents in the after ends of the coamings. You get access to the engine by opening the big hatch in the cockpit sole, and so long as you're not taking solid water over the coamings while you're trying to work on the engine, that big hatch has lots of merit.

Two doubles? Those comfortable-looking berths, one in the forward stateroom to port, and the other an enlarged quarter berth to starboard, are not what you find in most boats, although they'd be great for two couples cruising. But they're not so good for an all-male race to Bermuda, even if the pilot berth and the convertible settee (another double berth) are brought into play. But this boat was never intended to be an ocean racer; she'll be a two-couples cruiser, an around-the-buoys day racer, and, most of all, simply a grand daysailer that's easy to get underway, and delightful to sail after the mooring is dropped.

Is she strong? You bet! The fin is attached to the hull through a big bronze weldment that spreads the load so there's no critical weak link. It's the same construction that Joel used for the 74-foot ketch *Dragonera*, which was hammered by a Gulf Stream storm on her maiden voyage from Newport to Bermuda. *Dragonera* has cruised extensively since, with not a trace of weakness or failure.

But boats that are strong can also be light; this one's hull is light enough so that almost half her displacement is in her ballast keel. Her vertical center of gravity is almost 2 feet below the waterline, due both to the light-but-strong hull and the lightweight carbon-fiber mast. The tanks, batteries, and engine are located down low as well, which helps achieve this low center of gravity.

Here's just one example of Joel's design philosophy, as he expressed it when asked about his keel design:

"I have tried to make your design a high-performance sailing racer/cruiser without going to extremes. I dislike extreme boats because I find they often have limited usefulness under varying conditions. Going to a 9-foot draft seems to me counterproductive. It will limit your cruising grounds to some extent, and probably reduce the resale value of the boat. It will also have structural consequences, and the keelbolt arrange-

ment will have to be redesigned. In a heavy grounding, something that happens to the best of us, the very deep modern keels with narrow chord configuration and small footprint landing on the hull often cause severe hull damage because the impact forces are concentrated in such a small area. You will notice on the construction plan that the after end of the fin lands on a heavy structural bulkhead and at the after end of the bronze keel frame. This is done deliberately, in an attempt to minimize damage in a bad grounding."

Sounds like good reasoning to me.

Would I want a boat like this? I sure would, but I'd make a few minor changes to suit my whim and fancy. Starting forward, I'd give her a handsome cast-bronze stemhead fitting that would encompass the chocks and support the always-ugly-as-sin anchor roller assembly (which would be removable). The cove stripe would be routed into the upper hull, which I'd make a little thicker to allow for the depth of the groove, and her name would be carved into the transom. Both would be gilded with genuine gold leaf.

The toerail would be of varnished teak and set in from the hull about ⅛ inch (which is one of the options

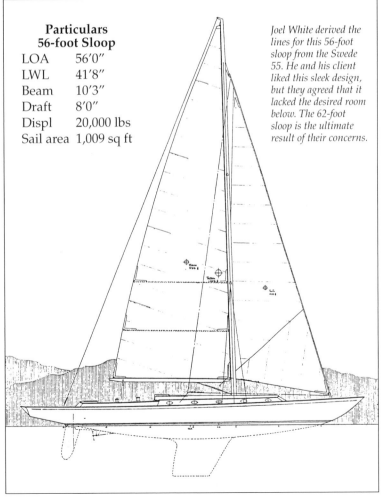

**Particulars
56-foot Sloop**

| | |
|---|---|
| LOA | 56'0" |
| LWL | 41'8" |
| Beam | 10'3" |
| Draft | 8'0" |
| Displ | 20,000 lbs |
| Sail area | 1,009 sq ft |

*Joel White derived the lines for this 56-foot sloop from the Swede 55. He and his client liked this sleek design, but they agreed that it lacked the desired room below. The 62-foot sloop is the ultimate result of their concerns.*

already shown on the drawing). There'd be a folding gallows near the after end of the doghouse in which to secure the boom. The boom would be of varnished spruce, made hollow for the reefing lines. I'd pay particular attention to the cockpit's appearance and use a fair amount of wood trim to avoid the look of a bathtub. Beauty is important here, because the cockpit is always in the foreground while sailing or sitting. The steering wheel would be turned-spoke traditional, with an outer wooden rim, and every block on the boat would be either wood- or bronze-shelled. In fact, there'd be absolutely no stainless showing anywhere, if possible, meaning that the winches and tracks, stanchions, and pulpit would be bronze.

Since there'd never be a reason for going way aft while under sail, I'd be inclined to eliminate the stern pulpit and try using that area to carry my tender when I didn't want to tow it. The tender would, of course, be a Nutshell Pram — never, never an inflatable!

Below deck, I'd make the door openings rectangular and have the doors, the bulkheads, and the berth fronts of raised-panel construction — or at least made to look like raised panels. There'd be a bare teak cabin sole and countertop. Otherwise, except for varnished edge trim, ladder, cabin sides, and cabin table, she'd be painted satin-finish, off-white. Cushions would be darkish green corduroy.

For the exterior colors, she'd have a light tan, Dynel-covered deck and cabintop, and a mast of the same color. Although the topsides (including the transom) would look lovely black, they'd soak up enough heat that there'd be a risk of the veneers coming unstuck, so a light, green-gray will have to do, along with a single, wide, dark red boottop, and black bottom. Cabin sides, including the edge trim, and both faces of the coamings would be of varnished teak, while the coaming tops would be left bare.

The systems would be few and simple. But, for singlehanding and for long runs, an autopilot would be great, and with an 8-foot draft, a fathometer would come in handy.

Finally, the sails. They'd be of off-white Dacron, as lightweight and soft as practical for easy furling, and would have parallel seams and narrow panels. Convincing a sailmaker to build a less-than-bulletproof sail takes some effort, but I believe the end result would be worth it. For running rigging, white Dacron, either three-strand or braided — no colored stuff!

If I had the money, I'd already have one of these slippery sloops on order. If I didn't quite have enough for the 62-footer, I'd go with the 56-foot *Vortex* variant.

*Plans from Joel White, Brooklin Boat Yard, P.O. Box 143, Brooklin, ME 04616.*

# Three Simple Skiffs for Oar and Outboard

—————— Designs by William and John Atkin, Ken Swan, and Charles W. Wittholz ——————
Commentary by Mike O'Brien

W e grew up in these skiffs. Many of us made childhood voyages of discovery in them. The little flat-bottomed boats weren't perfect — short and wide by the oarsman's standards; slow if powered by the specified engines, and downright scary if pushed by larger machinery. Still, they served their purpose and asked not much in return.

The design concept is simple. Start with a good flat-bottomed pulling boat. Make it wider for greater stability. Make it shorter for convenience and to keep weight and cost from spiraling out of control (all else being equal, effective "size" increases as the cube of the length). Add freeboard to achieve some gains in ability and capacity (moderately amplified windage presents no real problem here). Flatten the run, more or less, depending upon whether we want to emphasize the oars or the motor. What we're left with is a healthy waterfront skiff suitable for low-powered outboard motors and knockabout rowing.

William and John Atkin, aware of a pervasive prejudice against flat-bottomed boats, employed their talents in both drafting and design to create this "outboard fishing skiff." Many a handsome skiff looks too plain on paper to attract the uninitiated. Not Jebb. From the gentle sweep of the bottom-paint line (why do people insist on cutting the waterline dead straight these days?) to the sketched-in wood grain, the hint of seams in the cross-planked bottom, and the suggestion of the water's surface, this is a simple but carefully crafted drawing.

Jebb's moderately flat run (flat compared to most purpose-made rowing skiffs) will cause her transom to drag when she's loaded down some, but even a small engine will notice the increased resistance less than will the strongest oarsman. And, because a propeller's thrust is continuous, the skiff's carry (ability to glide between strokes of the oars) isn't crucial. The substantial bearing provided by reduced rocker and fairly broad transom will be welcome if Jebb sees service as a tender. Should the need arise, you'll be able to exit over the stern; this skiff won't dump you and run away.

Considerable flare will help ensure a friendly stability curve when Jebb is heavily loaded. The wide, flat bottom, with its beam carried well into the ends of the boat, promises plenty of initial stability.

Between them, the Atkins must have built more than a few skiffs. Their experience shows in the presence of two baselines on the drawings. A baseline at the top (24 inches above the LWL) will be used if you set the molds bottom-side up. Should you choose to build right-side up, a line 12 inches below the LWL represents your shop floor — a considerate touch that might save some arithmetic.

The construction details shown here represent fairly standard building practices for traditional skiffs in the designers' place and time. Chine logs, keel, frames, breasthook, and sheer moldings are got out of white oak. Planking is white cedar, ¾ inch for the bottom and ⅝ inch for the sides. If you can find good stock, cedar is a pleasant wood to work — and its aroma is little short of intoxicating. Of course, with appropriate thought given to framing and sheet thickness, you could sheathe Jebb's bottom with plywood. In any case, the lapped sides ought to be retained, as they make good sense structurally and aesthetically.

A long time ago, Charles W. Wittholz sketched a simple 11-foot 6-inch plywood skiff for Boris Lauer-Leonardi, then editor of *The Rudder* magazine. Taken with the concept, Lauer-Leonardi asked the designer to complete the plans. Later, nearly three full pages of that much-admired publication were devoted to the finished drawings. Wittholz credits the exposure with putting his career "on track" — a career that spanned more than 50 years.

Wittholz's cartoon suggested no fewer than 10 different names for the utility skiff. They alluded to function (Rod & Reel, Rod & Gun, Flatfish) and/or construction (Plyfly). The final name, Decoy, didn't appear until publication. Perhaps it was the editor's choice. By whatever name, this is an easily built, relatively lightweight (about 115 pounds), potentially leak-free skiff.

Decoy's narrow stern and somewhat slender (4-foot) overall beam imply, perhaps, that oars would provide her main propulsion. However, a small outboard could be hung directly on her transom. It was drawn to accommodate the standard motor shaft length of her day (short shaft, now) without having to be cut down.

I suspect that at least one consideration in determining Decoy's overall length was the availability of continuous, splice-free, 12-foot-long plywood panels during the 1950s. Today, you'll have to make your own — or have someone scarf the panels for you. Either way, it's no real problem.

Wittholz's extensive use of transverse framing in this little skiff leaves no doubt as to the rigidity of the bottom. Some of us might prefer a cleaner interior. Certainly, we could employ thicker plywood and fewer frames. But we should remember that, without the use of exotic materials, our results might prove heavier and/or more limp than the original.

During the early 1960s on Barnegat Bay, a Decoy lived just down the beach from me. Her owner (more fisherman than boatbuilder) had made a plain but fair job of putting her together. He fished the little skiff with varied results but with constant satisfaction. The boat received neither terrible abuse nor lavish care. In fact, her builder seemed hardly to think about her one way or the other. And that's the point — she was simply waterfront equipage.

I should mention that the skiff outlived the marshes she fished. They're clogged now with hydraulic fill and blocked by causeways that hurry people to somewhere or other.

Ken Swan's Nez Percé 13, with her run carried out straight, is a pure outboard fishing skiff. Probably the ash breeze will be rigged only for jogging around while fishing or in emergencies. (Given the reliability of contemporary outboard motors, running out of fuel constitutes the most likely crisis.)

When she is rowed, the Nez Percé ought to be kept down by the bow to avoid dragging half the bay around behind her transom. Installing the oarlock sockets at the forward thwart, as the designer indicates, will help ensure proper trim. The boat won't show her best with this attitude, but she'll row acceptably in smooth water. To track well, she'll need the substantial skeg shown in the drawings. Without it, despite a rower's best efforts, she'll be inclined to turn around and look herself in the eye.

As I said, Nez Percé is a powerboat. Pushed by a 5- to 10-horsepower outboard motor, she'll jump onto a plane more quickly and go faster than most of her production fiberglass competitors. (Unless worked into sophisticated composite layups, fiberglass tends to be neither a stiff nor a light medium — and builders seldom lavish sophistication on flat-bottomed skiffs.) The designer reports that a 4-horsepower Johnson outboard propels his own Nez Percé at a comfortable 9 miles per hour.

Swan intends for this boat to go together in true skiff fashion. The pre-cut plywood sides are fastened together at the stem, wrapped around a couple of frames, and pulled in by a Spanish windlass at the stern. Building time is about 60 hours.

Don't be fooled by Swan's spare drawing style. This is one handsome skiff. The dory-like flare and sheer give her strong character. I believe Nez Percé was modeled before being drawn on the flat. Skiffs seem to benefit from that design sequence.

So, here we have three good little skiffs: Decoy, designed primarily for rowing but able to carry a small outboard motor; Jebb, designed for a small outboard motor but able to be rowed; and Nez Percé, an efficient low-powered planing boat that can be rowed if need be. I'm tempted to build all of them.

*Jebb's plans are available from Atkin & Co., P.O. Box 3005, Noroton, CT 06820.*

*Charles Wittholz's plans are available through Mrs. Charles Wittholz, 100 Williamsburg Dr., Silver Spring, MD 20901.*

*Ken Swan sells plans for Nez Percé at P.O. Box 267, Hubbard, OR 97032.*

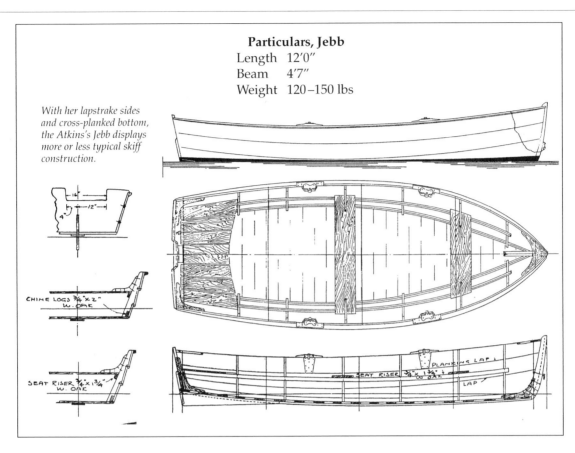

**Particulars, Jebb**
Length   12'0"
Beam     4'7"
Weight   120–150 lbs

*With her lapstrake sides and cross-planked bottom, the Atkins's Jebb displays more or less typical skiff construction.*

CHINE LOGS ¾"X 2"
W. OAK

SEAT RISER ¾"X 1¾"
W. OAK

SEAT RISER ¾"X 1¾"
W. OAK

PLANKING LAP

LAP

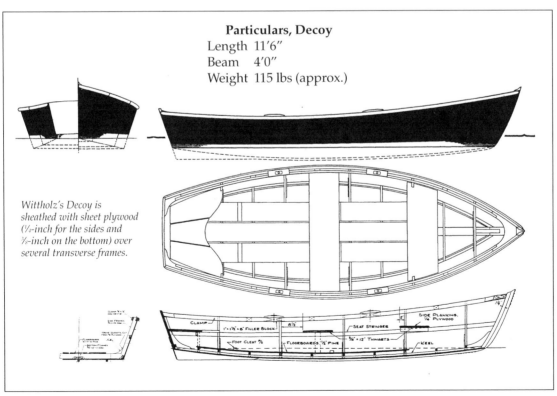

**Particulars, Decoy**
Length  11'6"
Beam    4'0"
Weight  115 lbs (approx.)

*Wittholz's Decoy is sheathed with sheet plywood (¼-inch for the sides and ⅜-inch on the bottom) over several transverse frames.*

CLAMP

1"X 1½"X 6" FILLER BLOCK

6½

SEAT STRINGER

SIDE PLANKING,
¼ PLYWOOD

FOOT CLEAT ⅝

FLOORBOARDS, ½ PINE

¾"X 12" THWARTS

KEEL

**Particulars, Nez Percé**
Length 13'6"
Beam 4'11"
Weight 190 lbs
Power 4–10 hp

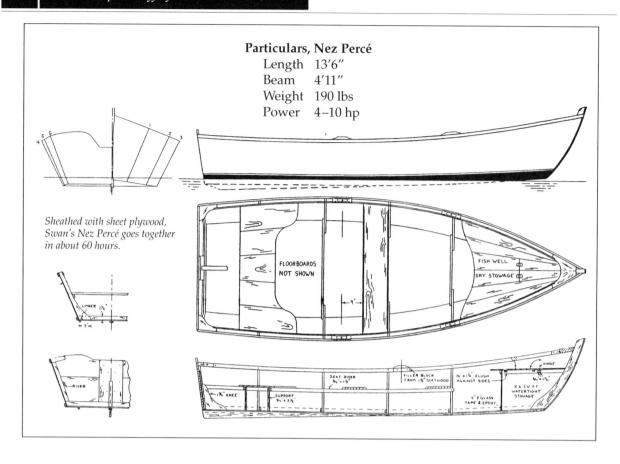

*Sheathed with sheet plywood, Swan's Nez Percé goes together in about 60 hours.*

# Two Outboard-Powered Garveys

Designs by Sam Devlin and Robert W. Stephens
Commentary by Mike O'Brien

Here we have two easily built modified garveys, each of strong character. Both are capable of performance that is equal, at least, to that of their stock fiberglass counterparts of fancier origin.

For want of a more formal definition, garveys can be thought of as sometimes well-modeled scows that originated in the shallow bays and creeks along the Jersey Shore. Put together by different builders for different purposes, individual garveys display the considerable variety expected from a generic type, but, as a class, they share light draft, ample initial stability, and extreme ease of construction. Planks hang naturally with little curve: you'll go a long way before finding much edge-set in any real garvey. Also, their shapes tend to be well suited for sheet construction.

Although the once-common sailing garvey is long dead (save for an occasional yacht), the breed survives in countless descendants powered by internal-combustion engines — either hung on their transoms or set in their bilges.

A few years back, Sam Devlin, a designer/boat-builder from Olympia, Washington, created the 14-foot prototype *Cackler* to serve as a duck-gunning skiff and yard workboat. The modified garvey was built with ⅜-inch plywood assembled over a series of ½-inch plywood bulkheads, stitch-and-glue fashion — a technique that makes good use of wood, epoxy, fiberglass tape, and the builder's time. Fast and rugged, the prototype has more than earned her keep. Impressed with his skiff's performance and versatility, Devlin made the construction plans available for other builders.

Should you choose to build a Cackler, you need do no true lofting, as the designer provides expansions for her sides, bottom, and transom. That is to say, he has peeled the boat and laid the parts out on the flat, revealing their true shapes. As the first step in construction, draw these shapes to full scale directly on the plywood that will become the boat's skin. Cut out the parts — a small circular saw is orders of magnitude better here than a slow, wandering sabersaw — and clamp the mirror-image, left and right panels together. After trimming the panels (with a plane) to ensure a perfect bilateral match, drill a series of ⅛-inch holes along a line ½ inch from the edges that will be sewn together. These holes are spaced at 2-inch intervals near the ends of the panels and are 6 inches apart elsewhere.

Assemble the boat by sewing the panels together with 6-inch lengths of mild-steel baling wire. After inserting the molds and aligning the structure, fillet the inside seams with a mixture of epoxy and wood flour. While they are still soft, the fillets should be covered with three layers of fiberglass tape set in epoxy. At this point, turn the boat upside down and remove the wire ties by heating the tip of each one with a torch until it glows red, then simply pull the wire out with a pair of pliers. Smooth the exterior chines, and sheathe and tape the outside of the hull with fiberglass and epoxy. Finishing the project requires the usual amounts of sanding and filling.

Cackler is a handsome boat. Although the top edges of the expanded sides are straight, flare and bend put a pleasant sheerline on the little skiff. And the motorwell, in addition to its practical value, makes the engine less obtrusive. In her own purposeful way, this boat ranks with the best.

Pushed by a 25-horsepower outboard, Cackler really moves out. But, won't she pound at speed? Well, yes, but so do virtually all small, fast boats of my acquaintance. When we were boys, we'd drive our flat-bottomed outboard skiffs into a steep harbor chop and suffer no more discomfort than the kids who owned sharp, store-bought runabouts. (Discomfort? We considered it great fun!) Of course, we sat way aft and steered with a tiller in the manner intended by Nature — the primitive remote controls of that day were, rightly, regarded as dangerous affectations. Come to think of it, back aft was a good place to be; given the right combination of wind, wave, and boat speed, everything forward of the midship thwart would vibrate into a fuzzy haze.

Aside from her forthright charm, Cackler's principal virtue might lie in her utility. From hunting to hauling lumber, she probably can perform many tasks better than the small fiberglass runabout that shares part of its name with New England's largest city — and Devlin's design will look better in the process. (Can I get sued for saying that?) No doubt you'll find good use for this boat — even if you don't take pleasure from blasting ducks out of the sky.

*B*ob Stephens drew his 19-foot Garvey Workboat for a specific purpose: A yard manager needed a skiff for general harbor work, but his boat would, on occasion, be called upon to run across the bay at speed and return with a heavy tow.

The idea was to run a fast, high-pitch propeller when traveling light, and switch to a more powerful low-pitch wheel before accepting the towline. With this tactic in mind, the designer drew a substantial motorwell that allows the outboard to tilt for the propeller exchange. The well's fringe benefits include better steering when handling a tow, reduced risk of damage in close quarters, and improved appearance. (For all their mechanical excellence, contemporary outboard motors seem to be aesthetically bad partners for traditional boats — designing a powerhead to complement both a garvey and, say, a Bayliner must be difficult at best.)

This garvey's construction is plain, straightforward "traditional" sheet plywood. The transverse frames are beveled and notched, and you'll therefore have sufficient opportunity to apply your woodworking skills. Though considered old-fashioned by some, this method of building does have advantages: It produces a stiff boat for a given weight, and it teaches basic boatbuilding techniques.

Although the plans call for planking the entire hull with ⅜-inch sheet plywood, you might want to consider using ½-inch plywood on the bottom. The structure is plenty strong as designed, but increased penetration resistance adds peace of mind in some situations. Certainly, many of us have pulled ½-inch ply around tighter corners, and Stephens tells me that it will lay down just fine here.

The designer has worked more than the normal amount of shape into this garvey, and both the bottom and topsides show considerable twist up forward. But all of the curves have been carefully worked out to ensure that the hull is developable. That is to say, it can be sheathed with sheet materials without forcing compound curves into the panels. Perhaps as a courtesy to students of naval architecture, Stephens has left the determinants intact on the finished drawings. (As used here, a determinant is a straight line on the side or bottom of the boat that, when extended, passes through the apex of the cone used to establish the curve of the developed surface.) At any rate, the drawings make interesting reading.

Along the shores of Barnegat Bay, garveys showing some deadrise in their forward sections are referred to as "chicken-breasted," but this somewhat impolite appellation seems inappropriate for a boat that is so well proportioned as Stephens's garvey.

*Plans for Cackler are available from Devlin Designing Boatbuilders, 2424 Gravelly Beach Loop N.W., Olympia, WA 98502.*

*Plans for the 19-foot Garvey Workboat are available from Robert W. Stephens, P.O. Box 166, Brooklin, ME 04616.*

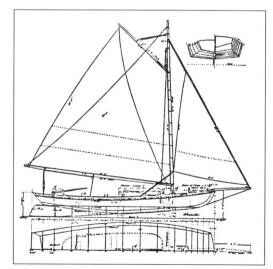

*Built in Absecon, New Jersey, in 1906, this sailing garvey displays the roots of the contemporary designs discussed here.*

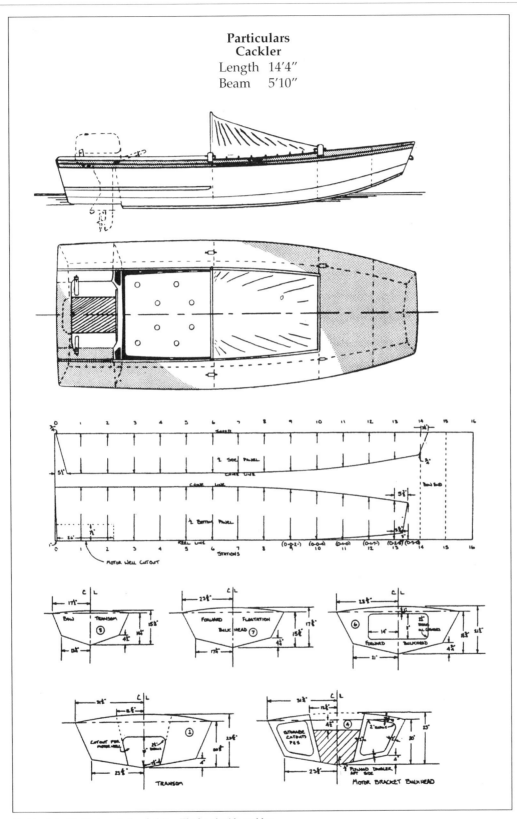

Cackler is built stitch-and-glue fashion. The boat's side and bottom panels are shown here in their expanded or "real" shape.

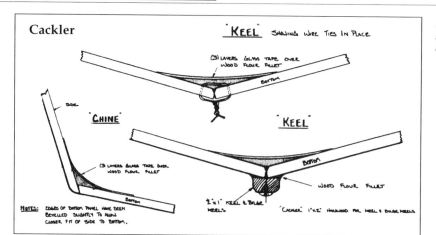

*Details of Cackler's
stitch-and-glue
construction.*

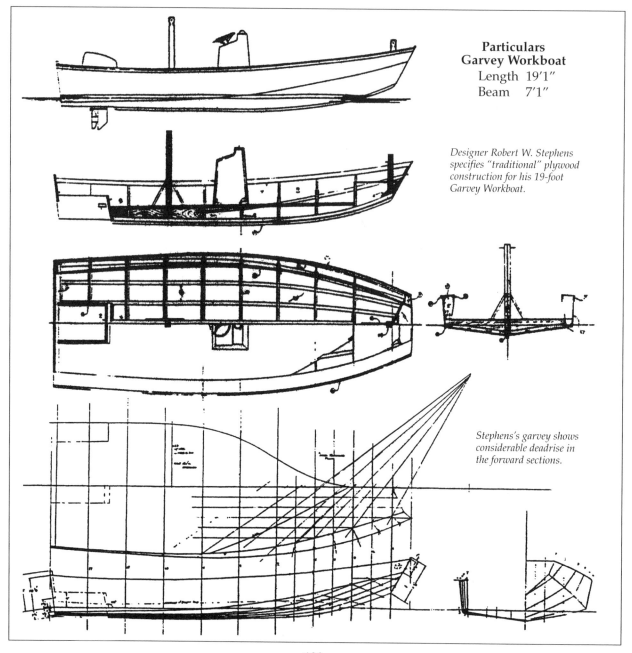

**Particulars
Garvey Workboat**
Length 19'1"
Beam 7'1"

*Designer Robert W. Stephens
specifies "traditional" plywood
construction for his 19-foot
Garvey Workboat.*

*Stephens's garvey shows
considerable deadrise in
the forward sections.*

# Two Low-Powered
# Inboard Skiffs

———— Designs by William and John Atkin ————
Commentary by Mike O'Brien

When I was a boy, commercial watermen kept low-powered inboard skiffs. Summer people used outboard motors. The professionals knew that small inboards ran quieter, were more reliable, and stretched a gallon of fuel miles farther than the cranky outboards of that era. Since that time, four decades of relentless outboard motor development have rendered small inboard skiffs virtually extinct.

Be that as it may, skiffs of the type shown here continue to offer some advantages. They carry their engine weight low and amidships — far better for a boat's handling than clamping the motor's mass high on the transom. The engine itself is protected, more or less, from salt water and theft.

Small inboards (with the exception of some air-cooled industrial engines) tend to produce pleasant sounds. Even if the amplitude of their noise equals that of outboards, the lower firing frequency contributes to a skipper's peace of mind. Some of us are also inclined to think that inboard skiffs look better than their outboard cousins. A modern, stylist-designed outboard motor hooked onto a traditional skiff can create an aesthetic Armageddon.

We should say up front that, unless you have access to an historic chunk of cast iron (such as the 6-horsepower Palmer specified here) or are willing to borrow the motor from your lawn mower, these rigs aren't inexpensive. This flaw, combined with the competition's easier maneuverability at low speeds and more convenient servicing (unscrew the motor, carry it to the dealer), might well have hastened the decline of the breed.

In profile above the waterline, our first little inboard boat looks to be a Sea Bright skiff, but it's not — not exactly. In fact, this design can claim descent from such wildly divergent ancestors as the Cape Ann dory, the Japanese sampan, and the Jersey skiff. Her story begins with Joshua Slocum (yes, "the" Joshua Slocum: controversial circumnavigator, author, and extraordinary seaman).

In 1887, Slocum and his wife and their two sons found themselves shipwrecked on the coast of Brazil. In need of a way home, the Captain built the 35-foot three-masted "canoe" *Liberdade*, and the family sailed her some 5,500 miles to New York. Years later, William and John Atkin received an old blueprint from a client. The faded, freehand lines had been drawn by Slocum's elder son, Victor, and they represented his rendition of *Liberdade*'s hull shape. Although Captain Slocum was said to have based his escape vehicle on a cross between a Cape Ann dory and a sampan, Victor and the Atkins apparently viewed it as a Jersey skiff. In any case, the Atkins reworked the old lines, reduced the scale, and turned out this nifty 15-foot inboard skiff. We can see the Cape Ann influence in her sections and the Jersey heritage in her overall appearance and construction. Perhaps the sampan influence was more apparent in the rigging and detailing of the original boat.

The most obvious difference between *Victor Slocum* and the deceptively dissimilar Sea Bright skiffs is the former's use of a common skeg in place of a box deadwood. On the beach, skeg-built boats tend to pitch, roll, and dig in. Sea Bright skiffs stand up straight and slide over the sand like sleds. Performance differences when fully afloat are likely to be more subtle. At any rate, the *Slocum*, with her high and buoyant ends, ought to be happy in summer waves and moderate surf — and the skeg will make for easier construction. Setting up a box deadwood looks simple in the hands of old-time boatbuilder Charlie Hankins and his peers, but builders trying it for the first time might want to close their shop doors.

For planking this skiff, the Atkins specify ⅝-inch-thick cedar over ⅞-inch-square steam-bent white oak frames on 8-inch centers. Bronze screws fasten the hood ends of the planks to the stem. Copper nails riveted over burrs are used at, and between, the frames. No sealant or caulking need be employed in planking up the sides, because the soft cedar strakes will work into each other to keep the skiff tight. The bottom, which is planked fore-and-aft with ⅞-inch cedar, should have its seams caulked with three or four strands of cotton.

For power, the Atkins suggest a 6-horsepower Palmer Baby Huskie (now long out of production) turning a 10-inch-diameter wheel with 6-inch pitch. Predicted performance is "a good 8 mph."

If *Victor Slocum* is a buoyant cork, *XLNC* (Excellency, right?) is a knife. With a beam of only 4 feet 4 inches on a length of 19 feet 2 inches, this flat-bottomed Atkin skiff promises speeds of more than 13 mph when pushed by an engine of 6 horsepower turning an 8-inch (diameter) by 7-inch (pitch) wheel.

The construction here is straightforward, in the style of most traditional skiffs. Four lapped ⅝-inch white cedar strakes make up each side. They are fitted and fastened in the same manner as the *Slocum*'s, but they'll be even easier to hang because of *XLNC*'s gentle curves and straight sections. The bottom goes together as would that for a cross-planked rowing skiff. It is more robust, with ¾-inch cedar planking, a ¾-inch by 6-inch white oak keelson, a couple of ¾-inch by 4-inch sister keelsons, and three 2½-inch by 4-inch white oak floor timbers (which support 3-inch-square white oak engine beds).

Long, slender powerboats are easy to like, and we can — as did the Atkins — make cogent arguments supporting their superiority. All else (particularly power and displacement) being equal, the longer, narrower skiff will tend to be faster and will throw less spray than will a shorter boat. Longer skiffs, if properly designed, will provide a more comfortable ride through the harbor chop, and they make better working platforms. Their easier curves allow for easier construction. (Is there anything in this world more difficult to plank up than a squat, apple-cheeked dinghy?)

All logic aside, there is something compelling about a long, narrow boat running at low rpm and high speed — making little fuss and less noise.

As Billy Atkin might have said: There you have it, Shipmates, two good little skiffs. Build them exactly as drawn, and they won't disappoint you.

*Plans for* Victor Slocum *and* XLNC *can be ordered from Atkin Boat Plans, P.O. Box 3005, Noroton, CT 06820.*

# Particulars
## *Victor Slocum*
LOA    15'0"
Beam   5'1"
Draft  1'2"
Power  6 hp

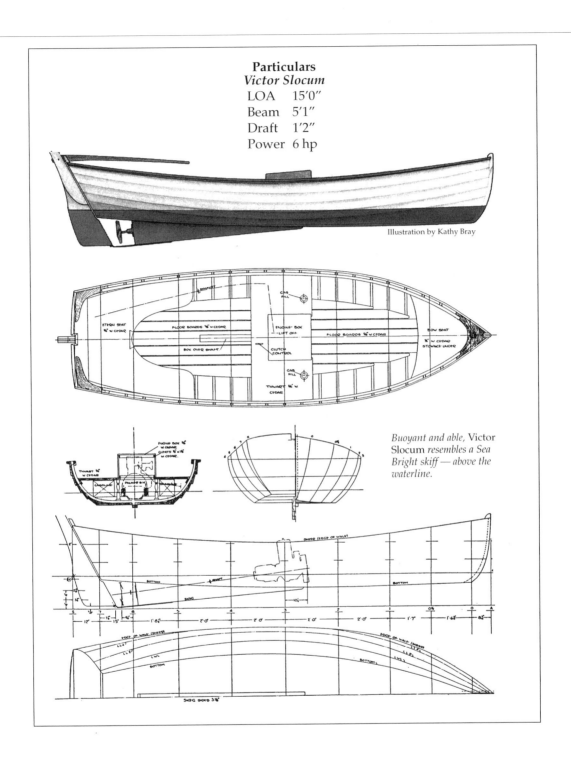

Illustration by Kathy Bray

*Buoyant and able,* Victor Slocum *resembles a Sea Bright skiff — above the waterline.*

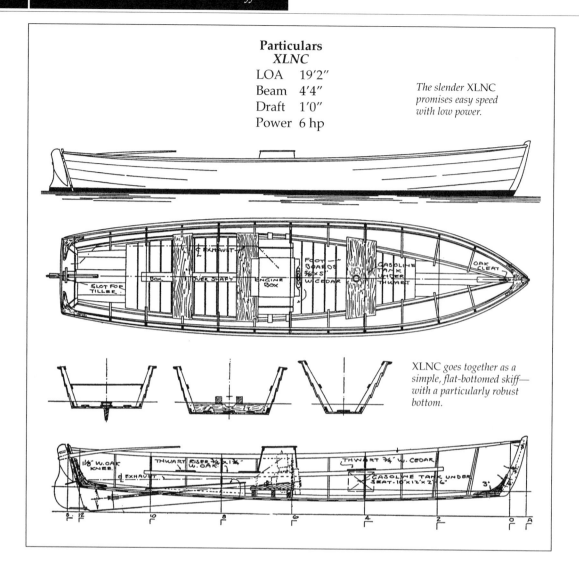

**Particulars**
*XLNC*

| | |
|---|---|
| LOA | 19'2" |
| Beam | 4'4" |
| Draft | 1'0" |
| Power | 6 hp |

*The slender XLNC promises easy speed with low power.*

*XLNC goes together as a simple, flat-bottomed skiff— with a particularly robust bottom.*

# LIX

# Three Plywood Composite Outboard Boats

Designs by Accumar, Headwater Boats, and Glen-L Marine
Commentary by Mike O'Brien

*A*mong traditional boatbuilding tasks, the beveling of chine logs must rank as one of the most satisfyingly pleasant operations. You sharpen your favorite plane to near perfection, and let it slice through the wood, spewing long curls. It feels fine, sounds fine, employs no unusual chemicals, and raises no dust — only wood shavings (and, so long as you don't eat them or set fire to them, they seem to pose no health hazards).

Some of us accept plywood composite construction techniques reluctantly, because they trade all of this fun for clouds of sanding dust and the stench of resins and catalysts. Psychologically comforting structural members are eliminated. A healthy fillet might well be stronger than a chine log, but it doesn't look stronger. Still, all having been considered, builders of plywood composite boats are on to something good. They produce clean, strong hulls that seem more tolerant of casual care than do boats of conventional manufacture.

So, how do you build a plywood composite hull? There are variations in name (stitch-and-glue, taped-seam, tack-and-tape, sewn-seam, Fast-G, etc.) that can indicate differences in technique, but in simplest terms: Draw the expanded (that is, flattened-out) shape of the hull panels on sheet plywood — no true lofting required. Cut out the panels (in the interest of your sanity and the hull's fairness, use a circular saw — not a sabersaw). Stitch the panels together (usually with copper wire) over a few frames or molds, and you have something that looks to be a boat. Cover the inside of the panel junctions with a fillet made from resin (usually an epoxy) mixed with a filler (this can be wood

flour and/or proprietary powders and fibers). After the resin cures, cut off or remove the wire stitches, and cover the seams inside and out with fiberglass tape. If you desire a yacht-smooth appearance, attack the areas near the taped panel junctions with sandpaper, surfacing filler, and patience — again, and again, and again. Finally, finish as you would any fiberglassed plywood boat.

On Bainbridge Island, Washington, Eric Hutchinson, proprietor of Good Enough Boatworks, succumbed to the lure of plywood/epoxy and asked Accumar's Scott Sprague to draw a stable, trailerable, easily built, outboard-powered fishing boat. The new design also would have to offer protection from the cold rain that seems to go along with catching blackmouth salmon in the Northwest. Sprague needed just a few days to respond with plans for the likable Good Enough 15.

The boat went together using the basic stitch-and-glue techniques described above. Apparently, the only intimidating part of the process involved pulling the bottom panels together up forward. Hutchinson claims he attempted to enlist the aid of Clark Kent but settled, instead, for a Spanish windlass and two threaded rods.

Despite the name of his shop, the builder had some trouble determining an appropriate level of finish. "I got sucked into the 'just a couple more hours' syndrome... days dragged into weeks," Hutchinson reports. In the end, he went off cruising and left the job to a friend. He seems pleased with the results.

The Good Enough 15 weighs less than 500 pounds, floats where she should, and makes 22.5 knots when pushed by a 25-horsepower outboard. In the words of contemporary copywriters, the small house combines protection with "full walk-around capability" on deck — a virtue mightily appreciated by anglers.

Preferring functional definitions, Tracy O'Brien of Headwater Boats (no relation to this writer) refers to his method of plywood composite construction as "taped-seam." For the fast-and-able Deadrise 19, he specifies that the epoxy fillets be covered with two layers of 24-ounce biaxial tape rather than several layers of 8- or 10-ounce woven fiberglass cloth. Essentially, biaxial cloth consists of multiple layers of nonwoven fiberglass fibers oriented at 45 degrees to the edge of the fabric. These diagonal strands are sewn to a thin fiberglass mat. The Chehalis, Washington, designer/builder points out that virtually every fiber in biaxial cloth crosses the joints between plywood panels, resulting in great strength for a given amount of material. Also, this strand orientation allows the tape to conform more easily to tightly radiused turns. (For these reasons, some experienced builders who use conventional woven fiberglass make their own tape by cutting across the weave of standard fiberglass cloth at a 45-degree angle. Store-bought fiberglass tape usually has its fibers woven parallel and perpendicular to the tape length.)

O'Brien's drawing technique results in a hull with a slightly different twist — or, rather, lack of same. At first glance, the Deadrise 19's panels do seem to show twist. But, in reality, all of its curved surfaces are cylindrical. Tracy accomplishes this feat during the design process by using station lines that are neither perpendicular to the design waterline plane in profile nor at right angles to the hull centerline in plan view. All else being equal, this should result in relatively low stress on the plywood sheets, and assembly of the hull panels should be easy — no small matter, as the lack of substantial molds and frames would make severe distortion of the plywood difficult to control.

Although the heavy, stark drawings shown here hardly flatter the Deadrise 19, this boat has a striking hull shape and a reputation as a strong, level runner. I might want to cut a stronger sheer into her, but unless I plan to haul pots over her rail or row her (not likely), logic won't be in my corner. (Logic might smile, though, at the resulting reduction of edge-set in the rails.) While we're at it, let's ditch the windshield and move the controls back to a nice console placed right, plop, amidships. And maybe fit an oval coaming, and... well, now you see why relationships between builders and designers can be strained at times.

Now, here's a building technique that lies some distance from ordinary. Glen-L Marine Designs has developed a construction method called FAST-G (Fold And Stitch Then Glue). Putting together the 15-foot 9-inch Console Skiff provides a thorough demonstration of this process: First, draw the expanded hull panel shapes on sheets of plywood and cut to the lines (full-sized patterns are supplied with the plans). Then, assemble the planking flat on the shop floor. Fold this weird, and large, wooden pancake into the shape of a boat hull. Stitch and glue everything together, and finish the hull with the usual filling and sanding.

You'll notice that the drawings show the bottom and side panels as being continuous up forward. Farther aft, two large darts in the flat panel form chines when the pancake is folded to form the hull. All of this scheming tortures some interesting curves into the sheet plywood.

Acknowledging the strength of the stitched-and-glued hull, Glen-L has drawn an open arrangement plan — just a console and a bench seat surrounded by uncluttered space. Few or no structural bulkheads and frames are needed for any of the boats described here. In fact, after one of these hulls is pulled into shape and has its floors and sole installed, you can take some liberties with the interior. Of course, various weights and centers ought to be kept in mind — to say nothing of aesthetics. Certainly, no major changes should be attempted without the advice and consent of the designers.

Having said that, I'm inclined to think that the Console Skiff has sufficient shape and beam to handle increased freeboard without degrading its appearance. If you'd like to be surrounded by higher sides, without incurring the wrath of Glen L. and Barry Witt (father and son), you might consider building their 16-foot 3-inch Cabin Skiff (not shown here) and omitting the house. Aside from the cabin boat's greater freeboard, the hulls appear to be identical.

*Plans for the Good Enough 15 are available from Scott Sprague, Accumar Corporation, 1180 Finn Hill Rd. N.W., Poulsbo, WA 98370.*

*Plans for the Deadrise 19, and kits as well as completed boats, can be had from Tracy O'Brien, Headwater Boats, 156 Bunker Creek Rd., Chehalis, WA 98532.*

*Plans and frame kits for the Console Skiff are sold by Glen-L Marine Designs, 9152 Rosecrans Ave., Bellflower, CA 90707.*

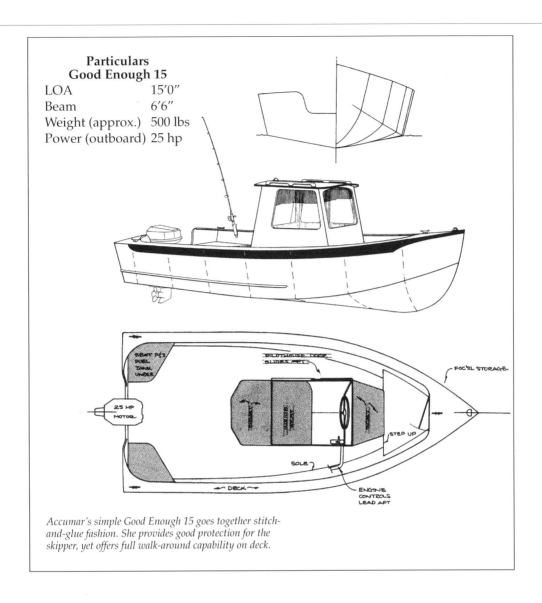

**Particulars**
**Good Enough 15**

| | |
|---|---|
| LOA | 15'0" |
| Beam | 6'6" |
| Weight (approx.) | 500 lbs |
| Power (outboard) | 25 hp |

*Accumar's simple Good Enough 15 goes together stitch-and-glue fashion. She provides good protection for the skipper, yet offers full walk-around capability on deck.*

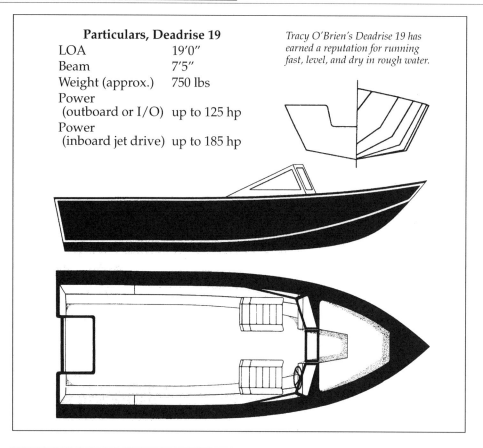

### Particulars, Deadrise 19

| | |
|---|---|
| LOA | 19'0" |
| Beam | 7'5" |
| Weight (approx.) | 750 lbs |
| Power (outboard or I/O) | up to 125 hp |
| Power (inboard jet drive) | up to 185 hp |

*Tracy O'Brien's Deadrise 19 has earned a reputation for running fast, level, and dry in rough water.*

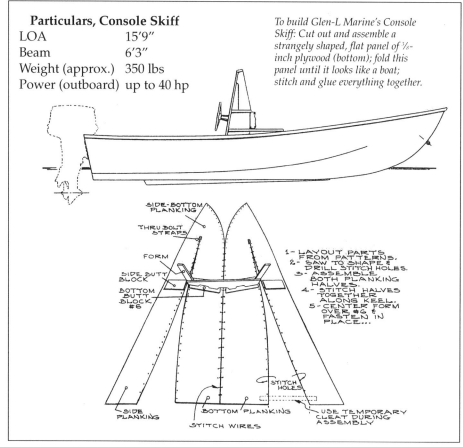

### Particulars, Console Skiff

| | |
|---|---|
| LOA | 15'9" |
| Beam | 6'3" |
| Weight (approx.) | 350 lbs |
| Power (outboard) | up to 40 hp |

*To build Glen-L Marine's Console Skiff: Cut out and assemble a strangely shaped, flat panel of ⅜-inch plywood (bottom); fold this panel until it looks like a boat; stitch and glue everything together.*

SIDE-BOTTOM PLANKING

THRU BOLT STRAPS

FORM

SIDE BUTT BLOCK

BOTTOM BUTT BLOCK #6

SIDE PLANKING

STITCH WIRES

BOTTOM PLANKING

STITCH HOLES

USE TEMPORARY CLEAT DURING ASSEMBLY

1- LAYOUT PARTS FROM PATTERNS.
2- SAW TO SHAPE & DRILL STITCH HOLES.
3- ASSEMBLE BOTH PLANKING HALVES.
4- STITCH HALVES TOGETHER ALONG KEEL.
5- CENTER FORM OVER #6 & FASTEN IN PLACE...

# Four Classic Outboard Cruisers

Designs by Weston Farmer and Howard I. Chapelle
Commentary by Mike O'Brien

Post-World War II America flaunted excess. Aggressively ugly automobiles serviced the ill-conceived tract houses that sprouted around nearly every city. As their contribution to this scene, boat designers — or at least boat promoters — contrived short, fat, and high plywood boxes that they marketed as "outboard cruisers." These monstrosities ran at high speeds only on the advertising pages of boating periodicals. In real life they were slowed by any sea larger than a ripple and by totally unreasonable fuel costs — a considerable achievement in those days of 23-cents-per-gallon gasoline.

Periodical advertising notwithstanding, not all naval architects lost their bearings. Fortunately for those of us who became posterity, the masters of the craft sailed through this period unaffected. Here's a quartet of clean-lined outboard cruisers that enjoyed no great popularity when introduced in the 1950s. Now, perhaps, we're ready for them.

Writing in *From My Old Boatshop* (Boat House Portland, Oregon, 1996), Weston Farmer referred to *Trumpet* as "the keystone piece in my ganglia of narrative design hooks...." Clearly, he considered her to be one of his most significant efforts, and her businesslike lapstrake hull does yield some surprises. From the turn of her bilge to the keel, her bottom is outlapped (reversed lapstrake). Farmer saw this as a way of providing "peeler strips" — longitudinal steps or ventilators — for the out-flying water. Though not everyone would agree in detail, he considered their function identical to that of the longitudinal strakes Ray Hunt was using on his early deep-V hulls at about

the same time. Citing work done by George Crouch 20 years earlier, Farmer took no credit for the idea.

*Trumpet*'s keel appears to be deliberately hogged. Her designer explained that this helps produce "inherent fore-and-aft trim components" resulting in a boat that lifts at speed but never points her nose at the sky. Farmer was quick to point out that the bottom isn't hooked. Indeed, the buttock lines are quite straight. In recent years, others have applied similar reasoning, with mixed results. One school of thought holds that the improved performance is offset by more complicated construction, and that adjustable trim tabs achieve about the same results more easily — if somewhat less elegantly. As may be, every photo we've seen shows *Trumpet* running level and looking fine. She's no easy boat to build, but those who have put her together say the work is well spent.

Sun Dance floated off Farmer's drawing table a few years before *Trumpet*. She's a straightforward piece of hull design and construction, and her layout is full of clever ideas and common sense. Compared to a trunk cabin, her raised deck provides greater working space and strength at a lower cost. Making it tight would be no trouble at all, whereas Farmer allowed that "no living man has yet made a cabin trunk that won't eventually leak."

Because she has no main bulkhead, *Sun Dance*'s interior lacks distinct boundaries. The cabin is open to the cockpit, and between them sits the steering station — Farmer jokingly called it a "semi-demi flying bridge." Whether we perceive the controls as being in the cabin or out in the cockpit seems to depend upon our degree of anxiety at the moment. Having had several childhood adventures aboard a boat with a similar layout, I can tell you that as the evenings became dark and cold, the bridge seemed to move below as if by magic. When things got scary, the dry ride, perfect vision, and good trim allowed by this arrangement seemed incidental to the psychological comfort it provided.

We remember Howard I. Chapelle for impressive books in which he showed lines taken off native American watercraft. His original designs are more obscure. As you might suspect, most of his work was heavy with the tradition and details of the boats he had measured while studying working watercraft. The two plans shown here display the Chesapeake flavor that marked much of his personal output. They are likable, easily driven skiffs with strong personalities.

In an uncharacteristically romantic description, Chapelle referred to *Waterman* as being "intended for use in open waters where a small boat must meet both sea and wind." At first glance she appears to be a typical outboard-powered deadrise, but closer inspection reveals that she's really a modified sharpie. The deadrise's deep, staved forefoot that would have made her softer and quieter in a chop was eliminated in the interest of easier construction. The designer meant that the bottom should be cross planked — "Chesapeake construction," he called it in the plans — but he showed optional longitudinal and plywood planking. For what it's worth, the traditional method, with its minimal transverse framing, creates a cleaner interior on paper and in fact.

Low and narrow by pleasure-boat standards, *Waterman* could earn her keep as a working skiff. When you're hauling several score crab pots over the side each day, an extra inch of freeboard is bad news. The cuddy certainly ought to be shortened if this boat is going to work for her living, but you might consider keeping the swinging "lift-top." It allows for useful headroom while at anchor and a low profile underway.

Hardly a new concept, this feature has been built into cruising canoes and other small boats for more than a century. The design details are well settled, and the system works — unlike some too-clever production "pop-tops."

In drawing the last boat in this little fleet, Chapelle called upon his reservoir of grace and skill as a designer. Admittedly, he opted for the prosaic in labeling her an "18-foot Sharpie Outboard Motor Camp Skiff." She deserves better. This boat's perfect proportions reflect Chapelle's respect for her type. He often warned his readers that flat-bottomed craft might be easily built, but designing them properly requires experience.

Chapelle drew the Camp Skiff with a lift-top, and he included a companionway slide for unlimited headroom. Making use of her depth, he pampered the skiff's crew with raised berths. The motor gets equally good treatment, as it is camouflaged by its own house — also fitted with a lift-top. Twin skegs guard the lower unit, and the engine can tilt up into its well. On deck, the crew is protected by a deep cockpit, healthy coamings, and wide side decks ("washboards," if you're on the Chesapeake). A scuppered deck box just forward of the trunk holds ground tackle and its associated mess.

The 18-foot Sharpie Outboard Motor Camp Skiff would be much at home poking around somewhere miles back in an Eastern Shore salt marsh. Looking hard at her drawings, I can almost smell the dried grass and hear the redwings. She's a "right" boat — no doubt about it. If you build her, give her a proper name.

*Plans for* Trumpet *and* Sun Dance *are available from Weston Farmer Associates, 18970 Azure Rd., Wayzata, MN 55391.*

*Plans for Howard I. Chapelle's Camp Skiff are available from the Smithsonian Institution, Division of Transportation, NMAH 5010/MRC 628, Washington, DC 20560.*

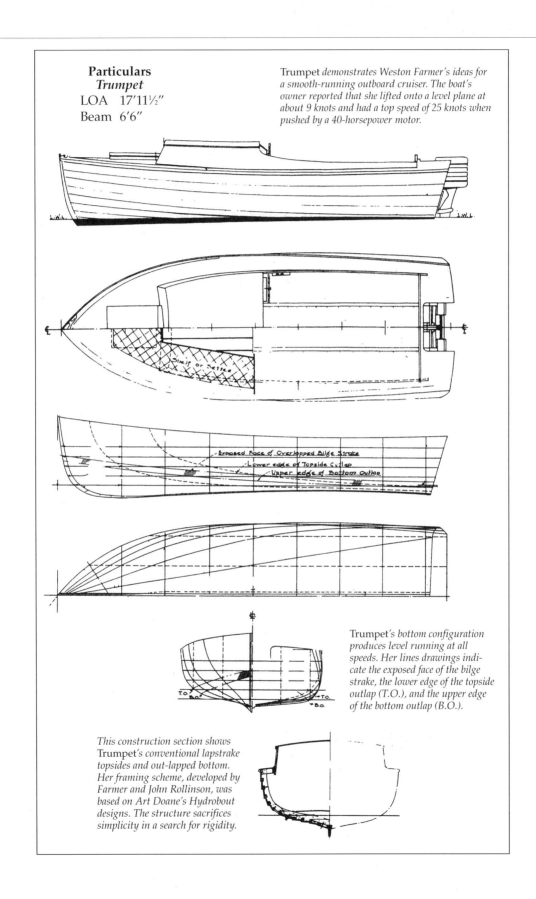

**Particulars**
*Trumpet*
LOA 17'11½"
Beam 6'6"

Trumpet *demonstrates Weston Farmer's ideas for a smooth-running outboard cruiser. The boat's owner reported that she lifted onto a level plane at about 9 knots and had a top speed of 25 knots when pushed by a 40-horsepower motor.*

Exposed Face of Overlapped Bilge Strake
Lower edge of Topside Cutlap
Upper edge of Bottom Outlap

Trumpet's *bottom configuration produces level running at all speeds. Her lines drawings indicate the exposed face of the bilge strake, the lower edge of the topside outlap (T.O.), and the upper edge of the bottom outlap (B.O.).*

*This construction section shows* Trumpet's *conventional lapstrake topsides and out-lapped bottom. Her framing scheme, developed by Farmer and John Rollinson, was based on Art Doane's Hydrobout designs. The structure sacrifices simplicity in a search for rigidity.*

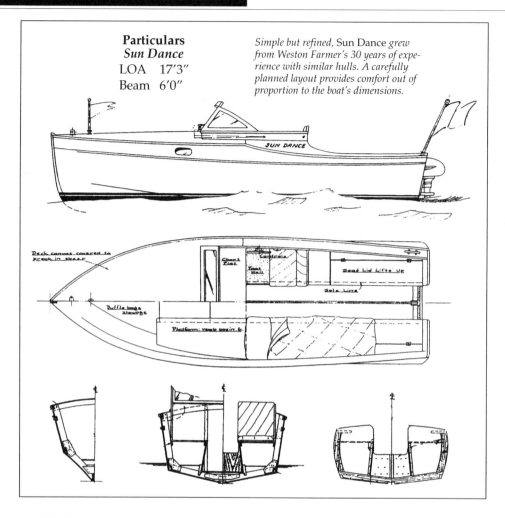

**Particulars**
*Sun Dance*
LOA   17'3"
Beam  6'0"

*Simple but refined, Sun Dance grew from Weston Farmer's 30 years of experience with similar hulls. A carefully planned layout provides comfort out of proportion to the boat's dimensions.*

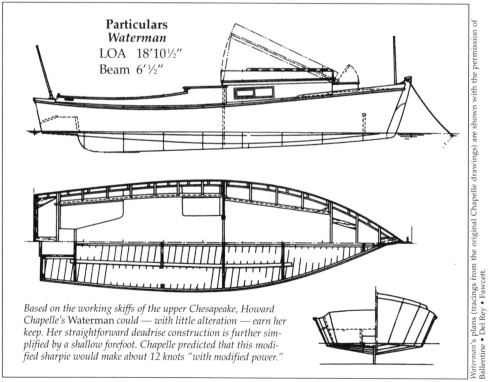

**Particulars**
*Waterman*
LOA   18'10½"
Beam  6'½"

*Based on the working skiffs of the upper Chesapeake, Howard Chapelle's Waterman could — with little alteration — earn her keep. Her straightforward deadrise construction is further simplified by a shallow forefoot. Chapelle predicted that this modified sharpie would make about 12 knots "with modified power."*

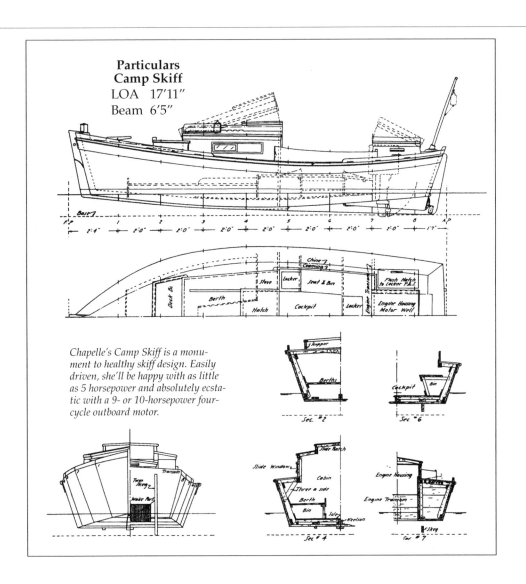

**Particulars
Camp Skiff**
LOA   17'11"
Beam  6'5"

Chapelle's Camp Skiff is a monument to healthy skiff design. Easily driven, she'll be happy with as little as 5 horsepower and absolutely ecstatic with a 9- or 10-horsepower four-cycle outboard motor.

# A Displacement Launch

Design by Eliot Spalding
Commentary by Mike O'Brien

With a cruising speed of about 8 knots, this likable launch will move too slowly to demand a helmsman's raw-edge, wheel-clutching attention; yet the scenery will pass at a rate sufficient to entertain the crew and the passengers. And I'll wager that *Decoy* will look as appropriate in the middle of the next century as she did last week. Eliot Spalding designed her nearly 20 years ago, but he could have completed the drawings half a century back down the road — this hull is not of a rapidly evolving type.

In a letter written before the ink had dried on the lines plan, Spalding explained the rationale for this design: "There seems to be an ever increasing number of practical boatmen who have had their bellies full of the 'thrill' of the spine-jarring pounding one gets in the high-speed-in-flat-water cracker boxes that have saturated the waterfront in recent years.... People who don't care for these plastic, flash, and chrome imitations of one another.... People who value comfort, safety, and economy over high speed; who want a boat with an easy motion and good maneuverability; who want a comfortable cockpit...and side decks wide enough to let someone go forward with at least some hope of arriving at the foredeck." Passionate words for a plain, but handsome, design.

Bob Knecht, who made some preliminary sketches and then commissioned this design, seemed to fit the profile described by Spalding. Knecht wanted a boat with "classic" lines — a launch that would be wide enough to accommodate his two-year-old daughter and her friends with safety and comfort. He hoped that the boat would be relatively heavy and steady on her feet and, yet, shoal of draft for casual gunkholing.

One more criterion: Knecht, an amateur builder, wanted to put the boat together on his own. To this end, Spalding drew a hull that shows easy lines and no severe compound curves. He specified strip planking (¾-inch by 1-inch pine). Although building a hull by stacking countless slivers of wood one atop another can be labor intensive, the process is straightforward. It avoids the seemingly arcane layout work associated with other planking schemes, and there's no worry of making catastrophically incorrect sawcuts through $200 sheets of plywood or wide planks of perfect cedar. The method lends itself well to start-and-stop boatbuilding; an amateur builder can hang as many strip planks as he wishes after coming home from the office. There is little materials waste when strip-building — if you don't consider the sawdust. Contrary to common opinion, round-bilged hulls need be no more difficult to build than their chined counterparts; in some cases, they might go together more easily.

The builder planned on running his boat up on the beach with fair regularity, and the scantlings were worked up with this in mind. Stem and keel are of 3-inch oak, and the ⅞-inch by 1¼-inch oak frames are bent in (on the flat) on 10-inch centers.

Spalding predicted that *Decoy*'s burdensome hull would punch to windward with authority and little reduction in speed. Generous reserve buoyancy forward would, he said, keep her from rooting and otherwise misbehaving when running off in rough water. A substantial external keel should help her head where she's pointed, as well. The keel sweeps up a few feet forward of the sternpost to allow improved water flow to the propeller. Pot warp also will have good access to the propeller, and we might consider adding a cage or other protection. As may be, the designer points out that the keel ought to keep this big little launch steady on her mooring: "A boat that sails around at anchor makes a poor boat for comfort."

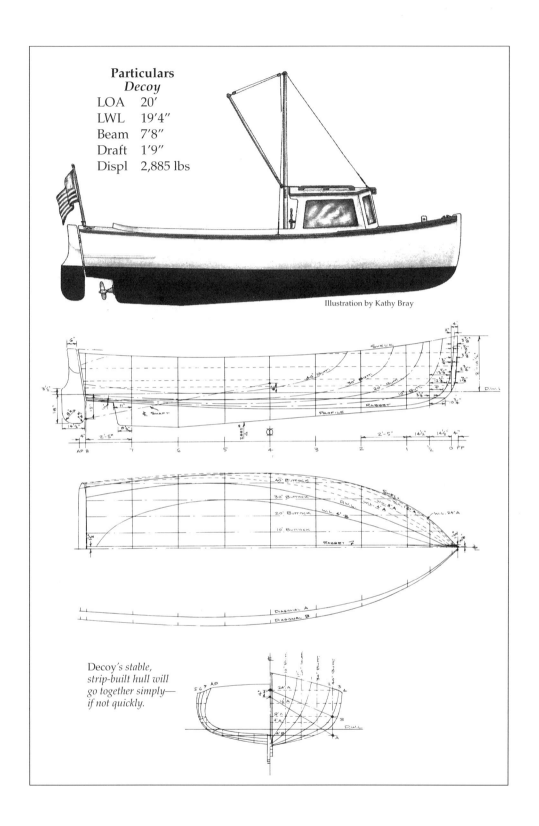

**Particulars**
*Decoy*
LOA    20′
LWL    19′4″
Beam   7′8″
Draft   1′9″
Displ   2,885 lbs

Illustration by Kathy Bray

Decoy's stable,
strip-built hull will
go together simply—
if not quickly.

To control *Decoy*, Spalding resorted to a wooden rudder hung from the transom. His designer's commentary suggests that he expected to be criticized for that decision: "No doubt, upon seeing this, many will accuse [me] of living in another age." He took pains to explain the choice: "For a low- or moderate-speed powerboat [an outboard rudder] has practical advantages compared to its under-hull counterpart. Being farther aft, it provides more effective turning action...and it is easily inspected." He added that an outboard rudder tends to be simple to build and inexpensive to install, as it requires no hole through the boat's bottom and no stuffing box or other sundry paraphernalia. I'll add that a well-crafted outboard rudder might enhance a boat's appearance — particularly a boat with a broad, flat, transom stern.

The large rudder, and the hull's gentle shape, persuaded Spalding to draw an auxiliary sailing rig (a single spritsail) for this powerboat. He cautions, however, that *Decoy* does not pretend to be a sailboat and,

"of course, will not sail to windward, although she will reach and run."

Other design options include an open version with an oval coaming forward that can accept a canvas dodger. Fitted with robust quarter rails and fenders, *Decoy* could work as a launch in any harbor — plain or fancy.

Knecht planned to finish the prototype with a shelter cabin as depicted in the drawing. In place of the specified Westerbeke Four-91, he had obtained an inexpensive rebuilt Atomic Four and expected to be on the water for less than $2,000 total cost. As sometimes happens, the boat was sold away before completion and has dropped from sight.

*Plans for* Decoy *are available from The WoodenBoat Store, P.O. Box 78, Brooklin, ME 04616; 800–273–7447.*

*You can write to designer Eliot Spalding at P.O. Box 22, South Freeport, ME 04078.*

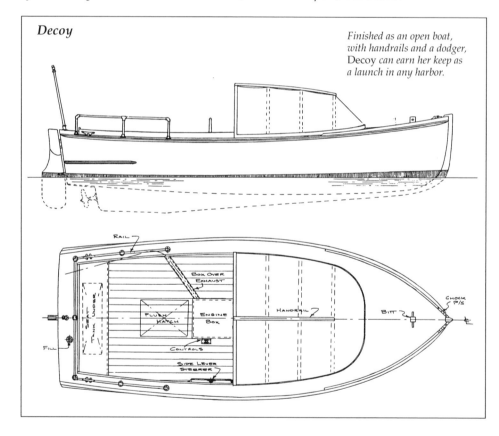

**Decoy**

*Finished as an open boat, with handrails and a dodger,* Decoy *can earn her keep as a launch in any harbor.*

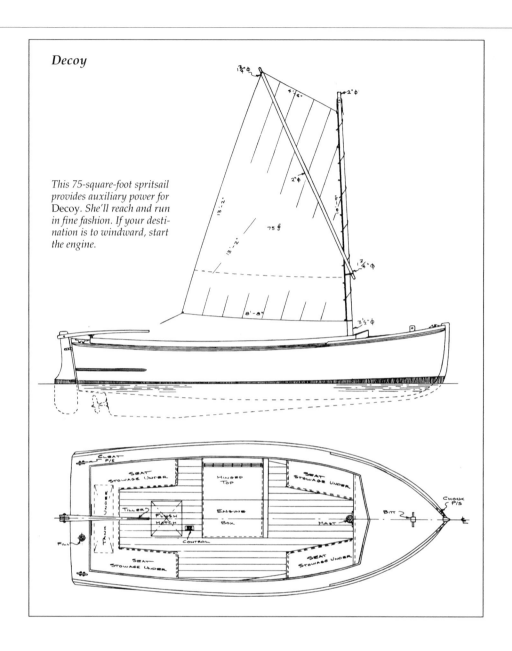

## Decoy

This 75-square-foot spritsail provides auxiliary power for Decoy. She'll reach and run in fine fashion. If your destination is to windward, start the engine.

# A Sheet-Plywood Lobster Skiff

Design by Arno Day
Commentary by Mike O'Brien

Typical Maine outboard lobster skiffs appear to be juvenile versions of the larger Maine inboard lobsterboats. They share strong sheerlines; shapely topsides, with considerable flare in the forward sections; firm bilges aft; and relatively low beam-to-length ratios. Tradition calls for strip-planking or plank-on-bent-frame carvel construction. Of late, some skiffs have been splashed in fiberglass and a few have been cold-molded. Altogether, they are a handsome and efficient breed.

A few years back, I visited Arno Day's shop in Sedgwick, Maine. This native of coastal Maine has been designing and building traditional lobsterboats and skiffs for more than fifty years. After we had conducted some now long-forgotten editorial business, he asked if I'd like to see his latest drawings. Of course — and I should have known from the look in his eyes that these new designs were out of the ordinary.

We walked from the shop, across the dirt driveway, and into his well-kept, barn-red house. In a room that appeared to have been intended for dining (but now was filled with splines, battens, ducks, and tubes of vellum), the designer pulled the dust cover off his drawing board. There, in place of the lines for his usual round-bilged hulls, were preliminary drawings for a series of straight-sectioned, multi-chined lobsterboats. Day explained that he had drawn the sheet-plywood hulls so that watermen might have easily built boats — boats they could put together themselves even if they had little experience as builders.

Among the drawings were sketches for a lean 21-foot outboard skiff that Day later would flesh out for builder Mark Abb as the Great Cove 21, the design you see here. Abb, an aspiring marine photographer, wanted to replace his chunky fiberglass runabout with a longer boat that would easily and smoothly traverse the sometimes rough waters of Penobscot Bay — a fast and steady camera platform.

Abb built his skiff using about 38 sheets of ¼-inch plywood (doubled all over to give a hull thickness of ½-inch) and 15 gallons of epoxy. He reckons that material for the hull (plywood, epoxy, solid timber, and fastenings) spoiled the better part of $2,000 [1995].

Total construction time amounted to nearly 1,600 man-hours spread through three winters. Some of that time must be charged to the inefficiencies of stop-and-start boatbuilding. (Untangle the extension cord, find the drill motor, get the epoxy working. Then, coil the extension cord, put the drill back where it ought to have been in the first place, clean the brushes....) And the showboat finish applied by Abb and painter Jack Powell couldn't be accomplished overnight. Working straight through and settling for a plain-vanilla appearance (i.e., lots of latex house paint), we might cut this time in half. The result wouldn't look half so well as Abb's expert work, but it would run the same.

Quick study of the construction drawings for the Great Cove 21 reveals a complex web of internal structure. Couldn't we knock more than a few hours off the building time by eliminating some of the transverse frames and longitudinal stringers? In fact, might we resort to stitch-and-glue construction, which would

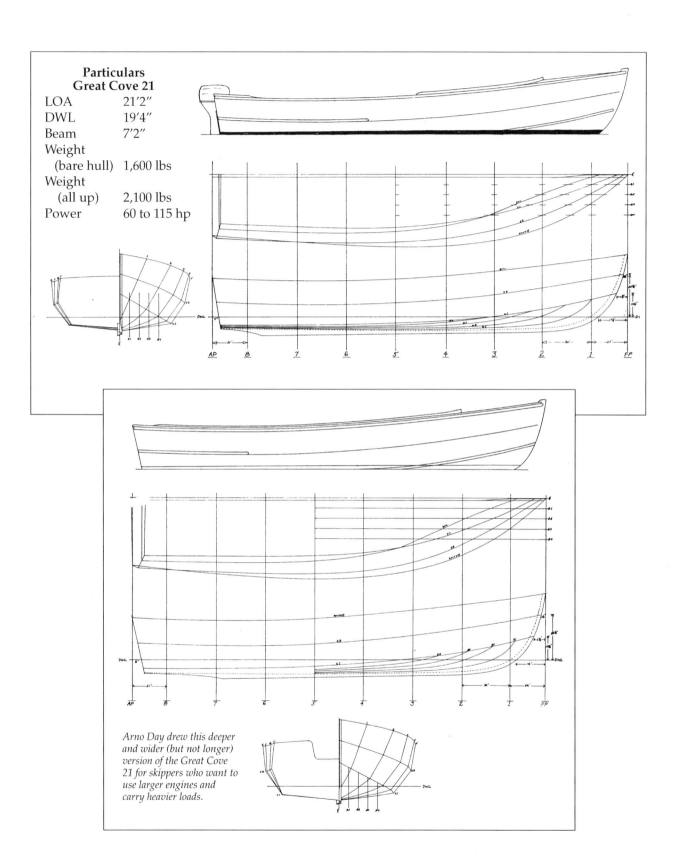

**Particulars**
**Great Cove 21**

| | |
|---|---|
| LOA | 21'2" |
| DWL | 19'4" |
| Beam | 7'2" |
| Weight (bare hull) | 1,600 lbs |
| Weight (all up) | 2,100 lbs |
| Power | 60 to 115 hp |

*Arno Day drew this deeper and wider (but not longer) version of the Great Cove 21 for skippers who want to use larger engines and carry heavier loads.*

drastically reduce our need for solid timber? Day responds that the traditional framed-plywood construction specified in his plans allows a builder to choose adhesives according to personal preferences and costs. (For most contemporary builders, stitch-and-glue dictates the use of epoxy.) I'll add that framing and beveling can be pleasant work. On the other hand, grinding down epoxified stitch-and-glue joints is, well — not grand fun. As may be, this hull shape seems suited to stitch-and-glue construction. If you want to convert this design (or other framed-plywood hulls) to stitch-and-glue, it can be done. The construction work will be messy, but the results will be clean, tight, and strong.

The prototype Great Cove 21 made a striking appearance as it slipped into Eggemoggin Reach on a cold day in late spring. Long, lean boats of simple line are almost always pleasurable to our eyes. Builder Abb cranked up the 115-hp Mercury, backed down clear of the trailer, and made a few careful low-speed passes by the pier. Builders are allowed their caution. On about the fifth turn around the float, he stopped to pick up designer Day. After a brief discussion, Day took the controls. He secured his cap with a tug at the visor, grabbed the throttle, and jammed it forward — hard forward, all the way forward. Designers are permitted their curiosity. For a moment the high-powered skiff paused and pointed at the sky, then it climbed over its own bow wave and screamed away at 35 knots.

The boat proved more than fast enough; but, as happens with prototypes, there were minor glitches. The "moment" required to jump onto a plane from a dead start proved to be longer than hoped, and, under certain combinations of throttle setting and motor trim, the boat tended to porpoise. (In fairness, it should be said that the powerful Mercury packed about 45 more horses than had been called for in the original design.) As may be, Abb corrected both of these problems simply by tacking ½-inch-thick wedges (shingles, if you will) to the boat's bottom at the stern.

Day has ensured that future Great Cove 21s will run perfectly by straightening the lower chines slightly in plan view and providing greater beam on the bottom back aft. The changes are reflected in the drawings shown here. Design at its best can be a cooperative venture. While recalling the evolution of this boat, Day explains, "I wrote the words, but Mark sang the song."

I suspect that designers are always designing. Not long after the epoxy on the prototype Great Cove had set up, Day unveiled drawings for a wider and deeper version of the big skiff. Hulls built to the new plans should be happy with more powerful engines and heavier loads, but they might sacrifice some of the fuel efficiency and gentle ride of the original. The prototype's beam-to-length ratio (about 1 foot of width for every 3 feet of length) coincides with the proportions of the traditional hulls that Day has designed and built for decades. The 8-foot beam specified in the new drawings seems more representative of contemporary high-powered lobsterboats.

Although the Great Cove 21 can run fast (35-plus knots), it seems most natural when loping along with an easy gait — say, 21 knots at 4200 rpm — leaving little fuss behind. It rides smoothly, banks predictably in high-speed turns, and demonstrates no handling vices. In the designer's words, "It works all right." That's high praise Down East.

*Plans for the Great Cove 21 are available from Arno Day, P.O. Box 23, Sedgwick, ME 04676.*

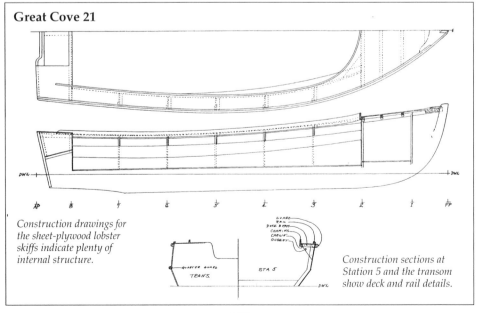

**Great Cove 21**

*Construction drawings for the sheet-plywood lobster skiffs indicate plenty of internal structure.*

*Construction sections at Station 5 and the transom show deck and rail details.*

# A Stretched Lobster Skiff

——— Design by Philip C. Bolger ———
Commentary by Mike O'Brien

Maine outboard-powered lobsterboats enjoy a reputation for efficient speed, good load-carrying ability, and handsome appearance. Philip C. Bolger began drawing an evolving family of these skiffs in the 1950s. His latest thoughts appear in the 21-foot 4-inch *Sometime or Never*.

This launch represents a stretched version of the designer's 16-foot *Shivaree*. The 16-footer has plenty of beam (7 feet), so Bolger simply increased the distance between mold stations from 2 feet to 2 feet 8 inches. He changed the stem's fore-and-aft offsets proportionally so the bow profile shows more rake. Heights and breadths were left untouched. These alterations increased the hull's displacement at the marked waterline from 1,750 pounds to 2,300 pounds. (If Bolger had scaled up all dimensions, rather than only the length, the resulting 21-foot 4-inch by 9-foot 4-inch boat would have pushed aside about 4,100 pounds of water.)

As almost any skiff builder knows, "stretching" boats is common practice. And creating a new design by sliding molds back and forth on a strongback sometimes works as well as sitting down at the drawing table. Bolger points out that stock-boat manufacturers of the 1930s often used the same molds for hulls built to different lengths. Matthews, for example, built standard 38-, 46-, and 50-foot power cruisers all based on the same molds. On a larger scale, ships are routinely chopped in half athwartships and lengthened by the insertion of new midbodies. We're told that this surgery often results in greater speed with the same power.

In addition to their virtues, some lobster skiffs share a common fault: they can be wet. Twenty years ago, I worked an 18-foot fiberglass cousin of this boat (not a Bolger design) on the Chesapeake. Driving into a steep chop resulted in a high-pressure shower. Warm Bay water — and my youth — made this behavior tolerable, but I worried about my fellow skiff owners to the north and east. Many of them coped, I learned later, by adding wooden spray rails low down on the fiberglass hulls.

Unless driven too fast while loaded too heavily, the skiffs shown here shouldn't need spray rails. Some time ago, while drawing a revised version of his *Seguin* (a 15-foot 6-inch by 7-foot design created in 1956), Bolger fined up the forefoot and recovered the lost volume by swelling the topsides higher and farther aft. The altered boat proved easier to plank than its predecessor, and it behaved better in rough water.

Traces of the new *Seguin*'s hollow-cheeked appearance can be seen in most of the designer's recent lobster-skiff derivatives. Bolger describes the shape as having "a nice blend of sharpness and buoyancy [so] that the boat is perfectly dry at all speeds, even in a chop with three people sitting forward." It would seem that the configuration reduces and redirects spray. The bow wave rolls down and out, rather than climbing the sides. When running off in a sea, the hull picks up displacement and stability early on, which helps prevent broaching.

Bolger assigns some numbers to *Shivaree*'s performance: "With two men, she made 29.8 statute miles per hour powered by an old Johnson 50-horsepower outboard. She planed level with her bottom and took sharp turns smoothly. With the same load, she made 15 miles per hour powered by the 25-horsepower Evinrude that's on her now.... You're welcome to infer that she would make close to 60 miles per hour with 100 horsepower, and I bet she would do close to 12 miles per hour with 15 horsepower. I like the way she can run slowly with the light 25 without dragging half the bay behind her — as opposed to how she behaves with the heavy 50."

The designer predicts that the new 21-foot 4-inch hull will run faster than his 16-foot *Shivaree* when pushed by the same 25-horsepower motor. If each boat has 50 horsepower strapped to its transom, he expects that they will be about even in speed — with the shorter gaining a slight advantage in smooth water. (Much of the shorter boat will be in the air, and its shape will be of less consequence, but the weight and surface friction of the longer boat still must be factored into the equation.) In rough water, the longer boat will win "by slicing through the crests more smoothly."

If a boat will be kept in the water, Bolger usually recommends carvel planking on bent frames for this type of hull ("set work," some would call it). He suggests that lapstrake, strip, or cold-molded construction might be more appropriate if the boat is to live on a trailer. In any case, the scantlings detailed on the 21-footer's plans are noted as being "suggestive only." The alternate construction sections shown here are taken from the drawings for the 16-foot *Shivaree*. British builder Paul Billings cold-molded the prototype *Sometime or Never* to a yacht finish.

The characteristics that make these boats well suited for their ancestral job of inshore lobstering allow them to perform all manner of waterfront tasks for pleasure or profit, and, as we have seen, they are amenable to being scaled up or down in size. In a letter, Phil Bolger expressed some ideas for the future of the type: "I've played with the idea of a further stretch, to 25 feet 6 inches, which would create an improved *Tartar* [an older design of similar intent]. I blew a great chance with that boat by giving her keel too much rocker. For that matter, stretching this hull to 30-odd feet would make a fine slicer. How about if we go to 70 feet — like a 1900s commuter?"

*Designer Philip C. Bolger can be reached at 29 Ferry St., Gloucester, MA 01930.*

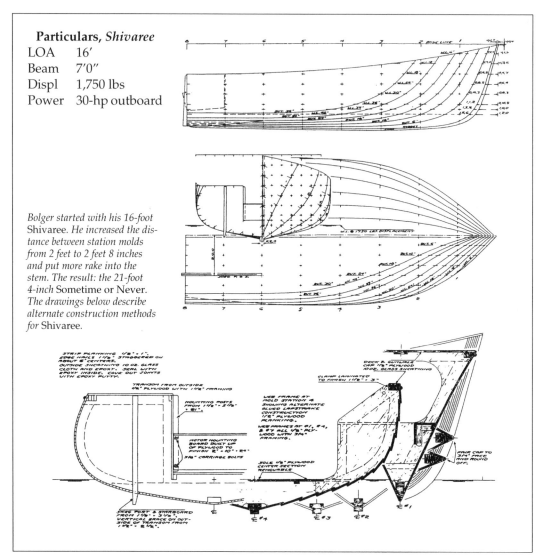

**Particulars,** *Shivaree*

| | |
|---|---|
| LOA | 16' |
| Beam | 7'0" |
| Displ | 1,750 lbs |
| Power | 30-hp outboard |

*Bolger started with his 16-foot* Shivaree. *He increased the distance between station molds from 2 feet to 2 feet 8 inches and put more rake into the stem. The result: the 21-foot 4-inch* Sometime or Never. *The drawings below describe alternate construction methods for* Shivaree.

**Particulars,** *Sometime or Never*

| | |
|---|---|
| LOA | 21'4" |
| Beam | 7'0" |
| Weight (empty) | 1,100 lbs |
| Nominal displ | 2,300 lbs |
| Power | 40-hp outboard |

*The stretched lobster-skiff hull combines a striking appearance with efficient performance.*

*Compared to older Bolger lobster skiffs,* Sometime or Never *shows a finer forefoot. The designer recovered the lost volume by swelling the topsides higher and farther aft.*

*The drawings indicate carvel planking, but plywood-lapstrake, strip, or cold-molded construction will be better if the boat must live on a trailer.*

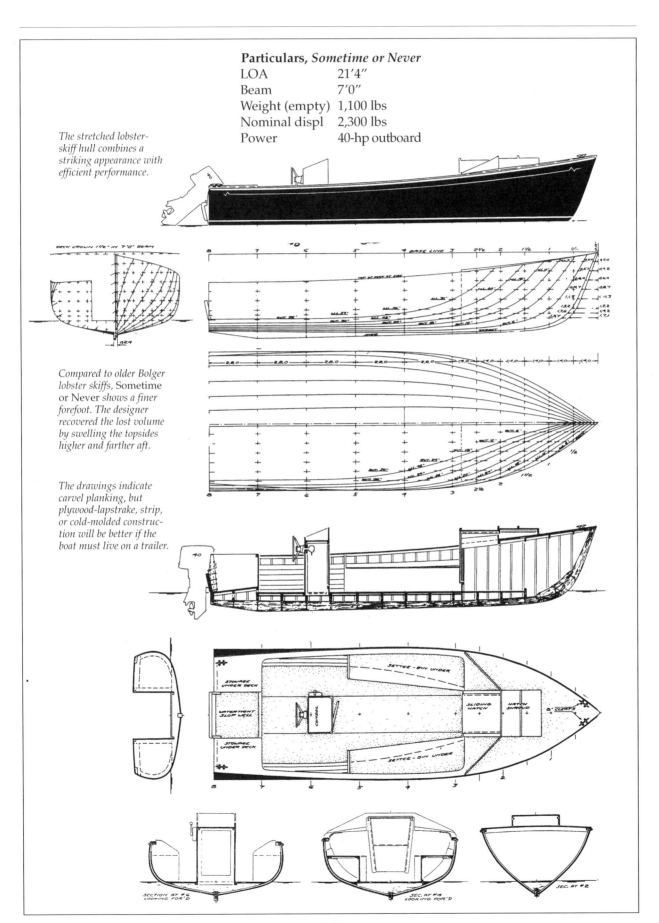

# LXIV

# A Seaworthy
# Double-Ended Powerboat

Design by George Calkins
Commentary by Sam Devlin

As a young boy growing up in Oregon, I had my heroes, but they weren't the ordinary movie-star type. They were the boat type, and one of them was a living legend on the Oregon coast — George Calkins, designer of the renowned Bartender.

The Bartender is probably George Calkins's most noteworthy contribution to boat design. As George tells it, in the 1950s his boatshop was busy building flat-bottomed plywood surf dories for use on the rough coast and bar crossings for which Oregon is famous. George was also actively involved in powerboat racing then, and began to favor V-bottomed boats over flat-bottomed ones — their speed relative to horsepower was better because of less surface friction. The V-bottoms were faster and much smoother in the lumpy seas along the shore.

George reasoned that the seaworthiness of a double-ended dory could be combined with the speed and ride of a V-bottomed powerboat. If a design like that could be worked out, then it would be the ideal vessel for going over the bar, fishing for the day, and getting back safely. By 1957 the first Bartender was off the drawing board, out of the shop, and launched. After the usual tinkering during initial sea trials, the prototype Bartender was deemed a success. This V-bottomed double-ender likely exceeded expectations.

The Bartender caught on. It rapidly developed a regional reputation for being seakindly, easy to handle, and fast. The U.S. Coast Guard thought well enough of the performance of this craft in those conditions to select it for service as a patrol boat, not only on the upper West Coast, but in other regions as well,

including the Great Lakes. The Bartender also went on duty in Australia, where it has been used by harbor patrols, state police, and surf rescue teams. Its adoption for official use by American and Australian coastal authorities lends a strong endorsement for this boat's ability in rough water.

Over time, the Bartender line expanded into four models: 19-, 22-, 26-, and 29-footers — all designed to be conventionally built using sheet plywood over closely spaced frames. All models but the smallest have a cabin, separated from the cockpit by a watertight bulkhead. And preferred power, for all but the smallest, is an inboard gas engine driving through a regular shaft, strut, and prop. There is a separate rudder and a very small keel, a shallow skeg on the bottom — not enough stock, really, to protect the prop or rudder. Some careful thought is therefore needed before attempting to beach a Bartender.

On that note I might mention that when I last visited his shop, George was putting the finishing touches on a new 26-foot Bartender built for his own use — the distinguishing feature of which is a Hamilton jet engine driving through a pump mounted at the base of the stern. The installation looks neat and is actually simpler than for an ordinary inboard. The jet pump, with its 8-cylinder gasoline engine, replaces the shaft, stuffing box, strut, propeller, and even the rudder of a standard inboard installation. Without all the underwater gear this Bartender draws mere inches and can be readily beached on a soft shore.

Bartenders, being planing boats, demand appropriate horsepower to yield best results. An emphasis

# Particulars
## Bartender, 22-footer
LOA   22'7"
LWL   18'7"
Beam  7'10"
Draft  1'6"
Displ  3,275 lbs

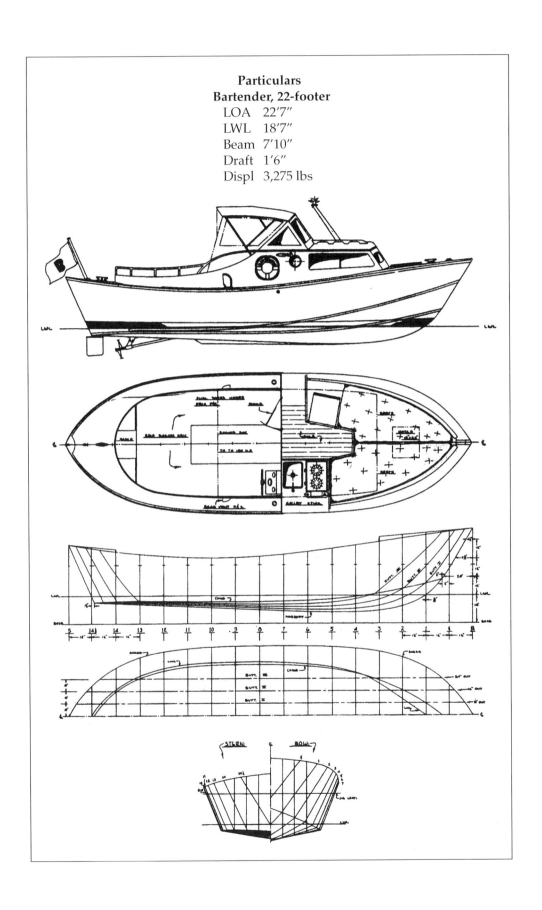

on gasoline engines, with their good power-to-weight ratios, is explicit in the Bartender line. For the 22-footer, the recommended power range is 70 to 200 horsepower; current specifications call for a 150-horsepower gas inboard, which, at 4,300 rpm a turning a 3-blade propeller, can deliver 32 miles per hour. However, the 26- and 29-foot models can carry the powerful lightweight diesels that are now available.

A look at the lines of a 22-foot Bartender shows a strongly sheered boat with a high bow and quite a bit of flare in its sections. The chine starts approximately 12 inches above the load waterline and disappears beneath the water about 4 feet aft of the entry; it then flattens out rather quickly and continues on that plane until meeting the stern. The chine — because this is a double-ender — in profile view seems to hog downward at the stern. Actually, this is just the chine meeting the V-bottom, aft of where we would ordinarily see a straight chine run out at the transom. The deadrise angle shallows from approximately 35 degrees at the entry to about 5 degrees at the stern. With its pronounced sections and slight increase in depth forward, one can expect this boat to assume a planing posture that is somewhat bow high.

All Bartenders wear spray rails that begin midway up the stem, about halfway between the chine and the sheer. The spray rails run down and disappear below the waterline amidships, then run parallel to the chine almost to the stern, where they widen a bit. These rails not only knock down the spray but also help the boat get up on plane faster under load. On a double-ended chine boat, the spray rails allow a separation of water along the sides: in a quick turn, this helps avoid a dangerous broach.

Notice how straightforward and essentially simple a V-bottomed, single-chined boat can be — and still look good. The Bartender has a very capable, seaworthy presence; here is a fine example of how the character and appearance of a boat can extend the life of the design. These boats of Calkins have been around for decades and are still being built by amateurs and professionals alike. Their styling, proportions, and salty good looks continue to appeal to a large market.

The Bartender plans are aimed at amateur construction. The 22-foot model lists eight sheets of drawings — including separate sheets for a framing schedule and cabin offsets and such details as the building jig, hardware, motor well, and spray rail. No full-sized templates are provided, so the hull must be lofted, but for framed plywood construction this is generally a beneficial step. Because of the fullness in both the bow and the stern, the plywood planking is rather light at ⅜ inch to facilitate bending over frames spaced on 16-inch centers. Bottom planking is ⅝-inch ply. The cockpit coaming, toerails, and rubrails must be steam-bent.

The Bartender line ranges from trailerable to must-be-moored. The 19-footer is an outboard-powered, partially decked, open boat; the 22-footer will berth two in a small cabin; the 26-footer can accommodate two in better comfort or four in a squeeze. The top of the line, the 29-footer, has full headroom and enough space on deck and down below for real voyaging.

The notion of high speed in an able vessel fits in on the Oregon coast. Powering out through breaking water over a rough bar is serious business — it takes a good boat, and very good boathandling. The Bartender has proven its worth in this part of the world, and elsewhere, and I expect it will continue to do so for a long time to come.

*Plans for the Bartender line are available from George Calkins, P.O. Box 222, Nordland, WA 98358.*

# A Traditional Lobsterboat

Design by Philip C. Bolger

Commentary by Joel White

Lobsterboats are so universal to the New England waterfront scene that not much thought is given to their origin or design. The coming of fiberglass to the lobster fleet has standardized the boats to the extent that a dozen or so hull builders, offering a range of models from 25 feet to 45 feet, produce virtually 95 percent of all the new boats hauling traps along the intricate New England coastline.

Don't underestimate the extent of the lobster fleet. In Maine alone, the annual catch of these succulent crustaceans averages about 20 million pounds [1987]. This translates to a lot of boats when you realize that the average daily catch of the fishermen is only 100 to 200 pounds.

Occasionally a design for a lobsterboat built of that old-time material, wood, crops up. There are still a few lobster fishermen who, for one reason or another, prefer a wooden boat. This little 28-footer designed by Phil Bolger of Gloucester, Massachusetts, and built by Dave Montgomery of Montgomery Boat Yard, Gloucester, for a local fisherman, shows a small inshore boat designed to work the fishing grounds close to her home port. For this reason, she does not need great speed and is designed to cruise at about 8 knots with her 6-cylinder Ford truck gasoline engine. Her beam is 10 feet, consistent with the trend in the fishing fleet to go toward beamy boats with length/beam ratios of around 3.

Gone are the days of the long, narrow Jonesporter type, which used to drive so easily and gracefully through the water. The modern lobster-catcher handles five times as many traps as did his grandfather, and needs much more carrying capacity and working space in his boat. Beam is the answer.

The lines of this boat show a nice, hollow waterline forward, with a 13-degree entry half-angle. This should make her dry and allow her to be driven against a chop without the feeling of butting into a wall. Her buttock lines in the run aft are somewhat curved, rising to a transom that just touches the water. This hull form is more easily driven than one with a straight run and immersed transom, but limits her speed to about 11 knots (wide open). If more speed had been needed, a straighter run would have been used, as well as a much larger engine.

The hull is a skeg model, meaning the rabbet line is lowest at about Station 4, and rises toward the stern in a fair curve; the sections have no reverse curve in the garboard area. Most of the backbone — the so-called skeg — is external to the hull. Skeg boats are a little easier to build than "built-down" boats, and probably drive a little more easily. Her displacement is given at 7,400 pounds.

The sections of this 28-footer show high bilges, with the bilge curve above the waterline, a plumb transom, and good flare in the forwardmost station. The sheer-line is quite high forward; Bolger says this is to allow easier planking of the flared bow area. I like the strong sheer on this little boat, both for looks and reserve buoyancy as well as for spray suppression. She draws 2 feet 9 inches and has a good amount of drag to her keel. This will help prevent broaching when running off before the seas, and also allows for a big propeller aperture with adequate tip clearance.

The rudder on this boat looks small to my Maine eyes, and has no balance. Lobstering demands great agility and good handling; a short turning radius is greatly prized in lobsterboats. A slightly larger rudder with a couple of inches of balance forward of the rudder stock would aid this.

While we're on the subject of propellers, notice the drawing for an alternate propeller location. Mr. Bolger says, "I'd like to see this scheme published and discussed, although it was not seriously considered for this boat. I've designed eight or ten auxiliaries with off-center props in a recess on one side of the deadwood, as shown. The object in each case has been to avoid having a hole in front of the rudder in a very shoal-draft sailing boat, and the props have all been two-blade folding types. None of them has any asymmetry effect under power, and all turn equally well either way, including backing up — in fact, they seem to me to handle at least as well as any centerline installation. It seems to me that this arrangement would be at least as effective as a cage in keeping pot warp out of the prop, with a hell of a lot less drag, and possibly improved steering as well, for the same reason that it improves the steering of the sailing boats."

It is an interesting idea, although I don't think it would take the place of a cage on a working lobsterboat. You have to be protected not only from fouling your own pot warp while hauling, but also the warps of your competitors all around you. The elimination of an aperture hole forward of the rudder is certainly a plus. A propeller working in clear water will always be more efficient than one in an aperture. In a sailboat, the cross-flow of water from leeward to windward through the aperture is detrimental to performance by forming eddies and turbulent water flow in the area behind the aperture. The propeller is nearly as well protected from grounding as with an aperture, but would be a little more susceptible to fouling pot warps and seaweed.

Her construction is straightforward and pretty standard for a small lobsterboat, with the exception of a couple of unusual features. One of these is the sternpost, which pierces the horn timber and rises into the hull, up to the level of the cockpit floor. While this is common in larger boats, it is not so common in small lobsterboats, where the horn timber is usually continuous and the sternpost is an external, bolted-on piece that can be removed. Bolger has a pair of hefty cheekpieces on either side of the horn timber to tie the stern securely to the rest of the backbone.

The other somewhat unusual feature is the long, massive engine bed resting on heavy floor timbers. This spreads the weight and thrust of the engine over a large part of the boat's bottom and will ensure that she isn't wracked by engine strains. I like this. I also like the way the protrusion of the skeg aft of the sternpost, which takes the rudder keel bearing, is a separate piece of wood allowing for easy replacement in case of damage in a bad grounding. Often this piece is a part of the main keel and is difficult to fix if broken.

I do think the skeg extension might have been a bit heavier in section, as the continuous turning and twisting involved in hauling lobster traps puts a lot of stress on this area.

Note that heavy floor timbers are shown in every other frame bay, and up forward (at least) they are not alongside the frames, but spaced away from them. This is preferable to the more commonly seen arrangement, where the floor timbers lie against the frames with the two members bolted together. My boatyard experience is that in older boats, the frames tend to break at these bolts because their section area is weakened by the bolt holes. Having the floor timbers separate from the frames, with the planking well fastened to them, makes a lot of sense.

Other than the above, the construction of this boat is normal. It is planked with $\frac{7}{8}$-inch cedar or pine, the frames are steambent oak, $1\frac{1}{4}$ inches by $1\frac{1}{2}$ inches, and the backbone is oak sided $4\frac{1}{2}$ inches. The deck and trunk top are $\frac{3}{4}$-inch plywood, while the cockpit floor is $1\frac{1}{4}$-inch cedar or pine.

The outboard profile and deck plan show the usual arrangement of a working lobsterboat. Traps are hauled from the starboard side amidships via an hydraulic pot-hauler mounted on the main bulkhead, the pot warp leading over a davit block hanging outboard of the rail. When the trap comes up, it is landed on the starboard rail, where it is opened and lobsters (if any) are removed; then the trap is re-baited and set again. The large cockpit area is needed for all the paraphernalia that goes with the trade — barrels of bait, bait pockets, and (as most boats now have) a lobster holding tank with circulating water to keep the catch in prime condition in the hot summer months. The profile shows the riding sail that some lobstermen like because it helps hold the bow of the boat into the wind and chop while hauling — although a photograph I have seen of the boat does not indicate that such a sail was rigged.

Don't write to Mr. Bolger saying that this little boat is just what you are looking for and that with the addition of two berths, an enclosed toilet, and a nice galley it would be the boat of your dreams! It simply won't work. Even by moving the bulkhead and engine aft, the space forward is limited and the headroom is less than 4 feet. Lobsterboats are designed to do one thing — get a man out to his traps, haul them, and get back. They are not small cruisers, much as people would like them to be.

*More information from Philip C. Bolger, 29 Ferry St., Gloucester, MA 01930.*

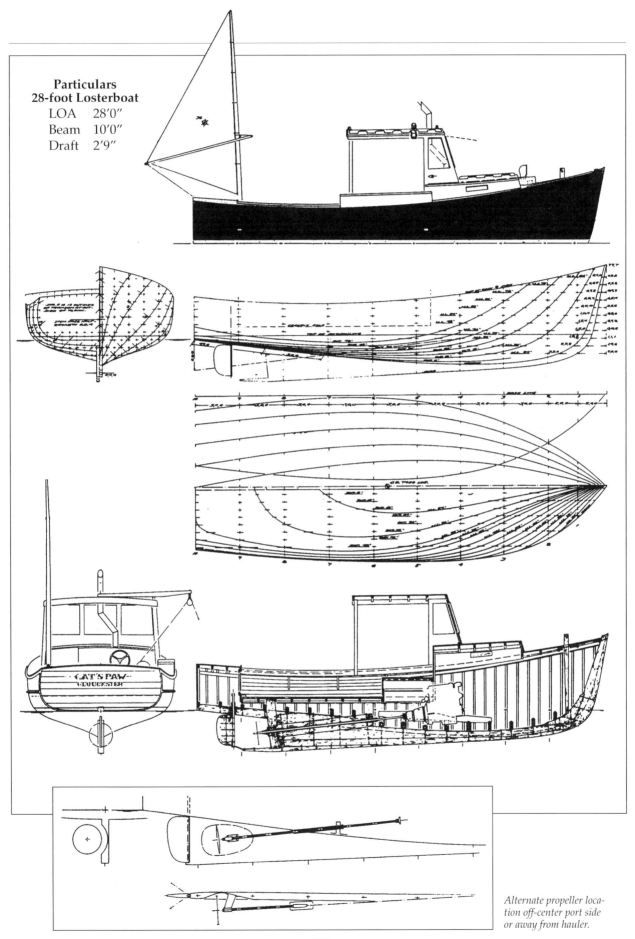

**Particulars**
**28-foot Losterboat**
LOA   28'0"
Beam   10'0"
Draft   2'9"

*Alternate propeller location off-center port side or away from hauler.*

# A Modern Maine Picnic Boat

—— Design by C.W. Paine Yacht Design, Inc. ——
Commentary by Joel White

*I*s there anyone who hasn't daydreamed of owning a snappy little open powerboat — something that looks great, goes fast, and makes a noise like Vroom? A boat that will get you from here to there in nothing flat, and will make you feel like the Aga Khan (or the Begum) when you shwoosh into Northeast Harbor, or Newport, or Key West, or wherever it is you want to make a bit of a splash. Sure you have, you're just a little reluctant to admit to the showoff inside your buttoned-down self.

Well, Charley, here's the boat for you! Nothing ostentatious or vulgar — not at all. In fact, this little gem is very refined and genteel, but believe me, heads will turn as you carve a lovely elliptical curve of a wake coming around the point on the way to the head of the harbor. Her gleaming varnished mahogany and ash, and the polished hardware, will add to the visual joys of the scene.

The Lincoln 28 is an elegant piece of work, both in design and construction. Her design is by C.W. Paine Yacht Design, Inc. of Camden, Maine. She was built by Bob Lincoln of RKL Boatworks, Mount Desert, Maine.

Paine's office is best known for designing handsome cruising sailboats, but in recent years there have been several solid powerboat designs, including the Able 40/42, credited to this busy firm. I mention the Able boat because I see a distinct similarity in design and looks between the Lincoln 28 and the larger sibling. Both have single-chined bottoms with straight sections, low-angle deadrise at the stern (10 degrees and 12 degrees, respectively) twisting into fine forward sections with

lots of deadrise. The after ends of the buttock lines are virtually straight and nearly parallel to the DWL, making for a hull that will run easily and is capable of speed/length ratios in the range of 3 to 6 (up to 30 knots for the Lincoln 28). A boat of this type will run with the bow up a few degrees, as the buttocks must take on some angle of attack relative to the water in order to achieve planing.

The bottom is entirely free of lifting strakes, chine flats, or external skegs. When the underwater design is right, and the hull and the powerplant are well matched, such devices are not needed.

I asked Mark Fitzgerald of Chuck Paine's office what were the principal criteria for the design of this boat, and he told me fun and good looks. It isn't often that an owner has his ideas so clearly and simply defined. And aren't these the qualities we should all be seeking in a pleasure boat?

A look at the outboard profile shows that a good deal of time and thought were spent to make the boat attractive. The sheer is strong, with a high bow for dryness, while the stern kicks up only slightly from the low point of the sheer, which is well aft. In plan view, the beam at the transom is somewhat less than you might find on many powerboats, thus avoiding the heavy-sterned look now so prevalent in highly powered craft. The transom is particularly interesting, as it is crowned rather heavily in the athwartship plane, and slightly crowned in the vertical plane. This gives a distinctive look not often seen in small yachts.

The windshield is nicely done. Its profile is kept low, and the side windows are carried well aft to emphasize

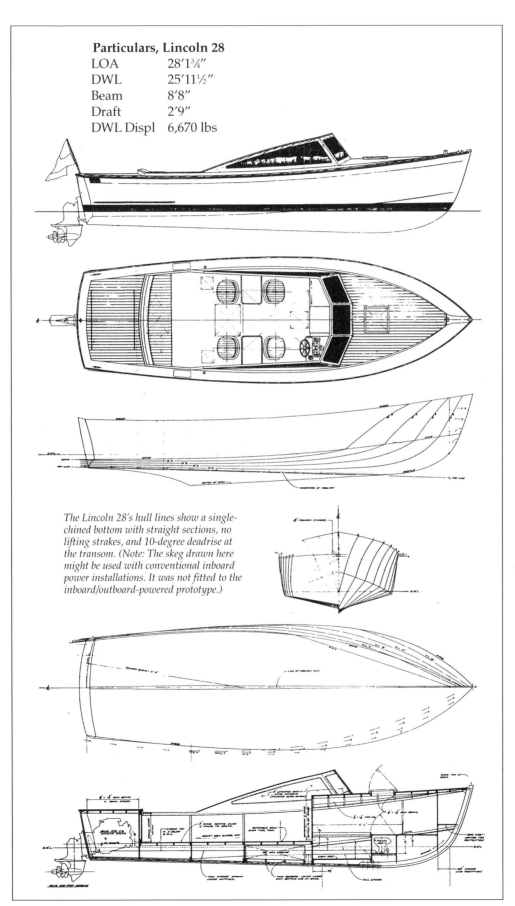

**Particulars, Lincoln 28**

| | |
|---|---|
| LOA | 28'1¾" |
| DWL | 25'11½" |
| Beam | 8'8" |
| Draft | 2'9" |
| DWL Displ | 6,670 lbs |

*The Lincoln 28's hull lines show a single-chined bottom with straight sections, no lifting strakes, and 10-degree deadrise at the transom. (Note: The skeg drawn here might be used with conventional inboard power installations. It was not fitted to the inboard/outboard-powered prototype.)*

the low, sleek look, and to protect those sitting in the aft seats. I might have been tempted to rake the forward windshield a bit more, but who's to say it would look better? It is certainly very handsome as is. The cockpit is well centered fore-and-aft in the boat, and is laid out with four swiveling chairs that have small lockers with countertops between them on each side. Under the forward deck there is room for a 6-foot 6-inch V-berth, with a marine toilet under a hinged cover in between.

The first boat, pictured here, was built with a Volvo 275-horsepower V-8 gasoline engine with stern drive, housed under a big hatch right aft. This leaves the center of the boat free from mechanical distractions, and gives the clean layout shown. Apparently, the boat can also be powered with a standard marine engine amidships driving a propeller through the usual shaft-and-strut arrangement, but you would lose the large and uncluttered lounging space in the cockpit as designed.

Fitzgerald had nothing but praise for the Volvo powerplant, and particularly the Duoprop stern-drive unit. He says the counter-rotating propellers give a very quick rise onto a plane, and allow sharp turns without any sign of cavitation. He claims the powerplant did much toward satisfying the fun part of the design equation.

Bob Lincoln is well known for building elegant canoes and small rowing craft. This boat was one of his early ventures into larger projects. The hull construction is cold-molded, with much use of epoxy glue. Planking starts with ½-inch by 1½-inch Honduras mahogany strips, covered by three layers of ⅛-inch veneer. The inner layers are diagonal red cedar, while the outer layer is mahogany laid fore-and-aft to look like traditional planking. The bottom is internally stiffened with a 1½-inch-thick hull girder on each side. At the after end, these are doubled in thickness to 3 inches and serve as engine beds. Amidships, these girders spread apart to cradle the 100-gallon gasoline tank under the cockpit floor.

The side decks are ½-inch plywood covered with fiberglass and painted white. The forward deck and the after engine hatches are laid mahogany strips with white epoxy in the seams, and finished bright. Trim is a combination of mahogany and ash, with most surfaces varnished. All this varnish means spring fitting out will be lengthy and costly, but if you want to feel like the Aga Khan, the price must be paid.

For taking a picnic to the outer islands, or just for an afternoon romp on the bay, I find it difficult to imagine a better way to travel.

*You can reach the designers at C. W. Paine Yacht Design, Inc., P.O. Box 763, Camden, ME 04843.*

# A Troller-Cruiser

——————— Design by William Garden ———————
Commentary by Maynard Bray

ere is a wonderful little cruiser based on the commercial salmon trollers of the Pacific Northwest. Like her progenitors she's not speedy, but she'll have their seakindly ways. She is thoroughly practical for a crew of two at all times, with space for sleeping guests on the 6-foot double berth formed by converting the pilothouse dinette. There's a basic galley opposite the dinette, plus good steering stations below deck and on deck over the engine box. Below, forward are V-berths with an enclosed toilet between. At the after end of the pilothouse, on the port side, is a hanging locker. A combination heating and cooking stove is part of the galley; it burns oil that is stored in a tank atop the pilothouse in the dummy smokestack. Altogether, this is a snug little cabin from which to watch the world slide by as Pollywog chugs along.

The self-bailing cockpit, which is accessed from the cabin through a Dutch door, has space for a couple of deck chairs under the shelter of a canvas awning. The fuel tank is located all the way aft in the cockpit where it is boxed in under a grating. Here the fumes are readily exhausted, and any spillage stays in the cockpit, where wiping up is easy — rather than draining to the bilge where it's not.

At the forward end of the cockpit, the engine box runs all the way to the port side, where it doubles as a standing platform for the helmsman. At least that's how the plan is drawn for the big Easthope engine shown. A modern engine of higher speed could hide under a much smaller box — although there'd still have to be an elevated helmsman's platform.

While on the subject of platforms, there's another important one outboard of the transom that can be used for swimming as well as for turned-up-on-its-side dinghy stowage when underway.

Pollywog was designed for Laurie Anderson, one of Bill's longtime friends, who built a Garden-designed, double-ended motorsailer some years ago. At this writing [1994], Pollywog's hull construction is well along. Two other boats of this same design are taking shape in Vancouver. Both are being built by veteran shipbuilder George Fryatt and will be powered by modern diesels. Laurie Anderson, however, found a vintage, heavy (1,300 pounds), slow-turning, two-cylinder Easthope gas engine. As you can see, the design was developed around it. The 1940 Easthope catalog states that "It's a pleasure to hear one run," and as Bill Garden describes it, "With lots of interesting exposed parts wiggling around, and the solemn stroke of the plunger pump and the rockers methodically doing their thing, and the big flywheel evening out the strokes, this old engine sounds especially fine when slowed to its 150-rpm idling speed."

Having ridden many times to and from Bill's island home aboard his 1904, 25-foot double-ended commuter *Merlin*, I have listened with great pleasure to the pukata, pukata, pukata of its three-cylinder Vivian (a cousin of Pollywog's Easthope), and I have studied the controls and other features that Bill had rigged up. I see a lot of *Merlin* in this boat: the pilothouse extensions, the handwheel reverse-gear control, the almost invisible, frameless, Plexiglas windshield, the businesslike visor wrapping around the front of the pilothouse, the at-the-ready life ring, and, of course, a proper mast for the masthead navigation light. But Pollywog, being a few feet longer than *Merlin* — with proportionally more cabin and less cockpit — falls into the cruiser instead of the commuter category.

The scantlings of West Coast working craft have always been on the heavy side (some mighty big trees grow there), and, as you can see, Pollywog is faithful to this tradition in that there's plenty of wood in her structure. The West Coast way of building may be unfamiliar to most readers, so let's examine how to go about it based on the notes Bill sent along with the drawings.

Note that the drawings show the hull is to be built upside down for easy and comfortable framing and planking. The harpins, which in this case also form the subdeck, are laid out using patterns picked up from the lofting. The true station spacing and length along the sheer are established from the lofted lines plan by bending a batten along the sheer in profile, marking the stations on it; then, while tacked down at Station No. 5, the batten is straightened out parallel to the baseline. The sheer half-breadths are measured out from these expanded station intervals and the points are faired on the loft floor, forming the basis for a harpin pattern. When the harpins themselves (consisting of the lumber harpins and one layer of ⅜-inch plywood glued and nailed when on the floor) are bent over the molds as required to conform to the sheer, their station line markings will fall properly on the stations. The molds, except for No. 9, are erected on the harpins. No. 9 is extended down to the shop floor in order to facilitate the transom construction.

Molds are placed abaft the stations in the forebody and forward of Station Nos. 6, 7, and 8, with No. 9 falling abaft the station line. (This placement clears the transom frame, which is steam-bent right along with the oak frames as noted later.)

With the molds and backbone in place, the stringers are bent around and beveled to fit against the stem. Then, the frame spacing is noted on them. Frame locations should already have been marked on the harpins and the keel, and frame-heel boxes cut into the latter. Using these top and bottom reference marks, a light batten simulating the frames can be used to mark the frame positions on the stringers.

Frames 1, 2, and 3 can be beveled and screwed to the stem. Back aft, the horn timber cheekpieces can be screwed to the backbone for marking, then removed to the bench, notched for the frame heels, and beveled for the planking back rabbet. Then, they can be screwed and glued back on to form the sides of the horn timber. After steaming until limber, the bent frames are secured at their heels, then wrapped around the stringers, and clamped before being secured to the harpins. A nice lather of pine tar or fiber gum should go in each frame-heel box. A ¼-inch plywood pad, epoxied to the clamp paws, will keep the clamps from marking the stringers or cutting into the hot oak frames.

As soon as a frame is in position, the clamps can be replaced with permanent screws at each stringer crossing — so the frames will be completely fastened by the time they have cooled. On heavier work, or where there is a really hard turn to the bilge, the turn is backed

up with a cluster of three or more stringers rounded off outboard, so as to avoid a sharp corner that might stress and fracture the hot oak frame. With the spread-out stringers shown, a light chamfer should be planed in to reduce corner stresses. Frames in the flare forward can be lightly shored-out as required to lay into fair curves.

This brings us to the transom, whose frame, or margin, is a similar-sized bent oak member. It is bent both to the curve of the hull and to the 12-foot radius of the curved transom. If the margin is so built, no prior transom expansion or pattern is required. To mark the curve in plan view on the two harpins and on each of the stringers, a 12-foot plywood radius-pattern is laid across each pair of stringers (and, in turn, across the two harpins), squared with the boat's fore-and-aft centerline, and positioned so its curved edge rests where the forward face of the transom will be. Since this also represents the after face of the steam-bent margins, the stringers and harpins can be marked where the pattern's curved edge crosses them. After the margins have been steamed, bent into place, and fastened, the laminated transom rim can be fitted. Then come the vertical framing members, which are notched into the rim and jogged around the bent margins. The centerline vertical frame is 4 inches wide — the same as the boat's backbone — so it can be secured to the horn timber with a pair of gussets.

With the transom framed up, the stringers and harpin ends can be cut off flush with the bent margin frame, and Mold No. 9 removed and discarded. Just prior to that, prop up and secure both harpins a foot or so forward of Station No. 9 so they will stay put when the mold is removed. Now, after you bevel the transom frame, the transom planking can be completed, the frames and rabbets faired up as required, and she's ready for the floor timbers and planking.

Planking can be worked from the garboards down, the stringers being used as easy steps. Alternatively, 2 by 4s can be run through athwartships to take conventional staging planks.

After dressing off the planking, caulking, and prime-painting, the hull is ready to turn over. The waterline can best be run in when she's right-side up. A pair of nylon slings, plus a pull, and a tail hold line will do to turn her over. A couple of chainfalls suspended from a strongback above will lift the hull high enough to clear away the horses.

Once the hull is right-side up, and the ⅜-inch deck lamination is glued and nailed down, she's ready for the really labor-intensive part of the job: about 2,500 to 3,000 hours of one-piece-at-a-time detail work. The superstructure can be simplified by deleting the cabin staving, and encapsulating the deck and house with a skin of fiberglass. There are countless ways to build and to finish her.

*Large-scale study plans, as well as a complete set of drawings for building, are available from Maynard Bray, c/o WoodenBoat Publications, P.O. Box 78, Brooklin, ME 04616.*

**Particulars, Pollywog**

| | |
|---|---|
| LOA | 27'0" |
| LWL | 27'0" |
| Beam | 9'0" |
| Draft | 3'0" |
| Displ | 9,861 lbs |
| Power | 15 bhp at 500 rpm |
| Propeller | 24 x 22", 3-blade, right-hand |
| Speed | 6.5 knots at 500 rpm |

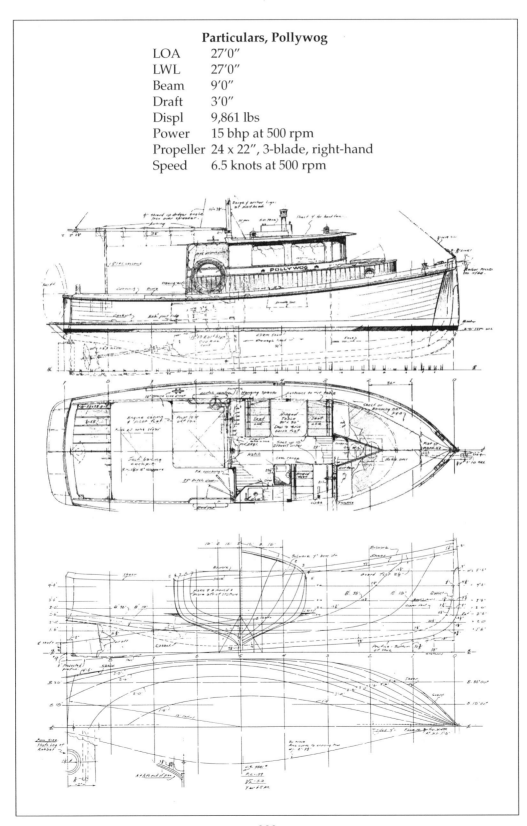

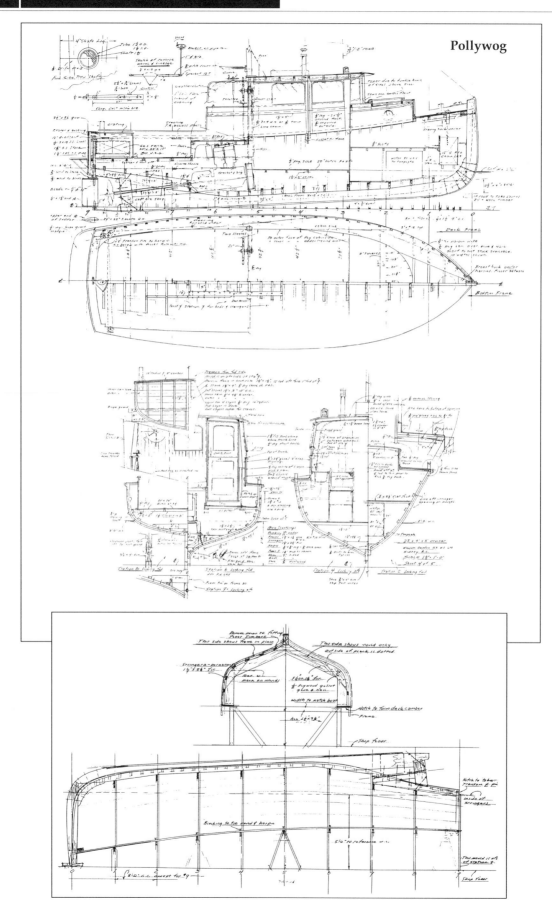

**Pollywog**

# Two Plywood Cruising Houseboats

Designs by Jay R. Benford
Commentary by Joel White

Although I have never had the inclination to be a live-aboard — to use a boat as my residence — should the urge overcome me, I would certainly consider Jay Benford's 35-foot Packet, or his Tramp. If the "*Suzy Q*" were to be my home, she must have more space — elbow room, that is, both real and psychological — than the average cruising sailboat. I always loved cruising on my 35-foot Nielsen cruising cutter *Northern Crown*, and I was content aboard her week after week. But, when the cruise was over, I was glad to get home to a tub or a shower, a comfortable armchair, and the golden retriever.

Benford's approach to designing boats that are to be used as houses (for these are true houseboats) is to maximize the volume by every trick he can think of. I applaud his single-mindedness.

Packet and Tramp have virtually identical hulls. The beam is 15 feet 4 inches, which is 3 or 4 feet more than might be expected on most 35-footers. The stern is elliptical, while the bow is bluff and full. The topsides are vertical, so the width at the chine is equal to the width on deck. The topsides continue up to form the walls of the lower superstructure, with only a small well deck on each side for access to docks or dinghies. The fo'c's'le is raised above sheer height (the sheer is the line of the heavy fendering that carries right around the hull; everything above that is superstructure). Although it is only 8 feet long, the fo'c's'le is roomy enough to contain a double stateroom.

Above the lower deck structures is the second tier of accommodations, but here the deckhouse sides are moved inboard enough to allow for an all-around walkway on the upper deck. The pilothouse floor is raised about 2 feet for better visibility and traditional looks. The height of the boat deck is 14 feet above the waterline, and the pilothouse roof is 2 feet higher! No place for sailors with a fear of heights. Launching and loading the dinghy over this cliff would be a bit scary for me. But all this beam and height adds up to interior volume, which translates to elbow room, and leads to marvelous spaciousness and comfort in what is essentially a small boat.

Another unorthodox approach to comfortable living is Benford's choice of systems. He says: "We've eliminated the need to use 'marine' hardware and equipment wherever possible. All the kitchen, laundry, bath, heating, and airconditioning equipment can be good-quality house equipment." This makes sense for long-term living aboard. Much of the time will be spent tied to a dock and plugged in to the shore-power system, so dependence on 110-volt electricity is no drawback. A generator set of ample size will keep things running while away from the dock — albeit with considerable noise and greater cost. I would want two lighting systems, one 110 volt and one 12 volt, so I could spend an evening reading without running the generator.

I find the lines plan for Benford's houseboats most interesting. In plan view, the deck line is shaped much like a Dutch shoe — wide and full ended. In profile, the lines remind me of a shoal-draft tugboat, with a deep-chested look that concentrates displacement amidships. The chine line (for, this is a chined hull) rises steeply toward the stem, while aft it rises gradually and shows a distinct hook at the stern. The hull sections are virtually flat aft and have a moderate 10-degree deadrise amidships. Forward, because of the high chine, the deadrise is steep (it reaches about 45 degrees at the first station abaft the stem). Because of the hull's extreme beam, she will have excellent stability at low angles of heel. No figures for displacement were given, but I ran my planimeter around the midship section and came up with an estimated displacement of 33,000 pounds, which is large for a 35-foot vessel.

This seems to be a good place to talk about the seaworthiness and stability of such a craft. I would not consider this an oceangoing boat, and I doubt that Benford does, either. While I had the planimeter out, I also ran it around the above-waterline profile of Packet. The windage (or sail area) came out to be 432 square feet, about what we might find in the rig of a 28- to 30-foot sailboat. A 25-mph breeze gives wind pressures of about 2½ pounds per square foot, while at 35 mph the pressure is nearly 5 pounds on each square foot. Thus, in a 35-mph gale on the beam, a force of more than a ton will be exerted on the superstructure, centered about 8 feet above the waterline. The boat will not capsize by any means, but she will heel some, and her action in the water will be affected. Because of her shoal draft she will certainly crab sideways in a beam breeze. If this imaginary gale were accompanied by heavy seas, as it surely would be in anything but the most sheltered waters, I would prefer to be elsewhere. But, as Benford says, the competent sailor waits for good weather whenever possible, even in the most capable craft.

For ordinary coastwise cruising, careful weather-watching will allow Packet/Tramp to go safely to her next destination. This sort of boat would be especially suited for cruising the big river systems of America — up the Hudson, into the Great Lakes, down the Mississippi to New Orleans, and across the Gulf to Florida, with many side excursions along the way. What a great way to see our country!

These boats are designed to be built of lumberyard materials. From the specifications sheet: "Good-quality plywood with fir framing is the basis for the whole boat. The sides of the houses are all double wall, with insulation built-in. The whole structure is glued and sealed with epoxy, and she is sheathed with a skin of Dynel or fiberglass cloth set in epoxy for abrasion and impact resistance." The hull is drawn with developable surfaces, so multiple skins of plywood can be glued together over the frame to make up the finished planking thickness of 1¼ inches.

Benford has also designed a version of this hull to be built in steel, with the superstructure and pilothouse of wood. The steel hull will have integral tanks for 300 gallons of fuel and 500 gallons of water, versus 250 and 400 gallons in the wooden version. Large liquid capacity is a boon to the liveaboard, reducing the frequency of fill-ups.

The specifications call for a Yanmar 50-horsepower diesel as standard power, with twin 30-horsepower diesels as an option. Benford says he would prefer a single diesel with bow thruster to twin diesels, and I agree with him. Twin screws mean twice as much maintenance, and twin propellers are more vulnerable than one on the centerline.

A 12-volt electric system, powered by three 8D batteries and a battery charger, is standard. Hydraulic steering, a pressure freshwater system with hot-water heater, and manual and electric bilge pumps also are included on the list of basic equipment. Optional extras include a 110-volt, 8-kilowatt generator, central air-conditioning, electronics, and phone and TV wiring.

Let's take a look at the accommodations offered in the two versions of this design. Packet has a small cockpit aft. Tramp does not, but she has a full-width well deck forward of the superstructure. A large hatch in this well deck leads to a cargo hold below. These differences in deck layout force certain changes in the accommodations: Packet has an amidships dinette with a small dining table opposite and the kitchen aft. Tramp has a lovely elliptical seat right around the stern, with a dropleaf table for eating and drinking, and the kitchen is farther forward. In both boats, the bathroom is on the main deck level under the pilothouse. A tub or shower is indicated on each boat, as well as a washer/dryer.

Climbing a set of stairs brings us to the upper deck. Each of these vessels has a roomy pilothouse with a raised settee for those who would keep the helmsman company and enjoy the view. Aft and down two steps is the master bedroom with double bed, dresser, and, on Packet, a washbowl. On the afterdeck under the canopy, there is room for a table, two chairs, and a small settee for comfortable, shaded lounging and dining outdoors. With the double stateroom in the fo'c's'le, each layout will sleep, feed, and seat four people. The only real drawbacks to these floor plans are the distances from the sleeping areas to the bathrooms — in each case, one must climb or descend a set of stairs to reach the facilities. It would be nice if a small head could be fitted on the upper deck. But there is no doubt that these boats can cruise four people nicely for long periods of time, and that a liveaboard couple would be very comfortably housed, whether tied to the dock or roaming free.

Benford has created a large number of designs on the houseboat theme. I have before me his booklet entitled "Small Ships" that includes many of this type, ranging in length from 35 feet to 100 feet. So Packet and Tramp have a long ancestry from which he has

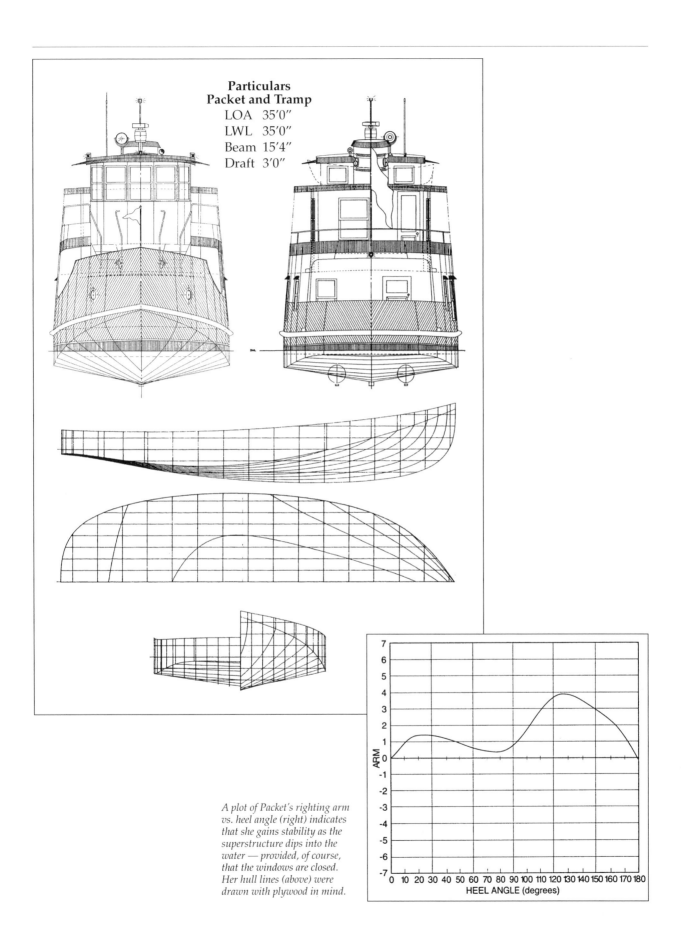

**Particulars**
**Packet and Tramp**
LOA  35'0"
LWL  35'0"
Beam  15'4"
Draft  3'0"

*A plot of Packet's righting arm vs. heel angle (right) indicates that she gains stability as the superstructure dips into the water — provided, of course, that the windows are closed. Her hull lines (above) were drawn with plywood in mind.*

selected the best features and added improvements while drawing these floating houses.

"Houses," Arthur Ransome wrote in *Racundra's First Cruise*, "are but badly built boats so firmly aground that you cannot think of moving them. They are definitely inferior things, belonging to the vegetable not the animal world, rooted and stationary, incapable of gay transition."

Here is your chance to have a house that is easily uprooted and fully capable of moving over our watery realm.

*More information from Benford Design Group, P.O. Box 447, St. Michaels, MD 21663.*

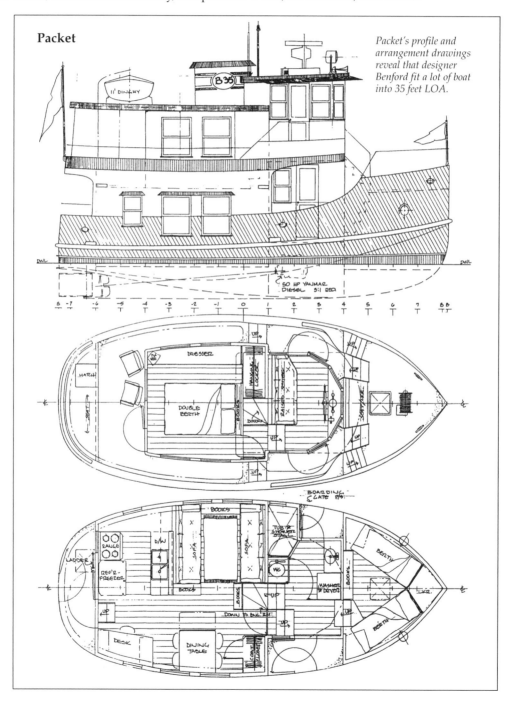

Packet

*Packet's profile and arrangement drawings reveal that designer Benford fit a lot of boat into 35 feet LOA.*

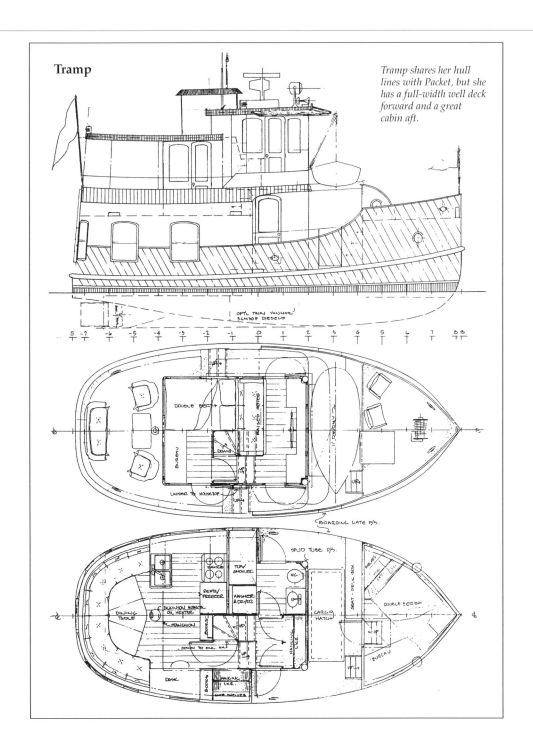

**Tramp**

*Tramp shares her hull lines with Packet, but she has a full-width well deck forward and a great cabin aft.*

— 239 —

# A Motor Cruiser with Workboat Character

Design by William Garden
Commentary by Maynard Bray

*I*approached our college library differently, to say the least, than did most engineering students. This was where I could look forward each month to the arrival of *The Rudder* magazine, for me an event of far greater importance than discovering solutions to differential calculus problems. Not only did the new issue bring the next installment of L. Francis Herreshoff's serialized "Compleat Cruiser," or a new marlinspike project by Hervey Garrett Smith, but design after design appeared from the drawing board of William Garden.

Bill Garden's work had undeniable charm. The boats looked salty, as though you could move right aboard. You could, in fact, be a little jealous of the pipe-smoking, bill-hatted sailormen that Bill drew lounging in a bunk with a book, standing at the helm, or just admiring the view from the deck. He would occasionally include a wonderful perspective of his newest design, perhaps grounded out for bottom painting with a sketch of the proud owner, brush and paintpot in hand, standing in the mud and taking in the lovely lines of his new craft. How I envied those happy little stick-figured men.

As time passed and styles changed, Bill Garden's boats became generally larger and more sophisticated, and included state-of-the-art megayachts — doomsday boats, as he sometimes calls them — and *The Rudder* went out of business altogether. Several years ago, through the generosity of Orin Edson, one of Bill's patrons, all of Bill Garden's drawings up to 1967 were donated to Mystic Seaport Museum. These included all of my favorites from *The Rudder* days as well as many more that had never been published — a total

of some 2,500 sheets all told, representing nearly 500 individual designs. To admit that I was pleased when my wife Anne and I took on the task of inventorying them, in situ at Bill Garden's West Coast office, would be a gross understatement. Being able to examine each of the drawings, as our limited time permitted, and question Bill about the backgrounds of various boats was about as good as it can get. Those plans are now at Mystic, and you'll have to go there to see the originals; but, believe me, the trip is well worth it. Alternatively, you can order copies by mail.

What this story is about is an entirely new design, but one that is obviously based on Garden's earlier style. It came about in the fall of 1992 while I was again at Toad's Landing (the name of Bill's island office/home near Sidney, British Columbia). We "just got to talking" about salmon trollers and halibut schooners and good, common-sense cruising craft for the West Coast. Out came a paper napkin (this was a conversation over lunch), and, before I knew it, here was a sketch of a 37-foot round-sterned powerboat laid out for cruising but with workboat character. We faxed that great little sketch back home to Anne, who wasn't with me on this trip, and I thought that would be the end of it.

But the wheels kept turning when everyone who saw the sketch was very enthusiastic, so Bill went into gear. High gear, in fact, which is his usual way of designing, anyhow. We pretended that Anne was the absentee client and that I was her on-site agent, paid to keep an eye on the designer. In about 40 hours over the next two weeks Bill went on to produce complete plans, and I'll feel forever privileged to have observed

**Particulars, *Dynamo***
LOA  38′6″
LWL  34′6″
Beam  11′0″
Draft  4′6″
Displ  15 tons

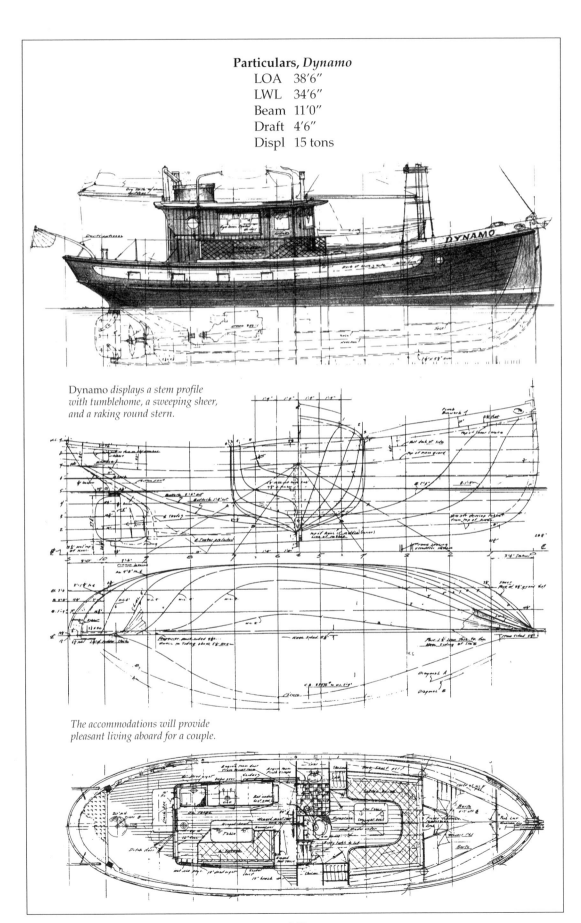

*Dynamo displays a stem profile
with tumblehome, a sweeping sheer,
and a raking round stern.*

*The accommodations will provide
pleasant living aboard for a couple.*

nearly every pencil line and to have shared in the excitement of turning four blank sheets of tracing paper into working drawings for the halibut schooner-cruiser that we called *Dynamo*.

*Dynamo* ended up with a raking round stern rather than the tugboat stern of the preliminary sketch, so she grew to 38 feet 6 inches in final form. Her draft was kept to 4 feet 6 inches as the reasonable minimum for seakeeping and the practical maximum for coastal cruising. From the start, the deckhouse was to be aft like a halibut schooner's and contain the galley and mess table as well as the steering station. We imagined this as a liveaboard boat for Anne and me (dreamers that we are), so our sleeping would be way forward in a double V-berth, which could be curtained off from the rest of the cabin. There'd be a couple more sleeping possibilities in that cabin, however, for occasional guests.

Arranging the cabin — sometimes called the main saloon — offered the greatest challenge and took the most head-scratching. The last of several versions, shown here, satisfied the requirements perfectly. This was to be the place where friends gather to enjoy each other's company in a snug and good-to-be-in space. When alone onboard, it was to be our living room. Comfortable seating — a low table, a fireplace, and plenty of natural lighting — was the chief consideration. Beyond that, a toilet room and lockers had to be worked in. I think the result is a cabin that most any sailorman or woman would enjoy being in.

*Dynamo*'s hull shape features hollow waterlines, a nice flare at the bow, a perky sheerline, a stem profile with tumblehome, and a sculpted pad that fairs the overhanging counter into the rudderstock. We're totally in love with it, and find that the inset waist, freeing ports, and lower guardrail add even more to this vessel's charm. Drawing the lines plan was almost a knee-jerk operation, since there seemed to be never a question in Bill's mind about what the general characteristics should be. He drew the lines plan, complete with table of offsets, in just over seven hours.

Six-cylinder Chrysler Crown gasoline engines used to be the power of choice — the old standby — for working vessels of this size before, say, 1960, when diesels came into widespread popularity. Bill, of course, grew up with them. Thus, the recently overhauled, but not yet committed blue-painted Crown that sat in his shop became the logical engine for this fantastic fantasy. Less noise, vibration, and smell are a gasoline engine's advantages over diesel, and Bill claims it will be years before the considerable added cost of a diesel could offset its greater fuel economy. So we're all content with gasoline and plan on a safe installation and careful management to mitigate its inherent hazards. (If a diesel were to be installed, one could hardly go wrong with an engine built by Bedford.)

There'll be an abundance of small craft carried aboard *Dynamo* for excursions. A pair of canoes will ride on the housetop, where they can be dropped or raised by davits. In chocks forward of the deckhouse will rest some kind of sailing dinghy or pulling boat that the main boom can handle, and a little tender can be snugged up under the stern davits as shown. This fleet of small craft should greatly enhance the big-boat cruising experience.

For anchoring, *Dynamo* carries a roller chock and a drum-type windlass on the foredeck in the usual West Coast fashion. A typical long-shanked, Babbit-type anchor will be used, along with a good length of chain rode, so that anchoring will be both easy and secure. For steadying the roll in a beam sea and boosting her along in a brisk, fair breeze, she'll carry some sails in a rig yet to be fully worked out. But she'll probably carry just enough sail area to qualify as a motorsailer.

*Dynamo* will be a very comfortable sea boat that can take about any weather. She'll push easily at 6 or 7 knots, using about 3 gallons (or 2 of diesel) an hour. At that rate and with 500 gallons of fuel equally divided between two wing tanks, she can cruise almost the entire length of either the East or West Coast without taking on fuel.

Construction is rugged, to say the least, since Bill gave the boat the same scantlings as her working counterparts might have had. There's plenty of wood (Douglas-fir, yellow and red cedar, and gumwood) for withstanding an occasional grounding, and she'll be able to lie alongside an exposed wharf without fear of damage. The keel is 5½ inches by 9½ inches, the beams supporting the foredeck are 2¼ inches by 3¾ inches, and the planking is 1¾ inches thick. These heavy timbers are quite different from the delicate Herreshoff-built yachts that I've come to know so well, but the service demands it, and the wooden-hulled commercial boats of the Northwest have proven how necessarily robust a hull must be. She's designed to be built utilizing the West Coast practice of bending the frames outside permanently installed fore-and-aft stringers, with a notched harpin along the forward sheer.

*Dynamo* represents low-key, leisurely cruising. She's not a boat for everyone, but she's a design with a lot of visual appeal and a load of practical utility.

*More information from Maynard Bray c/o WoodenBoat Publications, P.O. Box 78, Brooklin, ME 04616.*

# Dynamo

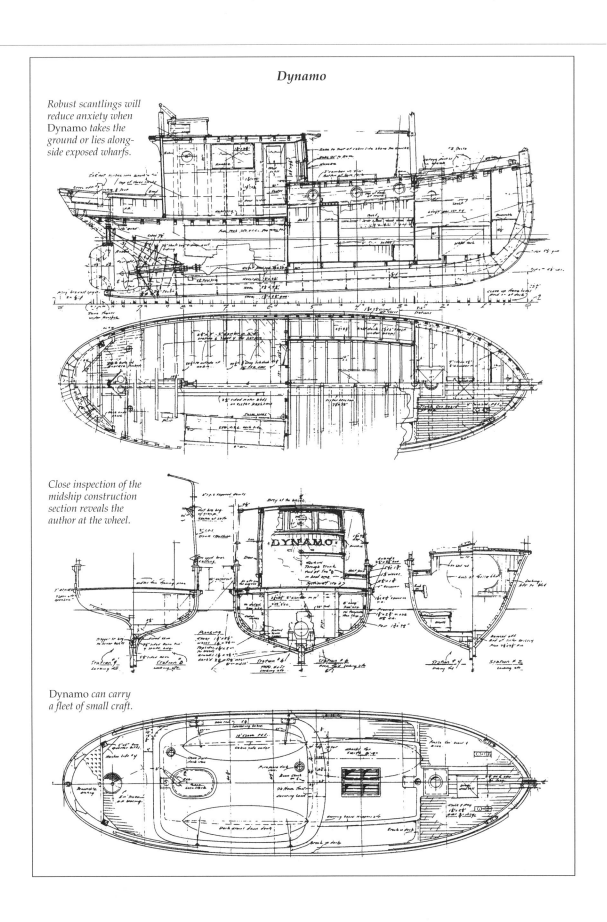

*Robust scantlings will reduce anxiety when* Dynamo *takes the ground or lies alongside exposed wharfs.*

*Close inspection of the midship construction section reveals the author at the wheel.*

Dynamo *can carry a fleet of small craft.*

# A Tunnel-Sterned Motor Cruiser

Design by Dave Gerr
Commentary by Joel White

The design for Summer Kyle first came to my notice in the form of a press release from Gerr Marine. While I tend to digest press releases with a considerable sprinkling of salt, anything from the board of Dave Gerr interests me, and Summer Kyle proved to be no exception. Designs from his office are usually no-nonsense, good-looking boats, with a considerable leaning toward traditional styling. A glance at the outboard profile of this design would seem to confirm this assessment.

Yet there is much about this boat that is not usual or traditional — once the outer veneer of the 1930s styling is peeled away. Most noticeable are her hull shape and her shallow draft; these two elements are integrally related to each other.

Quoting the press release: "Summer Kyle was designed for a client who wanted extreme shoal draft, economical operation at moderate speed, and relatively long range on a vessel he and his wife could live on for several months at a time — 'long exploring vacations.' He specifically requested 1920s to 1930s styling."

In order to achieve very shoal draft in a single-screw powerboat, Gerr has used a hull form derived from the old Sea Bright skiffs of the New Jersey coast — a narrow flat bottom, horizontal chines starting about Station 4 and running to the stern, and a tunnel stern (which Gerr credits to naval architect William Atkin). The tunnel, starting about amidships, is an inverted V-shape, with the box deadwood separating it into two tunnels from Station 6 to Station 9. From Station 9 to the transom, the tunnel is a single inverted V, with straight sections running from the submerged chines to the centerline of the transom above the designed waterline. The perspective lines sketch shows the shape clearly.

With the boat floating at rest on its designed waterline, about one-third of the 22-inch-diameter propeller is above water while the remainder is submerged. The shaft is horizontal, as the flat bottom construction allows the engine to be mounted low in the boat.

There is much that appeals about this tunnel configuration; the shoal draft will permit exploration of many places that are off-limits to deeper craft. Gerr states, "You can run at full cruising speed anywhere there's 24 inches of water or more — a simply incredible, almost unbelievable thing!" If I were running at 14 knots in 24 inches of water, I believe my heart would be in my throat the whole time for fear I might suddenly arrive at a place with only 18 inches of water!

The flat bottom is to be plated with ¼-inch copper-nickel plate, and the boat can be grounded out without fear of her falling over, another appealing trait. The propeller and rudder are well protected from damage by the box deadwood and skeg that support the bottom of the rudder.

I do have some concerns about this tunnel. A naval architect friend who has done dozens of designs with tunnel sterns tells me there are two definite no-no's in tunnel design: First, the top of the back end of the tunnel must be completely below water when the boat is at rest; otherwise, when the engine is put into reverse, the propeller will fill the tunnel with air bubbles and the boat will not back down. The second concern is that the rudder when turned must not close off the tunnel,

**Particulars, Summer Kyle**

| | |
|---|---|
| LOA | 41'6" |
| LWL | 39'2" |
| Beam | 11'6" |
| Draft | 1'7" |
| Displ | 15,960 lbs |
| Power | 170-hp Yanmar |
| Cruising speed | 12 to 14 knots |
| Top speed | 16 knots |

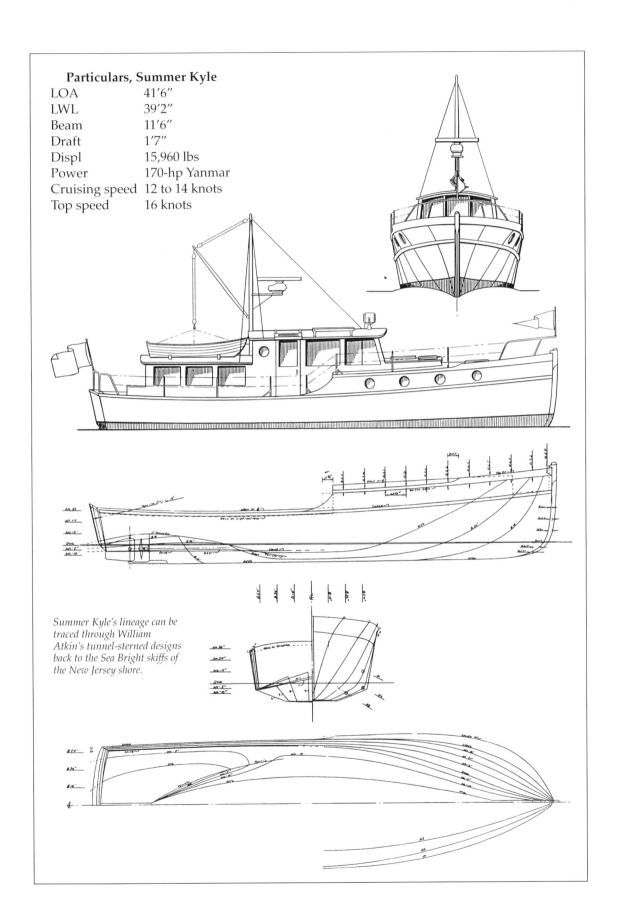

*Summer Kyle's lineage can be traced through William Atkin's tunnel-sterned designs back to the Sea Bright skiffs of the New Jersey shore.*

as there needs to be plenty of room for the slipstream from the prop to escape. Summer Kyle's design seems to violate the first rule. In talking to Gerr about this, he told me that Atkin had a number of boats built with this tunnel arrangement, some of which are still in service.

My friend also tells me that if there is too much hook downward in the after end of the tunnel, the boat will run bow-down and consequently be very wet. I can't judge if this will be a problem with Summer Kyle.

The arrangement plan is nicely set up for extended cruising for two, with the possibility of two more guests. The owner's cabin aft is large and pleasant, with a big double bunk, a dresser, and a good seat next to the bunk. However, the only head is forward, making it a bit of a trip from the after stateroom.

Amidships, the pilothouse floor is raised over the engineroom. There is plenty of seating, a large chart table to starboard, and a wet locker. In addition to regular floor hatches over the engine, the entire pilothouse floor is designed to be removed for complete access to the machinery below.

Down two steps from the forward cabin, the pilothouse contains the galley to port and a dinette with table opposite to starboard. This can convert to a double berth. The head is to port, with a shower and a hanging locker to starboard. Having a shower separated from the head is fine luxury on a small cruising boat. I have never liked entering a head compartment that appeared to have recently contained a lawn sprinkler, and which had the atmosphere of a tropical rain forest. Right forward, there is a space that can be used either as a workshop or for V-berths on each side. If extended cruising with two couples were contemplated, this would be the second stateroom. The head and shower doors are arranged to close off the forward space for privacy. Altogether, this is a conventional but excellent arrangement for a boat of this size.

Because of the space taken by the tunnel configuration and the steering gear mechanism, there is no cockpit where one can sit outside to enjoy fresh air and the sunset. Gerr has done his best to overcome this problem by making the pilothouse as airy as possible. Virtually all windows open, there is a sliding hatch cover over each side door, and there are larger sliding hatch covers over the steering and navigation stations. In addition, the after deck over the lazarette is big enough for a couple of folding deck chairs. Still, I would miss not having a cockpit.

The machinery specified includes a 170-horsepower Yanmar diesel, with 350 gallons of fuel tankage, giving about a 700-mile range at cruising speed, according to Gerr. Also specified are large battery banks, an inverter and converter, a hot water heater, an air conditioner, an 8-kilowatt generator, and an Espar hot-water cabin heater. With all this equipment properly installed and running, the crew should not suffer for lack of creature comforts.

Construction is to be strip-planked wood, glued with epoxy, and the outer surface sheathed with fiberglass laid in epoxy. This is a cost-effective way to build a boat of this size and should facilitate building the unusual shapes of the tunnel stern. While not specified, I imagine that decks and superstructure will be wood framed, plywood sheathed, and covered with fiberglass and epoxy. Or the decks could be teak veneered for a more yachty appearance.

Summer Kyle is an appealing boat for anyone wanting a medium-sized power cruiser. Her overall appearance is traditional, and I think quite good-looking. Her relatively narrow beam and long hull lines, combined with a single-screw diesel of moderate power, ensure a boat that is economical to operate and maintain. The raised forward deck configuration gives maximum usable space in the accommodations, while the many hatches, portlights, and windows will provide plenty of light and air below. The dinghy can be carried on the after cabintop and easily launched using the mast and boom. The mast will also be useful for carrying steadying sails. Gerr has done a fine job of providing all the necessary elements for fun, and for comfortable cruising.

I am envious of Summer Kyle's future owners. A September departure for a leisurely trip south on the Intracoastal Waterway, taking advantage of the good days to run, and exploring the countryside when the weather threatens, could take them to Florida and across to the Bahamas for a winter spent in tropical climes. The trip back home, following the spring north, might be the best of all.

*Plans for Summer Kyle are available from Gerr Marine, Inc., 838 West End Ave., New York, NY 10025.*

# Summer Kyle

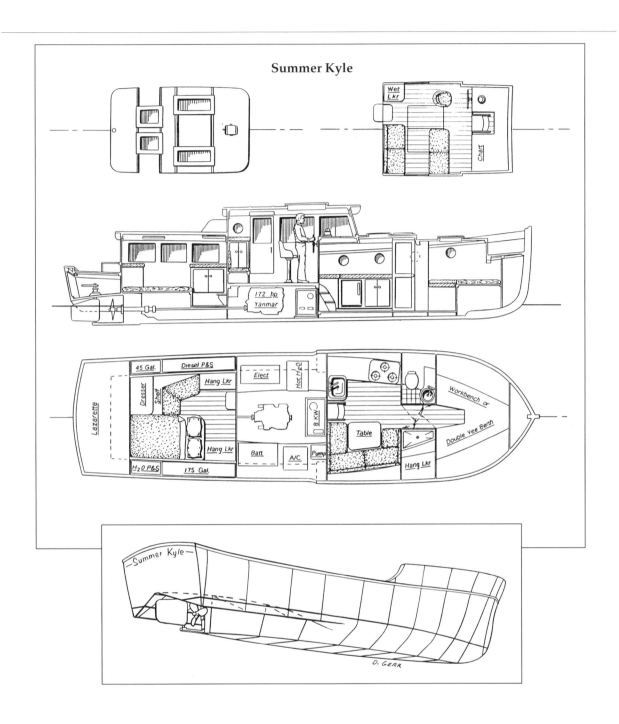

# Two Seagoing Powerboats

Designs by Robert P. Beebe and Eldredge-McInnis ———
Commentary by Joel White

Some time ago, Mike O'Brien and I discussed our desire to review the designs of real power-boats — not just flit-around-the-bay boats, but heavy-duty, long-range, oceangoing types. The happy result of these discussions was to renew my acquaintance with a book that I had read years ago, but whose virtues I had nearly forgotten. For anyone seriously interested in the oceangoing powerboat, Robert P. Beebe's *Voyaging Under Power* (third edition, revised by James F. Leishman, International Marine, Camden, Maine, 1994) is the place to start one's thinking. In the book Beebe set down, in clear and carefully reasoned fashion, the underlying principles of power, speed, and cruising range that govern the design of all seagoing power craft.

As Beebe is quick to point out in his book, the rules that govern power, speed, and cruising range are absolute, and can be easily determined by simple mathematics. Chapter 5, "Technicalities of the Seagoing Motorboat," includes a clear discussion of displacement/length ratio, speed/length ratio, prismatic coefficient, and how these non-dimensional tools of analysis are used when planning a long-distance cruiser. Even more useful are graphs from which it is possible to calculate the power requirements, achievable speed, and range in nautical miles that can be attained at varying speed/length ratios for any vessel for which you know the displacement. These graphs cover the speed/length range of 0.7 to 1.6, and it is within these limits that oceangoing powerboats operate.

Beebe shows us such a plot of approximate values for a 46-foot 8-inch cruiser of his own design that has a displacement of 31 tons and a fuel capacity of 1,200 gallons. At a speed/length ratio of 1.34, the upper limit of pure displacement running, the horsepower needed is 115, the speed 9 knots, and the range 1,500 nautical

miles. By slowing down to 7.5 knots and a speed/length ratio of 1.2, the power drops to 50 horsepower and the range increases to about 2,800 nautical miles! Back off to 6.8 knots, and the range rises to 4,000 nautical miles!

The book goes into all aspects of long-distance power cruising, including chapters on historical background and the philosophy of power voyaging, a number of Beebe's own designs for ocean cruisers, and a chapter containing the plans of several other designers; also cruising in Europe, 'round-the-world passage-making, the long-range galley (written in part by Beebe's wife, Linford), and a chapter on operating a seagoing motorboat.

Beebe, who was a career Navy officer and had a lifetime interest in naval architecture, makes some telling comments about modern trawler-yachts, and the fuzzy, sometimes exaggerated, claims made by their salesmen as to speed and power. He urges a potential buyer to take the known facts (engine horse-power, hull displacement, and fuel tankage) and apply his graphs and calculations before purchasing a boat for a trip to the South Seas. Most of these cruisers simply do not measure up in terms of range, or volume of hull needed to carry all the stores and fuel required for such a trip.

All of the above is preamble to looking at a couple of long-distance power vessel designs for which plans are published in Beebe's book. Both have been built and well tested. One of them, *Albacore III*, is a boat that I have seen and admired, as she originally made Brooklin, Maine, my home town, her home port. The other design is Robert Beebe's own boat *Passagemaker*, which he designed and had built in Singapore to test his theories and prove his point about the feasibility of ocean cruising in quite small power craft. Her maiden voyage (or, more accurately, maiden cruise) brought

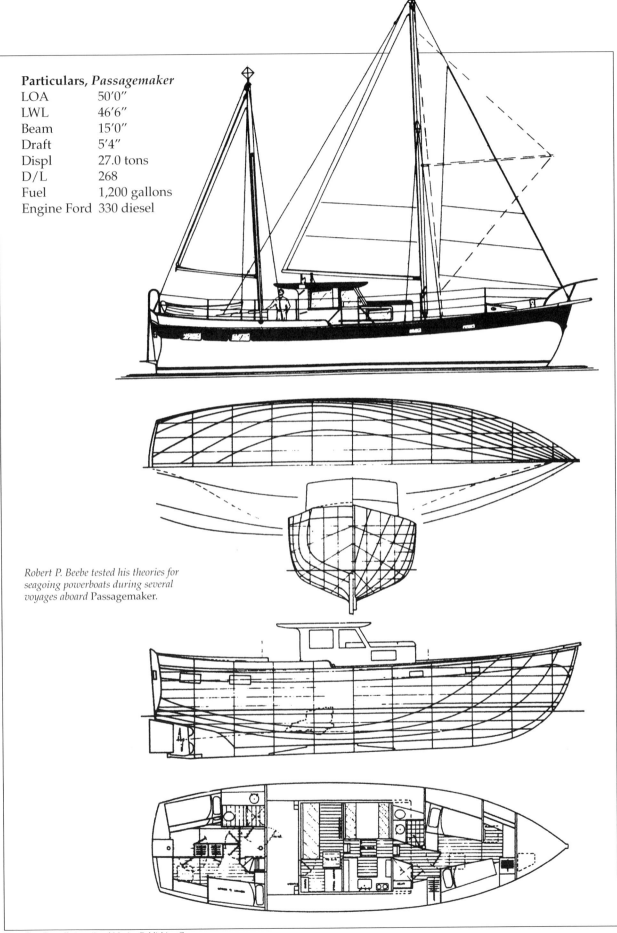

**Particulars,** *Passagemaker*
LOA        50'0"
LWL        46'6"
Beam       15'0"
Draft      5'4"
Displ      27.0 tons
D/L        268
Fuel       1,200 gallons
Engine Ford  330 diesel

*Robert P. Beebe tested his theories for seagoing powerboats during several voyages aboard* Passagemaker.

her home to California via the Indian Ocean, the Suez Canal, a long stopover in the Mediterranean, across the Atlantic by way of the Azores, through the Panama Canal, and home to San Diego after 21 months. Let's look at *Passagemaker* first.

Built at the Thornycroft yard in Singapore in 1963, *Passagemaker* is an extremely interesting boat. Her design does not compromise Beebe's stated aim, that of providing a long-range small powerboat capable of crossing oceans in safety (to both boat and crew). For cost reasons, she is a bare-bones sort of yacht, with minimum electronic equipment, and a very simple interior. She's planked with teak over laminated chengal frames, and has plywood decks with synthetic sheathing.

*Passagemaker's* lines show a fine-ended displacement-type hull, designed to run at speed/length ratios of 1.4 or below. Her transom stern is large, but lifted well clear of the water to reduce drag to a minimum. The buttock lines have considerable rocker, and the bow sections are V-shaped but without reversed flare in the upper sections. She has a single propeller protected by a skeg, which supports the lower rudder bearing. And bolted to her keel is 5,000 pounds of outside ballast. Beebe says that ballast for stability in really bad weather is what distinguishes the oceanic power vessel from the coastal cruiser. As he points out, you pay dearly for carrying it around, and most of the time you don't need it, but when the weather turns awful, you are darned glad it is with you.

I have never thought of *Passagemaker* as a particularly pretty boat. Her sheer aft is raised to provide headroom in an after cabin, and this brings it up to the same height as her bow, a profile that looks odd to my eyes. Beebe, in analyzing her performance after many thousands of miles of voyaging, admits that her bow could have been higher to enable her to keep going to windward in bad seas. But, aesthetics aside, her hull lines show a seaworthy and easily driven shape. The rounded forefoot profile, long, straight keel with a small amount of drag, and the large rudder right aft make for a hull that will track beautifully, steer easily, and run off before the sea without distress. Beebe was well pleased with her performance. With a slightly different sheer, she could be handsome, too.

*Passagemaker* has a small midship pilothouse with a short, deep cockpit just aft of it. This allows the watchkeeper to leave the helm and go outside for a look around without being exposed to the fatal danger of falling overboard. I use the word "fatal" in its most literal sense, because in mid-ocean, with the ship on autopilot, and the rest of the crew below sleeping or eating, falling overboard is not to be contemplated.

Going forward from the pilothouse, you descend three steps to the galley and dinette, where windows allow crew sitting at the table to look out. Three more steps down take you to the forward cabin that contains a head, a shower room, two bunks, and a couple of hanging lockers. There is also access to this compartment through a small companionway and ladder leading down from the forward deck.

Originally, the after cabin was a large, open space that housed a drafting table (to allow Beebe to pursue his design interests) and a convertible sofa that could be made into a double bed. Beebe readily admits that after months of voyaging, the layout did not work out well. At sea it was fine, but in port the lack of comfortable lounging space for the crew was a problem. The after cabin was later converted to two double cabins with a head; however this still did not solve the space problem in port.

In his book, Beebe goes into the matter of accommodation layout at great length and considerable detail. He is an advocate of double-decking (placing one space above another) as a means of getting more accommodations in a given length of hull. He has rules governing the allowable ratio of above-water profile area to below-water profile area (A/B ratio); these rules are the limiting factor as to how much double-decking can be done while maintaining safety at sea. There is not room here for a detailed discussion of his ideas — instead, I refer you to his book.

Another area of the seagoing experience, to which Beebe devotes an entire chapter, is roll dampening. He maintains that comfortable passages can be made only if the vessel's crew can operate without being subjected to day after day of serious rolling. The boat can stand it, but the crew cannot. His solution for the problem at manageable cost is the West Coast stabilizer or "flopper-stopper." This is a flat-plate paravane towed from extended poles on each side of the boat. When the boat rolls to starboard, the starboard stabilizer dives deeper; as the boat starts to roll to port, this vane provides a strong resistance to being pulled upward. Meanwhile, the port vane is diving, preparing to resist the roll in the opposite direction. Properly designed and installed, flopper-stoppers have proved quite effective. *Passagemaker* carried and used them on all her deep-water voyages.

*Passagemaker* was designed to have a cruising range of 2,400 nautical miles at a speed of 7.5 knots (speed/length ratio = 1.1). In practice, she did better than that, proving to be able to make 3,200 nautical miles on 1,200 gallons of fuel oil.

Altogether, *Passagemaker* is a most interesting concept, and the voyages carried out by Beebe proved the ideas behind the design to be sound. The dream of cruising to any part of the world in a small powerboat is not only viable, but affordable and fun.

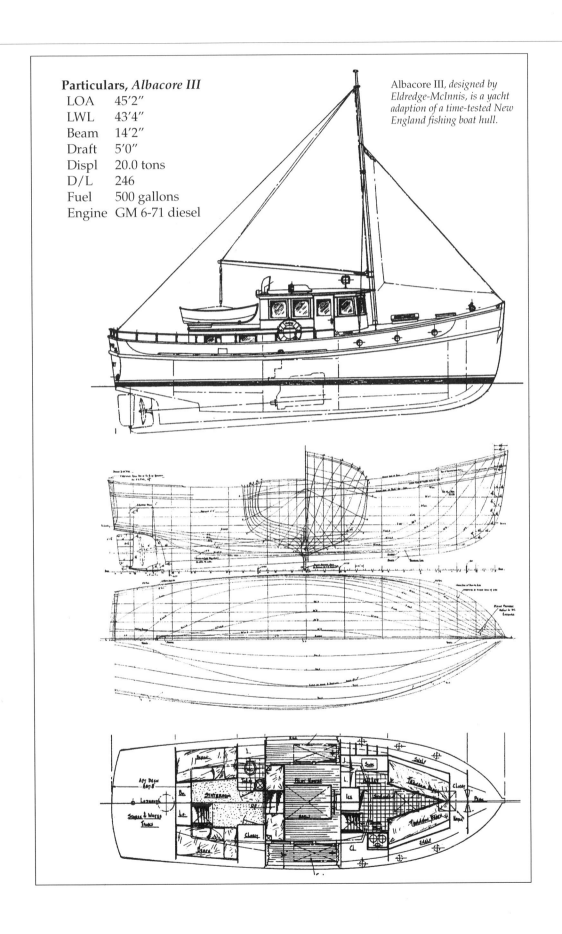

**Particulars,** *Albacore III*

LOA   45'2"
LWL   43'4"
Beam   14'2"
Draft   5'0"
Displ   20.0 tons
D/L   246
Fuel   500 gallons
Engine   GM 6-71 diesel

*Albacore III, designed by Eldredge-McInnis, is a yacht adaption of a time-tested New England fishing boat hull.*

*L*et's take a look at another rugged powerboat, this one by the well-known design firm of Eldredge-McInnis. *Albacore III* was intended to cruise in comfort from Maine to the Bahamas, where she served as a winter home for her owners. Her rather small fuel tanks, holding 500 gallons, would not place her in the ocean-crossing category, but the addition of larger tanks and flopper-stoppers would turn her into a go-anywhere vessel. Certainly her hull and superstructure are perfect for the job.

This lovely powerboat is a yacht adaptation of the time-tested New England fishing boat hull. Eldredge-McInnis Co. was a master at designing these boats, and indeed, much of their business for many years was supplying excellent designs to the fishing industry of the United States and Canada. Notice that the engine and the fuel tanks, the heaviest weights on the boat, are directly over the center of buoyancy, where trim will not be affected by the state of the fuel supply. She has no outside ballast, although I believe that she carried some inside. For crossing oceans, it might be well to bolt this to the bottom of the keel in the form of a cast lead shoe.

The large pilothouse over the engineroom contains not only the steering station, controls, and electronic gear, but also large seating areas and a table. This will be the social center of the ship. Down five steps toward the stern is the owner's cabin, with a wide berth on either side, toilet room, cabin heater, and a huge clothes closet. A companionway leads to the after deck.

Steps lead forward from the pilothouse down to the big galley to port. Across from this is a small single stateroom. Forward is a double stateroom, with two berths to port, and a toilet to starboard. Altogether, this is a very shippy and practical layout.

Her small pilothouse profile and low houses give this boat a very seagoing look and make for a low A/B ratio — just the thing for safety at sea. The mast sets two small riding sails. If *Albacore* were to be fitted for flopper-stoppers, this mast should be moved to the after end of her pilothouse, as Beebe recommends that the ends of the poles be 28 percent of the LWL forward of the stern to keep drag to a minimum.

Running *Albacore*'s dimensions through Beebe's formulas for power, speed, and range, we find that at 7.9 knots (S/L = 1.2) she requires 43 horsepower and burns 2.57 gallons per hour. With 500 gallons of fuel, this works out to a range of 1,532 nautical miles. By increasing her fuel capacity to 1,000 gallons, her range would be 3,073 miles, more than enough to cross oceans. Slow her down to 7.24 knots (S/L = 1.1), and 1,000 gallons will carry you 4,140 nautical miles!

*Albacore*'s lines are a delight to my eye. The sturdy, wide-beamed hull shows the skill of the Eldredge-McInnis firm at drawing this modified workboat shape. Because she does not have to carry heavy loads of fish and ice, her displacement/length ratio of 246 is a bit less than her fishing-boat sister might be. I also find it interesting that her D/L is less than *Passagemaker*'s 268. A glance at the two lines plans would lead me to think otherwise. It only proves that the eye is not infallible.

The large transom stern is well Veed, with very little area below the water to create drag. The sheer is perfect, with the bow considerably higher than the stern, and some flare has been worked into the forward sections. She has a nice hollow in the waterlines forward, which I remember as a very pleasing feature of the completed boat. She has deep (16 inches) bulwarks aft, dropping to half that forward, where the deck is raised over the forward stateroom. The nearly plumb stem, heavy stern, and large guardrails all around give her a purposeful, seaworthy air. Like *Passagemaker*, she has a single, large propeller protected by a skeg, and a big rudder right aft. I remember her well, with her white hull and buff and gray decks and trim, as an extremely handsome craft.

Ocean voyaging under power is not everybody's cup of tea, but the idea of traveling to the far corners of the world in one's own power cruiser will appeal to many. *Voyaging Under Power* makes a strong case for the practicality and pleasures of such a life, and it provides a tremendous amount of good advice to bolster the confidence of the prospective voyager.

Given good care and clean fuel, modern diesel engines are extremely reliable. The latest electronic navigation instruments can relieve much of the pressure on the navigator, although no one should go to sea without a sextant, time piece, and nautical tables — no matter how many electronic marvels are onboard. Weatherfax machines can offer early warning of impending bad weather, and suggest ways to avoid it. Long-range radio communication is easy and available to all. Thus, many of the hazards that faced early proponents of the long cruise under power have been reduced to manageable proportions. All one needs is the will to voyage, and a good ship underfoot.

*Passagemaker's plans are available from Beebe Plans Service, P.O. Box 881, Shelter Island Heights, NY 11965.*

*For* Albacore III's *plans, contact Alan McInnis, Eldredge-McInnis, Inc., P.O. Box F, Hingham, MA 02043.*

# A Deep-V Power Cruiser

—————— Design by C. Raymond Hunt Associates ——————
Commentary by Joel White

While a glance at the outboard profile gives the impression of a thoroughly up-to-date power craft, the design of *Sting Ray V* is more than 30 years old, for she was designed in 1962-1963 and built in 1964.

It was in 1960 that Ray Hunt and Dick Bertram revolutionized the offshore powerboat racing scene with *Moppie*, beginning the era of the deep-V hull. Since that time, this hull form has been used for powercraft of all types — sometimes in applications where other shapes might have served better. Certainly for fast motorboats in rough waters, the deep-V has proved to be a reliable and able performer. While "comfortable" is not the word I would use to describe a high-speed powerboat traveling across rough water, the deep-V hull form handles these conditions better than most, allowing small vessels to make difficult passages without self-destructing.

For those not familiar with the type, a deep-V hull has a bottom deadrise angle at the transom of 20 degrees or more. Usually this angle is carried forward to about amidships, giving parallel bottom sections in the after body. The forward-bottom is twisted to provide sharper deadrise as it approaches the stem. The topsides above the chines can be of any shape, but most hulls show considerable flare forward with straighter sections aft. The transom may have some tumblehome, as seen in the lines of *Sting Ray V*, or not. Many, but not all, deep-Vs have one or more spray strakes running from the stem aft to amidships, or even to the stern. These triangular-sectioned strips have horizontal bottom surfaces. Most designers feel that these surfaces give greater lift to the hull, reduce spray on the topsides, and introduce air under the boat, which helps to lower surface friction and drag. The penalty for spray strakes is some jarring and bang-

ing as the flat surfaces hit the approaching seas.

With all of the above as preamble, let's have a look at this particular boat as a fine example of the type. (It is of great interest to me to learn that these lines were drawn by Fenwick Williams, as I had not realized that he was working for Hunt in the early 1960s, and that he was involved with the evolution of the deep-V hull form.)

Remember that hull lines such as *Sting Ray*'s, which seem so normal to us today, were considered quite new and unusual in 1962. *Sting Ray*'s transom and after body have a constant deadrise of 22 degrees. As the body plan sections approach the centerline, the V becomes an arc of a circle running from the transom to the forebody, where this cylinder dies out and fairs into the sharper bow sections. While the lines plan shows the chine line well above the designed waterline for its full length, Stephen Weld of Hunt Associates states that *Sting Ray* floated with the chine barely immersed aft, and photographs seem to confirm this. The forward top sides show great flare blending into a radiused upper stem. The transom has a bit of tumblehome for looks.

We are told that the hull was built using entirely sawn-frame construction, and without the use of the steam-bent oak frames shown on the righthand side of the construction section drawing. The plan indicates double planking, mahogany over cedar, with a finished thickness of 1 inch. Four spray strakes are shown on the midship section, evenly spaced between the keel and the chine. Decks call for teak over thin plywood. Deckhouses are plywood over spruce framing, fiberglass covered. Throughout, construction scantlings are very much on the light side, as with all good high-speed power craft. Excess weight is the enemy of speed, performance, and fuel consumption.

A letter from Stephen Weld that accompanied the plans states that this is one of his favorites among the older Hunt designs of this hull form. He has this to say about *Sting Ray V*: "The central fact of *Sting Ray's* form and conception is that she is simple and light and makes her speed with small engines and small tanks (about 500 gallons; today's owner might demand 50 percent more). Her handsome, low after house is only possible because the fuel tanks are in the engine space, a situation impossible to achieve with the contemporary mix of large engines, large tanks, multiple generators and batteries, compressors, desalinators, water heaters, and so on.... Larger engines mean heavier structure and bigger fuel tanks, and seem to go with more gadgets and systems. The resulting boat is heavy and expensive; it will run fast, but its mid-range performance will be less graceful than that of a lighter boat. *Sting Ray* at moderate speed seems to move without the fuss and bow-up trim of a heavier boat."

These observations coincide exactly with my own. All that I would add to Mr. Weld's comments is that the heavier boat will have greatly increased fuel consumption as well, a point that we can hardly ignore in these times. We must start to enter efficiency into the design equation when developing modern powerboats.

The profile drawing and the photographs of *Sting Ray* show us a very handsome power vessel of medium size. The Hunt firm of designers has been turning out craft of this type for more than three decades, and no one does it better. The boats have a look of competency and correctness that is a pleasure to see. The low profile resulting from a hull of moderate freeboard and low deck structures speaks of safety and stability at sea.

Forward of amidships, a two-level cabinhouse gives light and headroom to the forward accommodations, and is followed by the windshield and pilothouse canopy over the raised bridge amidships. Under this bridge is the engineroom, which contains twin diesels and fuel tanks. The sides and after end of the pilothouse are mostly open — although canvas and plastic curtains were installed to enclose this space. The low after house contains the owner's stateroom and head. This is a truly luxurious space with a large berth on each side, three bureaus, a huge hanging locker, and a large head to port with its own shower room. A three-step ladder leads from this cabin to the small cockpit in the stern, under whose soles is the 10-kilowatt generator.

Three steps down from the bridge takes us to the forward quarters. The first area is labeled "deckhouse" and includes an L-shaped settee with table, two movable armchairs and a folding table to port, and, placed against the after bulkhead, the galley. The cook is provided with an electric range, a freezer under the counter, a large sink, and several lockers. Two large windows on each side make the deckhouse a light and airy place. Going forward, another step down takes us into the guest stateroom, with upper and lower berths to starboard, a bureau, and a bath and hanging locker to port. Yet another step down takes us forward to the fo'c's'le, with a single berth, a toilet and a lavatory, and sundry lockers and shelves, right up in the eyes of the boat. This is a perfect illustration of simple yet effective and comfortable accommodations, without the frills that many would deem necessary today.

Such a boat these days would probably have to include an office area, a sophisticated electronic and navigation center, TV viewing possibilities, and some sort of motorized launch carried on deck — handled by an onboard crane. All of these added complexities would make most owners feel that they required the services of a captain and/or engineer, who, of course, must have quarters suitable to the position. Suddenly our simple, comfortable cruiser of 55 feet is much more complex, much more expensive, larger and heavier, and much less efficient to run and maintain.

It used to be that people had yachts to enable them to get away from life's complexities and back to a simpler style for vacation relaxation. Now the cruising life is often more stressful than being home, what with keeping tight schedules despite the vagaries of weather, and hoping all the gadgets will work in a harsh marine environment. It is not my idea of fun. *Sting Ray V* offers more relaxation than one of her modern sisters with a full complement of high-tech equipment.

*C. Raymond Hunt Associates, Inc. can be reached at 69 Long Wharf, Boston, MA 02110.*

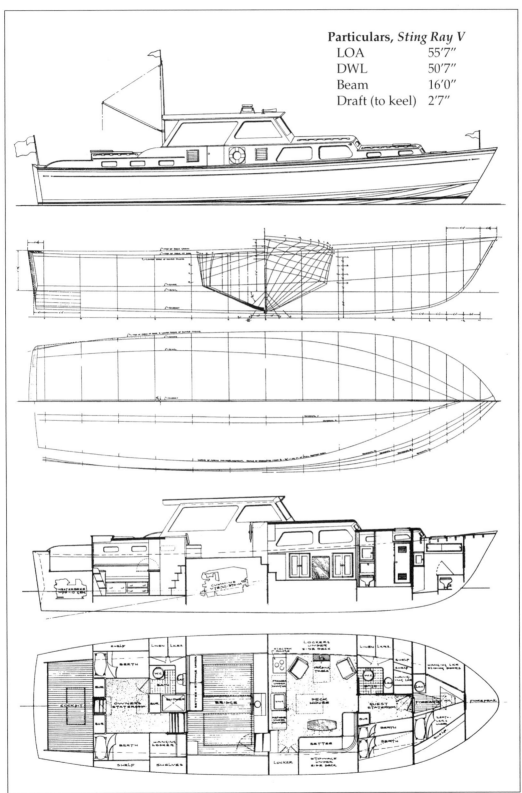

**Particulars, *Sting Ray V***

| | |
|---|---|
| LOA | 55'7" |
| DWL | 50'7" |
| Beam | 16'0" |
| Draft (to keel) | 2'7" |

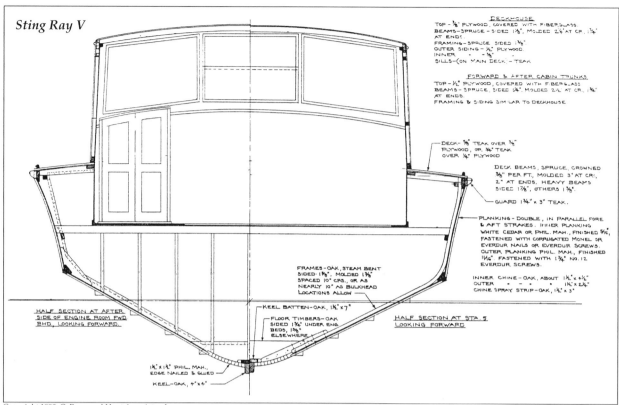

**Sting Ray V**

DECKHOUSE
TOP - 3/8" PLYWOOD, COVERED WITH FIBERGLASS.
BEAMS-SPRUCE - SIDED 1 3/8", MOLDED 2 1/4" AT CR., 1 3/4"
AT ENDS.
FRAMING-SPRUCE SIDED 1 3/8".
OUTER SIDING - 1/2" PLYWOOD.
INNER   "   - 3/8"   ".
SILLS-(ON MAIN DECK)-TEAK

FORWARD & AFTER CABIN TRUNKS
TOP - 1/2" PLYWOOD, COVERED WITH FIBERGLASS.
BEAMS-SPRUCE, SIDED 1 1/4", MOLDED 2 1/4" AT CR., 1 3/4"
AT ENDS.
FRAMING & SIDING SIMILAR TO DECKHOUSE.

DECK- 5/8" TEAK OVER 3/8"
PLYWOOD, OR, 3/4" TEAK
OVER 1/4" PLYWOOD

DECK BEAMS, SPRUCE, CROWNED
3/8" PER FT., MOLDED 3" AT CR.,
2" AT ENDS, HEAVY BEAMS
SIDED 1 7/8", OTHERS 1 3/8".

GUARD 1 3/4" x 3" TEAK.

PLANKING-DOUBLE, IN PARALLEL FORE
& AFT STRAKES. INNER PLANKING
WHITE CEDAR OR PHIL. MAH., FINISHED 9/16",
FASTENED WITH CORRUGATED MONEL OR
EVERDUR NAILS OR EVERDUR SCREWS.
OUTER PLANKING PHIL. MAH., FINISHED
1 1/16" FASTENED WITH 1 3/4" NO. 12
EVERDUR SCREWS.

INNER CHINE-OAK, ABOUT 1 1/2" x 4 1/2"
OUTER   "   -   "   "   - 1 1/2" x 2 1/2"
CHINE SPRAY STRIP-OAK, 1 1/2" x 3"

FRAMES-OAK, STEAM BENT
SIDED- 1 3/8", MOLDED 1 3/8"
SPACED 10" CRS., OR AS
NEARLY 10" AS BULKHEAD
LOCATIONS ALLOW

HALF SECTION AT AFTER
SIDE OF ENGINE ROOM FWD.
BHD., LOOKING FORWARD.

KEEL BATTEN-OAK, 1 1/2" x 7"

FLOOR TIMBERS-OAK
SIDED 1 3/4" UNDER ENG.
BEDS, 1 3/8"
ELSEWHERE

HALF SECTION AT STA. 5
LOOKING FORWARD.

1 1/2" x 1 1/2" PHIL. MAH.,
EDGE NAILED & GLUED

KEEL-OAK, 4" x 4"

# A Swordfisherman

—————— Design by Geerd Hendel ——————
Commentary by Joel White

I have always had a soft spot for long, low, fast, good-looking powerboats. And whenever I think of such a boat, *Porpoise* is the image that appears in my mind's eye. Oddly enough, I have never seen *Porpoise* in the flesh, only in pictures; the same is true of my relationship with Sophia Loren. This lack of personal contact in no way diminishes my respect for the ladies in question.

*Porpoise*'s hull is nearly perfect; I can think of no change that would make her better. Her superstructure is nearly so. Geerd Hendel, who designed this paragon, managed to blend the two elements, hull and superstructure, into a unified whole that delights the eye, or at least my eye.

The label on the plan sheets says "Commercial Sword Fisherman," but it is difficult to visualize her lying alongside the fish wharves of New Bedford or Nantucket, her scuppers running red with fish blood, and kegs, irons, dories, and miles of line scattered around her decks. As the pictures show, she is obviously a yacht that was designed with the emphasis on sportfishing and particularly swordfishing. The long bowsprit for ironing fish, and the unusual A-frame mast, with masthead lookout hoops and steering wheel aloft, are both geared toward taking the elusive and delicious swordfish. But it is not her bowsprit or mast that makes her design unique or distinctive — remove them and she would look better, if anything. The long, continuous flow of the sheerline, starting from a relatively low freeboard at the after end of the superstructure and rising steadily to the flaring clipper bow profile, is one element of the design that gladdens the eye. The low freeboard is made to appear even lower by the continuous guardrail at the deck edge.

The other element that contributes so much to the overall impression of the boat is the low, short deck-house structure. This superstructure is very much concentrated amidship, leaving a good deal of hull showing alone at the bow and the stern. The midships handrail, with a varnished teak railcap set on bronze stanchions, and a canvas weathercloth laced between the handrail and the caprail, was designed to give one a feeling of security while walking the sidedecks. It also does much to lower the apparent height of the deckhouse. I realize that I have spent a lot of words analyzing the appearance of this boat, but beauty is so rare and nowadays so neglected in the design process that it seems worthwhile to consider.

Most modern powerboats fall into two categories of appearance. The first is based on maximum interior volume on minimum overall length, and the resulting design looks like a condominium afloat — a Winnebago of the waterways. The other is based on the Buck Rogers spaceship concept. The aim here seems to be to design something that will float, but look as little like a boat as possible. Most such boats would be improved in looks with the addition of wings. The interior decor leans heavily on the use of shag carpeting, even on the overheads.

The lines of *Porpoise* show a graceful hull 60 feet long, with straight buttock lines aft that enable her to be driven at 18 to 20 knots. Her displacement of 47,500 pounds is quite light for her length.

Making a powerboat go fast is not complicated in principle — keep her light, and provide plenty of power. *Porpoise* was built in 1951, when diesels did not provide as much horsepower per pound of weight as they do now. Her twin General Motors 6-110s put out 275 horsepower at 1,300 rpm each, a total of only 550 horsepower. But her long, easy lines, and particularly her light weight allow her to achieve 18 knots, which is quite respectable. Her lines also show a long, straight skeg, with considerable drag in its length, providing good directional stability while running.

This skeg also gives the hull a great deal of structural stiffness. One of the tough problems in this type of boat is the need to keep weight low, for speed reasons, and yet build a hull strong enough to cope with offshore conditions without losing its shape or leaking. The details of her hull structure, shown in her construction section drawing and construction plan, are very instructive and interesting. Let's examine them in some detail.

*Porpoise*'s keel is oak, sided 5 inches, and tapering in depth from 2½ feet aft to about 7 inches in the forefoot area. On top of the keel is a 2-inch by 7-inch oak keel apron, or hog piece, which forms the back rabbet for the garboard plank. Her bent-oak frames are only 1⅜ inches by 1¾ inches, on 9-inch centers. Planking is only 1¼-inches in thickness, but it is double — an inner layer of ⅜-inch cedar covered by a ⅞-inch outer layer of Philippine mahogany. Double planking is much stiffer than single planking of the same thickness, and less apt to leak. The garboard and sheerstrake are single-thickness 1¼-inch Philippine mahogany. Every other frame has a 1¼-inch oak floor timber alongside. In addition to the centerline keel and apron construction, fore-and-aft rigidity is gained by use of deep 2-inch by 9-inch spruce stringers that tie into the massive 3½-inch-thick engine bearers amidships. There are four of these engine beds, each about 13 feet long. Attached to these beds, two stringers run aft to the stem, while two more run forward to within 6 feet of the stem. There is also a 3½-inch by 4½-inch spruce bilge stringer on each side, outboard of the vertical stringers.

*Porpoise*'s deck is 1¼-inch teak, laid on oak beams, which in turn rest on the oak clamp and shelf at the sheer. The bulwarks, which are about a foot high, have oak top timbers that pierce the covering board, are planked with 1⅛-inch pine, and are topped off with a 2-inch by 6-inch teak railcap. The superstructure is carefully designed to be as light as possible, with spruce framing and tops of canvas-covered pine. Mr. Hendel

must have been reassured by the knowledge that *Porpoise* was to be built at Camden Shipbuilding Co., under the supervision of master builder Malcolm Brewer.

*Porpoise*'s accommodations might be called spare for a 60-foot yacht. But like the rest of the design, they seem to fit the overall purpose — the swift pursuit of large game fish. The engineroom, containing the two diesels plus 860 gallons of fuel oil, occupies the middle 11 feet of the boat. Aft of the engineroom, under the open bridgedeck, is a nice owner's stateroom with two large bunks, a generous toilet room, and several lockers and a bureau. Forward of the engineroom there is a large refrigerator, a good-sized galley, and quarters for two crew — two V-berths forward and a toilet room. Opposite the galley are two bunks called "emergency" berths. So the layout provides accommodations for two aft, two crew forward, and berths for two more should they be required.

The boat can be run either from the open bridge deck in good weather, or the enclosed deckhouse in bad conditions. The layout of the deckhouse is not shown, other than a high seat across the back, but it is large enough to be a comfortable sitting-dining area. Access to the deckhouse is from the side decks on either side, through hinged doors. From the deckhouse, steps ascend to the bridgedeck aft, and descend to the galley forward. The crew can also reach their quarters through a hatch in the forward house.

*Porpoise* is unusual. She was not designed as an all-around boat, suitable to the needs of many. Instead, the design steadfastly aims toward one end — grace and speed at sea. Perhaps it is this single-mindedness of concept that makes her appeal so great. I would love to spend some time on the end of her swordfish stand, looking aft, watching her work her way through a long swell at 15 knots.

*Further inquiries on this design should be addressed to: Geerd Hendel, N.A., 144 Bayview St., Camden, ME 04843.*

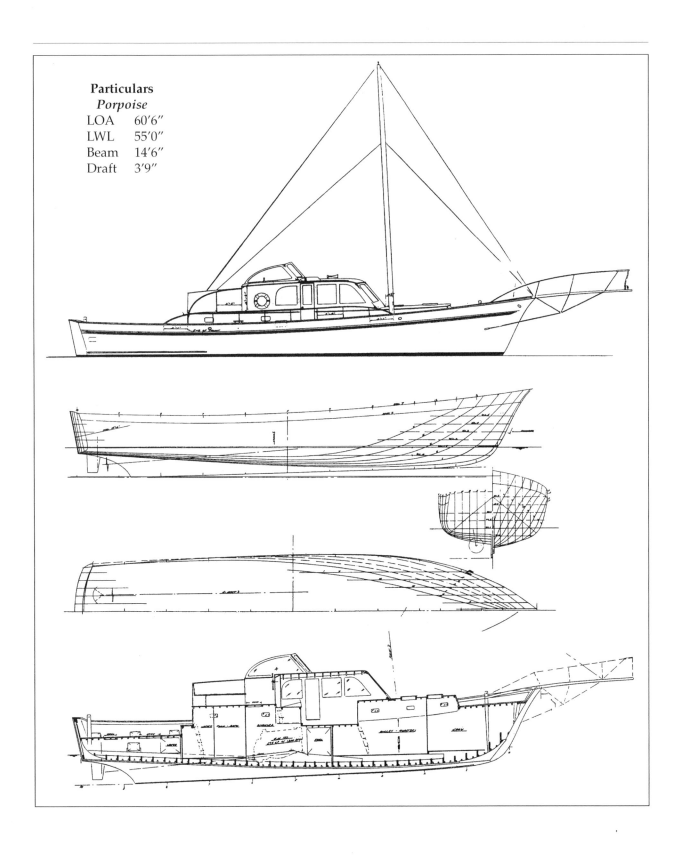

**Particulars**
*Porpoise*
LOA    60′6″
LWL    55′0″
Beam   14′6″
Draft   3′9″

*Porpoise*

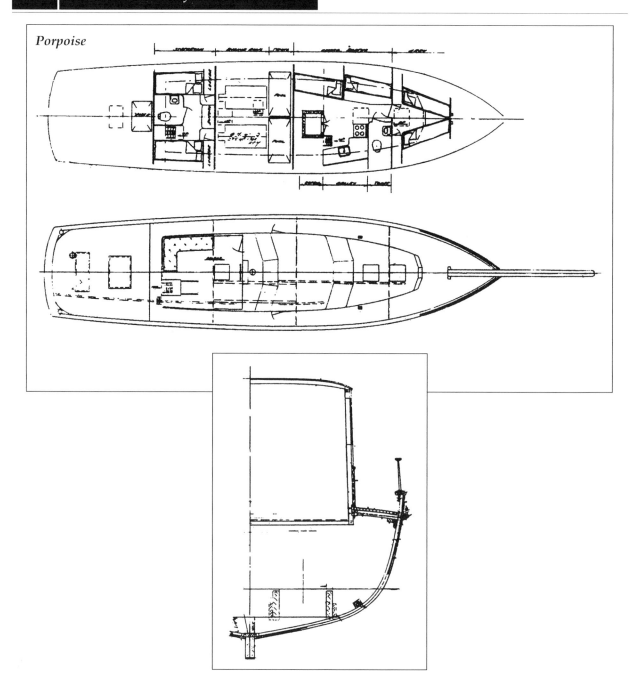

# Two Striking Power Yachts

Designs by William Garden ——
Commentary by Joel White

Here are drawings for a 92-foot express moto-ryacht, one of those rare ones of such a large size built of wood in recent years. I am not surprised to learn that the design is by William Garden. Let's have a look at *Czarinna*, a *rara avis*.

While this boat may be constructed of that "old-fashioned material," she cannot by any criteria be called "traditional." *Czarinna*'s styling is contemporary, almost space-age, though not what I would call European. I like it. She is big enough to carry off with style the overhanging roof of the afterdeck and the sharp outward flare of the bridge deck structure. On a smaller vessel, these details might look fussy, but at 92 feet they should be elegant. The steeply raked line of the stem and the heavy cant aft to the windshield and bridge structure give a feeling of speed and purpose that is just right for such a craft. Her low freeboard aft and the lengthy "arrow" of the forward cabin will make her seem even longer than she really is.

Powered by twin Caterpillars of 1,000 horsepower each, *Czarinna* is expected to cruise at 25 knots. The V-bottomed hull has a dead-straight rabbet line parallel to the waterline, and a constant deadrise of about 17 degrees from amidships to the stern. The chine is well lifted at the stem, and her forward sections are sharp and easy for smooth penetration in head seas. The topsides have continuous flare from stem to stern. A boarding platform across the stern and large transom doors make entering and leaving easy to manage without the need for a gangway. Space is provided for a skiff and a powered launch on the after boat deck, with suitable davits for launching.

Three steering stations are shown: an enclosed midship pilothouse, with the big Caterpillars booming away underneath, an open flying bridge that is reached by several steps up from the pilothouse, and a raised tower several feet up the mast that also has a set of controls.

The pilothouse will be a grand place. In addition to a full control station and battery of electronic equipment, there is a large L-shaped settee with a table in one corner, raised high enough for easy visibility out the large windows. Three glass skylights overhead will bring in even more light — so much so that on truly sunny days, some method of screening will be wanted. The flying bridge is also large, with a complete control station, two-person helmsman's seat, and a settee with table. At 25 knots, a lot of wind blows over this type of bridge, and I am sure the flared side wings are there to minimize the blast to those enjoying the view.

The interior of this vessel is most interesting. She is designed to operate with a minimum of professional crew — perhaps none. The only sign of crew's quarters is a tiny cabin right forward that almost appears as an afterthought. The forward half of the boat is occupied with three sumptuous double staterooms, each with a toilet. The largest cabin (I presume it is the owner's) sits just forward of the pilothouse. A long passageway runs down the port side for the entire length of the superstructure, connecting these staterooms with the saloon and galley, which are abaft the pilothouse. The compact U-shaped galley occupies the forward end of this space; the remainder contains living, dining, and lounging areas, with movable furniture to suit. Large windows provide light and air, and give good views of the scenery zipping by. It is interesting that the floor for these living areas is raised well above the waterline — about 18 inches, I would say. This gives more floor width and better window views. There must be a huge amount of space under the cabin sole forward. Aft, it is taken up with fuel and water tanks.

An express cruiser, even one 92 feet long and 25

knots fast, must of necessity be light, and the construction plans of this vessel show this to be true. For instance, *Czarinna*'s main keel is only sided 7½ inches and is capped with a 4½-inch by 9½-inch keelson. She has a full set of steam-bent frames, 2 inches by 3 inches on 12-inch centers, passing on the inside of the chine. Longitudinal stiffness is assured by four box-section stringers running the full length of the vessel, bolted to the frames and the floor timbers. As with many West Coast craft, she has a harpin to connect the deck structure to the hull.

The hull is triple planked, the inner layers being diagonal cedar, the outer mahogany laid fore-and-aft. The superstructure is plywood over light framing, and I imagine it will be fiberglass sheathed for waterproofing and a smooth finish — neat, light but strong, and well thought out. It would be a treat to see her under construction.

Two thousand imperial gallons of diesel fuel in four aluminum tanks, and four hundred imperial gallons of water in two tanks of stainless steel, occupy most of the space under the saloon floor. A quick estimate indicates she might use 85 gallons per hour at cruising speed, giving her 24 hours of endurance and a range of about 600 nautical miles. Slow her down some, and she will do much better than that. But it is a bit daunting to think of pouring a couple of barrels of fuel through her every hour.

Czarinna's plans make a fascinating engineering document, showing the wealth of detail and practical experience needed to build such a craft. For those of us not quite ready to take on a 92-footer, we offer you *Tlingit*, another Bill Garden design that is a bit smaller (only 62 feet overall).

This motor canoe is diametrically opposite to the express cruiser in concept. She is a small boat greatly stretched in length to attain speed without wake and, thus, maximize fuel economy. Her bottom is flat, and her topside frames are straight. She is a giant, double-ended dory, built with 2-by-4s and sheet plywood, and powered by an old three-cylinder Easthope gasoline engine. She burns 2 gallons per hour while making 10 knots.

Designed a number of years ago as a simple launch to transport people to and from an island in the Gulf of Georgia, she was originally flush decked except for a small midship cockpit with pilothouse over most of it.

When Bill Garden purchased *Tlingit* for his own use as a camp cruiser he added a small cabin trunk forward of the pilothouse that contains two berths, a tiny galley, and a toilet. These changes are shown on the plans published here. Another nice touch is the addition of a little self-bailing cockpit forward of the cabin trunk. This cockpit allows two crew members to sit in comfort while enjoying the scenery. About the only noise to be heard up here is the rush of the water past the bow. The old-fashioned three-cylinder Easthope, developing 30 horsepower at about 750 rpm, contributes low-level, low-frequency sounds; it is visually interesting on account of the myriad external parts wiggling about.

*Tlingit* is a far cry from the double staterooms, huge galley, and flying bridge of *Czarinna*. She is simply a long, skinny launch, economical to build and operate. But she illustrates how diverse the world of boat design can be, and that for every gain there is a price to pay. If you simply need to transport a few people a limited distance economically, it would be difficult to beat *Tlingit*. If you must provide shelter, comfort, elbow room, and high-speed transport, it can be done, but the stakes are higher — and so are the costs involved. Both these vessels are fine examples of the designer's art.

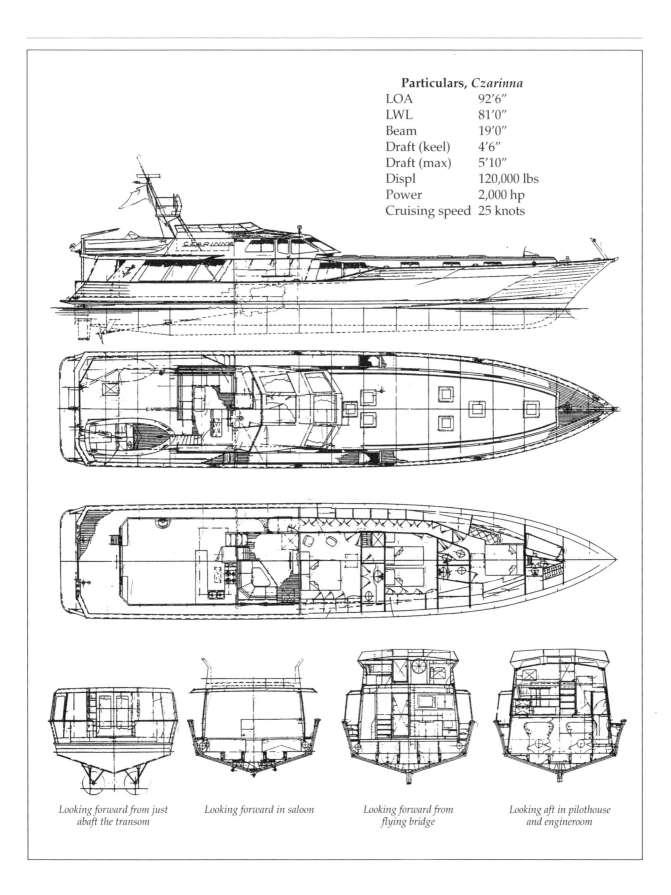

**Particulars,** *Czarinna*

| | |
|---|---|
| LOA | 92'6" |
| LWL | 81'0" |
| Beam | 19'0" |
| Draft (keel) | 4'6" |
| Draft (max) | 5'10" |
| Displ | 120,000 lbs |
| Power | 2,000 hp |
| Cruising speed | 25 knots |

*Looking forward from just abaft the transom*

*Looking forward in saloon*

*Looking forward from flying bridge*

*Looking aft in pilothouse and engineroom*

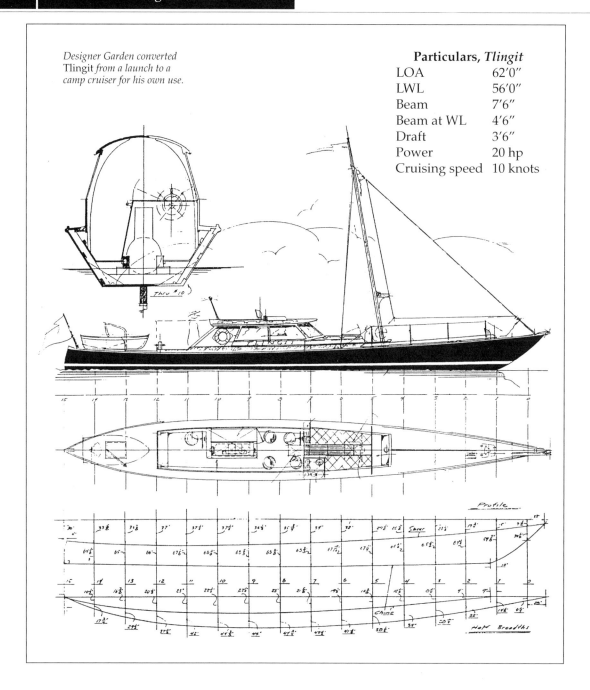

*Designer Garden converted*
Tlingit *from a launch to a*
*camp cruiser for his own use.*

**Particulars,** *Tlingit*

| | |
|---|---|
| LOA | 62′0″ |
| LWL | 56′0″ |
| Beam | 7′6″ |
| Beam at WL | 4′6″ |
| Draft | 3′6″ |
| Power | 20 hp |
| Cruising speed | 10 knots |